The Joy of Dreamweaver® MX: Recipes for Data-Driven Web Sites

About the Author

Paul Newman is President of BRAVE NEW WURLD, a web design firm in Vancouver, British Columbia. He has a B.A. in English and Creative Writing from Binghamton University and an M.F.A. in Film Production from the UCLA Department of Film, Television, and Digital Media.

Paul's computer experience dates back to 1985, when he bought one of the first Apple Macintosh computers in his senior year of college. He has been building web sites since 1997, and his clients include RaikaUSA.com, VoiceoverAmerica.com, Officetek.com, and BarbaraTyson.com.

Paul lives in Vancouver with his wife, Barbara, and their two dogs.

The Joy of Dreamweaver® MX: Recipes for Data-Driven Web Sites

Paul Newman

McGraw-Hill/Osborne

New York   Chicago   San Francisco
Lisbon   London   Madrid   Mexico City   Milan
New Delhi   San Juan   Seoul   Singapore   Sydney   Toronto

McGraw-Hill/Osborne
2600 Tenth Street
Berkeley, California 94710
U.S.A.

To arrange bulk purchase discounts for sales promotions, premiums, or fund-raisers, please contact **McGraw-Hill**/Osborne at the above address. For information on translations or book distributors outside the U.S.A., please see the International Contact Information page immediately following the index of this book.

The Joy of Dreamweaver® MX: Recipes for Data-Driven Web Sites

1234567890 CUS CUS 0198765432

ISBN 0-07-222464-9

Publisher	Brandon A. Nordin
Vice President & Associate Publisher	Scott Rogers
Acquisitions Editor	Jim Schachterle
Project Editor	Katie Conley
Acquisitions Coordinator	Tim Madrid
Technical Editors	Michael Buffington, George Petrov
Copy Editor	Robert Campbell
Proofreaders	Cheryl Abel, Mike McGee
Indexer	Irv Hershman
Computer Designers	Tabitha M. Cagan, Kelly Stanton-Scott, Melinda Moore Lytle
Illustrators	Michael Mueller, Lyssa Wald
Series Designer	Kelly Stanton-Scott
Cover Design & Series Illustrator	Jeff Weeks

This book was composed with Corel VENTURA™ Publisher.

For Barbara, fearless dreamer

Contents at a Glance

Contents

Acknowledgments

Thanks to my editor, Jim Schachterle, and to Tim Madrid, Katie Conley, Kelly Stanton-Scott, Robert Campbell, and everyone else at McGraw-Hill/Osborne. It's a sign of the times that my editor and I have never met. I don't even know what he looks like. Throughout this book's development, Jim has been the unflappable voice of reason at the other end of the line. Charlie to my Farrah. Thank you, Jim, for your unwavering support.

Thanks also to my technical editors, George Petrov and Michael Buffington, for their careful attention to detail. Michael is the author of the *ColdFusion 5 Developer's Guide*, and George is the author of many first-rate Dreamweaver MX extensions, including Pure ASP File Upload.

I'd also like to thank Ray West and Tom Muck—authors of *Dreamweaver MX: The Complete Reference*—and their technical editor, extension guru Massimo Foti. Ray, Tom, Massimo: thanks for your generosity and patience in answering my questions. If the Dreamweaver community is unusually supportive, it's largely due to these gentlemen.

A recipe book like this couldn't be written without the contributions of many great chefs. Thanks to the following people and organizations who generously granted permission to reproduce their code and use their extensions: Greg Alton at CFDev.com, Paul R. Boon and Stefan Van As at DWfile.com, George Petrov and Waldo Smeets at UDzone.com, Scott Mitchell at 4GuysFromRolla.com, Michael E. Brandt, Massimo Foti, Tom Muck, Owen Palmer, Nicholas Poh, Daniel Short, Tom Steeper, Jaro von Flocken, and Nate Weiss. And thanks to Macromedia, for its ongoing commitment to making the best software money can buy.

Special thanks to my family—Oscar, Kopper, Jon, Sara Jo, Hinde, and Gary—for cheerleading this book when it was just a crazy idea.

Most of all, thanks to my wife, Barbara, for tolerating a husband who spent six months toiling away in the dungeon. You are the real dream weaver.

Introduction

Dreamweaver has come a long way since the introduction of Dreamweaver UltraDev 1 in June 2000. Back then, what set UltraDev apart from products like FrontPage was that Macromedia actually seemed to listen, and respond, to what developers wanted. From the outset, Dreamweaver was more intuitive and efficient than its competition. It didn't rewrite your code or clutter your documents with proprietary tags, and it generated web pages that were cross-browser compatible. When Macromedia added support for data-driven sites with the release of Dreamweaver UltraDev, it was like a dream come true.

Dreamweaver MX is another enormous leap forward. That Dreamweaver MX supports ASP.NET, within months of its final release, is nothing short of astounding. In addition, Dreamweaver's tight integration with ColdFusion MX—not to mention other Macromedia products—is bound to win over HomeSite and ColdFusion Studio users. Add to this its enhanced support for PHP and JSP—and cutting-edge technologies like XML, CFCs, and web services—and Dreamweaver MX emerges as a formidable rapid application development tool.

What is arguably best about Dreamweaver MX is its extensibility. If Dreamweaver doesn't include a feature you want, you can write it yourself. Macromedia has tried to make Dreamweaver MX backward-compatible with as many Dreamweaver UltraDev 4 extensions as possible, and developers are already releasing new and updated extensions optimized for Dreamweaver MX. In the next several months, developers will undoubtedly release new extensions that teach Dreamweaver to perform tricks its creators never could have imagined. That's what separates DMX from the pack. Other programs let you dabble in the kitchen. Dreamweaver is the galloping gourmet of web design software.

The purpose of this book is not only to show you what Dreamweaver MX can do "out of the box," but to push the software to its limits. Over the past several years, I have scoured web sites and newsgroups, pored over books and magazines, and "burnt a lot of toast" in search of simple, reliable recipes for the most demanding Dreamweaver dishes.

In *The Joy of Dreamweaver MX*, I want to share this hard-won knowledge with you. Using step-by-step recipes, this book illustrates how to implement features that DMXers can really sink their teeth into. Use the book to flex your culinary muscles—to learn new skills and experiment with new flavors and ingredients—and before you know it, you'll be a Dreamweaver MX Master Chef! Here's my guarantee to you: If you follow the recipes carefully, and remember to have fun along the way, soon you'll be creating the kinds of hearty web sites even your mother would be proud to serve.

Who Should Read This Book

I wrote *The Joy of Dreamweaver* MX because this is the book I wanted when Dreamweaver UltraDev 4 was released. Plain and simple.

If you've ever used any web design software, this book is for you. If you're a web designer eager to make the transition to web developer, this book is for you. If you're an experienced Dreamweaver UltraDev user who wants to add a few new tricks to your repertoire, this book is for you.

For most users of Dreamweaver MX, the burning question is "How'd they do that?" Or, more to the point, "How do *I* do that?" *The Joy of Dreamweaver* MX provides the answers—the "secret" recipes, if you will. This book doesn't dwell on the rudiments: it assumes you already know how to boil water and separate an egg. Instead, *The Joy of Dreamweaver* MX offers the kinds of soup-to-nuts solutions that aren't documented in the manual.

Written for the moderate to advanced Dreamweaver MX user, *The Joy of Dreamweaver* MX offers step-by-step recipes for creating data-driven web sites using ASP and ColdFusion MX. Part I, "Setting the Table," explains how to install and configure the software needed to complete this book. Part II offers recipes to get you acquainted with Dreamweaver MX, including an advanced contact form, a guestbook, and a news section. Part III is the "meat and potatoes" of the book: recipes for user authentication, file uploads and downloads, content management, batch updates and deletes, nested repeat regions, and much more.

Armed with this book, and Dreamweaver MX, you have everything you need to create the data-driven web sites of tomorrow. In addition, the companion web site, **www.newmanzone.com**, includes all the databases, code, and extensions needed to reproduce the book's sample web applications.

What's in the Book

The Joy of Dreamweaver MX is organized into three parts:

Part I: "Setting the Table: Get Cookin' with Dreamweaver MX"   Focuses on what you need to create data-driven web sites using Dreamweaver MX. This includes detailed instructions on how to obtain and install Dreamweaver MX and the database software necessary to complete the book.

Part II: "Appetizers: Some Recipes to Get You Started"   Walks you through constructing the Newman Zone web site, which includes an advanced contact form, a guestbook, a downloads page, and a news section. Part II also includes coverage of Access parameter queries and SQL Server stored procedures.

Part III: "Entrees: Building a Data-Driven Web Application"   Uses advanced features to construct a fully functional site for a fictitious realtor named Chip Havilmyer. The realty site includes a password-protected admin section, content management, file upload functionality, and a preview image feature. Part III also includes coverage of nested repeat regions, batch updates, batch deletes, and the @@IDENTITY variable.

Part I: Setting the Table: Get Cookin' with Dreamweaver MX

Part I ensures that you have everything you need to complete this book's recipes.

Chapter 1 Guides you through installing Dreamweaver MX and gives you a quick tour of its most exciting new features.

Chapter 2 Explores the requirements for developing web applications with Dreamweaver MX, including choosing a server model, and installing a web server and an application server.

Chapter 3 Provides a rundown of Dreamweaver MX database options, including Microsoft Access, SQL Server, and MSDE.

Chapter 4 Looks at Dreamweaver's integration with other products, including Fireworks MX, HomeSite+, and TopStyle.

Part II: Appetizers: Some Recipes to Get You Started

Part II—Chapters 5–10—is devoted to creating the Newman Zone web site. Coverage includes an advanced guestbook and contact form, a download counter, and a data-driven news scroller.

Chapter 5 Explains how to set up a mail server and send e-mail from an advanced contact form using JMail and `<cfmail>`.

Chapter 6 Builds on the previous chapter to create an advanced guestbook that previews the entry before it's submitted and sends e-mail to two recipients.

Chapter 7 Shows you how to filter Dreamweaver MX recordsets using Microsoft Access parameter queries.

Chapter 8 Introduces you to SQL Server stored procedures and explains how to use them to generate Dreamweaver MX recordsets.

Chapter 9 Shows how to increment a download counter and stream files to a browser using the ADO Stream object and the `<cfcontent>` tag.

Chapter 10 Explains how to create a news section and link it to a data-driven DHTML scroller on your home page.

Part III: Entrees: Building a Data-Driven Web Application

In Part III—Chapters 11–20—you construct a web application for a fictitious realtor named Chip Havilmyer. The Realty site includes coverage of many advanced features, including file uploading, user authentication, batch updates and deletes, and online HTML editors.

Chapter 11 Offers a six-step plan for developing complex, data-driven web sites, from defining a site's goals to publishing the completed site.

Chapter 12 Explains how to insert a record into a database and retrieve the new value of the `@@IDENTITY` variable.

Chapter 13 Simplifies file uploads using Pure ASP File Upload and ColdFusion's `<cffile>` tag.

Chapter 14   Demonstrates how to preview an image locally before it's uploaded to a remote web site.

Chapter 15   Explains how to adapt Dreamweaver's Insert Record server behavior to enable batch deletes via check boxes.

Chapter 16   Shows how to make batch updates to a database using a single HTML form.

Chapter 17   Takes the mystery out of nested repeat regions and horizontal loopers.

Chapter 18   Demonstrates how to integrate two popular content-management tools—ActivEdit and PD On-Line HTML Editor—with Dreamweaver MX.

Chapter 19   Explains how to use Dreamweaver's User Authentication server behaviors to restrict access to a web site.

Chapter 20   Covers issues concerning web site administration.

How to Read This Book

Unlike most recipe books, *The Joy of Dreamweaver* MX is best read from start to finish. If you complete the chapters in order, *The Joy of Dreamweaver* MX enables you to construct two functional web sites: Newman Zone and Realty. The Newman Zone site applies to Part II (Chapters 5–10), and the Realty site applies to Part III (Chapters 11–20).

The recipes are designed to gradually introduce you to increasingly advanced Dreamweaver MX features, and many of the chapters build on skills—and incorporate files and databases—covered in previous chapters. This is especially true of Chapters 7–9 in Part II, and Chapters 12–14 in Part III. I highly recommend that you complete the recipes in order the first time you read the book. After that, you can use the chapters as a reference—as you would with any other cookbook—whenever you need to remember how to prepare your favorite dish.

Formatting Conventions

The Joy of Dreamweaver MX uses a number of formatting conventions to make the recipes as clear and easy to follow as possible. To begin with, code listings and code fragments (functions, variables, etc.) are rendered in a fixed-width font (i.e., Courier). This also applies to file paths and filenames:

◆ Switch to Code view and locate the `Response.Write` method on line 20.

◆ Copy this folder into your server's root directory (e.g., `C:\Inetpub\wwwroot`).

In code listings, an arrow symbol (⏎) indicates that the code should appear on a single line, even though it wraps on the printed page. If the code is different for ASP and ColdFusion, the server model is indicated in parentheses:

L 1-1
```
<%=Replace((rsGuestbook.Fields.Item("Comments").Value), ⏎
vbNewLine, "<br>")%> (ASP)
#Replace(Replace(rsGuestbook.Comments, chr(10), "<br>"), ⏎
chr(13), "<br>")# (ColdFusion)
```

Key presses and key combinations are identified using small caps:

◆ Press F12 to preview the page in a browser.

◆ Select the table and press SHIFT-CTRL-ALT-C to center it.

Steps that require menu selections are indicated like this:

◆ Choose File | Save and save the file as `index.asp`.

◆ Choose Start | Programs | Macromedia ColdFusion MX | Administrator.

At the beginning of every chapter is a list of ingredients. Where possible, the ingredients have been included in the book's supporting files. However, some chapters require you to download and install third-party Dreamweaver MX extensions. A complete list of the ingredients for *The Joy of Dreamweaver MX*—and links to download them—can be found at **www.newmanzone.com/ downloads**. The book's supporting files are available from **www.newmanzone.com** and **www.osborne.com/downloads/downloads.shtml**.

Part

Setting the Table: Get Cookin' with Dreamweaver MX

Chapter 1

Dreamweaver MX: Cleaner, Whiter, Brighter

INGREDIENTS

File(s)	Type	Server Model(s)	Source
GettingStarted	Folder	ASP/CF	Dreamweaver MX
temperature.cfm	ColdFusion template	CF	*Sample Code*
globalcar.css	Style sheet		*Sample Code*
whois.cfm	ColdFusion template	CF	*Sample Code*

 from the desk of Paul Newman

In Part I of *The Joy of Dreamweaver MX*, we're going to focus on what you need to get cookin' with Dreamweaver MX. In Chapter 1, we'll install Dreamweaver MX and take a tour of its new features. In Chapter 2, we'll delve into the requirements for developing web applications with Dreamweaver MX, including choosing a server model, and installing a web server and an application server. In Chapter 3, we'll discuss Dreamweaver MX database options, including Microsoft Access, SQL Server, and MSDE. In Chapter 4, we'll take a look at Dreamweaver's integration with other products, including Fireworks MX, HomeSite+, and TopStyle.

At this point, I assume you've already purchased Dreamweaver MX, or downloaded the trial version from **www.macromedia.com/software/dreamweaver/download**. To whet your appetite, here's a quick rundown of some of Dreamweaver's new features:

◆ New integrated workspace

◆ Multiple document interface (MDI)

◆ Dockable panels and panel groups

◆ Support for new server technologies

◆ Support for the latest web standards

◆ Optimization for ColdFusion MX

◆ New coding features

◆ Customizable Insert bar

◆ Improved New Document dialog box

◆ Enhanced Dreamweaver templates

◆ Enhanced table editing with Layout view

◆ Simplified database connections

After installing Dreamweaver MX, we'll set up the lessons in the *Getting Started* guide. We'll also take a look at some of Dreamweaver's most exciting new features, including web services and ColdFusion components (CFCs).

Installation Checklist

The system requirements for installing Dreamweaver MX can be found in the Release Notes on Macromedia's web site: **www.macromedia.com/go/dreamweavermx_releasenotes**. If you're planning to use Dreamweaver MX to design web applications—and you better be, since that's what this book is all about—you may want to read "Installing a Web Server" and "Installing an Application Server" in Chapter 2 before you proceed.

The following are the Windows system requirements for Dreamweaver MX:

◆ 300 MHz or better Intel Pentium II processor or equivalent

◆ Windows 98 SE, Windows Me, Windows NT 4, Windows 2000, or Windows XP

- Microsoft Data Access Components (MDAC) 2.6 or greater
- Netscape Navigator or Internet Explorer 4.0 or later
- 96MB of free available system RAM (128MB recommended)
- 275MB of available disk space
- 800×600 resolution color display or better (1024×768, millions of colors recommended)

If you're planning to run Dreamweaver MX on Windows XP, invest in the Pro edition, which includes Microsoft Internet Information Services (IIS). In addition, consider purchasing at least 256–512MB of RAM if you intend to run several MX applications at once. To download MDAC (Microsoft Data Access Components), go to **www.microsoft.com/data/download.htm**.

Note Although Windows Millennium Edition (Me) is supported by Dreamweaver MX, Personal Web Server (PWS) and IIS are not compatible with Windows Me. Practically speaking, this makes Windows Me unsuitable for developing web applications with Dreamweaver MX.

If your system meets the minimum requirements, you're ready to install Dreamweaver MX.

Installing Dreamweaver MX

To install Dreamweaver MX, run the setup file from the CD-ROM (`Dreamweaver MX Installer.exe`). If you downloaded Dreamweaver MX, double-click the executable file in Windows Explorer.

Complete the following steps to install Dreamweaver MX:

1. The first screen is the InstallShield Wizard for Dreamweaver MX. Click Next to proceed with the installation.

2. Read the License Agreement and click Yes.

3. Enter your name and Dreamweaver MX serial number and click Next. (The serial number can usually be found on the CD-ROM sleeve. If you downloaded Dreamweaver MX, you can retrieve your serial number from the Macromedia Download Center.)

Note If you're installing the trial version of Dreamweaver MX, some of these screens may be different. For example, you won't be prompted to enter a serial number.

4. On the next screen, check the components you wish to install and click Next.

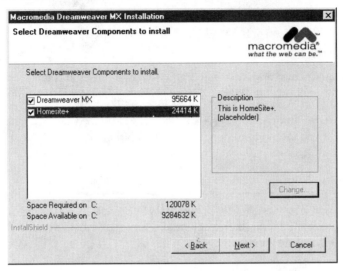

5. The next screen allows you to customize the installation folder. Unless you want to install Dreamweaver MX on another network drive, accept the default option and click Next.

6. The Default Editor screen allows you to choose which files types are associated with Dreamweaver MX (ASP, ASPX, CFM, JSP, etc.). Make your selections and click Next.

7. The next screen informs you that Setup has enough information to start copying files. If you wish to change any of the settings, click the Back button. Otherwise, click Next.

8. After installing Dreamweaver MX, Setup installs HomeSite+ (if selected) and the latest version of Macromedia Extension Manager.

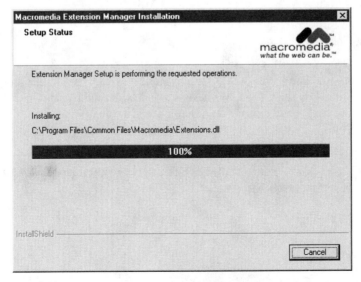

9. At this point, the InstallShield Wizard Complete screen appears. Click Finish.

10. "Welcome to Dreamweaver MX" opens in your default browser. This page contains late-breaking information about Dreamweaver MX, including links to the Release Notes, technical support, and other resources.

When you're finished with the ReadMe page, close your browser and restart your computer (it's always a good idea to reboot after installing any new software). After restarting, place a shortcut to Dreamweaver MX on your Desktop or the Quick Launch toolbar.

Setting Up the *Getting Started* Lessons

To get acquainted with Dreamweaver MX, we'll set up the lessons in the *Getting Started* guide.

In Windows Explorer, create a new folder under your root drive called `Sites` (e.g., `C:\Sites`). Locate the `GettingStarted` folder installed by Dreamweaver MX—usually `C:\Program Files\Macromedia\Dreamweaver MX\Samples\GettingStarted`—and copy it into the `Sites` folder (e.g., `C:\Sites\GettingStarted`).

To launch Dreamweaver MX, double-click the shortcut on your Desktop or choose Start | Programs | Macromedia | Macromedia Dreamweaver MX. The first time you launch Dreamweaver MX, you're presented with the Workspace Setup dialog box.

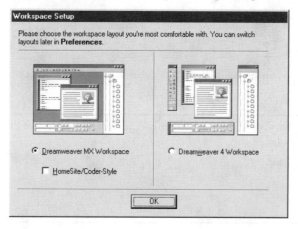

Accept the default option and click OK. This opens Dreamweaver MX with its new integrated workspace (see Figure 1-1).

Dreamweaver MX detects any previous installations of Dreamweaver or Dreamweaver UltraDev and imports the Site definitions into the new Site panel.

Insert bar

Document toolbar

Welcome window

Panel groups

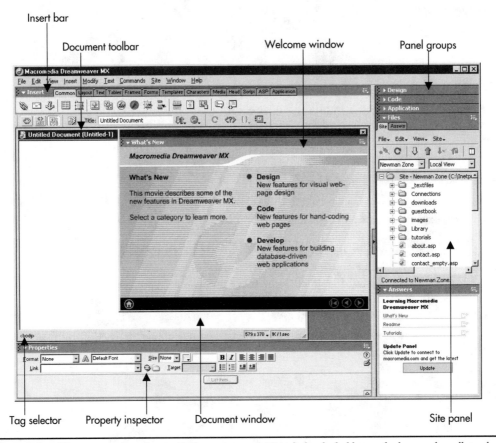

Tag selector   Property inspector   Document window   Site panel

Figure 1-1   *The integrated workspace in Dreamweaver MX includes dockable panels that can be collapsed or expanded as needed.*

New Feature

The Site panel is the successor to the Site window in Dreamweaver 4 and Dreamweaver UltraDev. The Site panel includes a built-in file explorer, which allows you to browse to any file on your hard drive without leaving Dreamweaver MX.

If you want to follow along with the rest of this chapter, set up the sample ColdFusion site as described in the *Getting Started* guide. To access the *Getting Started* guide, click Tutorials on the Answers panel. This opens *Using Dreamweaver MX*. Expand *Getting Started* and select "Setup for Sample ColdFusion Site." Follow the instructions to define the Global Car - ColdFusion site and create the connGlobal data source in ColdFusion Administrator.

Note

The purpose of this chapter is to expose you to some of the new features of Dreamweaver MX. If you haven't set up your web server or application server yet, you can return to this section after completing Chapter 2. If you're planning to use ASP, you can still set up the sample ASP site, but you won't be able to create the examples that use web services and ColdFusion components.

Once you've defined the Global Car site, the Site panel should look something like this:

Double-click `customerComment.cfm` and `customerInsert.cfm` to open the files in the Document window. Notice that Dreamweaver's new Multiple Document Interface (MDI) allows you to work with several open documents at once. To switch documents, select a tab on the bottom of the Document window, or press CTRL-TAB.

Select "Developing a Web Application in Dreamweaver MX" in the *Getting Started* guide and follow the instructions to complete the lessons.

New and Improved Features

If you completed the lessons in the *Getting Started* guide, you learned how to display database records on the Customer Comments page and insert a new record using Dreamweaver's Record Insertion Form application object. If you want some more practice, click Tutorials on the Answers panel and complete the "Building a Master-Detail Page Set Tutorial" and the "Building an Insert Record Page Tutorial."

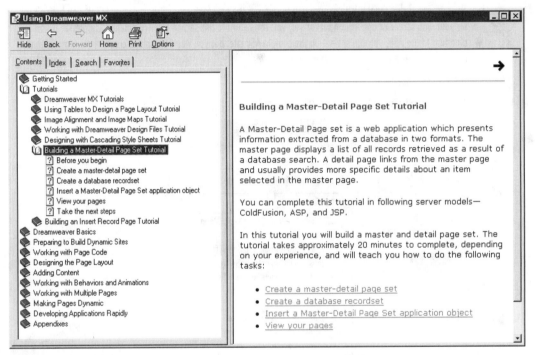

You'll also find useful information in the sections called *Making Pages Dynamic* and *Developing Applications Rapidly*.

New Document Dialog Box

The *Getting Started* guide exposes you to some of Dreamweaver MX's new features, including the Databases panel and the Insert bar. To expand on the *Getting Started* guide, we'll add two more pages to the Global Car - ColdFusion site.

Open the Global Car site in Dreamweaver MX and choose File | New or press CTRL-N. This launches the New Document dialog box. Select the General tab and click the Page Designs category. In the right-hand pane, select UI: Search. Click Create.

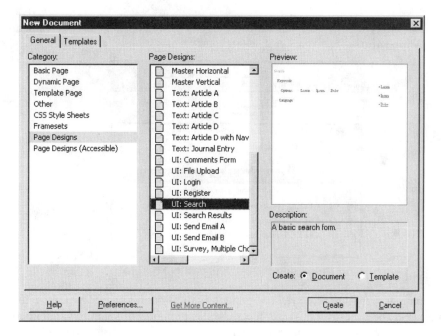

Dreamweaver MX generates a simple search page with a text field, three radio buttons, and a drop-down menu. Choose File | Save (or press CTRL-S) and save the page as **temperature.cfm**. We're going to use this page to invoke a ColdFusion component (CFC).

ColdFusion Components (CFCs)

Select the page's title in the Document toolbar (View | Toolbars | Document), and change it from Untitled Document to **Temperature Converter**. To construct a page that converts Fahrenheit to Celsius, and vice-versa, we're going to invoke a sample CFC that installs with ColdFusion MX.

Note

ColdFusion components (CFCs) are similar to the ASP Component Object Model (COM) in the sense that they "encapsulate application functionality and provide a standard interface for client access to that functionality. Clients access component functionality by invoking methods on components." For more information, consult the *ColdFusion MX Documentation* (Help | Using ColdFusion).

Open the Components panel (Window | Components) and choose CF Components from the drop-down menu. Click the Refresh button. Dreamweaver MX searches the web server for ColdFusion components. Expand the first component package, `CFDOCS.exampleapps.cfc`. This package contains one component: `tempconverter`. Click the plus (+) button to reveal the component's functions. The `tempconverter` CFC has one function: `convert`. Click the plus (+) button again. The `convert` function accepts two optional parameters or arguments: `scale` and `temperature`.

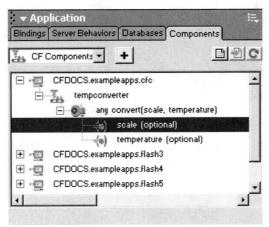

To obtain more information about the component, right-click on `tempconverter` in the Components panel and choose Get Description. (If you're prompted to log in to ColdFusion Administrator, enter the password you created when you installed ColdFusion MX.) ColdFusion's CFC Explorer displays information about the component, including its properties, methods, and location on the server.

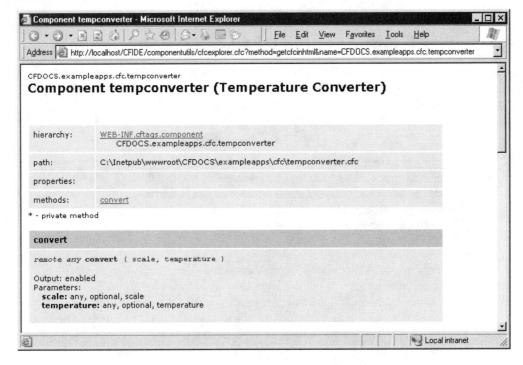

In Dreamweaver MX, choose View | Code (or press CTRL-`) to switch to Code view. Scroll to the bottom of the page and place your cursor to the left of the closing `</body>` tag (line 45). In the Components panel, select the `convert` function and click the Insert icon on the panel toolbar. Alternatively, you can drag and drop the function from the Components panel into the Document window. To invoke the function, Dreamweaver MX inserts the following code:

```
<cfinvoke
 component="CFDOCS.exampleapps.cfc.tempconverter"
 method="convert"
 returnvariable="convertRet">
</cfinvoke>
```

To invoke the function's two arguments, we'll use ColdFusion's new `<cfinvokeargument>` tag. Insert the following code *before* the closing `</cfinvoke>` tag:

```
<cfinvokeargument name="scale" value="#FORM.scale#">
<cfinvokeargument name="temperature" value="#FORM.temp#">
```

To display the results of the component call, we'll output the variable specified in the `returnvariable` attribute: `convertRet`. Insert the following code *after* the closing `</cfinvoke>` tag:

```
<cfif FORM.scale IS "F">
<cfoutput><p align="center"> ↵
Results: #FORM.temp# Fahrenheit = #convertRet# Celsius</p></cfoutput>
<cfelse>
<cfoutput><p align="center">↵
Results: #FORM.temp# Celsius = #convertRet# Fahrenheit</p></cfoutput>
</cfif>
```

Finally, select all of the code we just inserted and select the CFML Flow tab on the Insert bar. Click the cfif button. Complete the opening `<cfif>` tag as follows:

```
<cfif isDefined("FORM.temp")>
```

The final code should look like this:

```
<cfif isDefined("FORM.temp")>
<cfinvoke
 component="CFDOCS.exampleapps.cfc.tempconverter"
 method="convert"
 returnvariable="convertRet">
<cfinvokeargument name="scale" value="#FORM.scale#">
<cfinvokeargument name="temperature" value="#FORM.temp#">
</cfinvoke>
<cfif FORM.scale IS "F">
<cfoutput><p align="center"> ↵
```

```
Results: #FORM.temp# Fahrenheit = #convertRet# Celsius</p></cfoutput>
<cfelse>
<cfoutput><p align="center">
Results: #FORM.temp# Celsius = #convertRet# Fahrenheit</p></cfoutput>
</cfif>
</cfif>
```

Save your work and switch back to Design view.

> **Note**
>
> When you see the arrow symbol (✐) in a code listing—such as the previous listings—it indicates that the line continues without wrapping, even though it wraps on the printed page. Pay close attention to these critters, as improper carriage returns can cause your script to "bomb."

As you probably noticed, the values of the component's two arguments are ColdFusion `FORM` variables: `#FORM.scale#` and `#FORM.temp#`. To complete the Temperature Converter page, we have to revise the page's form accordingly.

In the Document window, place your cursor to the right of the drop-down menu and choose Modify | Table | Delete Row, or press CTRL-SHIFT-M. Select the third radio button and its description—"Dolor"—and press the DELETE key. Select the first radio button and use the Property inspector to change its name from `radiobutton` to `scale`. Tab to the Checked Value text box and enter **F**. In the Document window, select "Lorem" and type **Fahrenheit**. Select the second radio button and use the Property inspector to change its name to `scale`. Enter **C** in the Checked Value text box. In the Document window, select "Ipsum" and type **Celsius**.

Select "Keywords" in the Document window and type **Temperature**. Select the text field and use the Property inspector to name it `temp`. Select "Options" in the Document window and type **Scale**. Finally, select the submit button and use the Property inspector to change its Label from Go to Convert. The completed page should look like this:

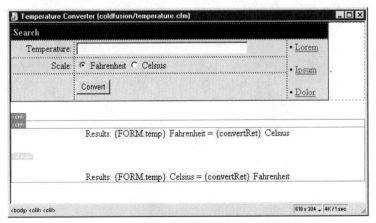

Save your work and press F12 to preview the page in a browser. Enter **212** in the text field and click Convert. The browser displays the results:

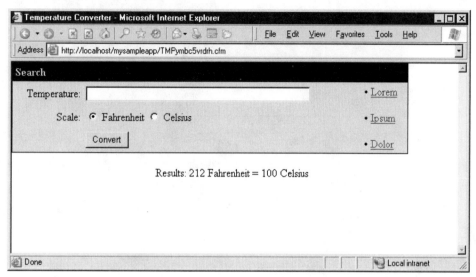

Click the Celsius radio button and enter **100** in the text field. Click Convert. The `tempconverter` CFC converts the boiling point of water to Fahrenheit.

To "upload" the completed version of the Temperature Converter page to your remote folder, select `temperature.cfm` in the Site panel and click the Put File(s) icon (the blue arrow) on the panel toolbar. You can view the completed page by browsing to the following URL on your local server: **http://localhost/mysampleapp/temperature.cfm**.

Improved CSS Support

Although the Temperature Converter page invokes a fairly simple ColdFusion component, it gives you an inkling of how powerful CFCs can be. To change the appearance of the page, we'll take advantage of Dreamweaver's improved CSS (cascading style sheets) support.

Open the Global Car - ColdFusion site in Dreamweaver MX and press CTRL-N to launch the New Document dialog box. Select the General tab and click the CSS Style Sheets category. In the right-hand pane, choose Full Design: Arial, Blue/Green/Gray and click Create.

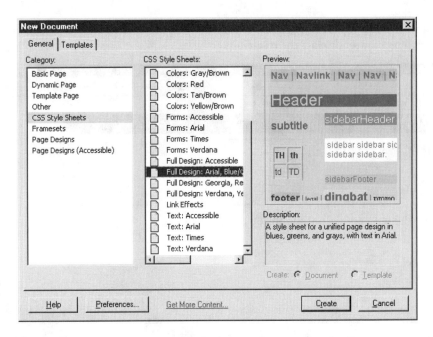

Dreamweaver MX generates an external style sheet and opens it in the Document window. Choose File | Save (or press CTRL-S) and save the style sheet as `globalcar.css`. Press CTRL-W to close the style sheet.

To attach the style sheet to the Temperature Converter page, double-click `temperature.cfm` in the Site panel. Open the CSS Styles panel by clicking the expander arrow on the Design panel group, or choose Window | CSS Styles.

Click the Attach icon on the bottom of the CSS Styles panel. This opens the Link External Style Sheet dialog box. Click Browse and double-click `globalcar.css`. Click OK to link the style sheet to the Temperature Converter page.

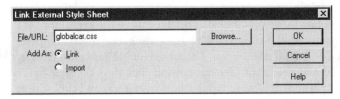

Save your work and select `temperature.cfm` and `globalcar.css` in the Site panel. Click the Put File(s) icon. Press F12 to preview the page in a browser. The new CSS styles are applied to the Temperature Converter page.

To edit the style sheet, select the Edit Styles radio button on the CSS Styles panel. The CSS Styles panel displays all of the styles defined on the page. To edit a style, double-click it in the

CSS Styles panel. This opens the CSS Style Definition dialog box. To force Dreamweaver MX to use an external editor, such as TopStyle, right-click inside the CSS Styles panel and choose Use External Editor. Now, when you select a style and click the Edit icon, the style sheet opens in TopStyle.

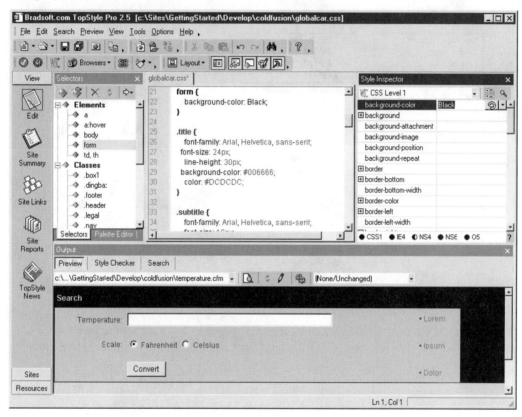

What's more, TopStyle uses the current Dreamweaver MX document as the preview file. See Chapter 4 for more on Dreamweaver MX/TopStyle integration.

XHTML Support

The next example we'll create is a page that obtains WHOIS information about a registered domain name. Open the Global Car - ColdFusion site in Dreamweaver MX and press CTRL-N to create a new document. Select the General tab and click the Dynamic Page category. In the right-hand pane, select ColdFusion and check the Make Document XHTML Compliant check box. Click Create.

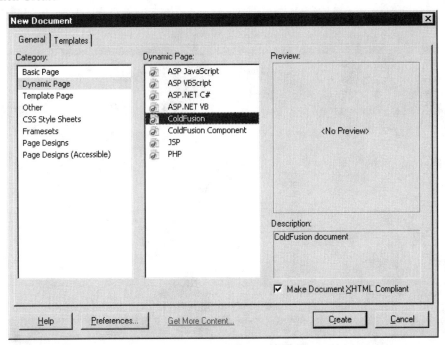

Dreamweaver MX creates an XHTML-compliant CFML page. Press CTRL-S and save it as whois.cfm. What makes this page XHTML-compliant? Switch to Code view and examine the first three lines:

```
<?xml version="1.0" encoding="iso-8859-1"?>
<!DOCTYPE html PUBLIC "-//W3C//DTD XHTML 1.0 Transitional//EN"
"http://www.w3.org/TR/xhtml1/DTD/xhtml1-transitional.dtd">
<html xmlns="http://www.w3.org/1999/xhtml">
```

According to the W3C, the XML declaration on the first line is not required, but "XHTML document authors are strongly encouraged to use XML declarations in all their documents." The mandatory DOCTYPE declaration must reference one of three DTDs (document type definitions): XHTML 1.0 Strict, XHTML 1.0 Transitional, or XHTML 1.0 Frameset. Line 3 designates the page's XHTML namespace, **http://www.w3.org/1999/xhtml**, using the xmlns parameter.

Note

XHTML 1.0, as you probably know, is the successor to HTML 4.01. To allow XHTML pages to be read by XML-enabled devices, XHTML enforces stricter tag rules than HTML 4.01. For instance, in XHTML 1.0, all tags must be lowercase (e.g., `<img>` instead of `<IMG>`), and all tag elements must be closed (e.g., `<br />` instead of `<br>`). For more information, visit **http://www.w3.org/TR/xhtml1**.

What's great about Dreamweaver's new XHTML support is that, once you identify a document as XHTML-compliant, Dreamweaver MX conforms to the XHTML specification whenever you add new content.

To convert an existing document to XHTML, open the file in Dreamweaver MX and choose File | Convert | XHTML. Keep in mind that some older browsers do not support XHTML and may render the page incorrectly.

Code Validation

Dreamweaver MX knows how to write "well-formed" XHTML, but there may be times when *you* make a mistake. That's where Validator comes in. To validate the WHOIS page, let's create an obvious XHTML error. Switch to Code view and insert a `<br>` tag between the `<body>` tags.

Save the page and choose Window | Results | Validation. This opens the Validation tab of the Results panel. Click the Validate icon—the green arrow—and choose Settings. Check XHTML 1.0 Transitional in the Validator preferences and click OK.

In the Results panel, click the Validate icon and choose Validate Current Document. Dreamweaver MX reports the following nesting error: "'br' should be closed before closing 'body.'" If you double-click the error, Dreamweaver MX switches to Split view (a.k.a. Code and Design view) and highlights the offending line. Change the `<br>` tag to `<br />` and run Validator again. The Description column says "No errors or warnings found."

Note

Throughout *The Joy of Dreamweaver MX*, I'll refer to Code and Design view as Split view. My apologies to Macromedia.

To change Dreamweaver's default validation back to HTML 4.0, choose Edit | Preferences and select the Validator category. Check the HTML 4.0 check box. Notice that you can also use Validator to validate ColdFusion tags, SMIL, WML, and JavaServer Pages. For XML validation, choose File | Check Page | Validate as XML. For additional validation services, visit **http://validator.w3.org**.

Web Services

To create the WHOIS page, we're going to use the Components panel to generate a web service proxy. Open whois.cfm in Dreamweaver MX and open the Components panel (Window | Components). Choose Web Services from the drop-down menu and click the plus (+) button. In the Add Using WSDL dialog box, enter the following URL:

http://ws.cdyne.com/whoisquery/whois.asmx?wsdl

Where did I get this URL? Click the globe icon and choose xMethods UDDI.

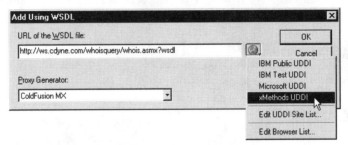

This launches the XMethods web site (**http://www.xmethods.net**) in your default browser. XMethods is a free registry of SOAP, WSDL, and UDDI web services. Scroll down the page and click the "Whois" link in the Service Name column. This takes you to a page with additional information about the web service.

Note

According to the W3C, WSDL (Web Services Description Language) is an "XML format for describing network services as a set of endpoints operating on messages containing either document-oriented or procedure-oriented information." Yep. For more acronyms, visit **http://www.w3.org/TR/wsdl**.

In Dreamweaver MX, make sure ColdFusion MX is selected in the Proxy Generator drop-down menu and click OK. According to *Using Dreamweaver MX*: "The proxy generator creates a proxy for the web service and introspects it. Introspection is the process where the proxy generator queries the internal structure of the web service proxy, and makes its interfaces, methods, and properties available through Dreamweaver."

In the Components panel, click the plus (+) button next to the WhoIS web service. This exposes the web service's three methods, along with their data types: getEmailforDomain, getWhois, and message. Expand getWhois. The getWhois method accepts two parameters: licenseKey and query.

We know, from the XMethods web site, that we can use 0 as the licenseKey parameter to test the web service. The query parameter is simply the domain name we want information about (e.g., macromedia.com).

To implement the web service on the page, we're going to create a simple form. Place your cursor in the Document window and type the following heading: **WHOIS Web Service**. Select "WHOIS Web Service" and choose Heading 3 from the Format drop-down menu on the Property inspector. In the Document window, insert a paragraph after the heading and select the Forms tab on the Insert bar. Click the Text Field button. When prompted to add a form tag, click Yes. Place your cursor inside the form boundary—the red dashed rectangle—and click Button on the Insert bar. Finally, select the text field and use the Property inspector to name it whois.

Switch to Code view and insert a new line after the closing </form> tag. In the Components panel, right-click the getWhois function and choose Insert Code. (You can also drag-and-drop the function into the Document window.) To invoke the getWhois function, Dreamweaver MX inserts the following code:

```
<cfinvoke
 webservice="http://ws.cdyne.com/whoisquery/whois.asmx?wsdl"
 method="getWhois"
 returnvariable="aString">
     <cfinvokeargument name="query" value="enter_value_here"/>
     <cfinvokeargument name="licenseKey" value="enter_value_here"/>
</cfinvoke>
```

In the first <cfinvokeargument> tag, replace enter_value_here with #FORM.whois#. In the second <cfinvokeargument> tag, enter 0 in the value attribute.

To output the results of the query, enter the following code after the closing </cfinvoke> tag:

```
<cfoutput><h3>WHOIS Results for #FORM.whois#</h3>
<p>#ParagraphFormat(aString)#</p></cfoutput>
```

Finally, select all of the code we just inserted (lines 14–22) and select CFML Flow on the Insert bar. Click the cfif button. Once again, Dreamweaver MX wraps the selection in `<cfif>` tags. Complete the `<cfif>` statement as follows:

```
<cfif isDefined("FORM.whois")>
```

The completed code should look like this:

```
<cfif isDefined("FORM.whois")>
<cfinvoke
 webservice="http://ws.cdyne.com/whoisquery/whois.asmx?wsdl"
 method="getWhois"
 returnvariable="aString">
      <cfinvokeargument name="query" value="#FORM.whois#"/>
      <cfinvokeargument name="licenseKey" value="0"/>
</cfinvoke>
<cfoutput><h3>WHOIS Results for #FORM.whois#</h3>
<p>#ParagraphFormat(aString)#</p></cfoutput>
</cfif>
```

Save your work and press F12 to preview the page in a browser. Enter a domain name in the text field and click Submit.

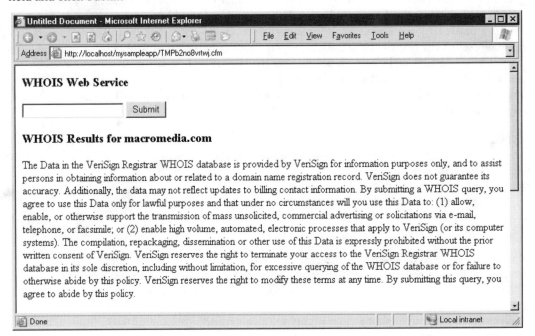

The results of the WHOIS query are displayed in the browser. Scroll down the page and you'll see the registrant's contact information.

How do you like that? You generated a proxy, invoked a function, and consumed your first web service in under 15 minutes!

Summary

In this chapter, we installed Dreamweaver MX and set up the *Getting Started* lessons. In addition, we toured some of Dreamweaver's most compelling new features:

◆ Improved New Document dialog box

◆ ColdFusion components (CFCs) support

◆ Improved CSS support

◆ XHTML support

◆ Enhanced code validation

◆ Web services support

In the next chapter, we'll install a web server and an application server—if you haven't already—and review the server models supported by Dreamweaver MX.

Chapter 2

Utensils: Choosing the Right Tools for the Job

INGREDIENTS

Software	Type	Source
Personal Web Server (PWS)	Web Server	Microsoft
Internet Information Services (IIS)	Web Server	Microsoft
ColdFusion MX Server Developer Edition	Application Server	Macromedia

 from the desk of Paul Newman

I n order to complete the recipes in *The Joy of Dreamweaver MX*, you need to install both a web server and an application server on your computer.

A *web server* is software that serves files—e.g., web pages, media files, Flash movies—in response to browser requests. Popular web servers include Microsoft Personal Web Server (PWS), Microsoft Internet Information Services (IIS), Apache HTTP Server, and Sun ONE Web Server.

An *application server* is middle-tier software that helps a web server process specific pages. For instance, if IIS receives a request for a page with a `.cfm` extension, it hands it off to ColdFusion Server. The application server processes the server-side code—for example, a database query—and returns the document to IIS, which serves it to the browser as regular HTML.

In some cases, a web server can also double as application server. For example, when you install Personal Web Server or IIS, it is automatically configured to interpret ASP pages. If you install the .NET Framework, IIS also functions as an application server for ASP.NET pages.

In this chapter, we're going to look at requirements for the different server models supported by Dreamweaver MX. We'll also review the steps to install and configure a web server (IIS) and an application server (ColdFusion) on the Windows platform.

Which Server Model?

Although the examples in this book are presented in ASP/VBScript and ColdFusion MX formats, Dreamweaver MX now supports five different server models: ASP, ASP.NET, ColdFusion, JavaServer Pages (JSP), and PHP/MySQL. This section reviews the requirements for getting each server model up and running on your system. Ultimately, the server model you choose to develop web applications is based on many factors, including:

♦ **Platform**   Which operating systems does the server support? Is it compatible with hardware you already own?

♦ **Ease of use**   How difficult is the programming language to learn and use? How difficult is the server to administer?

♦ **Cost**   Is the software open-source, like Apache? If not, does the manufacturer offer a free developer version?

♦ **Reliability**   What is the server's history and reputation? Stable? Buggy?

♦ **Performance**   How many simultaneous connections are supported? What sort of speed and response can you expect?

♦ **Connectivity**   Does the server include drivers for all the data sources you intend to use?

♦ **Security**   How vulnerable is the server to attack? Does it support secure sockets (SSL)? How is user access controlled?

♦ **Scalability**   Can the software grow with your company, or will you have to migrate your applications to another server model?

♦ **Extensibility**   How well does the server integrate with the latest Internet technologies, such as web services, XML, and WebDAV?

Since all of Dreamweaver's server models can be deployed on Windows, you may want to experiment with several of them before you make your decision. In fact, I encourage you to configure your system for both Active Server Pages and ColdFusion MX, so you can use this book's examples to compare their features.

Active Server Pages (ASP)

Dreamweaver MX supports two flavors of ASP: ASP/VBScript and ASP/JavaScript. Unlike ASP.NET, Active Server Pages can be developed on virtually any Windows machine.

To install ASP on your system, you have two options: Personal Web Server (PWS), or Internet Information Services (IIS). If you're running Windows NT 4.0, 2000, or XP Professional, install Internet Information Services. For details, see "Installing a Web Server," later in this chapter.

To develop Active Server Pages on Windows 95/98, you need to install Personal Web Server, a slimmed-down version of IIS. PWS is available from many different sources, but the version distributed with the NT 4.0 Option Pack seems to be the most reliable: **http://www.microsoft.com/ ntserver/nts/downloads/recommended/NT4OptPk**.

Note

At the time of this writing, Personal Web Server is not compatible with Windows Me.

When you visit the Windows NT 4.0 Option Pack web page, choose Windows 95 from the drop-down menu to obtain PWS for Windows 95/98. Download the files to your computer and run `install.exe` to begin the installation. Make sure to select the Custom installation option,which enables you to install additional components, such as the Active Server Pages documentation files.

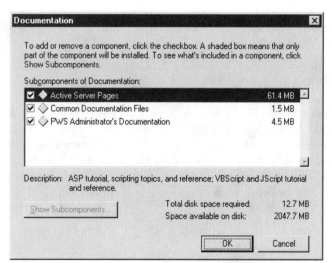

After installation, PWS is configured to run whenever Windows starts, and can be opened and administered via the icon in your system tray.

ASP.NET

Dreamweaver MX supports two flavors of ASP.NET: ASP/VB and ASP/C#. If you're already familiar with VBScript, making the transition to Visual Basic .NET shouldn't be too difficult. Microsoft's new language, C# (pronounced C-sharp), is closer to true object-oriented programming (OOP) languages such as C++ and Java. One of the many advantages of ASP.NET over ASP is that ASP.NET pages are compiled on the server, rather than interpreted, resulting in improved performance.

To develop ASP.NET applications, you need to install the .NET Framework. To download the .NET Framework, go to **http://asp.net/download.aspx**. There you will find two versions of ASP.NET 1.0: the .NET Framework Redistributable (21 MB) and the .NET Framework SDK (131 MB). If you intend to experiment with Dreamweaver's new .NET features, such as web services, choose the latter option. The .NET Framework SDK requires IIS 5.x running on Windows NT 4.0 (SP 6a), Windows 2000, or Windows XP Professional. As an added bonus, the .NET Framework SDK also includes MSDE (Microsoft Data Engine), a lightweight version of SQL Server.

The .NET Framework Redistributable, on the other hand, purportedly runs on Windows 98, Windows Me, Windows NT 4.0, Windows 2000, and Windows XP. However, the .NET Framework Redistributable also requires IIS, which effectively rules out Windows 98, Me, and XP Home.

Finally, ASP.NET requires MDAC 2.6 or later. To download MDAC (Microsoft Data Access Components), go to **www.microsoft.com/data/download.htm**.

ColdFusion MX

The ColdFusion MX application server can be installed on many different web servers, including IIS, Apache, iPlanet, and Netscape. The following is a list of Windows operating systems and web servers supported by ColdFusion MX:

- **Operating systems**   Windows 95, Windows 98, Windows Me, Windows NT 4.0, Windows 2000, Windows XP
- **Web servers**   IIS 4.0, 5.x, Apache 1.3.12-1.3.22, Apache 2.x, JRun HTTP Server, iPlanet 6.x, iPlanet 4.x, Netscape 3.6x

ColdFusion MX Server is available in three editions: Developer, Professional, and Enterprise. The free ColdFusion MX Server Developer Edition is bundled with Dreamweaver MX and MX Studio, or may be downloaded from Macromedia's web site: **http://www.macromedia.com/software/coldfusion/downloads**. After 30 days, the trial edition converts to the developer edition. The developer edition is a fully functional, nonexpiring version of ColdFusion Server for local development purposes only (in other words, it's accessible only from a single IP address).

At the time of this writing, Macromedia plans to offer editions of ColdFusion MX Server for Macromedia JRun, IBM WebSphere Application Server, Sun ONE Web Server, and BEA WebLogic Server.

For details on installing ColdFusion MX see "Installing an Application Server," later in this chapter.

JavaServer Pages (JSP)

In order to develop JavaServer Pages on your computer, you need at least the Java 2 SDK Standard Edition (J2SE) and a JSP application server. The Java 2 SDK includes the Java Runtime Environment (JRE) and a JDBC driver that lets you connect to ODBC data sources such as Access databases. The Java 2 SDK is a free download from Sun Microsystems: **http://java.sun.com/ j2se/1.4/download.html**.

Once the J2SE is installed, you can download and install the free developer edition of Macromedia's JRun application server: **http://www.macromedia.com/software/jrun/trial**. (The developer edition is a fully functional, nonexpiring version of JRun Server for local development purposes only.) The following is a list of operating systems and web servers supported by JRun Server:

◆ **Operating systems**   Windows 95/98/NT/2000/XP; Solaris 2.6, 7, 8; Red Hat Linux 6.0, 6.1; HP-UX 11.0; IBM AIX 4.2, 4.3; SGI IRIX 6.5; Compaq Tru64 UNIX 4.0

◆ **Web servers**   Apache; Microsoft IIS; Microsoft Personal Web Server; Netscape Enterprise Server; Netscape FastTrack Server; O'Reilly WebSite Pro; Sun iPlanet Web Server; Zeus Web Server

For help with installing and configuring JRun Server, read Macromedia's tutorial on "Setting Up a JSP Development Environment": **http://www.macromedia.com/support/ultradev/ installation/installing_jrun**. Although this tutorial was written with Dreamweaver UltraDev 4 in mind, most of it still applies to Dreamweaver MX.

Of course, you're not limited to using JRun Server to develop JavaServer Pages with Dreamweaver MX. Common JSP application servers include IBM WebSphere, BEA WebLogic, and Sun ONE Web Server (formerly iPlanet Web Server).

Tip   Although ColdFusion MX includes an embedded server based on JRun technology, it is not a full-blown JSP application server. If you want to develop web applications using both JSP and ColdFusion MX, you need to purchase ColdFusion MX for J2EE (Java 2 Enterprise Edition) Application Servers. This line of products supports integrating ColdFusion MX with Macromedia JRun, IBM WebSphere, Sun ONE, or BEA WebLogic.

Another popular (and free) option is Tomcat/Apache/MySQL, although it's not for the faint of heart. Part of Apache's open-source Jakarta Project, Tomcat server is a Java servlet and JSP container. Tomcat can be used in a development environment as a stand-alone web server or integrated with Apache HTTP Server and MySQL database server. James Goodwill has written an excellent tutorial on "Installing and Configuring Tomcat" on Windows and Linux: **http://www.onjava.com/pub/a/onjava/2001/03/29/tomcat.html**. For more information, visit the Jakarta Project: **http://jakarta.apache.org/tomcat**.

Hypertext Preprocessor (PHP)

Although Linux is unquestionably the most popular platform for developing PHP applications, Dreamweaver MX currently supports only the Windows and Macintosh operating systems. In order to develop PHP pages with Dreamweaver MX, you need to install the following software:

◆ Web server (e.g., IIS, Apache)

◆ PHP application server

◆ Database server (e.g., MS SQL, MySQL)

Although PHP can be configured to work with Microsoft SQL Server, Dreamweaver MX currently supports the PHP/MySQL server model. The easiest way to install PHP is to download and run the Windows InstallShield installer from **http://www.php.net/downloads.php**. This installs PHP with built-in MySQL support and automatically configures it for use with PWS or IIS.

To download MySQL database server, go to **http://www.mysql.com/downloads**. For help with installing MySQL Server, visit **http://www.mysql.com/doc/W/i/Windows_installation.html**. Once installed, MySQL server is administered from a command line. If you prefer a graphical user interface to MySQL, you can download MyCC (MySQL Control Center) or MySQLGUI from **http://www.mysql.com/downloads/gui-clients.html**.

To download Apache HTTP Server, go to **http://httpd.apache.org**.

Installing a Web Server

This section reviews the steps for installing and configuring Microsoft Internet Information Services (IIS), the web server bundled with Windows NT, 2000, and XP Professional. In addition to offering built-in ASP support, IIS integrates with application servers such as ColdFusion, JRun, and PHP.

Installing Internet Information Services (IIS)

Installing IIS on Windows is gloriously simple. Open the Control panel and choose Add or Remove Programs (make sure you're in Classic View). Click Add/Remove Windows Components.

This launches the Windows Components Wizard. Scroll down the list to see if there's a check next to Internet Information Services (IIS). (Notice the description for IIS mentions Web support and Active Server Pages.) If not, check IIS and click Details.

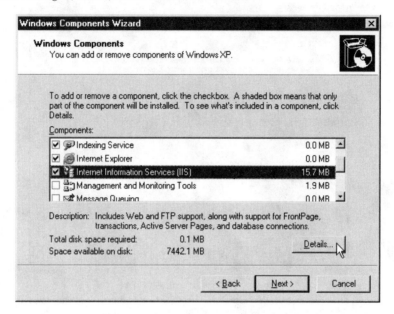

On the next screen, make sure Internet Information Services Snap-In and World Wide Web Service are checked. If you plan to send mail using <cfmail>, or a COM object such as JMail, check SMTP Service as well (for more on setting up a mail server, see Chapter 5).

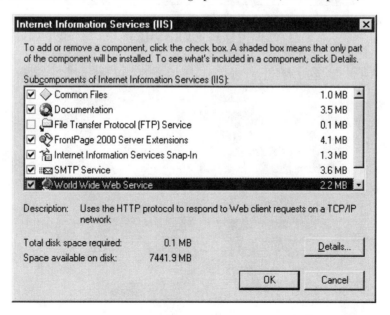

Click OK to close the subcomponents dialog box. Click Next to install IIS.

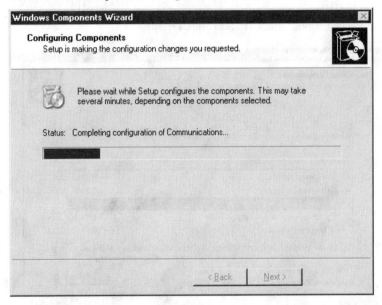

Click Finish and close the Control Panel. Internet Information Services, and any other components you may have selected, are now installed. To test the installation, launch your browser and type **http://localhost/** in the address bar. Press ENTER. You should see a welcome page like this one:

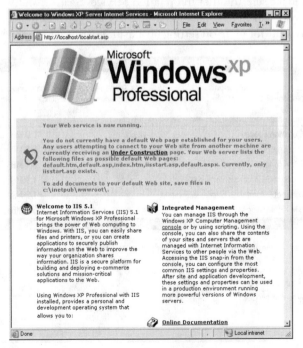

In addition, Internet Information Services Documentation opens in a second browser window. The IIS Documentation contains information about administering Internet Information Services, and an Active Server Pages Guide.

If you receive a "Permission denied" error, try typing **http://localhost/IISHelp/**. If that doesn't work, and you're running Windows XP Professional, you may have to disable XP's firewall (Microsoft enables it by default). To do this, open the Control Panel and choose Network Connections | Local Area Connection. On the General tab, click Properties. Click the Advanced tab and uncheck the option that enables the Internet Connection Firewall. If you must use the Internet Connection Firewall, leave the option checked and click Settings. On the Services tab, place a check next to Web Server (HTTP) and click OK.

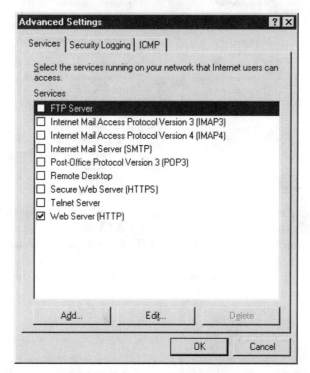

Click OK again to close the Local Area Connection Properties dialog box, and close the Local Area Connection Status dialog box.

Administering IIS

Internet Information Services is administered via the IIS Snap-in. To launch the IIS Snap-in, open the Control Panel and choose Administrative Tools | Internet Information Services. Better still, create a shortcut to the IIS Snap-in on your Desktop. To do this, right-click on the Desktop and choose New | Shortcut. In the Location text box, type **%SystemRoot%\System32\ inetsrv\inetmgr.exe** and click Next. Name the shortcut **IIS Snap-in** and click Finish.

Double-click IIS Snap-in on your Desktop to open Internet Information Services. In the left-hand pane, expand the console tree and select Default Web Site. The files and folders under C:\inetpub\wwwroot are displayed in the right-hand pane, as well as any virtual directories.

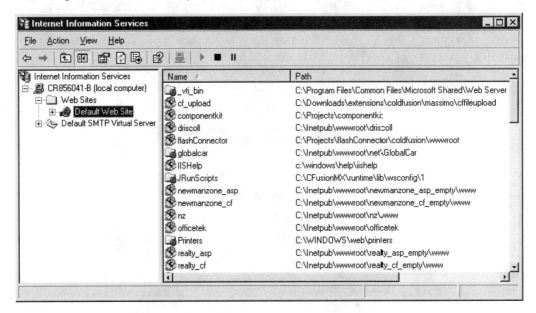

Notice that at least one virtual directory has already been created: IISHelp. If you open C:\inetpub\wwwroot in Windows Explorer, you'll see that there is no actual directory called IISHelp. However, if you browse to **http://localhost/IISHelp** on your local server, IIS serves the contents of the C:\Windows\Help\iishelp folder listed in the Path column.

A *virtual directory*, as opposed to a physical directory, is like a shortcut to the specified folder and its contents. To illustrate this, let's create a virtual directory for a site we'll be using later in the book: newmanzone_asp.

Creating a Virtual Directory

If you haven't already, download the supporting files for this book from **www.newmanzone.com** or **www.osborne.com/downloads/downloads.shtml**. Unzip the files to a folder on your hard drive (e.g., C:\Downloads) and copy the newmanzone_asp_empty folder into the web server's wwwroot directory (i.e., C:\Inetpub\wwwroot\newmanzone_asp_empty).

In the IIS Snap-in, right-click Default Web Site and choose Refresh. The folder you just copied into the server root, newmanzone_asp_empty, appears in the right-hand pane. In the left-hand pane, select Default Web Site and choose Action | New | Virtual Directory. This opens the Virtual Directory Creation Wizard. Click Next and enter **newmanzone_asp** in the Alias text box. Click Next.

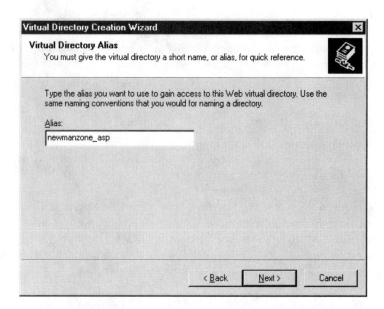

On the next screen, enter **C:\Inetpub\wwwroot\newmanzone_asp_empty\www** in the Directory text box (or click Browse to select the folder using a Windows Explorer–style directory tree). Click Next.

On the Access Permissions screen, make sure Read and Run Scripts (Such As ASP) are checked and click Next. On the final screen, click Finish to close the Virtual Directory Creation Wizard.

To test the virtual directory, launch your browser and enter the following URL in the address bar: **http://localhost/newmanzone_asp/**. The following error message appears:

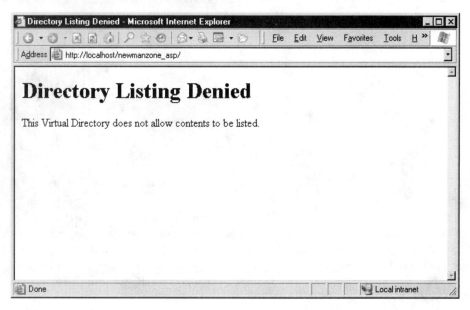

This is because directory browsing is disabled in IIS by default. That's a good thing: we don't want people snooping through our files. Change the URL in the address bar to **http://localhost/ newmanzone_asp/index.htm** and press ENTER. The Newman Zone splash page appears.

To display the Newman Zone home page without entering the full URL, we have to enable the default document.

Enabling the Default Document

When you create a virtual directory in IIS, the following default documents are enabled automatically: `default.htm`, `default.asp`, `iisstart.asp`. If you have ColdFusion MX Server or JRun Server installed on your machine, the list may also include `index.cfm` or `index.jsp`.

The default document in the root of the Newman Zone site is `index.htm`. To enable this document, right-click `newmanzone_asp` in the IIS Snap-in and choose Properties. Select the Documents tab and click Add. Enter **index.htm** in the Add Default Document dialog box and click OK. The new entry, `index.htm`, appears in the list of default documents. You can use the up and down arrows to change the priority of the default documents.

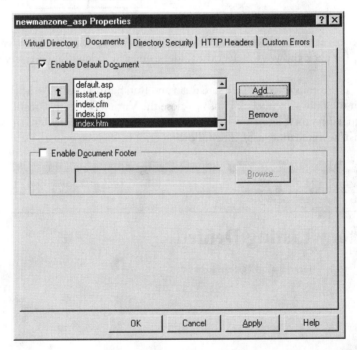

Click OK and browse to the following URL on your local server: **http://localhost/ newmanzone_asp/**. Instead of an error message, the Newman Zone splash page appears.

The IIS Snap-in offers a myriad of options for configuring Internet Information Services— everything from custom error messages and application mappings to script debugging and permissions. While a complete discussion of these options is beyond the scope of this book, you can learn more about IIS administration in the Internet Information Services Documentation: **http://localhost/IISHelp**.

Installing an Application Server

This section reviews the steps for installing and configuring the ColdFusion MX Server. The free developer edition can be installed from the Dreamweaver MX CD-ROM, or downloaded from Macromedia's web site: **http://www.macromedia.com/software/coldfusion/downloads**.

Installing ColdFusion MX Server

Before you install ColdFusion MX Server on your machine, read the Release Notes (**http://www.macromedia.com/support/coldfusion/releasenotes.html**) and make sure your computer meets the software's system requirements.

To install ColdFusion MX Server, run the installation file on the Dreamweaver MX CD-ROM. If you downloaded ColdFusion MX from Macromedia's web site, double-click the setup file in Windows Explorer.

Note

When you install ColdFusion MX, you're given the option to upgrade your existing ColdFusion installation. If you do *not* accept this option, ColdFusion MX installs on its own stand-alone server (ColdFusion MX and existing ColdFusion installations cannot share the same web server). The Standalone server allows you to test ColdFusion MX without affecting your existing ColdFusion 5 applications.

Complete the following steps to install ColdFusion MX Server:

1. If you're installing ColdFusion MX Server on a computer with a previous ColdFusion installation, a message box will appear, asking if you wish to upgrade to ColdFusion MX. Choosing Yes will migrate your previous ColdFusion settings to ColdFusion MX. If you choose No, ColdFusion MX will be installed on a stand-alone server (see previous note).

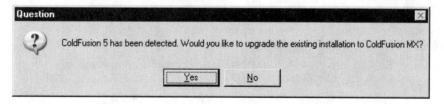

2. If you chose Yes in step 1, the ColdFusion MX Install Wizard backs up files and folders from your previous installation. Depending on your system, this may take several minutes. Click Next.

3. On the following screen, read the license agreement and click Next.

4. On the Customer Information screen, enter your name and serial number and click Next.

Note

If you're installing the trial version of ColdFusion MX Server, some of these screens may be different. For example, you won't be prompted to enter a serial number.

5. If you chose the option to upgrade ColdFusion Server in step 1, you are now offered the choice to install ColdFusion MX on your default web server (e.g., PWS, IIS), or on the Standalone server. (The Standalone server is suitable for development purposes only.) Make your selection and click Next.

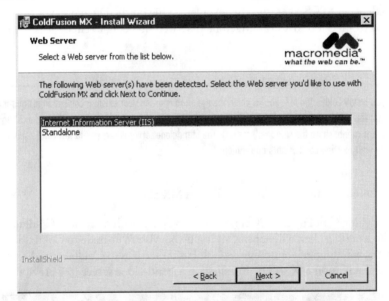

6. Unless you want to install ColdFusion to a different folder, accept the defaults on the Webroot Folder screen and click Next.

7. The Custom Setup screen enables you to choose which ColdFusion components are installed. Make your selections and click Next.

8. The Select Passwords screen prompts you to create a password for accessing ColdFusion Administrator. Enter your password in the Password and Confirm text boxes. Unless you

want to create a different password for ColdFusion Remote Development Services (RDS), select the option to "Use the same password as above" and click Next.

9. The next screen allows you to review the installation settings. If you wish to make any changes, click the Back button. Otherwise, click Next.

10. The Install Wizard installs ColdFusion MX on your computer. When the installation is complete, click Finish.

11. A browser pop-up window opens, informing you that ColdFusion Server was successfully installed. Close the pop-up window and log in to ColdFusion Administrator using the password you created in step 8.

12. The first time you log in to ColdFusion Administrator, a pop-up window appears, asking if you want to migrate the settings from a previous ColdFusion installation. Click Continue. (If you click Skip, you have to edit the Windows Registry to run the migration wizard at a later time.)

13. After the migration is complete, any problems encountered by the migration wizard will be listed. Click OK.

14. ColdFusion Administrator launches, and a pop-up window appears, with quick links to "Getting Started with ColdFusion MX," "Example Applications," and "Documentation."

We already know the installation of ColdFusion MX Server was successful, because we were able to log in to ColdFusion Administrator. To verify database connectivity, click "Example Applications," and then click "check for example applications installed on this server." A list of ColdFusion MX Example Applications appears in the browser. Under Beginner Examples, click "Database Search #2 - Data Drill Down." If you're able to search items by name or category, ColdFusion's data sources are working properly.

If you encounter any problems, consult the *ColdFusion Documentation* (**http://localhost/cfdocs/dochome.htm**), or visit the ColdFusion Support Center (**http://www.macromedia.com/support/coldfusion**).

Log out of ColdFusion Administrator and restart your computer (it's always a good idea to reboot your computer after installing new software).

Using ColdFusion Administrator

Most of the work you'll be doing in ColdFusion Administrator involves customizing the server settings, or creating data sources. In this section, we'll create a new ColdFusion data source, and explore ColdFusion's example applications.

To launch ColdFusion Administrator, choose Start | Programs | Macromedia ColdFusion MX | Administrator, or browse to **http://localhost/CFIDE/administrator** on your local server. Enter the password you created when you installed ColdFusion MX and click Login.

Creating a ColdFusion Data Source

ColdFusion Administrator is organized into five main sections: Server Settings, Data & Services, Debugging & Logging, Extensions, and Security. To add a new data source, click Data Sources in the table of contents on the left. A list of ColdFusion data sources appears in the frame on the right. Notice that data sources migrated from a previous ColdFusion installation use ODBC Socket drivers.

Note

Because ColdFusion MX Server's architecture is now based on Java technology — ColdFusion MX actually rests atop J2EE 1.3–compliant infrastructure services — ColdFusion uses JDBC (Java Database Connectivity) drivers to connect to data sources such as Access and SQL Server databases. In order to connect to System DSNs created with Windows ODBC Data Source Administrator, you need to use the ODBC Socket driver (essentially a JDBC-ODBC bridge).

To create a sample data source in ColdFusion MX, we'll use the Access database that installs with Office 2000: Northwind.mdb. (If you don't have Office 2000 or later, you can use the movies.mdb database that is included among this book's supporting files. You'll find it in the Chapter11 folder.) In the Add New Data Source area, enter **Northwind** in the Data Source Name text box, and choose Microsoft Access from the Driver drop-down menu. Click Add.

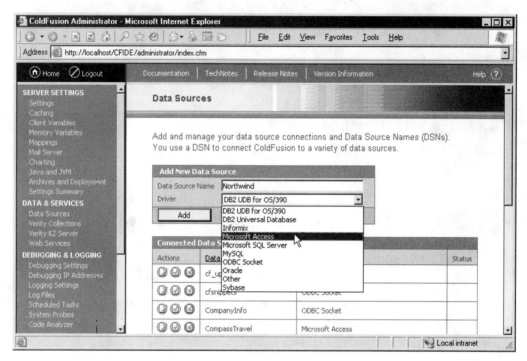

On the next page, click Browse Server to select the database file. ColdFusion Administrator uses a Java applet to display a Windows Explorer–style directory tree. Drill down to C:\Program Files\Microsoft Office\Office\Samples. Select Northwind.mdb and click Apply. The path to Northwind.mdb is entered in the Database File text box.

Click Show Advanced Settings and select the check box next to Enable Long Text Retrieval (CLOB). (This option is required to display Microsoft Access Memo fields.) Click Submit to create the data source. Northwind appears in the list of ColdFusion data sources, and "ok" appears in the status column.

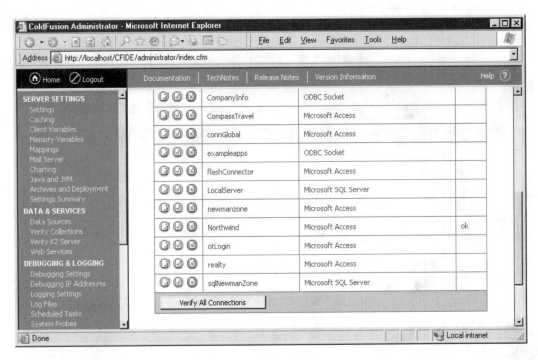

The Northwind data source is now available to Dreamweaver MX and other applications that support Remote Development Services (RDS), such as Macromedia HomeSite+.

Example Applications

One of the best ways to learn about ColdFusion's new features and capabilities is to browse its Example Applications. In ColdFusion Administrator, click Home in the table of contents on the left. This launches Welcome to ColdFusion MX in a browser pop-up window. Click "Example Applications," and then click "check for example applications installed on this server."

The ColdFusion MX Example Applications are organized into five categories: "Beginner Examples," "Intermediate/Advanced Examples," "New in ColdFusion MX," "Flash MX and ColdFusion MX Native Connectivity," and "Old Applications." Click "Web Services" under "New in ColdFusion MX."

The Web Services Example uses a sample web service that installs with ColdFusion MX. (You'll find it under Web Services in ColdFusion Administrator.) Babel Fish, as you probably know, is AltaVista's language translation service. Type **Hello, how are you?** in the text area on the left and click Translate! ColdFusion invokes the Babel Fish web service and returns the phrase in Spanish.

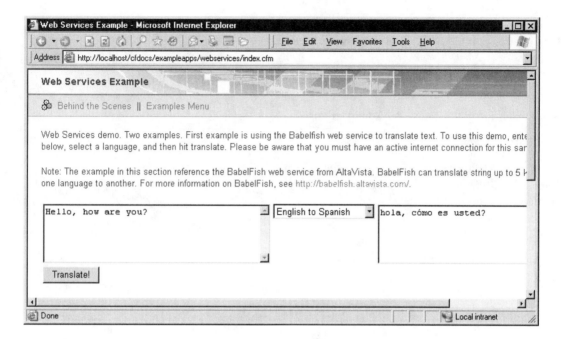

To find out how this was done, click the "Behind the Scenes" link. This opens a page with a list of source files, key tags, and functions. Click the link to `index.cfm`. ColdFusion displays the server-side markup used to invoke the Babel Fish web service and display the form results. Take some time to explore the remaining ColdFusion example applications and study the source code to see how they work.

For more information on using ColdFusion Administrator, see "Administering ColdFusion MX" in the *ColdFusion Documentation*: **http://localhost/cfdocs/Administering_ColdFusion_MX/ contents.htm**.

Summary

In this chapter, we touched on the differences between web servers and application servers. We also reviewed the requirements for setting up the five server models supported by Dreamweaver MX. Finally, we walked through the steps to install a web server (IIS) and an application server (ColdFusion MX) on the Windows platform.

We also covered some of the more common administrative tasks associated with Internet Information Services and ColdFusion Server:

◆ Creating a virtual directory (IIS)

◆ Enabling a default document (IIS)

◆ Logging in to ColdFusion Administrator

◆ Creating a ColdFusion data source

In the next chapter, we'll examine the differences between file-based databases (e.g., Microsoft Access) and client/server databases (e.g., SQL Server). In addition, we'll explore some of the options for managing and deploying databases.

Chapter 3

Ingredients:
The Care and
Feeding of
Databases

INGREDIENTS

File	Type	Server Model(s)	Source
global.mdb	Access database	ASP/CF	Macromedia
newmanzone.sql	SQL script	ASP/CF	*Sample Code*

 from the desk of *Paul Newman*

In order to create a data-driven web site, you need a database. Because of the widespread availability of Microsoft Access, most of the recipes in this book use Access 2000 databases. The one exception is Chapter 8, which requires SQL Server or Microsoft Data Engine (MSDE). In this chapter, we'll briefly compare the strengths and weaknesses of file-based databases (e.g., Microsoft Access) and client/server databases (e.g., SQL Server). We'll also look at how to obtain the database software required to complete this book. Finally, we'll explore the concept of relational databases.

As a bonus, the last two sections cover subjects that pertain to SQL Server or MSDE users: "Using Access Projects" and "How to Deploy and Manage Remote Databases." These sections walk you through setting up an Access project and using Data Transformation Services (DTS) to transfer your SQL Server database to a remote server. If you don't have a copy of SQL Server or MSDE, or you simply have no intention of using a client/server database, feel free to ignore these sections.

File-Based vs. Client/Server Databases

For the most part, databases fall into two broad categories: file-based databases and client/server databases.

A *file-based database*—e.g., Microsoft Access, FileMaker Pro, FoxPro, dBASE—is a self-contained file, like a Microsoft Word document. The advantage of a file-based database is that all of its information—tables, queries, reports, etc.—is contained in a single file that you can easily distribute (e.g., `newmanzone.mdb`). File-based databases—sometimes called desktop databases—tend to be far less expensive than client/server databases. In addition, file-based database programs usually offer a more intuitive, user-friendly interface than client/server databases (for instance, you can create queries in Microsoft Access without knowing anything about Structured Query Language). On the whole, these factors make file-based databases easier to learn, use, and maintain, which accounts for their popularity.

The disadvantage of a file-based database is that it's not optimized for use on a web server. For instance, Microsoft Access supports a maximum of 255 concurrent users, and a maximum of 2 gigabytes of data per `.mdb` file. According to Microsoft, "If users of your solution will be frequently adding and updating data, an Access file-server is generally best for a maximum of about 25 to 50 users" (see **http://msdn.microsoft.com/library/default.asp?url=/library/en-us/odeopg/html/ deovrfileservervsclientserver.asp**). This essentially restricts the use of Access to smaller, more controlled environments, such as a local network or intranet. File-based databases are also more susceptible to data corruption if the application (e.g., Microsoft Access) isn't shut down properly, or the computer crashes.

A *client/server database*—e.g., SQL Server, MySQL, Oracle, DB2, Sybase—is a robust, enterprise-level database that supports virtually unlimited connections.

> **Note**
>
> For our purposes, the *client* is the browser requesting a web page, and the *server* is the computer on which the database software is installed. The client/server implementation is also referred to as a two-tier architecture.

Client/server databases offer powerful features such as remote management, scheduled backups, transactions, replication, enhanced security (e.g., stored procedures), faster query processing, and much more. According to Microsoft, "In a client/server system, the network database server processes all requests for data on the server itself. The [client] doesn't request data at the file level, but sends a high-level request to the server to execute a specific query and return its results. The primary advantage of this technique is that network traffic is reduced because only the result set of the query is returned to the workstation."

The disadvantage of client/server databases is that enterprise database software is expensive and more difficult to set up and administer. In addition, most client/server databases don't have a user-friendly interface like Microsoft Access. To address this, SQL Server includes a set of visual database tools, and third-party vendors offer data modeling tools such as ERwin, System Architect, and ER/Studio. Moreover, client/server databases don't shield you from Structured Query Language (SQL), the standardized language of relational database management systems.

Throughout *The Joy of Dreamweaver MX*, we'll be using Microsoft Access databases to create the Newman Zone and Realty sites. While Access is adequate for development purposes, in a real-world scenario, consider using a more reliable database format. Later in this chapter, we'll explore a solution that offers the best of both worlds: Access projects that enable you to manage powerful database engines without sacrificing the familiar interface of Microsoft Access.

Installing the Database Software

Before you can complete the tutorials in this book, you need to install Microsoft Access 2000 or later. If you wish to complete Chapter 8, you also need SQL Server 2000, or Microsoft Data Engine (MSDE). This section provides information on how to obtain the software.

Obtaining Microsoft Access

Microsoft Access can be purchased as a stand-alone program or as part of Microsoft Office. Because the databases that accompany this book were created with Access 2000, you need Office 2000 or later to open them.

To order a 30-day trial of Office XP, visit the following link: **http://www.microsoft.com/office/ evaluation/trial.asp.**

Obtaining SQL Server 2000

At the time of this writing, Microsoft offers a 120-day trial of SQL Server 2000. You can order the trial version on CD-ROM, or download all 325 megabytes from Microsoft's web site: **http://www.microsoft.com/sql/evaluation/trial/2000/download.asp.**

Obtaining Microsoft Data Engine (MSDE)

Microsoft Data Engine (MSDE), also known as SQL Server 2000 Desktop Engine (MSDE 2000), is a royalty-free database engine that is fully compatible with SQL Server. Currently, there are two ways to obtain MSDE: purchase Microsoft Office (2000 or later), Visual Studio (6.0 or later), or Visio 2000; or download and install the .NET Framework SDK (**http://www.asp.net/download.aspx**).

Note

The redistributable version of MSDE, which appears on the Office 2000 Developer CD, apparently lacks the "design-time UI components" to interface with Microsoft Access projects. If you plan to manage MSDE using Microsoft Access, install the version that is bundled with Office Professional.

If you have a licensed copy of Office 2000 or later, you'll find MSDE on the CD-ROM. To install MSDE, double-click the setup file (e.g., `D:\Sql\x86\Setup\Setupsql.exe`). To install MSDE 2000 from the Office XP CD, double-click `Setup.exe` in the `MSDE2000` folder.

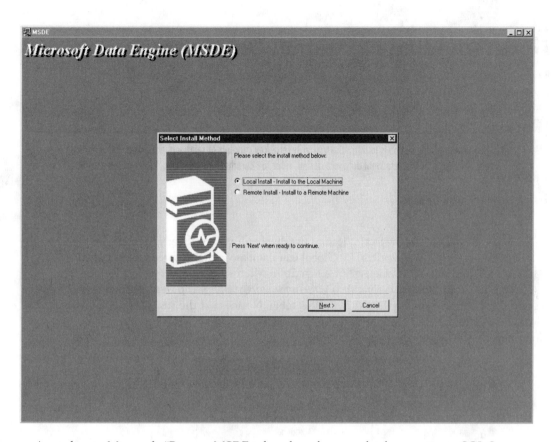

According to Microsoft, "Because MSDE is based on the same database engine as SQL Server, most Access projects or client/server applications can run unchanged on either version." Keep in mind, however, that MSDE imposes a two-gigabyte size limit (per database) and is optimized for five users. While this is adequate for development purposes, MSDE should not be used in a production environment.

Understanding Relational Databases

Throughout this book, we'll be using relational databases to create the Newman Zone (`newmanzone.mdb`) and Realty (`realty.mdb`) sites.

Note

The purpose of this section is to introduce you to several key concepts of relational databases. For a more comprehensive look at relational database design, refer to "Recommended Reading," later in this section.

If you completed the *Getting Started* lessons in Chapter 1, you've already been exposed to a relational database: `global.mdb`. The Global Car database contains three tables: COMMENTS, LOCATIONS, and REGION. Open `global.mdb` in Microsoft Access (the default location is `C:\Program Files\Macromedia\Dreamweaver MX\Samples\Database\global.mdb`) and examine the LOCATIONS table. Notice that the REGION_ID column consists of numbers, rather than the names of geographical regions.
Now open the REGION table.

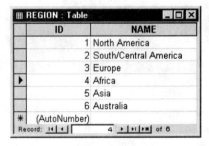

The REGION table contains two columns: ID and NAME. As you've probably guessed, the numbers in the ID column correspond to the REGION_ID column in the LOCATIONS table. In other words, the two columns—LOCATIONS.REGION_ID and REGION.ID—are *related*. Hence the term *relational* database.

Note

Since related columns frequently use the same name, SQL dot notation prefixes columns with table names to avoid ambiguity. For example, the Newman Zone database contains two related tables: News and Months. Each table has a column called MonthID. To distinguish these two columns, we refer to them as News.MonthID (foreign key) and Months.MonthID (primary key).

So how do the two columns know they're related? The truth is, they don't. As far as the columns are concerned, they're complete strangers. It's up to you to establish the relationship. This can be done in a number of ways. For example, Microsoft Access enables you to define relationships using the Relationships window (Tools | Relationships). In SQL Server, you can create a database diagram (see Figure 3-1).

Notice the endpoints on the relationship line in Figure 3-1. The key symbol indicates a primary key column, and the figure-eight symbol indicates a foreign key column. These tables are said to have a *one-to-many* relationship.

Primary Keys and Foreign Keys

What distinguishes a relational database management system (RDBMS) from a flat-file database is that a relational database contains two or more related tables. These tables are related through the use of primary keys and foreign keys.

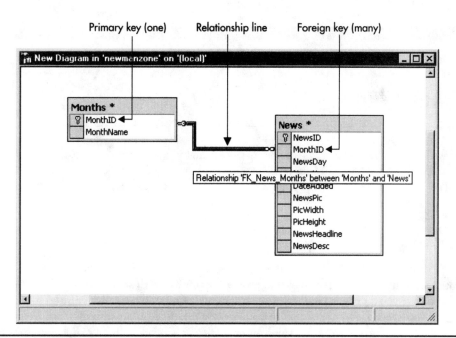

Figure 3-1   *This SQL Server database diagram illustrates a one-to-many relationship between*
Months.MonthID *(the one side) and* News.MonthID *(the many side).*

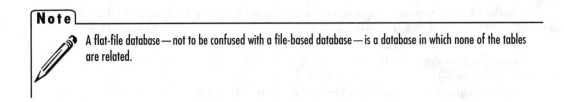

Note

A flat-file database—not to be confused with a file-based database—is a database in which none of the tables are related.

A *primary key* is used to uniquely identify a database record. The primary key column is usually a number that automatically increments each time a new record is added. (Microsoft Access calls this data type an AutoNumber column; SQL Server refers to it as an Identity column.) No two rows can have the same primary key value—otherwise, it wouldn't be a unique identifier—and primary keys cannot have a NULL value. In addition, only one column in a table can be designated as the primary key. While not all database management systems require you to define a primary key when you create a table, it's generally considered good practice. In fact, Microsoft Access will prompt you if you don't:

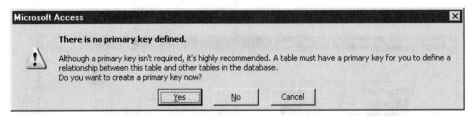

A *foreign key* is a column whose value matches the primary key column of another table. In the Global Car database, the LOCATIONS.REGION_ID column is a foreign key to the REGION.ID column. The relationship between the primary key and the foreign key is used to enforce the concept of *referential integrity*.

Referential Integrity

According to SQL Server *Books Online* (Start | Programs | Microsoft SQL Server | Books Online), "Referential integrity is a system of rules that ensure relationships between rows in related tables are valid and that you do not accidentally delete or change related data...Referential integrity between tables is enforced by default when you create a relationship in your database diagram. An enforced relationship ensures each value entered in a foreign key column matches an existing value in the related primary key column."

In practical terms, referential integrity is a way to protect the integrity of your data. To illustrate this, let's return to the example of the Global Car database (global.mdb). The

LOCATIONS.REGION_ID column is a foreign key to the REGION.ID column. If we were to create a query that joins the two tables, the result might look something like this:

CODE	LOCATION_NAME	ADDRESS	CITY	STATE_COUNTRY	NAME
BWI	Baltimore-Washington International	Airport Blvd	Baltimore	MD	North America
DEN	Denver International	100 Pena Blvd	Denver	CO	North America
DFW	Dallas Ft Worth International	3838 North Bound Service Road	Dallas/Ft Worth	TX	North America
MCI	Kansas City International Airport	902 Tel Aviv Ave	Kansas City	MO	North America
MSP	Minneapolis/St Paul Intl Airport	4300 Glumack Drive	Minneapolis	MN	North America
YGK	Kingston Airport	676 Princess St.	Kingston	Ontario	North America
YQG	Windsor International	Windsor Airport	Windsor	Ontario	North America
CWB	Afonso Pena	Av. N. Sra Da Aparecida 904	Curitiba	Brazil	South/Central America
CZM	Aeropuerto Intl De Cozumel	Cozumel Airport	Cozumel	Mexico	South/Central America
EZE	Eze	Autopista Tte Ricchierei	Buenos Aires	Argentina	South/Central America
FRA	Frankfurt Airport	General Aviation Terminal - Fran	Frankfurt	Germany	Europe
LHR	Heathrow Airport	Heathrow Airport	London	United Kingdom	Europe
MUC	Franz-Josef-Strauss Airport	Franz-Josef-Strauss Airport	Munich	Germany	Europe
PMO	Punta Raisi	Punta Raisi Airport - Sicily	Palermo	Sicily	Europe
PNA	Noain	Airport	Pamplona	Spain	Europe
TPS	Vincenzo-Florio Airport	Vincenzo-Florio Airport	Trapani	Italy	Europe
CAI	Cairo International Airport	Cairo International Airport	Cairo	Egypt	Africa
CPT	Cape Town Airport	Cape Town Airport	Cape Town	South Africa	Africa
KIX	Kansai International Airport	Senshu-kuko Kita	Osaka	Japan	Asia
NRT	New Tokyo International Airport	Chiba 282-8601	Narita	Japan	Asia
SIN	Singapore Changi Airport	Singapore Changi Airport	Singapore	Singapore	Asia

Record: 1 of 23

Notice that the NAME column contains geographical locations—North America, Africa, Asia, etc.—rather than numbers. This is accomplished by creating an *inner join* between the two tables. When you create a query in Design view, Microsoft Access uses Structured Query Language (SQL) to retrieve the data. Here's what the query looks like in SQL view:

```
SELECT LOCATIONS.CODE, LOCATIONS.LOCATION_NAME, LOCATIONS.ADDRESS,
LOCATIONS.CITY, LOCATIONS.STATE_COUNTRY, REGION.NAME, LOCATIONS.TELEPHONE,
LOCATIONS.FAX
FROM REGION INNER JOIN LOCATIONS ON REGION.ID = LOCATIONS.REGION_ID;
```

This query could also be written using an *equijoin*:

```
SELECT LOCATIONS.CODE, LOCATIONS.LOCATION_NAME, LOCATIONS.ADDRESS,
LOCATIONS.CITY, LOCATIONS.STATE_COUNTRY, REGION.NAME, LOCATIONS.TELEPHONE,
LOCATIONS.FAX
FROM LOCATIONS, REGION
WHERE LOCATIONS.REGION_ID = REGION.ID;
```

In both instances, we're querying the database for records in which the value of LOCATIONS.REGION_ID (the foreign key) is equal to REGION.ID (the primary key).

Now what would happen if we were to try to remove the first record (North America) from the REGION table? If referential integrity is enforced, Microsoft Access refuses to delete the record because the LOCATIONS table includes related records (foreign keys).

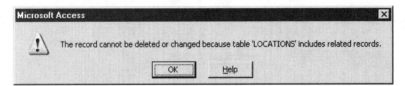

If, on the other hand, referential integrity is not enforced, the database permits the record to be deleted. This results in *orphaned* records in the LOCATIONS table—child records that are related to a parent record that no longer exists. If we were to run the query again, none of the North American locations would be returned.

CODE	LOCATION_NAME	ADDRESS	CITY	STATE_COUNTRY	NAME
CWB	Afonso Pena	Av. N. Sra Da Aparecida 904	Curitiba	Brazil	South/Central America
CZM	Aeropuerto Intl De Cozumel	Cozumel Airport	Cozumel	Mexico	South/Central America
EZE	Eze	Autopista Tte Ricchierei	Buenos Aires	Argentina	South/Central America
FRA	Frankfurt Airport	General Aviation Terminal - Fra	Frankfurt	Germany	Europe
LHR	Heathrow Airport	Heathrow Airport	London	United Kingdom	Europe
MUC	Franz-Josef-Strauss Airport	Franz-Josef-Strauss Airport	Munich	Germany	Europe
PMO	Punta Raisi	Punta Raisi Airport - Sicily	Palermo	Sicily	Europe
PNA	Noain	Airport	Pamplona	Spain	Europe
TPS	Vincenzo-Florio Airport	Vincenzo-Florio Airport	Trapani	Italy	Europe
CAI	Cairo International Airport	Cairo International Airport	Cairo	Egypt	Africa
CPT	Cape Town Airport	Cape Town Airport	Cape Town	South Africa	Africa
KIX	Kansai International Airport	Senshu-kuko Kita	Osaka	Japan	Asia
NRT	New Tokyo International Airport	Chiba 282-8601	Narita	Japan	Asia
SIN	Singapore Changi Airport	Singapore Changi Airport	Singapore	Singapore	Asia
CBR	Canberra	Canberra Airport	Canberra	Australia	Australia
CNS	Cairns	Cairns Airport	Cairns	Queensland	Australia

qLocations : Select Query

Record: 1 of 16

Instead, the query returns 16 records, even though the LOCATIONS table contains 23 rows. This demonstrates the value of relational database design. By adhering to certain rules, such as referential integrity, we avoid the possibility of database corruption.

If relational databases are so complicated, you may be wondering why you should use them in the first place. In addition to maintaining data integrity, relational databases offer a number of important advantages over flat-file databases. For instance, a well-designed relational database

- ◆ Eliminates redundant data
- ◆ Improves database performance
- ◆ Provides greater flexibility
- ◆ Helps prevent human error
- ◆ Organizes data more efficiently

There's no getting around the fact that relational databases aren't simple. The process of designing a *normalized* database is an art form in itself, and many thick books have been devoted to the subject.

Recommended Reading

Don't worry if all of this seems overwhelming right now. The purpose of this section is to introduce you to these concepts and lay the groundwork for Part II. If you're new to databases, pick up a copy of *Database Design for Mere Mortals* (Addison-Wesley, 1997) by Michael J. Hernandez. When you're ready for the more advanced stuff, read Kenneth W. Henderson's *The Guru's Guide to Transact-SQL* (Addison-Wesley, 2000), or Rob Vieira's *Professional SQL Server 2000 Programming* (Wrox, 2000). A good quick reference guide to Structured Query Language is *Sams Teach Yourself SQL in 10 Minutes* (Sams, 2001) by Ben Forta.

Using Access Projects

If you don't have a copy of SQL Server, Microsoft Data Engine (MSDE) is a perfectly viable alternative. However, MSDE does have one important drawback: it doesn't include SQL Server's visual database tools, such as Enterprise Manager and Query Analyzer. Fortunately, you can still work with MSDE in a graphical environment by creating an Access project.

> **Note**
>
> This section, and the one that follows, covers advanced topics relating to SQL Server. If you're new to databases, or you haven't installed SQL Server or MSDE, you may want to return to this material at a later time.

An Access project (e.g., `newmanzone.adp`) enables you to manage SQL Server and MSDE databases from within Microsoft Access. These can be databases on your computer, a local area network, or a remote web server. When you manage a SQL Server or MSDE database using Microsoft Access, the database's tables, views, and stored procedures are stored on the database server, and any forms, reports, or data access pages are stored in the Access project (`.adp`) file.

If you're just starting to learn SQL Server, Access projects enable you to add, edit, and delete tables, views, and stored procedures in a familiar graphical environment. To illustrate this, let's create an Access project that connects to a SQL Server version of the Newman Zone database.

If you haven't done so already, now would be a good time to download this book's supporting files from **www.newmanzone.com** or **www.osborne.com/downloads/downloads.shtml**. To create the Newman Zone database on SQL Server, you need to run the SQL script, `newmanzone.sql`, in Query Analyzer (you'll find `newmanzone.sql` in the `databases` folder). Refer to "The SQL Server Database" in Chapter 6 for step-by-step instructions.

Connecting to SQL Server or MSDE

To connect to SQL Server or MSDE from Microsoft Access, we have to create an Access project. Launch Microsoft Access and select the option to create a new database using Access database wizards, pages, and projects:

This launches the New dialog box. On the General tab, select Project (Existing Database) and click OK. Name the Access project file and click Create to save it to a location on your hard drive. Complete the following steps to create the Access project:

1. On the Connection tab of the Data Link Properties dialog box, select your SQL Server from the drop-down menu. To connect to a remote SQL Server, enter the domain name or IP address of the server.

2. In step 2, enter the username and password you use to log in to SQL Server. (A new installation of SQL Server defaults to sa, for system administrator, and a blank password.)

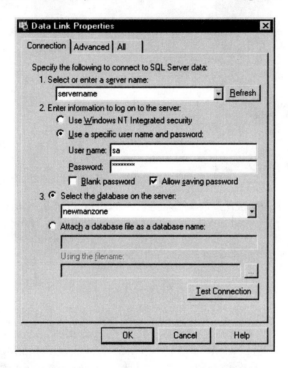

3. In step 3, select the SQL Server or MSDE database you wish to link to Microsoft Access.

4. Click Test Connection. A confirmation message appears: "Test connection succeeded."

5. Click OK to launch the new Access project.

Notice that the interface to the SQL Server database is virtually identical to that of an Access database.

The main difference is that Queries are replaced by Views, and two new items appear in the list of Objects: Database Diagrams and Stored Procedures. As you already know, database diagrams are used to define relationships in SQL Server, much like the Relationships window of an Access database. Stored procedures are discussed in greater detail in Chapter 8.

Manipulating Database Objects

The best part about using an Access project to manage a SQL Server or MSDE database is that you work with objects in much the same way that you would if it were an Access database.

As an example, let's create a new table in the Newman Zone database. If it's not open already, open the Newman Zone project file in Microsoft Access (e.g., `newmanzone.adp`). Select Tables, under Objects, and double-click Create Table In Design View. Enter `testTable` in the Choose Name dialog box and click OK.

Complete the following steps to create the sample table:

1. Enter **TestID** in the first Column Name cell, and choose int from the Datatype drop-down menu.

2. To make `TestID` an Identity column, clear the Allow Nulls check box—Identity columns can't contain NULL values—and check the Identity check box. (The Identity column is SQL Server's equivalent to an AutoNumber column.) Unlike Microsoft Access, SQL Server allows you to specify the starting value of the Identity column (Identity Seed) and the value to increment each time a new record is added (Identity Increment).

3. Enter **TestText** in the second cell of the Column Name column, and select varchar from the Datatype drop-down menu. The varchar data type is roughly equivalent to Text in Access databases.

4. Enter **TestYesNo** in the third cell of the Column Name column, and choose bit from the Datatype drop-down menu. The bit data type is equivalent to Yes/No in Access databases.

5. Enter **TestMemo** in the fourth cell of the Column Name column, and choose text from the Datatype drop-down menu. The text data type is roughly equivalent to Memo in Access databases.

Note

The SQL Server text data type is actually much larger than an Access Memo field and should be used only when varchar is not an option. The varchar data type holds up to 8,000 characters, whereas the text data type supports a maximum of 2,147,483,647 characters. For more information, search "data types" in SQL Server *Books Online*.

---

6. Finally, place your cursor in the `TestID` cell and click the Primary Key icon on the Database toolbar. Alternatively, you can right-click inside the `TestID` cell and choose Primary Key. As with Access databases, an icon appears to identify the column as a primary key.

Column Name	Datatype	Length	Precision	Scale	Allow Nulls	Default Value	Identity	Identity Seed	Identity Increment
TestID	int	4	10	0			✓	1	1
TestText	varchar	50	0	0	✓				
TestYesNo	bit	1	0	0	✓				
TestMemo	text	16	0	0	✓				

testTable : Table

7. Close Design view and click Yes when prompted to save your changes to the design of `testTable`.

The new table appears in the list of SQL Server database tables. To add data to the table, simply double-click `testTable` to open it in Datasheet view. Enter new records just as you would with an Access database. If you prefer to enter and update data using forms, you can launch Form Wizard or AutoForm (Insert | AutoForm) to generate forms automatically.

While the interface for creating tables is similar to that of Access databases, the process of creating views and stored procedures has more in common with Query Designer and Query Analyzer in SQL Server. For more on creating views and stored procedures, see Chapter 8. For more on using Access projects to manage SQL Server databases, check out *Professional SQL Server Development with Access 2000* (Wrox, 2000) by Rick Dobson.

How to Deploy and Manage Remote Databases

If you develop sites using Microsoft Access, deploying the database to a remote server is easy: simply upload the .mdb file and you're good to go. For developers making the transition from Microsoft Access to SQL Server, however, one of the main obstacles is how to deploy a local SQL Server database to a remote location (e.g., your domain hosting provider).

SQL Server provides a tool for exchanging data among different servers and data sources: Data Transformation Services (DTS). In this section, we'll use DTS to transfer a local SQL Server database, newmanzone, to a remote SQL Server.

Connecting to a Remote SQL Server

Before we can connect to a remote SQL Server, we have to register it in Enterprise Manager. Registering a remote SQL Server is a two-step process: add the server alias using the SQL Server Client Network Utility, and register the alias in Enterprise Manager.

Using the Client Network Utility

To run the Client Network Utility, choose Start | Programs | Microsoft SQL Server | Client Network Utility. On the General tab, make sure TCP/IP appears in the list of enabled protocols. If not, select TCP/IP in the Disabled Protocols list and click Enable.

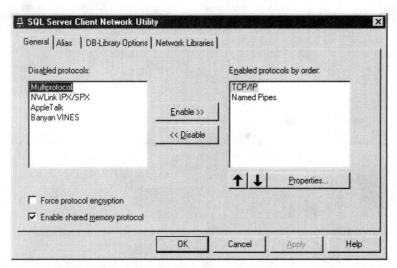

To create an alias for the remote server, select the Alias tab and click Add. Enter a name for the remote server in the Server Alias text box, and select the TCP/IP radio button under Network Libraries. In the Server Name text box, enter the domain name or IP address of the remote server (e.g., www.mysite.com). Leave a check next to Dynamically Determine Port and click OK (the default port for SQL Server is 1433).

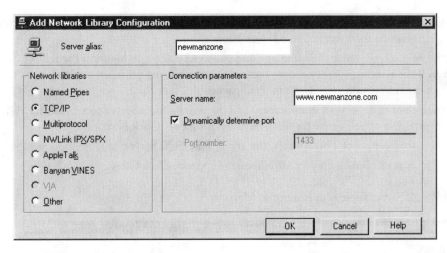

The Server Alias appears in the list of remote servers. Now we can use this alias to register the server in Enterprise Manager. Click OK to close the Client Network Utility.

Registering a Remote Server

To register a remote SQL Server, launch Enterprise Manager (Start | Programs | Microsoft SQL Server | Enterprise Manager). Select the desired SQL Server Group in the console tree and choose Action | New SQL Server Registration (or click the Register Server button on the toolbar). This launches the Register SQL Server Wizard. Click Next and complete the following steps to register a new SQL Server:

1. On the Select A SQL Server screen, select the alias you created with the Client Network Utility and click Add.

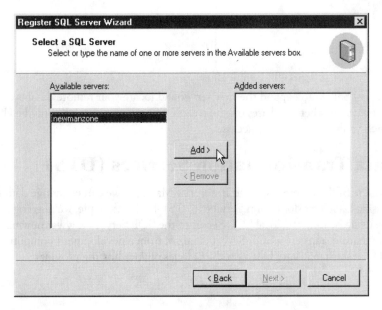

2. On the next screen, choose your desired authentication method—Windows Authentication or SQL Server Authentication—and click Next.

3. On the next screen, enter the username and password you use to log in to the remote SQL Server. If the remote SQL Server was created by your hosting provider, you may need to contact them to obtain your username and password. Click Next.

4. On the Select SQL Server Group screen, add the remote SQL Server to an existing SQL Server group, or create a new top-level SQL Server group. Click Next.

5. On the last screen, click Finish to register the remote SQL Server.

6. If registration succeeds, a confirmation message appears. Click Close.

The new SQL Server appears in Enterprise Manager.

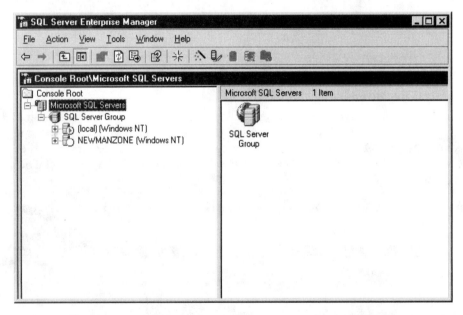

Click the plus (+) button to expand the new server and locate your remote database. Although you may see the names of other databases on the remote SQL Server, you will only be able to edit databases to which you've been granted access.

Using Data Transformation Services (DTS)

Now that the remote SQL Server appears in Enterprise Manager, we can exchange data between the two servers using Data Transformation Services (DTS). In this example, we're going to transfer the newmanzone database from the local SQL Server to the SQL Server on **www.newmanzone.com**.

The following routine transfers a SQL Server database from a development computer to a remote server. These steps may vary based on the policies of your hosting provider.

1. Create and test the SQL Server database on your development computer. When you are satisfied it is working properly, contact your hosting provider and ask them to create a new, blank SQL Server database on the remote server.

> **Note**
>
> Some hosting providers offer an online control panel that enables you to add, delete, back up, and restore SQL Server databases on your own. If you create the remote database yourself, make sure to write down the database name, username, and password for later.

2. Register the remote SQL Server by following the steps listed in the previous section.
3. Launch SQL Server Enterprise Manager and expand the `Databases` folder on your local SQL Server.
4. Select your database in the console tree and choose Tools | Data Transformation Services | Export Data. This launches the DTS Import/Export Wizard.
5. On the first screen, make sure your local SQL Server appears in the Server drop-down menu, and that the database you wish to transfer appears in the Database drop-down menu. Select your desired authentication method and enter your username and password, if needed. Click Next.

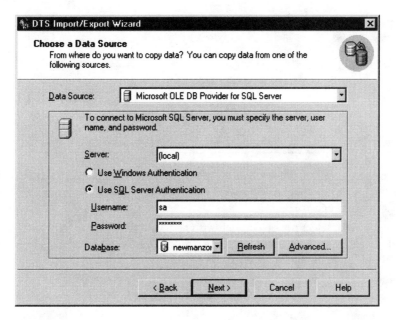

Note

You're not limited to using SQL Server data sources. If you select the Data Source drop-down menu, you should see drivers for Microsoft Access, Excel, dBASE, Visual FoxPro, and other data sources.

6. On the next screen, select the destination SQL Server from the Server drop-down menu. Select your authentication method and enter your username and password. Select the destination database—the blank database you created earlier—from the Database drop-down menu and click Next.

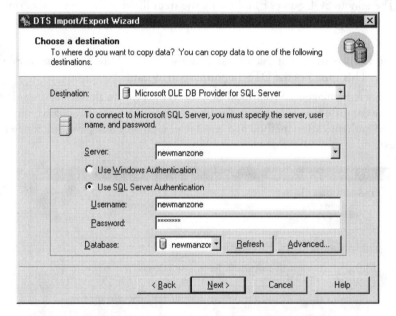

7. On the next screen, select the option to "Copy objects and data between SQL Server databases." This allows you to select additional objects, such as stored procedures and referential integrity constraints. Click Next.

8. On the next screen, select the objects you wish to copy to the remote SQL Server. To change the security and table options, clear Use Default Options and click Options. When you finish making your selections, click Next.

9. On the next screen, you can choose to run the transformation immediately, or save it as a DTS package. Make sure a check appears next to Run Immediately and click Next.

10. The final screen reviews your selections. To make any changes, click the Back button. Otherwise, click Finish to start the transfer.

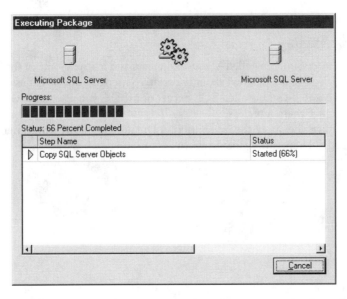

11. When the transfer is complete, click Done to close the Executing Package dialog box.

In Enterprise Manager, expand the destination database in the console tree and select Tables. The tables you transferred should appear in the right-hand pane. Select a table and choose Action | Open Table | Return All Rows to confirm the data was completely transferred. Repeat this with the other tables in the database.

	GuestbookID	PostDate	FirstName	LastName	City	State	Country	Email
▶	1	11/24/2001	Robert	Redford	Park City	UT	USA	sample@sample.com
	2	12/5/2001	Joanne	Woodward	New Haven	CT	USA	sample@sample.com
	3	12/7/2001	George Roy	Hill	Minneapolis	MN	USA	sample@sample.com
	4	12/8/2001	Katharine	Ross	Hollywood	CA	USA	sample@sample.com
	5	12/11/2001	William	Goldman	Highland Park	IL	USA	sample@sample.com
	6	12/15/2001	Cloris	Leachman	Des Moines	IA	USA	sample@sample.com

Data in Table 'Guestbook' in 'newmanzone' on 'NEWMANZONE'

You may find that, because of the remote SQL Server permissions, some of the database objects fail to transfer. If this is the case, use Enterprise Manager and Query Analyzer to recreate any missing objects—e.g., views, stored procedures, primary keys—on the remote SQL Server.

Once you've completely transferred all of the objects from your local SQL Server to your remote SQL Server, you can use Enterprise Manager, or an Access project, to manipulate the data as if the database were on your local computer. Depending on the speed of your Internet connection, these actions may take a little longer than they would on a SQL Server installed locally.

Summary

At this point, you've successfully installed Microsoft Access and learned some of the key concepts of relational databases. You've also learned about the relative strengths and weaknesses of file-based and client/server databases. If you installed SQL Server or MSDE, you also discovered how to use Access projects to manage them more easily.

In the next chapter, we'll explore the integration of Dreamweaver MX with other products, including Fireworks MX, HomeSite+, and TopStyle.

Chapter 4

Organizing Your Kitchen: The Macromedia Workflow

INGREDIENTS

File	Type	Server Model(s)	Source
Chapter4.htm	HTML document	ASP/CF	*Sample Code*
Chapter4.css	Style sheet	ASP/CF	*Sample Code*
Chapter4.cfm	ColdFusion template	CF	*Sample Code*

 from the desk of *Paul Newman*

With the release of Flash MX, Macromedia gave us a first look at the technology of the new MX brand: a new authoring environment, dockable panel groups, and tight integration with ColdFusion MX. Soon after came the preview releases of Dreamweaver MX and Fireworks MX, demonstrating Macromedia's commitment to a consistent workspace across its product line. With the announcement of Macromedia Studio MX—a package that bundles Dreamweaver MX, Flash MX, Fireworks MX, Freehand 10, and ColdFusion MX— Macromedia has ushered in "a new integrated family of client, tool, and server technologies for creating rich Internet applications that promise significantly more intuitive, responsive, and effective user experiences across platforms and devices" (**http://www.macromedia.com/ macromedia/proom/pr/2002/mx_wrapper.html**).

The key word here is *integration*. Macromedia is banking that web developers will prefer to work with a single suite of integrated tools, rather than rely on a different product for each phase of a site's development. The MX brand is an important first step in this direction, and it's a safe bet that future Macromedia releases will offer even tighter product integration.

In this chapter, we'll explore some of the ways Dreamweaver MX integrates with Fireworks MX, TopStyle Pro, and HomeSite+. In order to complete the examples in this chapter, you need to create a new folder in your server root—and define a new site in Dreamweaver MX—called Chapter4 (e.g., `C:\Inetpub\wwwroot\Chapter4`). For details on defining a site in Dreamweaver MX, see Chapter 5.

Fireworks MX Integration

While Dreamweaver's integration with Flash still leaves something to be desired, the integration with Fireworks keeps getting better and better. One of the most notable enhancements is improved "round-tripping." Prior to Dreamweaver MX, a developer's workflow might have resembled this: create a logo in Fireworks and save the PNG file in a folder reserved for images (e.g., `C:\images\ mysite\logo.png`). Export the GIF image from Fireworks to the folder that contains the web site (e.g., `C:\Inetpub\wwwroot\mysite\images\logo.gif`).

Thanks to improved Dreamweaver MX/Fireworks MX integration, you can now save your Fireworks source files in your site, and Dreamweaver "remembers" where to find them. With a little advanced planning, you'll never again have to search for the PNGs you used to generate your web site's images.

Using Image Placeholders

A convenient new feature of Dreamweaver MX is the ability to use placeholder images when "comping," or prototyping, a web page. This allows you to experiment with the visual layout of the page before you create the final images.

To demonstrate this, launch Dreamweaver MX and open the Chapter4 site (if you haven't defined a site called Chapter4, use an existing site, such as Global Car). Choose File | New, or press CTRL-N, to open the New Document dialog box. Select Page Designs in the Category pane, and select Text: Article D in the Page Designs pane. Click Create.

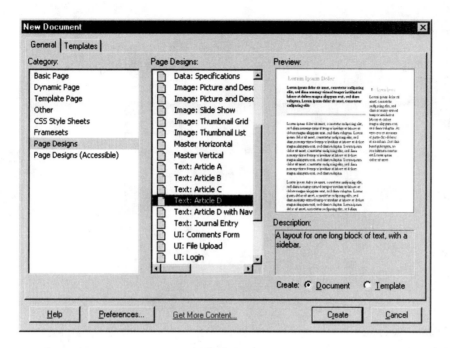

Dreamweaver MX generates a new document based on the template. Press CTRL-S and save the page as Chapter4.htm. Throughout this chapter, we'll use this template to construct a newsletter for a fictitious real estate agent named Chip Havilmyer (you'll learn more about Chip in Part III). Use the Site panel (Window | Site) to create a new folder in the Chapter4 site called Assets. This is where we'll store the site's images. Create a subfolder of Assets called PNG. This is where we'll store the Fireworks source files.

To create the image placeholder, place your cursor at the start of the paragraph that follows the horizontal rule, and choose Insert | Image Placeholder. This opens the Image Placeholder dialog box. Enter **Chip** in the Name text box, and set the dimensions to 150×150. Choose a background color for the placeholder and enter **Chip Havilmyer** in the Alternate Text box. Click OK.

Dreamweaver MX inserts the image placeholder into the body of the page. Select the image placeholder in the Document window. If you examine the Property inspector, you'll see that it identifies the image as a placeholder, and even enables you to edit some of its attributes. Click Create.

This launches a new document in Fireworks MX sized to the dimensions of the image placeholder. To create the image, copy and paste a photo into the canvas of the Document window. (If you don't have a photograph at hand, use the picture of Chip Havilmyer in the `Chapter11` folder of this book's supporting files.) Open the Optimize panel (Window | Optimize) and change the default file format from GIF to JPG (choose JPG - Better Quality from the Settings drop-down menu). When you're finished, click Done.

Fireworks MX prompts you to save the source file, `Chip.png`, in the root of the Chapter4 site. Instead, save it in the `PNG` folder we created earlier. The Save As dialog box is replaced with the Fireworks Export dialog box. Save `Chip.jpg` in the `Assets` folder of the Chapter4 site.

Focus returns to Dreamweaver MX, and the new image is inserted into the Document window. Using the Property inspector, choose Left from the Align drop-down menu. Notice that in addition to displaying the source of the GIF image, the Property inspector "remembers" where we saved the Fireworks source file. This enables us to edit and re-export this image at any time with the click of a button.

T i p   How does Dreamweaver MX remember where we saved the PNG file? If you open the `Assets` folder in Windows Explorer, you'll notice a subfolder called `_notes`. Inside this folder is an XML document called `chip.jpg.mno`. If you open this document in a text editor, you'll see that it contains four lines, one of which stores the path to the Fireworks source file: `<infoitem key="fw_source" value="/Assets/PNG/Chip.png" />`.

To demonstrate this, let's add a drop shadow to `Chip.jpg`. Select the image in the Document window and click Edit on the Property inspector shown next.

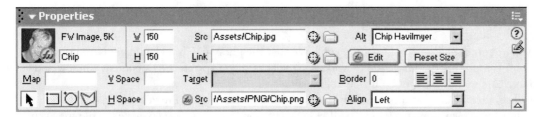

The image's source file, `Chip.png`, opens in Fireworks MX. In order to add a drop shadow, we need to make the canvas a little larger. From the Fireworks menu, select Modify | Canvas | Canvas Size. Enter **170** in the width and height text boxes, and select the Anchor button in the upper-left corner. Click OK.

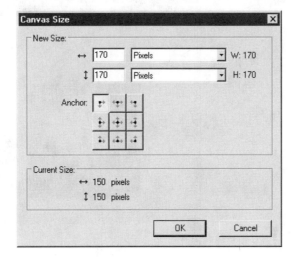

Select Chip's photo in Fireworks' Document window and open the Properties panel (Window | Properties). Click the plus (+) button next to Effects and choose Shadow and Glow | Drop Shadow. A drop shadow is added to Chip's photo. Click Done.

The updated image is inserted into Dreamweaver's Document window (you may have to reapply the image's Align attribute). Behind the scenes, Fireworks MX saves the revised source file (`Chip.png`) and re-exports `Chip.jpg` to the `Assets` folder.

Save your work and press F12 to preview the page in a browser. It doesn't get much easier than that!

Optimizing Images

If you examine the Property inspector, you'll see that the photo of Chip Havilmyer is 5 kilobytes in size. To optimize the image in Fireworks MX, select `Chip.jpg` in the Document window and choose Commands | Optimize Image in Fireworks.

The source file appears in a window identical to Fireworks' Export Preview dialog box. Use the Quality drop-down menu to change the JPEG compression from 80 to 70. To make the file size even smaller, you can uncheck Sharpen Color Edges. As you change the optimization settings, Fireworks previews the image and updates its file size. When you're finished, click Update.

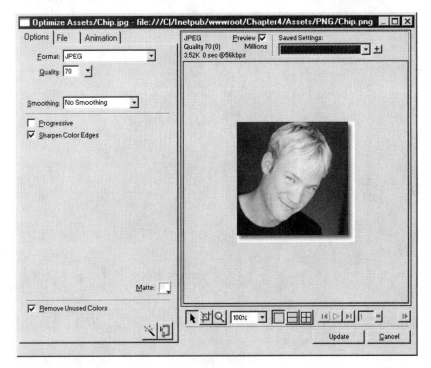

The optimized image appears in Dreamweaver's Document window. Select `Chip.jpg` and examine the Property inspector. The file size is now 4K.

If you use Dreamweaver's built-in FTP feature, you probably don't want to upload your PNG files every time you synchronize your site. To address this, click the plus (+) button to expand the `Assets` folder in the Site panel. Right-click the `PNG` folder and choose Cloaking | Cloak.

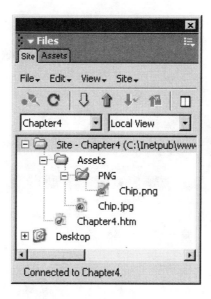

Cloaking excludes files and folders from operations such as Get, Put, Synchronize, and Find and Replace. In addition, cloaked files don't appear in the Assets panel.

Other Fireworks integration features you might want to explore include

◆ Editing a Fireworks pop-up menu in Dreamweaver

◆ Editing a Fireworks table in Dreamweaver

◆ Creating a web photo album

◆ Using the Quick Export button in Fireworks MX

For more on Dreamweaver/Fireworks integration, see "Dreamweaver Integration with Other Applications" in *Using Dreamweaver MX*.

TopStyle Pro Integration

Although TopStyle Lite is bundled with Dreamweaver MX, you need TopStyle Pro (2.51 or higher) to take advantage of the latest integration features. Fortunately, the trial version of TopStyle Pro allows unlimited usage. To download TopStyle Pro, visit Bradbury Software's web site: **http:// www.bradsoft.com/topstyle/download**. To support future development of TopStyle, please register the software if you decide to keep it.

Once the software is installed, Dreamweaver MX automatically detects TopStyle Pro and makes it the external editor for style sheets. To make TopStyle Pro the default editor for *embedded* styles, launch Dreamweaver MX and open the CSS Styles panel (Window | CSS Styles). Open a web page, such as `Chapter4.htm`, and right-click inside the CSS Styles panel. Make sure Use External Editor is checked.

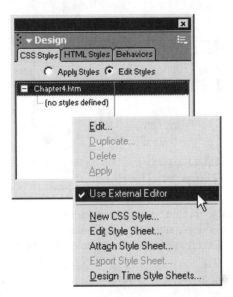

If you installed TopStyle Pro after installing Dreamweaver MX, you can enable integration using TopStyle's options. Launch TopStyle Pro and choose Options | Options, or press F8. Select Third Party Integration on the left, and click Enable Dreamweaver Integration. While you're at it, you may want to click Enable HomeSite Integration as well.

For more on Dreamweaver/TopStyle integration, visit Bradbury Software's web site: **http://www.bradsoft.com/topstyle/thirdparty/dmx/index.asp**.

Editing Style Sheets

After you've enabled the integration of Dreamweaver MX and TopStyle Pro, you can invoke TopStyle Pro by double-clicking any style defined in the CSS Styles panel. To demonstrate this, we'll create an external style sheet for the Chapter4 site. Open `Chapter4.htm` in Dreamweaver MX and click the New CSS Style icon on the CSS Styles panel toolbar. This opens the New CSS

Style dialog box. Select the Redefine HTML Tag radio button and choose body from the Tag drop-down menu. Select the (New Style Sheet File) option and click OK.

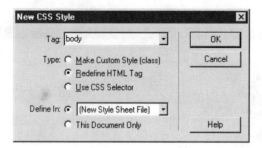

Dreamweaver MX prompts you to name the external style sheet. Enter Chapter4.css in the File Name text box and click Save.

In the CSS Style Definition dialog box, select Georgia, Times New Roman, Times, serif from the Font drop-down menu, and choose 10 from the Size drop-down menu. Click OK.

Dreamweaver MX generates the new external style sheet. If you examine the CSS Styles panel, you'll see that Chapter4.css appears below Chapter4.htm. Now we can use Dreamweaver MX and TopStyle Pro to edit styles defined in an external style sheet (i.e., Chapter4.css), or embedded styles defined in an HTML document (i.e., Chapter4.htm).

Note

An embedded CSS style is one that is defined in the current document — usually *embedded* between the <head> tags — rather than in an external style sheet. An inline style is one that appears within an HTML element (e.g., <input type="button" style="font-size:10px">).

To switch between using Dreamweaver MX and TopStyle Pro to edit your CSS styles, simply right-click inside the CSS Styles panel and check (or uncheck) Use External Editor.

Using the Output Panel

TopStyle Pro's integration with Dreamweaver MX includes a great new feature: any time you launch TopStyle Pro to edit a style, the current Dreamweaver MX document is used to preview it. To illustrate this, open the CSS Styles panel and double-click Chapter4.css.

TopStyle Pro opens Chapter4.css in an integrated workspace, not unlike Dreamweaver MX. Notice that Chapter4.htm appears in the Output panel (if you don't see the Output panel, choose

View | Output or press CTRL-D). Like Dreamweaver MX, TopStyle Pro generates a temporary version of the document to preview the page. (In other words, TopStyle doesn't mess with your original document.)

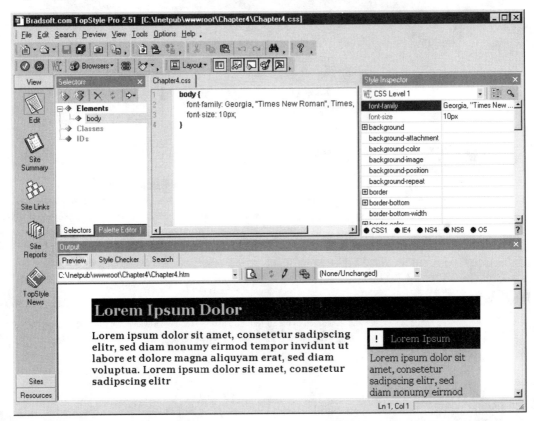

Above the Output panel are the Selectors panel, the Editor panel, and the Style Inspector. The Editor panel contains the style sheet itself, in a format resembling Code view in Dreamweaver MX.

Let's change the font color to Slate Gray. In the Editor panel, place your cursor between the opening and closing { } brackets. The Style Inspector lists the selector's available properties.

Note

Cascading Style Sheets use the following syntax: `selector {property:value}`. The selector can be an HTML element, a Class, or an ID. The property is the attribute you want to change, such as font-size, color, border, padding, etc. For example, a CSS declaration that changes all anchor tags to red would look like this: `a {color:#FF0000}`. Multiple properties are separated by a semicolon (;).

Scroll down to color in the Style Inspector and place your cursor inside the value column. Click the Color Picker icon and select Slate Gray. Click OK to close the Color Picker dialog box.

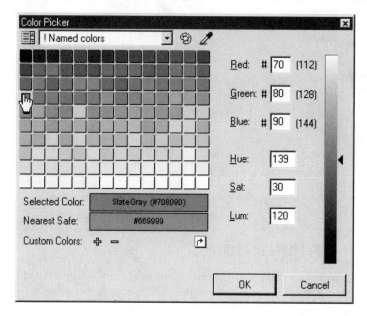

The new property appears in the Editor panel: `color: #708090`. Notice that the text in the Output panel is now gray.

Let's create a new selector for the horizontal rule (`<hr>`) tag. In the Selectors panel, click the New Selector button. This launches TopStyle's Selector Wizard. Click Simple to create a selector that applies to an HTML element. In the left pane, scroll down and select `hr`. Click Add, and then click OK.

The `hr` selector appears in the Editor panel, and Style Insight displays a list of available properties. Select color, and then select Teal, from the Style Insight pop-up menus. Examine the Output panel: the horizontal rule is now green. Choose File | Exit or press ALT-X to close TopStyle Pro. Click Yes when prompted to save your changes to `Chapter4.css`.

When you return to Dreamweaver MX, the changes to the style sheet are reflected in the Document window. In addition, the new selector appears in the CSS Styles panel.

To configure TopStyle Pro to use preview documents that contain server-side code—e.g., ASP, ColdFusion, PHP—you need to add a mapping. To do this, choose Options | Options in Top Style Pro and select Mappings in the Preview category. Click Add and enter the physical path to your site's root folder in the Map From text box. Enter the virtual directory in the Map To text box (e.g., **http://localhost/Chapter4/**). Click OK.

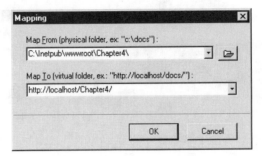

Check the option to Use Mappings When Previewing and click OK. Now you can use TopStyle's Output panel to preview new styles using dynamic, as well as static, web pages.

HomeSite+ Integration

While it's true that Dreamweaver MX now incorporates many of the features of HomeSite and ColdFusion Studio, there are still times when you need the tools of an external code editor. If you selected the option to install HomeSite+ when you installed Dreamweaver MX, the integration of these two products is already enabled.

In this section, we'll learn to use a handy-dandy HomeSite+ tool that has yet to be assimilated into Dreamweaver MX: SQL Builder.

Remote Development Services (RDS)

Launch Dreamweaver MX and open the page we were working on earlier, `Chapter4.htm`. Choose File | Save As and save the file as `Chapter4.cfm`.

Note

This section requires ColdFusion MX Server. ASP users may want to sit this one out.

Before we can insert a query into the page, we need to edit the Site Definition for Chapter4. Choose Site | Edit Sites, and double-click Chapter4. Select the Testing Server category on the Advanced tab of the Site Definition dialog box. Choose ColdFusion from the Server Model drop-down menu and click OK. Click Done to close the Edit Sites dialog box.

Chapter4 is now defined as a ColdFusion site. In order to view the data sources defined in ColdFusion Administrator, open the Databases panel (Window | Databases) and click RDS Login.

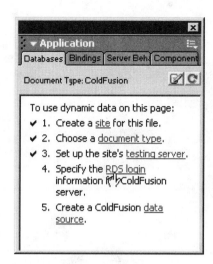

Enter the password you created when you installed ColdFusion MX and click OK. Dreamweaver MX uses Remote Development Services (RDS) to display your ColdFusion data sources in the Databases panel.

Note

ColdFusion Remote Development Services (RDS) is a component of ColdFusion Server used by ColdFusion Studio, HomeSite+, and Dreamweaver MX to provide HTTP-based access to files and databases. You can use RDS to manage files and databases on any local or remote server hosting ColdFusion, provided you have RDS login access. RDS is enabled in ColdFusion Administrator by default.

Open the Bindings panel (Window | Bindings) and choose Recordset (Query). Enter **rsLocations** in the Name text box, and choose the connGlobal data source we created in Chapter 1. Select LOCATIONS from the Table drop-down menu and click Test. The REGION_ID column consists of numbers, rather than geographical locations. To address this, we need to create a SQL statement that joins two related tables (LOCATIONS and REGION). This is where HomeSite+ comes in. Click OK, and then click OK again to close the Recordset dialog box.

Adding HomeSite+ Mappings

If it's not open already, open Chapter4.cfm in Dreamweaver MX and choose Edit | Edit with HomeSite+.

Because HomeSite+ is an advanced text editor, it doesn't feature a Design view like Dreamweaver MX. Instead, HomeSite+ consists of an Edit tab and a Browse tab. The Edit tab is akin to Code view in Dreamweaver MX. The Browse tab displays the current document using an internal browser. Before we can use the Browse feature, we have to add a server development mapping, as we did with TopStyle Pro.

Select Debug | Development Mappings (or press ALT-M) and choose your local server from the RDS Server drop-down menu. If you haven't configured your RDS Server yet, choose Add RDS Server from the drop-down menu. Enter an optional nickname for the server in the Description text box, and type **localhost** in the Host Name text box (if you're connecting to a remote RDS Server, enter its domain name or IP address). Under Macromedia RDS Security, enter the password you created when you installed ColdFusion MX and click OK.

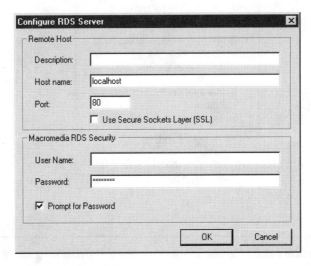

To create the development mapping for the Chapter4 site, click Add. As with TopStyle Pro, enter the physical path to the site's root folder in the HomeSite+ Path text box, and enter the URL it resolves to in the Browser Path text box. Click OK.

Chapter4 is added to the list of HomeSite+ mappings. Click OK to close the Remote Development Settings dialog box. Now select the Browse tab in HomeSite+. `Chapter4.cfm` is displayed as it appears in Internet Explorer.

Using SQL Builder

Although Dreamweaver's advanced Recordset dialog box provides some options for building SQL SELECT statements, it's not much use when it comes to creating queries that use joins. To simplify the creation of an advanced query, we'll use the SQL Builder tool included with HomeSite+.

In HomeSite+, select the Edit tab and choose Tools | SQL Builder. This opens the Select Database Query dialog box. Choose your RDS server from the drop-down menu and expand the connGlobal data source. Select the LOCATIONS table and click New Query.

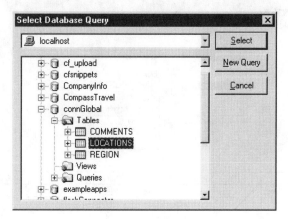

The interface of SQL Builder is similar to Query Design view in Microsoft Access, and Query Designer in SQL Server. The three panes, from top to bottom, are the Table pane, the Properties pane, and the SQL pane.

Since we selected the LOCATIONS table in the first dialog box, it already appears in the Table pane. To add the REGION table, click the Add Tables icon on the SQL Builder toolbar. Select REGION and click Add. Click Done to close the Add Tables or Views dialog box. (Alternatively, you can right-click inside the Table pane and choose Add Table | REGION.)

As you may recall from Chapter 3, the REGION and LOCATIONS tables are related by matching columns (REGION.ID is the primary key and LOCATIONS.REGION_ID is the foreign key). To create the join—in this case, an equijoin—select the ID column in the REGION table and drag and drop it onto the REGION_ID column in the LOCATIONS table. A join line appears between the two tables. If you mouse over the join line, you'll see a tooltip indicating that REGION.ID = LOCATIONS.REGION_ID.

To select the data returned by the query, double-click the following columns in the Table pane, or use the drop-down menus in the Properties pane: LOCATIONS.LOCATION_NAME,

LOCATIONS.ADDRESS, LOCATIONS.CITY, LOCATIONS.STATE_COUNTRY, REGION.NAME. The SQL pane updates to reflect each selection.

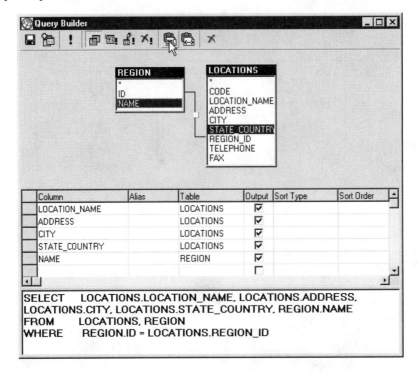

Click the Copy SQL To Clipboard icon on the SQL Builder toolbar. To exit SQL Builder, click the red "X" and click No when prompted to save and insert the new query. Click Cancel to dismiss the Select Database Query dialog box.

This returns you to `Chapter4.cfm` in HomeSite+. Highlight the SQL `SELECT` statement on line 2—`SELECT * FROM LOCATIONS`—and press CTRL-V to paste the query we just copied to the clipboard.

```
SELECT     LOCATIONS.LOCATION_NAME, LOCATIONS.ADDRESS,
LOCATIONS.CITY, LOCATIONS.STATE_COUNTRY, REGION.NAME
FROM       LOCATIONS, REGION
WHERE      REGION.ID = LOCATIONS.REGION_ID
```

Press CTRL-S to save `Chapter4.cfm` and exit HomeSite+. In Dreamweaver MX, click Yes when prompted to reload the file. Open the Bindings panel and double-click the `rsLocations` recordset. The advanced Recordset dialog box opens because the query cannot be represented in Simple mode.

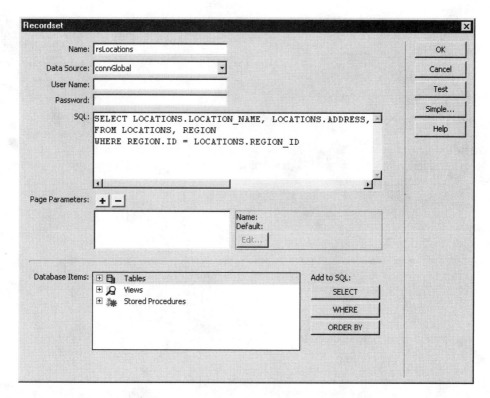

Click Test. Instead of numbers, the query returns geographical locations. Click OK to close the Test SQL Statement dialog box. Click OK again to close the Recordset dialog box.

Congratulations! You did it. Now you can take advantage of SQL Builder in HomeSite+ to create advanced queries.

Summary

In this chapter, we explored the ways Dreamweaver MX integrates with other products, including Fireworks MX, TopStyle Pro, and HomeSite+. Some of the topics we covered include

- ◆ Using image placeholders in Dreamweaver MX
- ◆ Editing a Fireworks image from Dreamweaver
- ◆ Using the Optimize Image command
- ◆ Cloaking files and folders in the Site panel
- ◆ Enabling TopStyle Pro integration

- Previewing styles in TopStyle Pro
- Adding TopStyle mappings
- Configuring RDS Servers in HomeSite+
- Adding HomeSite+ mappings
- Using SQL Builder to create advanced queries

In the next chapter, we'll finally get down to the business of whipping up recipes. Our first appetizer is an advanced contact form. Roll up your sleeves and tie on your apron, because there's a lot of work to be done in Chapter 5.

Part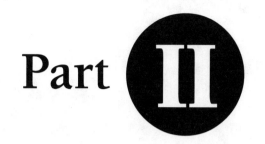

Appetizers: Some Recipes to Get You Started

Chapter 5

Advanced Contact Form

INGREDIENTS

File	Type	Server Model	Source
contact.asp	Active Server Page	ASP	*Sample Code*
contact.cfm	ColdFusion template	CF	*Sample Code*
Conditional Region 2	Server Behavior	ASP	Waldo Smeets
IsDefined	Object	CF	*Sample Code*
JMail	Object	ASP	*Sample Code*
Check Form 4.66	Behavior		Jaro von Flocken

 from the desk of Paul Newman

Now that we've got all that drudgery out of the way, let's cook something: an advanced contact form. This is our first recipe because contact forms are essential ingredients of web sites, but most of them aren't very well designed—in terms of either function or appearance. In fact, poorly designed forms are one of the most frequently cited reasons that shoppers abandon online orders.

How many times have you submitted a form, only to be told that several fields weren't completed? You click the Back button and the entries disappear. Or you submit the form, but the script bombs without a user-friendly error message. You'd be amazed at how many high-profile web sites don't employ some kind of error-handling.

One of the reasons my wife insists on using a traditional fax machine—instead of a computer fax program—is that it gives her visual confirmation the fax was sent. It goes in one side, it comes out the other. "How else do I know they got it?" she says. She's got a point.

Web-based forms should provide confirmation messages. Once again, you'd be surprised how many sites don't offer this basic courtesy. This is why web surfers often submit forms more than once: it isn't clear to them that the information was processed. By employing a simple error-checking routine, we can confirm to the visitor that the message was sent, display the contents of that message, even CC the visitor on the e-mail.

Because we want our contact form to be better, here's what we're going to do:

- Design a visually pleasing and intuitive form
- Validate user input using JavaScript
- Show the visitor a friendly error message if the script fails
- Display a confirmation message if the script succeeds

And we're going to do all of this on a single page (hooray!).

Setting Up the Newman Zone Site

If you haven't already, now would be a good time to go to **www.newmanzone.com** or **www.osborne.com** and download the supporting files for *The Joy of Dreamweaver MX*. It's OK, I'll wait.

Unzip the files to a folder on your hard drive. You should see 12 folders, each containing a different web site:

Site	Server Model
newmanzone.net	ASP.NET/VB
newmanzone.net_empty	ASP.NET/VB
newmanzone_asp	ASP/VBScript
newmanzone.net_empty	ASP/VBScript

Site	Server Model
newmanzone_cf	ColdFusion
newmanzone_cf_empty	ColdFusion
realty.net	ASP.NET/VB
realty.net_empty	ASP.NET/VB
realty_asp	ASP/VBScript
realty_asp_empty	ASP/VBScript
realty_cf	ColdFusion
realty_cf_empty	ColdFusion

In this chapter, and the remainder of Part II, we will focus on the Newman Zone site (we'll get to the Realty site later, in Part III). Copy the folder for your server model to the root of your local web server (e.g., C:\Inetpub\wwwroot). You should use the empty version of the site, unless you want to preview the completed pages.

Note

The examples in this book are presented in ASP/VBScript and ColdFusion MX formats. The ASP.NET versions of the Newman Zone and Realty sites are included to demonstrate new features of Dreamweaver MX.

If you're using Windows 95/98, launch Personal Web Manager and create an alias called newmanzone_asp (or newmanzone_cf) that points to the www directory in the newmanzone_asp_empty (or newmanzone_cf_empty) folder:

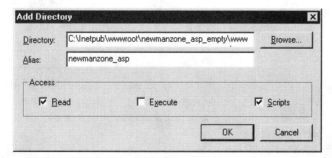

If you're using Windows NT/2000/XP, launch Internet Information Services (IIS) and create a virtual directory called newmanzone_asp (or newmanzone_cf) that points to the www directory in the newmanzone_asp_empty (or newmanzone_cf_empty) folder.

To preview the Newman Zone site, type the following URL into your browser's address bar: **http://localhost/newmanzone_asp/** (or **http://localhost/newmanzone_cf/**).

You should now be looking at the Newman Zone splash page. If I'm not winking at you from the splash page (i.e., you haven't set up your server), please refer to "Installing a Web Server" in Chapter 2.

Defining the Site in Dreamweaver MX

Before we can whip up our first appetizer, we need to define the Newman Zone site. Launch Dreamweaver MX and choose Site | New Site from the menu. Click the Advanced tab.

The Site Definition dialog box consists of seven categories. At this stage, we only need to be concerned about the first three: Local Info, Remote Info, and Testing Server.

Local Info

The Local Info category prompts you to name your site and identify its location on your hard drive. Enter **Newman Zone** as the site name. In the next text box, browse to the folder you set up earlier (e.g., `C:\Inetpub\wwwroot\newmanzone_asp_empty\www`) and click Select.

Note

Web developers use different terms to refer to staging and production servers. Since Macromedia uses the local/remote metaphor, this will be the convention used throughout this book. The local server is where you create and test your web site. The remote server is where the flawless, completed site is published for all the world to see.

Leave the Refresh Local File List option checked. In the next text box, browse to the images folder (e.g., `C:\Inetpub\wwwroot\newmanzone_asp_empty\www\images`) and click Select to make it the Default Images Folder for the Newman Zone site.

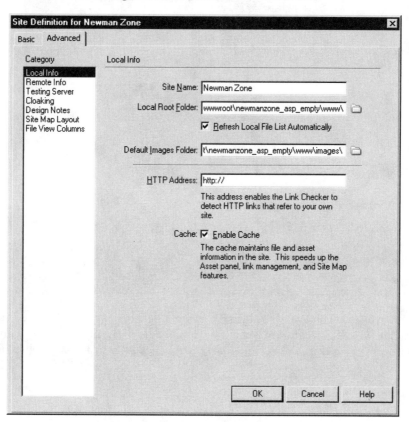

You can leave the HTTP Address text box empty for now, but make sure Enable Cache is checked.

Remote Info

Select the Remote Info category and choose FTP from the Access dropdown menu. Enter the information required by your hosting provider. The reason we're configuring FTP access is that some features, such as JMail, may require the components of a remote server in order to function. Click Test to verify the connection to your remote server.

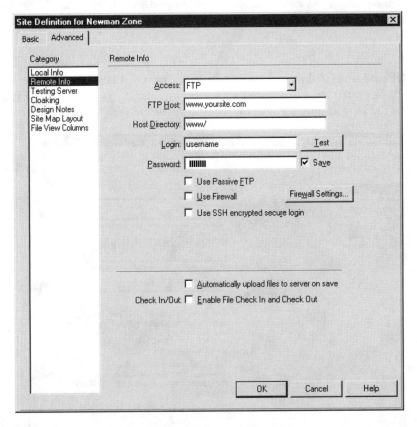

If you're not a fan of Dreamweaver's built-in FTP feature, or you simply prefer to use a stand-alone program like WS_FTP, feel free to ignore this category. If, on the other hand, you just won't sleep until you've mastered the Remote Info options, click Help to access Dreamweaver's context-sensitive help system.

Testing Server

The Testing Server category (formerly "Application Server") enables you to specify the local or remote server Dreamweaver MX uses to preview your files.

Choose your Server Model from the drop-down menu—either ASP VBScript or ColdFusion—and accept Dreamweaver's defaults. Notice that because you entered a value for the Local Root Folder in the Local Info category, Dreamweaver MX automatically enters it as the location of the Testing Server Folder. Confused? All this means is that your Local Root Folder and your Testing Server Folder are one and the same. (This is possible only if your web server—e.g., IIS, PWS, etc.—is installed on your local computer.)

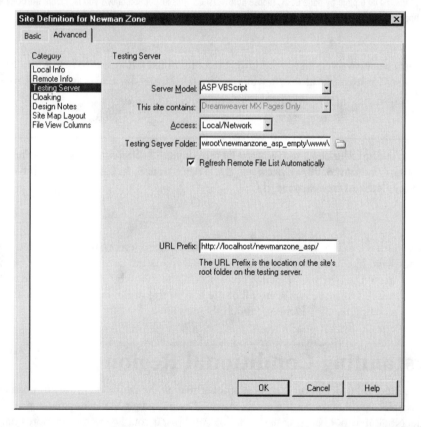

If your web server runs on a different machine—for instance, on a local area network (LAN)—you need to specify it in the Remote Info category, and upload the files before you can preview them. For more information, see "Setting Up a Web Application" in *Using Dreamweaver MX* (choose Help | Using Dreamweaver or press F1).

New Feature

A new option in the Testing Server category enables you to choose whether the site contains Dreamweaver MX Pages, UltraDev 4 Pages, or Both Versions. (Currently, this option only affects ColdFusion users.) This is one of those good news/bad news situations. The good news is, Macromedia has completely redesigned Dreamweaver MX to write "improved and easier-to-understand" ColdFusion code. This shift to more traditional, tag-based ColdFusion code comes in response to user requests and is sure to appeal to coders migrating from ColdFusion Studio. The bad news is, the new ColdFusion code Dreamweaver MX generates is not compatible with the ColdFusion code generated by UltraDev 4. In order to work with ColdFusion code you created in UltraDev 4, choose the UltraDev 4 Pages Only option. This gives you access to the old UltraDev 4 server behaviors. To be prompted on a page-by-page basis, choose Both Versions. This last option allows you to update UltraDev 4 pages using the old server behaviors, and create new pages using the new server behaviors.

The last entry we want to change is the URL Prefix text box. Change it to **http://localhost/ newmanzone_asp/** (or **http://localhost/newmanzone_cf/**). This is the alias you created earlier, remember?

Note

If you're using ColdFusion MX, and you choose the option to install the Standalone server, the URL Prefix is **http://localhost:8500/newmanzone_cf/**. In most other cases, the ColdFusion URL Prefix is **http://localhost/newmanzone_cf/**.

Now you won't have to type http://localhost/newmanzone_asp_empty/www to preview your site. (It may not seem like much now, but trust me, you'll thank me later.)

Click OK to create the new site. A dialog box informs you that "the initial site cache will now be created." Click OK. Dreamweaver scans all of the files in the site in order to track changes. When the scan is complete, click Done to launch the new site.

Understanding Conditional Regions

Despite what a die-hard coder would say—you know the type, he insists on using Notepad even though HomeSite+ would make his life much easier—Dreamweaver MX generates some pretty effective code. No, it may not be the easiest to follow, and yes, it could benefit from more comments, but on the whole, it does its job, and it does it well. One of the ways Dreamweaver MX writes efficient and reusable code is by employing conditional regions.

As you probably know, a *conditional region* displays different parts of a web page based on different conditions. These conditions might include

◆ Has the visitor logged in?

◆ Was a form value passed to the page?

♦ Is the requested recordset empty?

Sound familiar? Yep. When you apply the Show Region If Recordset Is Empty SB (server behavior), you are creating a conditional region. If the recordset contains a value, that region is displayed on the page. If the recordset is empty, alternative content is shown (e.g., "No records found").

We're going to use this approach in our Advanced Contact Form, as well as the Advanced Guestbook in the next chapter. In both cases, we will be displaying different regions—and executing different blocks of code—based on the existence of form values.

Dreamweaver-Generated Code

One of the things you may have noticed, if you've spent some time looking under Dreamweaver's "hood," is that an Insert Record page posts the results to itself. In other words, if the page in question is `insert.asp`, the form's action page is also `insert.asp` (one and the same page).

Caution

The default behavior of an HTML form when the `action` attribute is omitted or left blank is to submit to itself. The default method is `get`. However, it's not good practice to omit these `<form>` attributes, because doing so can produce unexpected results in certain browsers.

To better understand the code Dreamweaver MX generates, open one of your existing sites and track down a page with an Insert Record server behavior applied to it.

Note

If you don't have an existing site, you may want to complete the *Getting Started* lessons as described in Chapter 1. Alternatively, you can define a new site using one of the completed projects from this book.

Find a page with an Insert Record SB and use Dreamweaver's tag selector to select the `<form>` tag. Examine the Property inspector. The Action text box contains the following code:

```
<%=MM_editAction%> (ASP)
<cfoutput>#CurrentPage#</cfoutput> (ColdFusion)
```

Switch to Code view and locate the following statement (press CTRL-F to search the source code, if necessary):

```
MM_editAction = CStr(Request.ServerVariables("SCRIPT_NAME")) (ASP)
<cfset CurrentPage=GetFileFromPath(GetTemplatePath())> (ColdFusion)
```

What does this mean? Dreamweaver declares a variable (`MM_editAction` or `CurrentPage`) and sets its value to the location of the current page. This way, if you move the page to another folder in your site, the form's `action` attribute remains intact. Just to prove this, create a new blank ASP or ColdFusion page and try it out yourself. Place your cursor in the body of the document, switch to Code view, and type the following:

```
<%= CStr(Request.ServerVariables("SCRIPT_NAME")) %> (ASP)
<cfoutput>#GetFileFromPath(GetTemplatePath())#</cfoutput> (ColdFusion)
```

When you run the page on your local server, it should display the root-relative URL of the current document (e.g., `/newmanzone_asp/filename.asp`) or its filename (e.g., `filename.cfm`). We're going to apply this same technique to our contact form.

If-Else Statements

Dreamweaver MX submits the form's data back to itself by setting the action page to the location of the current document. But how does the page know the user clicked the submit button? Yes, Virginia—the `If-Else` statement.

Still have that Insert Record page open? Notice the hidden field that appears at the end of the form.

Tip

Can't see the hidden field? Select View | Visual Aids | Invisible Elements.

Here's what the hidden field looks like in Code view (these examples are from the *Getting Started* lessons):

```
<input type="hidden" name="MM_insert" value="insertLocation"> (ASP)
<input type="hidden" name="MM_InsertRecord"⤸
value="insertLocation"> (ColdFusion)
```

The hidden field is what tells the page when to run the Insert Record code block. Now hit CTRL-F and search the source code for `MM_insert` (or `MM_InsertRecord`). Find the start of the Insert Record code block:

```
If (CStr(Request("MM_insert")) <> "") Then (ASP)
<cfif IsDefined("FORM.MM_InsertRecord") AND ⤸
FORM.MM_InsertRecord EQ "insertLocation"> (ColdFusion)
```

In plain English, the code is saying: "If `MM_insert` exists, then insert the posted form values into the database." At the end of the Insert Record code block, appropriately enough, is an `End If` (or `</cfif>`) statement. If `MM_insert` doesn't exist, the code block to insert a record never runs, and the page's form is displayed.

We're going to use an `If-Else` statement to create conditional regions on the Advanced Contact Form. If a specific form value is passed to the page, we will send an e-mail and display a confirmation message. Otherwise, we will display the form.

Building the Page Blocks

All right, let's get to work. Open the Newman Zone site you defined in Dreamweaver MX earlier, and double-click the Contact Information page (`contact.asp` or `contact.cfm`, depending on your server model).

As you can see, I've already done some of the grunt work for you. I've created two distinct regions on the page: a contact form, and a confirmation message. I've also added a horizontal rule to visually separate them (you can delete it later).

The form consists of six fields: `FirstName`, `LastName`, `Phone`, `Email`, `Comments`, and `Mode`. The value of the hidden field, `Mode`, is `submit`. The values of the other fields will be supplied by our visitor. Once the form is submitted, we'll display the results in the confirmation message.

If you didn't read this chapter's list of ingredients, better go download Waldo Smeets' Conditional Region extension and install it using Macromedia Extension Manager.

Tip

You can find a complete list of all the extensions used in this book at **www.newmanzone.com/downloads**. When you click a link, you'll be prompted to save the file, or redirected to the author's web site to download it. Newer versions of these extensions, optimized for Dreamweaver MX, will be added as they become available.

ColdFusion users: the isDefined extension is included among the supporting files you downloaded earlier (look in the `extensions` folder).

The Conditional Region Extension (ASP)

The first step is to make these page blocks conditional regions. We'll do this using Waldo Smeets' Conditional Region 2 extension (if you haven't already, please install Conditional Region 2 using Macromedia Extension Manager).

Note

This example is in ASP. ColdFusion users should skip ahead to the next section: "The IsDefined Extension."

Place your cursor to the left of the horizontal rule and, moving upward, select everything between the horizontal rule and the contact image. From the Server Behaviors panel, choose Conditional Region | Request and Script. Select `Request.Form` from the drop-down menu and enter **Mode** in the Name text box. The default Condition is Equals (=), so tab down to the Script text box and enter two quotation marks (an empty string). Click OK.

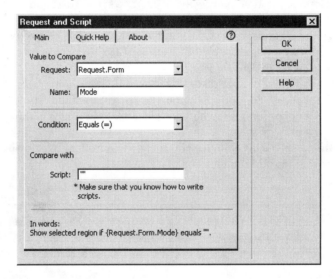

This tells the page that if a particular form value (`Mode`) is empty, show the selected region. Here's what's going on behind the scenes:

```
<% If (Request.Form("Mode")) = ("") Then 'script %>
```

The server behavior also places the following ASP code at the end of the selection:

```
<% End If ' end If (Request.Form("Mode")) = ("") script %>
```

Save your work and press F12 to preview the page in a browser. Why, you may ask, do we still see both regions? Because we haven't added the `Else` part of our `If-Else` statement.

Select the ASP server markup tag—it's the little yellow icon labeled "ASP"—and CTRL-drag it below the confirmation region. A plus (+) sign appears, indicating that you're copying the selection (see Figure 5-1). What we're doing is copying the `End If` statement to the end of the confirmation message.

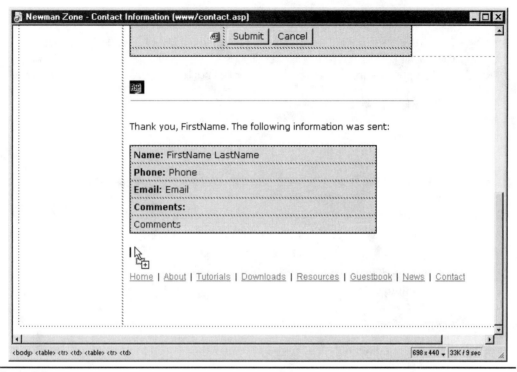

Figure 5-1   *Drag the server markup tag while holding down the* CTRL *key.*

That leaves us with two End If statements. So go back to the first one, select the server markup tag, and click Edit on the Property inspector. Replace the existing code with an Else statement:

```
<% Else 'process form and send e-mail %>
```

Save your work and press F12 to preview the page in a browser. Eureka! The confirmation region has disappeared. That's because the form field, Mode, has no value. In fact, the Request object's Form collection contains no values whatsoever, because no form was posted to this page. Now try hitting the Submit button. There's that pesky horizontal rule (this might be a good time to delete it). If you don't see the confirmation region, you may want to go back over the last couple pages and make sure you didn't miss a step.

The IsDefined Extension (ColdFusion)

To create conditional regions in ColdFusion, we'll use the IsDefined extension (if you haven't already, please install the isDefined extension using Macromedia Extension Manager). Once installed, the isDefined object appears on the CFML Flow tab of the Insert bar.

Follow these steps to create the conditional regions in ColdFusion:

1. In the Document window, select everything between the contact image (`contact.gif`) and the library item at the bottom (`navlinks.lbi`).

2. Switch to Code view (CTRL-`) and verify that you've made a clean selection (lines 39–117).

3. Select the CFML Flow tab on the Insert bar and click the isDefined button.

4. Select FORM from the drop-down menu and enter **Mode** in the text box. Click OK. Dreamweaver MX wraps the selection with `<cfif>` tags.

5. While you're still in Code view, change the opening `<cfif>` statement to the following (the new code is shaded):

   ```
   <cfif NOT isDefined("FORM.Mode")>
   ```

   Adding the NOT modifier tells ColdFusion to display the contact form only if FORM.Mode is *not* defined.

6. Switch back to Design view and select the horizontal rule. Click the cfelse button on the Insert bar. The `<hr>` tag is replaced by `<cfelse>`. Notice that Dreamweaver MX switches to Split view to show you where the code was inserted.

7. Add the following ColdFusion comment after the `<cfelse>` tag:

   ```
   <!--- process form and send e-mail --->
   ```

   This way, you'll remember what you were doing when you look at this code tomorrow.

Switch back to Design view. Notice the gray `<cfelse>` icon in the Document window. Also notice the `<cfif>` icon at the top of the page. Dreamweaver MX adds a thin gray border to identify the conditional region. (Beats server markup tags, doesn't it?)

Save your work and press F12 to preview the page in a browser. Click Submit. Do you see the confirmation region? Good job.

The Confirmation Message

The confirmation message would look a lot more professional if it didn't display text placeholders such as "Thank you, FirstName." So let's replace them with form variables.

Displaying Form Variables (ASP)

Select "FirstName" in the Document window and select the ASP tab on the Insert bar. Click the Trimmed Form Element button. Dreamweaver MX wraps `FirstName` in a `Request.Form` statement and uses the `Trim` function to remove any blank spaces:

```
Trim(Request.Form("FirstName"))
```

While the statement is still selected, click the Output button:

```
<%= Trim(Request.Form("FirstName")) %>
```

The selection is wrapped in a shorthand `Response.Write` statement. Switch back to Design view.

Tip

If you hold your cursor over a button on the Insert bar, its name is displayed as a tooltip. To force the Insert bar to display button names, choose Edit | Preferences and select the General category. Under Editing Options, choose Text Only, or Icons and Text, from the Insert Panel drop-down menu. If you select the option to display Icons and Text, you may need to click the arrow on the left side of the Insert bar to display all of the objects.

Repeat these steps with the remaining text placeholders: "FirstName," "LastName," "Email," "Phone," and "Comments." Your page should now resemble Figure 5-2.

Press F12 to preview the page in a browser. Fill out the form and click Submit. Did you enter any carriage returns in the `Comments` field? If so, you probably noticed that your formatting wasn't preserved. Let's fix this. Select {Form.Comments} in the Document window and switch to Code view:

```
<%= Trim(Request.Form("Comments")) %>
```

Change this statement to the following:

```
<%= Replace(Request.Form("Comments"), vbNewLine, "<br>") %>
```

Try the form again. The VBScript `Replace` function replaces all occurrences of line breaks (vbNewLine) with the HTML <br> tag.

Now you've got a fully functioning Advanced Contact Form. Only one problem: it doesn't send e-mail.

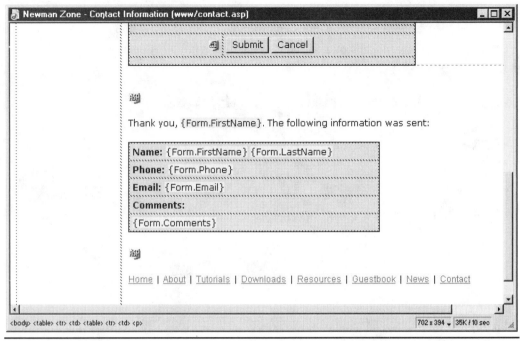

Figure 5-2 *Without Dreamweaver's translators, these form variables would be displayed as server markup tags.*

Displaying Form Variables (ColdFusion)

Select the "FORM.FirstName" placeholder in the Document window and select the CFML Basic tab on the Insert bar. Click the Surround with # button. Dreamweaver MX wraps FORM.FirstName with ColdFusion pound (#) signs. While #FORM.FirstName# is still selected, click the cfoutput button. Tag editor opens with a list of possible attributes for the <cfoutput> tag. Leave the attribute text boxes empty and click OK. The form variable is wrapped in <cfoutput> tags.

 Tag editor — not to be confused with Quick Tag Editor — is another feature that should be familiar to ColdFusion Studio users. When you click certain buttons on the Insert bar, tag editor offers you a list of possible attributes for the selected tag. Tag editor can also be invoked by clicking a tag on the tag selector and pressing CTRL-F5. Clicking the Tag Info button on tag editor toggles a context-sensitive listing from the Reference panel.

Repeat these steps with the remaining text placeholders: "FirstName," "LastName," "Email," "Phone," and "Comments." Your page should now resemble Figure 5-2.

Press F12 to preview the page in a browser. Fill out the form and click Submit. Did you enter any carriage returns in the Comments field? If so, you probably noticed that your formatting wasn't preserved. Let's fix this. Select {FORM.Comments} in the Document window and switch to Code view:

```
<cfoutput>#FORM.Comments#</cfoutput>
```

Change this statement to the following:

```
<cfoutput>#ParagraphFormat(FORM.Comments)#</cfoutput>
```

Try the form again. The ColdFusion ParagraphFormat function replaces double newline characters with HTML paragraph (<p>) tags. Check the Macromedia Exchange for extensions that automate this feature: **www.macromedia.com/exchange**.

Tip

ParagraphFormat only replaces occurrences of two CR/LF sequences. For greater control over formatting, use ColdFusion's Replace function.

Now you've got a fully functioning Advanced Contact Form. Only one problem: it doesn't send e-mail.

Sending E-mail

These days, most domain hosting providers offer you some means of sending e-mail from web-based forms. For our purposes, this will involve either ColdFusion's <cfmail> tag or Dimac's w3 JMail component. Since both of these solutions require setting up a mail server, that's what we're going to do next.

Setting Up a Mail Server

If you're developing Dreamweaver MX sites on Windows NT/2000/XP, you're in luck: Internet Information Services comes with its own SMTP (Simple Mail Transfer Protocol) server.

Windows 95/98 developers, on the other hand, will need to install a separate mail server in order to test the contact form locally. Whereas Microsoft SMTP Server runs as a service on Windows NT/2000/XP, ArGoSoft Mail Server runs as a small icon in your system tray. It's a good choice for Windows 95/98 for several reasons: it's relatively easy to set up, it has a small memory footprint, and—best of all—it's free.

Microsoft SMTP Server

The steps for installing and configuring Microsoft SMTP Server are not as complicated as some people would have you believe. Simply open the Control Panel and choose Add/Remove Programs | Add/Remove Windows Components. Select Internet Information Services (IIS) and click Details. See if SMTP Service is checked. If it's not, check it and click OK.

Once SMTP Server is installed, you need to configure it to send e-mail from your local machine. Open the IIS Snap-In or choose Administrative Tools | Internet Information Services from the Control Panel. Expand the console tree until you see Default SMTP Virtual Server. Right-click it and choose Properties.

Follow these steps to configure SMTP Server:

1. On the General tab, choose your IP address from the drop-down menu. If it doesn't appear automatically, click Advanced to add it to the list. (If you don't know your IP address, type **ipconfig /all** at a command prompt and copy it down. You'll find some other useful information there as well, such as your host name and DNS servers.)

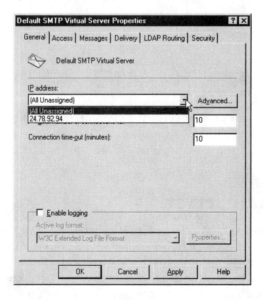

2. On the Access tab, click Relay. This opens the Relay Restrictions dialog box. Select the first radio button—Only The List Below—and click Add. Enter your IP address and click OK. Your computer should now appear in the list of domains with relay access to SMTP Server. This means that you can now send e-mail to recipients outside your domain or local network (LAN).

C a u t i o n

If you choose the second relay option, All Except The List Below, anyone who knows your domain name or IP address could potentially use your server to send bulk e-mail.

3. On the Delivery tab, click Advanced. Enter your IP address in the Fully Qualified Domain Name text box and click Check DNS. A confirmation dialog box will appear if SMTP Server is able to resolve your IP address to a valid domain name.

Click OK to close the Default SMTP Virtual Server Properties window. SMTP Server should now have enough information to send e-mail. However, there's one more step. If you're developing Active Server Pages, you may need to register an e-mail component on the server (see the next section, "Installing ASP E-mail Components"). ColdFusion users need to define a mail server in ColdFusion Administrator (see the later section, "ColdFusion Administrator Mail Server Settings").

ArGoSoft Mail Server

Setting up ArGoSoft Mail Server on Windows 95/98 is a little more complicated than setting up Microsoft SMTP Server.

The first time you run the program, an icon appears in your system tray. Double-click the ArGoSoft icon to launch the program's main interface, and choose File | Options. Complete the following steps to configure ArGoSoft Mail Server:

1. On the General tab, enter the address of your DNS server and make sure Allow Relay is checked. (If you don't know your DNS server address, see step 2. Otherwise, skip to step 3.)

2. To launch Windows' IP Configuration utility, choose Start | Run, type **winipcfg**, and click OK. If you're connected to the Internet via DSL or cable modem, choose your Ethernet Adapter from the drop-down menu. Click More Info. Copy down your host name, DNS server, and IP address for later.

3. On the Local Domains tab, enter your server's domain name in the text box and click Add. This is where it gets a little tricky. If you don't know your server's domain name, you will have to perform a reverse lookup of your IP address. There are many sites on the Internet that provide this service free of charge. Click OK to close the Options window.

4. Choose Tools | Users to open the User Setup window. Click the Add New User button.

5. On the General tab, create a User Name and Password for the new mail account. Click OK to close the User Properties window.

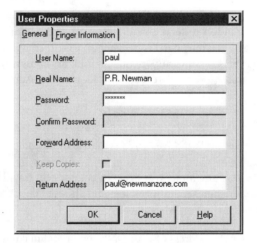

If you run into any problems—and it can take a bit of tinkering to get the settings just right—click Help or read the information posted at **www.argosoft.com**.

Tip

If you don't have a domain name, or a fixed IP address, you may want to consider a dynamic DNS service such as TZO (**www.tzo.com**).

You should now be able to use ArGoSoft Mail Server to send e-mail from ColdFusion templates and ASP components such as JMail.

Installing ASP E-mail Components

A number of companies have created COM objects for use on the Microsoft platform. Although installing an e-mail component on your local server is not necessary to complete this book, it does save you the trouble of uploading files to your remote server every time you want to test them. In this section, we will focus on five of the most widely used e-mail components, including Microsoft's own implementation, CDONTS.

Company	Terms	Requirements
JMail (www.dimac.net)	Free	-Windows NT/2000/XP -mail server
AspMail (www.serverobjects.com)	Trial software	-Windows 95/98 or Windows NT/2000/XP
AspEmail (www.persits.com)	Free	-Windows 95/98 or Windows NT/2000/XP -mail server
SMTPMail (www.softartisans.com)	Advertising	-Windows 95/98 or Windows NT/2000/XP
CDONTS (www.microsoft.com)	Free	-Windows NT/2000/XP -mail server

JMail: Windows NT/2000/XP

If you're running Windows NT/2000/XP and have already set up Microsoft SMTP Server, download JMail Personal Edition from Dimac. The installation routine automatically registers `jmail.dll` on your server. Personal Edition is free for personal use and for students. If you want to install JMail for commercial use, you need to purchase a site license for JMail Professional ($49).

AspMail: Windows 95/98 or Windows NT/2000/XP

Of the five components, AspMail is probably the easiest to install. This is because AspMail doesn't require an external SMTP server in order to function. It also works on Windows 95/98. To install AspMail, copy `smtpsvg.dll` into your `C:\Windows\System32` directory.

> **Note**
>
>
> The installation path for AspMail is different on Windows 95, NT, and 2000. Go to **www.serverobjects.com** for installation instructions.

To register AspMail on your server, choose Start | Run, type **regsvr32 smtpsvg.dll**, and click OK. If registration succeeds, you will see a confirmation message. When the evaluation period expires, you can purchase a Single CPU license for $49.95.

AspEmail: Windows 95/98 or Windows NT/2000/XP

AspEmail's basic functionality is free, but its "Premium Features" will cease to work after 30 days. It also requires an external SMTP server. The setup program, `AspEmail.exe`, automatically registers `AspEmail.dll` on your server. For more information, and sample code, visit **www.aspemail.com**.

SMTPMail: Windows 95/98 or Windows NT/2000/XP

The free version of SMTPMail adds a promotional header and footer to your e-mail, so it's useful only in a development environment. Like ASPMail, SMTPMail doesn't require an external SMTP server in order to function. In addition, the setup program automatically registers `sasmtp.dll` on your server. The full version of SMTPMail costs $129.

CDONTS: Windows NT/2000/XP

In case you were wondering, CDONTS stands for Collaboration Data Objects for Windows NT Server. What is this propensity for acronyms? (Don't get me started.)

If you're running Windows NT, you've already got `cdonts.dll` in the `C:\winnt\system32` directory. All you have to do is register it on the server. However, Microsoft, in its infinite wisdom, elected not to include CDONTS in later versions of its operating system.

Fortunately, if you have a copy of `cdonts.dll` gathering dust somewhere, it will still work on Windows 2000 and XP. Just copy the DLL into your `C:\Windows\System32` directory and register it by entering **regsvr32 cdonts.dll** at a command prompt. You should receive a confirmation message like this:

If you need to interface with Microsoft Exchange, you might want to consider using one of Microsoft's other CDO objects: `cdo.dll` (Windows 2000) or `cdosys.dll` (Windows XP).

ColdFusion Administrator Mail Server Settings

For those using ColdFusion to create the contact form, there's one more step before you can send e-mail using the `<cfmail>` tag. You need to define your mail server using ColdFusion Administrator's Mail Server Settings page.

Browse to ColdFusion Administrator (e.g., **http://localhost/cfide/administrator/**) and log in using the password you created when you installed ColdFusion Server. Choose Mail Server from the table of contents on the left.

On the Mail Server Settings page, enter the domain name or IP address of your mail server. Check the Verify Mail Server Connection check box and click Submit Changes. You should receive the following message: "Connection Verification Successful."

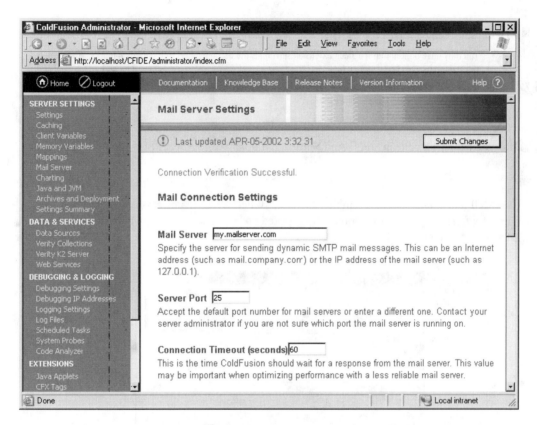

Log out of ColdFusion Administrator and restart ColdFusion Server. You can now send e-mail from ColdFusion templates using the `<cfmail>` tag.

Sending E-mail Using JMail (ASP)

In this example, we will use the JMail extension to send e-mail from the contact page when the form is submitted. If you don't have the JMail component installed on your server, you can find other extensions for sending e-mail at the Macromedia Exchange. For instance, the UltraSuite 4000 Extensions Package includes a number of AspMail extensions. Visit **www.ultrasuite.com** for details.

Launch Dreamweaver MX and open the contact page we created earlier (`contact.asp`). In the Document window, place your cursor to the right of the server markup tag between the conditional regions. Select the ASP tab on the Insert bar and click the JMail button. Enter your e-mail address in the To text box, and **"Newman Zone Contact Form"** in the Subject text box.

Note

You may have noticed that the JMail extension surrounds the default values with quotation marks. When you use this extension, only literal strings (e.g., `"paul@newmanzone.com"`) need be enclosed in double quotes. Variables, functions, and objects, such as `Request("Email")`, can be entered directly.

Enter the following code in the From (Name) text box:

```
Request("FirstName") & " " & Request("LastName")
```

The JMail dialog box should resemble Figure 5-3. Click OK. Dreamweaver MX switches to Split view to show you the location of the inserted code (it should appear right after the `<% Else %>` statement).

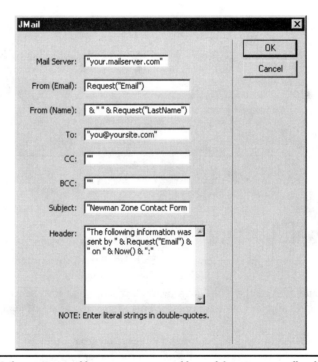

Figure 5-3   *The JMail extension enables you to enter variables and functions as well as literal strings. You can even mix and match.*

Notice the code on lines 98–103:

```
For i = 1 To Request.Form.Count
  FieldName = Request.Form.Key(i)
  FieldValue = Request.Form.Item(i)
  JMail.Body = JMail.Body & _
  FieldName & ": " & FieldValue & vbNewLine
Next
```

The `For-Next` loop places all of the form's name/value pairs into the body of the e-mail, right after the header. For greater control over formatting, replace the `For-Next` loop with the following code:

```
JMail.Body = JMail.Body & _
"Name: " & Request("FirstName") & " " & Request("LastName") & vbNewLine & _
"Phone: " & Request("Phone") & vbNewLine & _
"E-mail: " & Request("E-mail") & vbNewLine & _
"Comments: " & Request("Comments")
```

That's it! Save your work and press F12 to give it a test drive. If you run into any problems, make sure you entered a valid mail server and double-check your syntax. In addition, some mail servers are configured to send e-mail only from the local domain or IP address. (Remember the Relay Restrictions dialog box in Microsoft SMTP Server?) In other words, if your domain is `xyz.com`, and you enter **jack@abc.com** in the From text box (see Figure 5-3), the mail server may refuse the message.

Sending E-mail Using <cfmail> (ColdFusion)

Thanks to the `<cfmail>` tag, sending e-mail in ColdFusion is considerably easier than it is in ASP. At minimum, all you need is the following code:

```
<cfmail
to="you@yoursite.com"
from="#FORM.Email#"
subject="Newman Zone Contact Form"
>
#FORM.Comments#
</cfmail>
```

To insert the `<cfmail>` tag into the Contact Information page, we'll use one of Dreamweaver's new features: tag editor. Open `contact.cfm` in Dreamweaver MX and select the CFML Advanced tab on the Insert bar. Place your cursor to the right of the `<cfelse>` icon and click the CFMail button. In the General category, enter the information shown here (replace `you@yoursite.com` with your actual e-mail address):

```
Tag Editor - Cfmail

  General                    Cfmail - General
  Dynamic Content
  Message Body
  MIME Attachment                  To:  you@yoursite.com
  Server Settings
                                 From:  #FORM.Email#

                              Subject:  Newman Zone Contact Form

                                   CC:

                                  BCC:




                                                              ▷ Tag Info

                                              OK          Cancel
```

Select the Message Body category and choose Plain Text from the drop-down menu. Enter the following code in the Message text box:

```
The following message was sent by#FORM.Email# on #DateFormat(Now())#↵
at #TimeFormat(Now())#:

Name: #FORM.FirstName# #FORM.LastName#
Phone: #FORM.Phone#
E-mail: #FORM.Email#
Comments: #FORM.Comments#
```

Leave the other categories empty and click OK (if you've defined a mail server in ColdFusion Administrator, the Server Settings aren't necessary). Once again, Dreamweaver MX switches to Split view to show you where the code was inserted. Notice that the body of the e-mail message appears within the opening and closing `<cfmail>` tags. Unfortunately, tag editor strips carriage returns out of the message body. With any luck, this issue will be resolved by the time you read this. If not, restore the carriage returns in Code view.

Save your work and press F12 to preview the page in a browser. Fill out the form and click Submit. Did you receive the e-mail? If not, check ColdFusion's `Mail` folder for undelivered messages (e.g., `C:\CFusionMX\Mail\Undelivr`). A `.cfmail` file in the `Undelivr` folder usually means that your mail server isn't configured properly. Review "Setting Up a Mail Server," or consult the ColdFusion Documentation (**http://localhost/cfdocs/dochome.htm**).

Form Validation

This section will be brief (you're welcome). All we have to do is apply Jaro von Flocken's Check Form behavior to validate the contact form before it's submitted.

Open the Contact Information page in Dreamweaver MX and select `<form>` on the tag selector.

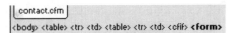

From the Behaviors panel—*not* the Server Behaviors panel—choose yaromat | Check Form. Select each field name, in turn, and check the Required check box. When you get to the `Email` field, select the radio button to validate an e-mail address. For the `Comments` field, choose the second radio button and enter a number to make it required. Click OK to close the Check Form dialog box.

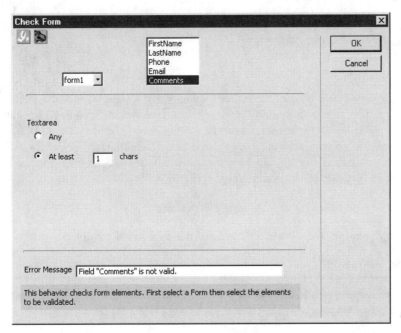

Save your work and press F12 to preview the page. If your browser allows you to submit the form without completing the fields, make sure you've selected the form's `onSubmit` event in the Behaviors panel.

While we're here, let's do one last thing: select `<form>` on the tag selector. The Action attribute should still be empty. Using the Property inspector, enter the code we discussed at the beginning of the chapter:

```
<%= CStr(Request.ServerVariables("SCRIPT_NAME")) %> (ASP)
<cfoutput>#GetFileFromPath(GetTemplatePath())#</cfoutput> (ColdFusion)
```

Now you can move and rename the contact page to your heart's content, and it will always post to itself.

Error-Handling

At this point, you could upload the Contact Information page, and chances are, it will work flawlessly. *As long as you haven't made any mistakes.* So in the interest of being thorough, let's trap ASP and ColdFusion errors and display a friendly message to the visitor if something goes wrong.

The Err Object (ASP)

To trap errors in ASP, we'll use the VBScript `Err` object. Open `contact.asp` in Code view and locate the JMail code block (around line 155). The JMail extension already checks for errors and, if it finds any, stuffs `Err.Description` into a variable called `strError`:

```
If Err Then 'Create error variable
strError = Err.Description
End If 'End check for errors
```

All we need to do is check if `strError` has a value and, if so, display it to the visitor. Otherwise, we'll display the confirmation message. This means nesting an `If-Else` statement inside our existing `Else` statement (don't worry, it's not as complicated as it sounds).

In the Document window, place your cursor to the left of "Thank you." Select the ASP tab on the Insert bar and click the If button. Dreamweaver MX switches to Split view and the blinking cursor is positioned between `If` and `Then`. Type **strError = ""**:

```
<% If strError = "" Then 'Display confirmation %>
```

Add a comment to remind yourself why you inserted the code in the first place.

 Tip VBScript comments are preceded by an apostrophe (`). I won't belabor the importance of comments. If you've ever returned to a project after a long absence, you know how helpful they can be.

Switch back to Design view and place your cursor to the left of the last server markup tag on the page. Click the Else button on the Insert bar. Add a comment to the `Else` statement on line 198:

```
<% Else 'Display error message %>
```

Enter the following code *after* the `<% Else %>` statement:

```
<p align="left">An error occurred: <b><%= strError %></b>.</p>
Please notify <a href="mailto:webmaster@yoursite.com">
webmaster@yoursite.com</a>.
```

Place your cursor at the end of this error message and click the End button on the Insert bar. Once again, add a comment to the `End If` statement:

```
<% End If 'end check strError variable %>
```

Now let's test the page. Scroll up to the JMail code block and delete the e-mail address after the `JMail.AddRecipient` method (around line 163). Save your work and press F12. When you submit the form, the page should resemble Figure 5-4.

Switch back to Design view. Notice that the Contact Information page now consists of *three* conditional regions: the form, the confirmation message, and the error message.

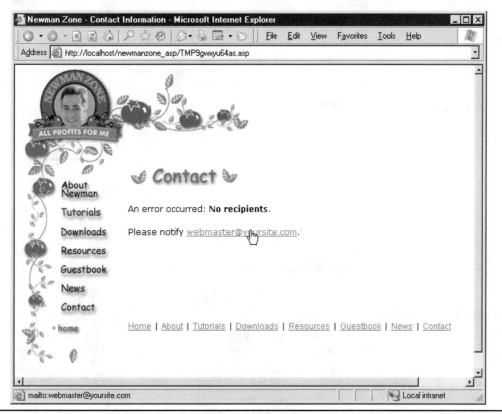

Figure 5-4   *The error message provides a brief description and an e-mail address to notify the Webmaster.*

That's it! You've created an error handler for the contact page. If you're feeling ambitious, try modifying the code to append errors to a log file and e-mail the Webmaster. For a complete list of JMail's properties and methods, visit **www.dimac.net**.

By the way: don't forget to restore your e-mail address to the `JMail.AddRecipient` line!

The <cferror> Tag (ColdFusion)

Error handling in ColdFusion requires a little more work up front but ultimately offers greater control over the appearance of error messages. In order to trap errors in the contact form—and throughout the site—we'll create two new ColdFusion templates: `Application.cfm` and `Errors.cfm`.

◆ **Application.cfm**   A special file that is automatically *included* at the beginning of every ColdFusion template when you place it in the site's root folder (e.g., `C:\Inetpub\wwwroot\newmanzone_cf_empty\www`). You don't even have to use the `<cfinclude>` tag. (In this respect, it's similar to ASP's `global.asa` file.) You can use `Application.cfm` to define application-wide variables, data sources, error routines, and so forth.

◆ **Errors.cfm**   A custom error template that is specified by the `<cferror>` tag in `Application.cfm`. (This page doesn't have to be called `Errors.cfm`—I just couldn't think of a better name.) When exception errors occur in the Newman Zone site, `Errors.cfm` is used to display a custom error message. However, the user is not redirected to this page: the browser's address bar still displays the location of the page that generated the error.

> **Note**
>
> According to Macromedia, the term "exception error" is used to describe any "events that disrupt an application's normal flow of instructions." These can include internal errors, syntax errors, and error responses from external services, such as an ODBC driver.

We'll take advantage of two new Dreamweaver features, tag editor and Code Hints, to help us build these pages.

The Application.cfm Page

Create a new, blank document in Dreamweaver MX named `Application.cfm`, and save it in the root directory of the Newman Zone site (www). Switch to Code view and delete the default HTML markup tags.

Select the CFML Advanced tab on the Insert bar, and click the cferror button. Choose Exception from the Error Type drop-down menu and type **Errors.cfm** in the Message Template text box (we'll create that page in a minute). Enter your e-mail address in the Administrator Email text box, and type **any** in the Exception text box. Click OK to insert the `<cferror>` tag.

If an exception error occurs in the Newman Zone site, the `<cferror>` tag specifies `Errors.cfm` as the template to display the error message.

Caution

If you do not create the `Errors.cfm` page in the next step, ColdFusion will return the following error on every page in the Newman Zone site: "Error attempting to resolve the template Errors.cfm." This is because ColdFusion is unable to find the error template specified in `Application.cfm`.

Pretty straightforward, right? Save your work and close `Application.cfm`.

The Errors.cfm Page

Open `template.cfm` in Dreamweaver MX and save a copy as `Errors.cfm`. (I always keep a file like this in the site's root directory to use as the basis for new pages.) Use the Document toolbar (View | Toolbars | Document) to change the page's title from [Title] to Error. Select the first paragraph, "This is a Headline," and replace it with "We're Sorry...." Select the three paragraphs below it and replace them with the following:

An Error Occurred:

ERROR

Please notify webmaster.

In the Document window, select the word "ERROR." On the Insert bar, select the CFML Basic tab and click the Surround with # button. Dreamweaver MX switches to Split view and wraps ERROR with ColdFusion pound signs. While #ERROR# is still selected, click the cfoutput button on the Insert bar and click OK. Place your cursor between ERROR and the closing pound sign (#), and type a period (.). Code Hints appears with a list of ColdFusion ERROR variables (how cool is that?). Select `Diagnostics` and press ENTER (you can also type the first letter to jump to the desired item in the list).

New Feature

Although Code Hints resembles Tag Hints in Quick Tag Editor, it has more in common with Tag Insight in ColdFusion Studio. You'll come across Code Hints in Code view (or Code inspector), when it suddenly pops up with a list of available tag attributes; function parameters; or object properties, methods, and variables. To set Code Hints preferences, choose Edit | Preferences | Code Hints.

Now select "webmaster" in the Document window and repeat the same steps to wrap it in pound signs (#) and `<cfoutput>` tags. Select `webmaster` and replace it with `ERROR`, followed by a period (`.`). When Code Hints appears, select `Mailto` (this is the variable we defined in `Application.cfm`).

Finally, let's make the Webmaster's e-mail address a hyperlink. Select `#Error.MailTo#` and click the Email Link button on the Insert bar (you'll find it on the Common tab). Enter **#ERROR.MailTo#** in the E-mail text box and leave Text empty. Click OK.

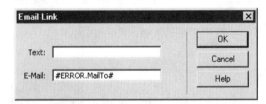

The completed code should look like this:

```
<p><b class="headline">We're Sorry...</b></p>
<p><b>An Error Occurred:</b></p>
<p><b><cfoutput>#ERROR.Diagnostics#</cfoutput></b></p>
<p>Please notify <cfoutput><a href="mailto:#ERROR.MailTo#">
#ERROR.MailTo#</a></cfoutput>.</p>
```

Save your work and close `Errors.cfm`.

Now all we have to do is create an error. Open `contact.cfm` and locate the `<cfmail>` tag in Code view (around line 164). Remove the following attribute: `to="you@yoursite.com"`. Save the page and press F12 to preview it in a browser:

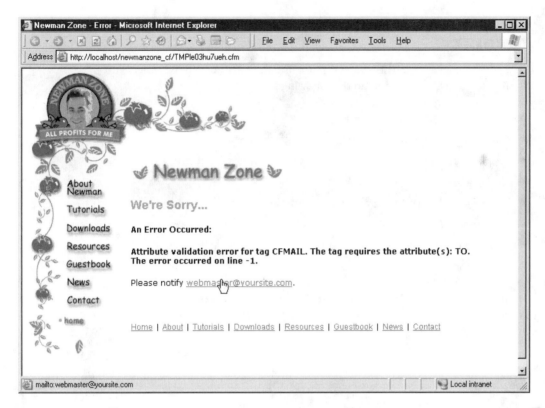

Not bad for ten minutes' work. All right, so maybe it was fifteen.

Keep in mind, you can add additional error variables to `Errors.cfm`, and additional application variables to `Application.cfm`, to customize your site even further. Also, don't forget to restore the `to` attribute to the `<cfmail>` tag (`to="you@yoursite.com"`) or you'll keep raising the same error.

Summary

Whew! We covered a lot in this chapter. I promise, the next one will be easier.
In this chapter, you learned to do the following:

◆ Define a new site in Dreamweaver MX

◆ Create conditional regions using `If-Else` statements

◆ Display form variables using `Request.Form` and `<cfoutput>`

◆ Set up a mail server and install ASP components

◆ Define a mail server using ColdFusion Administrator

◆ Send e-mail from a web-based form

◆ Validate form input using JavaScript

◆ Trap errors to display a user-friendly message

In the next chapter, we're going to build on what we've learned to cook up an advanced guestbook. This time, the visitor will be able to preview the guestbook entry before the form is submitted.

Chapter 6

Advanced Guestbook

INGREDIENTS

File	Type	Server Model(s)	Source
newmanzone.mdb	Access database	ASP/CF	*Sample Code*
newmanzone.sql	SQL script	ASP/CF	*Sample Code*
index.asp	Active Server Page	ASP	*Sample Code*
index.cfm	ColdFusion template	CF	*Sample Code*
Conditional Region 2	Server Behavior	ASP	Waldo Smeets
JMail	Object	ASP	*Sample Code*
IsDefined	Object	CF	*Sample Code*

 from the desk of Paul Newman

I n this recipe, we are going to build on what we learned in the last chapter to create an advanced guestbook. The guestbook will consist of two pages: the View Guestbook page, which displays the latest guestbook entries, and the Sign Guestbook page, which allows visitors to add entries of their own. This time, we'll create *three* conditional regions on the Sign Guestbook page: one to display the form, another to preview the entry before it's submitted, and a third to display a confirmation message. In addition, we'll e-mail the visitor to thank him for signing.

The techniques covered in this chapter can easily be put to other uses, such as a Customer Testimonials or Bug Reports page. If you decide to create such a page, you may want to restrict access to authorized users (employees, beta testers, etc.). For more on this, see Chapter 19.

To sum up, the Advanced Guestbook will consist of the following sections:

◆ **View Guestbook**   The default page with the guestbook entries

◆ **Sign Guestbook**   An HTML form with eight fields

◆ **Preview Guestbook**   A preview of the new guestbook entry

◆ **Thank You**   A confirmation region that e-mails the visitor

This time, only the View Guestbook page has been created for you. It'll be up to you to create the Sign Guestbook page and its conditional regions. Before we can get started, however, we need to set up the Newman Zone database.

Setting Up the Newman Zone Database

To complete this tutorial, you need to download the Newman Zone database from **www.newmanzone.com** or **www.osborne.com**. If you downloaded the supporting files earlier, you'll find two Access 2000 databases in the `databases` folder: `newmanzone.mdb` and `realty.mdb`. These databases contain the sample data that will be referenced—in screenshots and code listings—throughout this book. You'll also find `newmanzone.mdb` in the `db` directory of the Newman Zone site you set up in Chapter 5 (e.g., `C:\Inetpub\wwwroot\newmanzone_asp_empty\db`).

Creating the ODBC Data Source

To connect to the Access 2000 database, `newmanzone.mdb`, we'll create a new System DSN (Data Source Name) using Windows' ODBC Data Source Administrator.

Open the Windows Control Panel and launch ODBC Data Source Administrator. Select the System DSN tab and click Add. From the list of available drivers, choose Microsoft Access Driver (*.mdb) and click Finish.

Enter **newmanzone** in the Data Source Name text box, and an optional description. Click Select and browse to the location of `newmanzone.mdb` on your hard drive (e.g., `C:\Inetpub\wwwroot\newmanzone_asp_empty\db\newmanzone.mdb`). Click OK to close the Select Database dialog box.

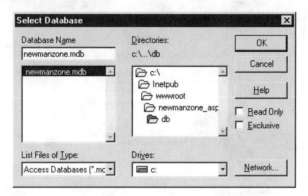

Click OK again to close the ODBC Microsoft Access Setup dialog box.

Creating the ColdFusion Data Source

To create the ColdFusion Data Source for the Newman Zone site, log in to ColdFusion Administrator (e.g., **http://localhost/cfide/administrator**) and choose Data Sources from the table of contents.

In the Add New Data Source region, enter **newmanzone** in the Data Source Name text box, and choose ODBC Socket from the Driver drop-down menu. Click Add.

Note

ColdFusion MX uses JDBC database drivers to communicate with data sources. DSNs created with Windows' ODBC Data Source Administrator are referred to as ODBC Socket connections.

On the next page, the ODBC DSN we created earlier is automatically selected in the drop-down menu. Notice that all of your other System DSNs appear in the menu as well. Enter an optional description and click Show Advanced Settings.

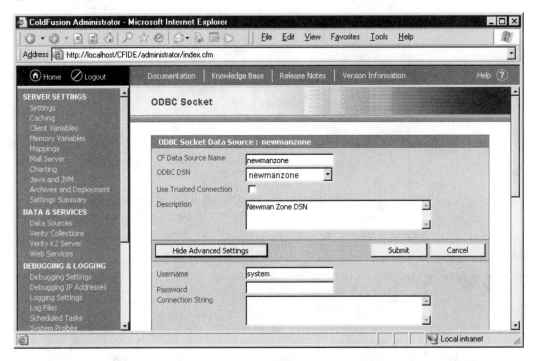

In the Advanced Settings, make sure Enable Long Text Retrieval (CLOB) is checked (CLOB is required for Microsoft Access Memo fields). Click Submit.

The newmanzone data source is added to ColdFusion Administrator, and "ok" appears in the Status column. This data source is now available to Dreamweaver MX and other programs that support Remote Development Services (RDS), such as HomeSite+ and ColdFusion Studio.

The SQL Server Database

To create the newmanzone database on SQL Server, locate the SQL script, `newmanzone.sql`, in the `databases` folder you downloaded earlier. The SQL Server database comes into play in Chapter 8, "Filtering Recordsets Using Stored Procedures."

Follow these steps to install the SQL Server database:

1. Launch SQL Query Analyzer (you may be prompted to log in) and choose File | Open.

2. This brings up the Open Query File dialog box. Browse to `newmanzone.sql` on your hard drive and click Open. The SQL script loads into the Query window.

3. Choose Query | Execute, or press F5. Query Analyzer executes the script and creates the newmanzone database on SQL Server.

4. Choose Tools | Object Browser | Show/Hide. The newmanzone database should appear in the Object Browser. If it doesn't, right-click your SQL Server in the Object Browser and choose Refresh.

5. To verify the installation, we'll query the Guestbook table. Choose File | New and open a blank Query window.

6. Choose newmanzone from the Current Database drop-down menu and enter the following SQL statement in the Editor pane:

```
SELECT * FROM Guestbook
```

7. Choose Query | Execute or press F5 to run the query. The table's six guestbook entries should be displayed in the Results pane.

Close Query Analyzer and click No when prompted to save the query.

If you have any problems setting up the SQL Server database, you can also upsize newmanzone.mdb using the Microsoft Access Upsizing Wizard, or SQL Server Data Transformation Services (DTS).

The View Guestbook Page

Now for the good stuff. Launch Dreamweaver MX and open the Site panel (choose Window |
Site or press F8). Expand the `guestbook` folder to reveal the View Guestbook page
(`index.asp` or `index.cfm`, depending on your server model). Copy and paste the View
Guestbook page and rename the copy `sign.asp` or `sign.cfm` (we'll use this later as the basis
of the Sign Guestbook page).

Open the View Guestbook page. As you can see, I've already created placeholders for the data.

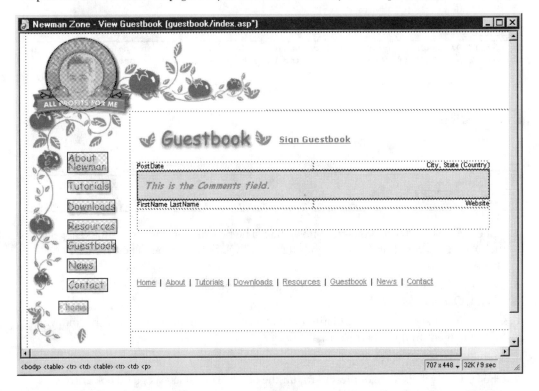

I've also created six sample guestbook entries in the Newman Zone database that we'll use to
populate the page.

The Guestbook Table

The `Guestbook` table is fairly straightforward, consisting of 11 fields or columns. The field
names and Access data types are listed in Table 6-1.

Take a moment to examine the Newman Zone database and familiarize yourself with its tables,
queries, and so forth.

Field Name	Data Type	Field Size	Default Value
GuestbookID	AutoNumber		
PostDate	Date/Time		Date()
FirstName	Text	50	
LastName	Text	50	
City	Text	50	
State	Text	2	
Country	Text	50	
Email	Text	255	
Website	Text	255	
Active	Yes/No		-1
Comments	Memo		

Table 6-1   *The Guestbook Fields and Their Corresponding Access Data Types*

Displaying the Guestbook Entries

In this section, we'll design the View Guestbook page. If it's not already open, open `index.asp` (or `index.cfm`) and follow these steps to complete the page:

1. From the Bindings panel, choose Recordset (Query) to create a new recordset. If the Recordset dialog box opens in Advanced mode, click Simple.

Note

If you're using ColdFusion, you may be prompted to log in to ColdFusion Remote Development Services (RDS). Enter the password you created when you installed ColdFusion Server and click OK. If you're using ASP, click Define and choose New | Data Source Name (DSN). Enter **newmanzone** in the Connection Name text box, and choose newmanzone from the Data Source Name (DSN) drop-down menu. Click Test to verify the data source and click OK. The new connection appears in the Connections dialog box. Click Done.

2. Enter **rsGuestbook** in the Name text box, and choose newmanzone from the Connection (or Data Source) drop-down menu.
3. Select `Guestbook` from the Table drop-down menu and click the All Columns radio button.
4. Filter the recordset to display entries only if the `Active` column is not equal (<>) to 0. (A value of 0 in the `Active` column is equivalent to false, or unchecked.)

5. Finally, sort the recordset in Descending order according to the `PostDate` column (this displays the latest entries first). Click Test to verify the recordset. The SQL statement should return six records. Click OK to close the Recordset dialog box.

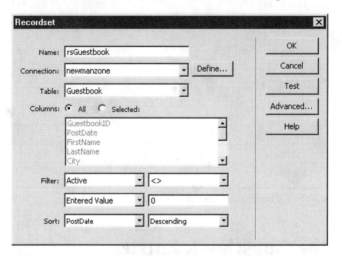

6. Select "PostDate" in the Document window, and expand the `rsGuestbook` recordset in the Bindings panel. Select the `PostDate` column and click Insert.

7. Repeat step 6 with the remaining `rsGuestbook` columns: `FirstName`, `LastName`, `City`, `State`, `Country`, `Website`, and `Comments`. Bind each recordset column, in turn, to its respective placeholder in the Document window.

Throughout this book, we'll be binding text and images to database columns. To do this, make your selection in the Document window, then select the corresponding database column in the Bindings panel and click Insert.

8. In the Document window, select the HTML table that contains the guestbook entry (it's the third `<table>` tag from the left on the tag selector).

9. Choose Repeat Region from the Server Behaviors panel and select the All Records radio button. Click OK.

10. Select {rsGuestbook.Comments} in the Document window and switch to Code view:

```
<%=(rsGuestbook.Fields.Item("Comments").Value)%> (ASP)
#rsGuestbook.Comments# (ColdFusion)
```

Change this line to the following:

```
<%=Replace((rsGuestbook.Fields.Item("Comments").Value),↵
vbNewLine, "<br>")%> (ASP)
```

```
#Replace(Replace(rsGuestbook.Comments, chr(10), "<br>"),⏎
chr(13), "<br>")# (ColdFusion)
```

This preserves the formatting if visitors enter carriage returns in the Comments field. (For the record, chr(13) and chr(10) are the ASCII characters for carriage return and line feed, respectively. In ASP, you can also use vbCrLf or vbNewLine to insert a carriage return/line feed.)

11. Next, we'll make the signer's name and web site hyperlinks. Select {rsGuestbook.FirstName} and {rsGuestbook.LastName} in the Document window (you may need to SHIFT-CLICK to get both of them). Right-click on the selection and choose Make Link. Click the Data Sources radio button and select Email from the rsGuestbook recordset. Add mailto: to the beginning of the URL text box and click OK.

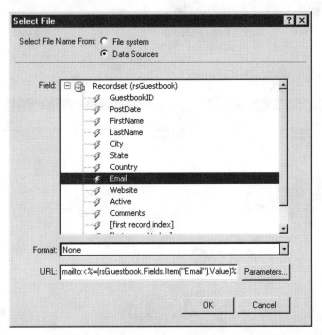

12. Repeat step 11 with {rsGuestbook.Website}, binding the placeholder in the Document window to the rsGuestbook.Website column. Use the Property inspector to change the link's target to _blank.

Save your work and press F12 to preview the page in a browser. Notice that the first guestbook entry doesn't have a web site. To address this, we'll create an If-Else statement that displays alternative text if the Website column is empty.

Select {rsGuestbook.Website} in the Document window and switch to Code view. Place your cursor before the opening <a> tag and click the If button on the ASP tab of the Insert bar

(ColdFusion users should click the cfif button on the CFML Flow tab). Complete the `If` statement as shown here:

```
<% If (rsGuestbook("Website") <> "") Then %>(ASP)
<cfif rsGuestbook.Website IS NOT ""> (ColdFusion)
```

Place your cursor after the closing `</a>` tag and click the Else (or cfelse) button on the Insert bar. Type **No URL Given**:

```
<% Else %>No URL Given (ASP)
<cfelse>No URL Given (ColdFusion)
```

Finally, click the End button to complete the `If-Else` statement (ColdFusion users should drag and drop the closing `</cfif>` tag into place):

```
<% Else %>No URL Given<% End If %>(ASP)
<cfelse>No URL Given</cfif> (ColdFusion)
```

Save your work and press F12. That's better.

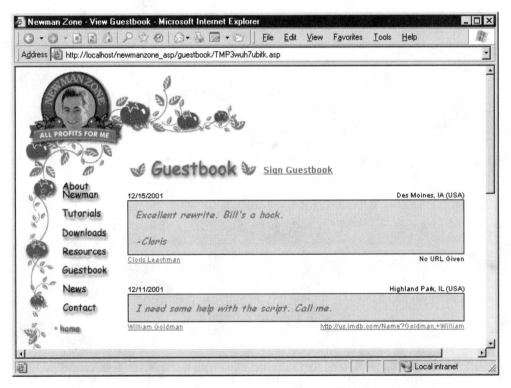

Before we proceed to the Sign Guestbook page, let's make one more edit. To display the date in a user-friendly format, we'll apply a date function to the `PostDate` column. Select {rsGuestbook.PostDate} in the Document window and switch to Code view:

```
<%=(rsGuestbook.Fields.Item("PostDate").Value)%>
```
(ASP)
```
#rsGuestbook.PostDate#
```
(ColdFusion)

Change this line to the following:

```
<%=FormatDateTime((rsGuestbook.Fields.Item("PostDate").Value), 1)%>
```
(ASP)
```
#DateFormat(rsGuestbook.PostDate, "dddd, mmmm d, yyyy")#
```
(ColdFusion)

That's it! Preview the page in a browser. Notice the new date format. If you run into problems, review the preceding steps to make sure you didn't skip over anything. Pay close attention to any steps that require hand-coding.

The Sign Guestbook Page

A guestbook is pretty meaningless if visitors can't sign it, so that is what we'll address next. The Sign Guestbook page consists of three conditional regions:

- **Sign Guestbook**   Displays an HTML form
- **Preview Guestbook**   Previews the entry before it's submitted
- **Thank You**   Confirms the new entry and sends e-mail

Open the Sign Guestbook page (`sign.asp` or `sign.cfm`) in Dreamweaver MX and use the Document toolbar (View | Toolbars | Document) to change its title to Sign Guestbook.

The Sign Guestbook Region

In the Document window, select the Guestbook image (`guestbook.gif`) and replace it with the Sign Guestbook image (`images/headers/sign-gbk.gif`). Delete the Sign Guestbook link.

Use the ENTER key to insert a paragraph after the Sign Guestbook image. Choose File | Open and browse to the supporting files you downloaded earlier. Find the original version of the Contact Information page (`contact.asp` or `contact.cfm`) and open it in Dreamweaver MX. Select `<form>` on the tag selector and copy the contact form to the clipboard. Close the Contact Information page and paste the contact form into the Sign Guestbook page, below the Sign Guestbook image.

Select `<form>` on the tag selector and change the form's name to `signGuestbook`. Select the hidden field marker (it looks like an "H" with a page curl) and use the Property inspector to change its value to `preview`. Change the label of the submit button to Preview as well.

Delete the `Phone` field and add the remaining guestbook fields to the form: `City`, `State`, `Country`, `Website`. The quickest way to do this is to copy and paste a table row (`<tr>`) and rename its label and text field. When you're finished, the form should consist of the elements listed in Table 6-2.

We don't have to worry about the other columns in the `Guestbook` table—`GuestbookID`, `PostDate`, and `Active`—because the database supplies their default values. However, if you

Name	Label	Input Type	Notes
FirstName	First Name:	text	
LastName	Last Name:	text	
City	City:	text	
State	State:	text	
Country	Country:	text	
Email	Email:	text	
Website	Web site:	text	
Comments	Comments:	textarea	
Mode		hidden	value="preview"

Table 6-2 *The Completed Sign Guestbook Form Consists of Nine Elements*

want to "hide" new guestbook entries until you approve them, add a hidden form field called Active and set its value to 0.

Press CTRL-S to save your work.

The Preview Guestbook Region

The Preview Guestbook region previews the new entry before it's submitted. In the Document window, select the HTML table that contains the guestbook placeholders, and wrap it with <form> tags (see Figure 6-1). To wrap the selection, press CTRL-T to open Quick Tag Editor. (You can cycle through Quick Tag Editor's three modes—Edit Tag, Wrap Tag, Insert HTML— by pressing CTRL-T repeatedly.) Make sure you're in Wrap Tag mode, and type **form** (or choose Form from the Tag Hints pop-up menu).

Click <form> on the tag selector and name the new form previewGuestbook. Follow these steps to complete the Preview Guestbook region:

1. Insert the Preview Guestbook image (images/headers/preview-gbk.gif) into the previewGuestbook form we just created. Use the ENTER key to insert a paragraph after the image, and add the following instructions for the visitor: **Below is a preview of your guestbook entry. Click Sign to submit it.**

2. Copy the two buttons from the signGuestbook form and paste them into the previewGuestbook form. Use the Property inspector to change the first button's label to Sign. (You can change the button names as well, but it's not necessary.)

3. To display the form variables, we'll use the same technique we employed on the Contact Information page. In the Document window, select the "FirstName" placeholder. Select the ASP tab on the Insert bar, and click Trimmed Form Element. While the form variable is still selected, click the Output button. (ColdFusion users should click the Surround with # button on the CFML Basic tab, followed by the cfoutput button.)

4. Repeat step 3 with the remaining form variables: LastName, City, State, Country, Website, and Comments.

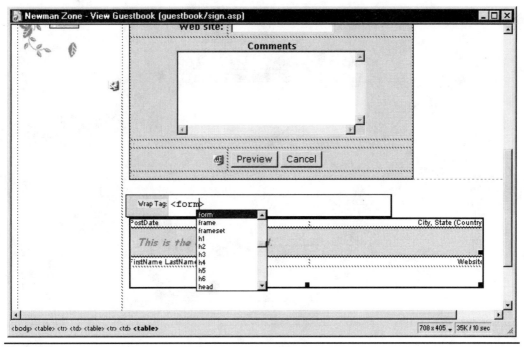

Figure 6-1 *You can wrap tags around the current selection by pressing CTRL-T until you enter Wrap Tag mode.*

5. Select "PostDate" in the Document window and switch to Code view. Replace the selection with the following code:

```
<%= Date() %> (ASP)
<cfoutput>#DateFormat(Now(), "mm/dd/yy")#</cfoutput> (ColdFusion)
```

6. Next, we'll add hidden fields to store the values of the `signGuestbook` form. Place your cursor inside the `previewGuestbook` form—it doesn't really matter where—and click Hidden Field on the Forms tab of the Insert bar.

7. Using the Property inspector, name the hidden field `FirstName`, and enter the following code in the Value text box:

```
<%= Request.Form("FirstName") %> (ASP)
<cfoutput>#FORM.FirstName#</cfoutput> (ColdFusion)
```

8. Repeat steps 6 and 7 with the remaining form variables: `LastName`, `City`, `State`, `Country`, `Email`, `Website`, and `Comments`. (You can skip `PostDate`, since its value is supplied by the database.)

9. Finally, insert one more hidden form field. Name it **Mode** and enter **sign** in the Value text box.

The Preview Guestbook region should now resemble Figure 6-2. Press CTRL-S to save your work.

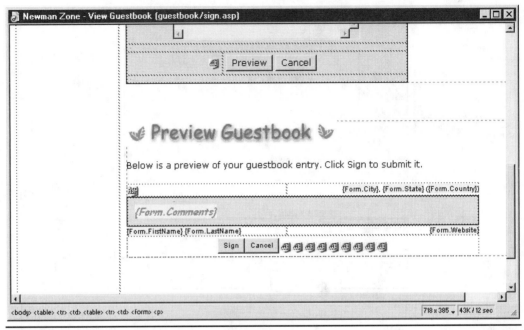

Figure 6-2 *The Preview Guestbook region of the Sign Guestbook page*

The Thank You Region

The confirmation region has two purposes: thank the visitor for signing the guestbook, and send two e-mail messages.

First, add a paragraph after the `previewGuestbook` form and insert the Thank You image (`images/headers/thanks.gif`). Insert another paragraph and type the following: **Thank you, FirstName, for signing the guestbook**. Press ENTER to insert another paragraph, and type **View Guestbook**. Select "View Guestbook" and link it to the View Guestbook page (`index.asp` or `index.cfm`).

In the Document window, select "FirstName" and click Trimmed Form Element on the ASP tab of the Insert bar. While the form variable is still selected, click Output on the Insert bar. (ColdFusion users should click Surround with # on the CFML Basic tab, followed by the cfoutput button.)

Sending E-Mail Using JMail (ASP)

Once again, we're going to use the JMail extension to send e-mail as the confirmation region loads. This time, we're going to send one e-mail to the guestbook owner, and a second e-mail to the visitor, thanking him for signing.

In the Document window, place your cursor to the left of the Thank You image. Select the ASP tab on the Insert bar and click the JMail button. Fill out the text boxes as shown next and click OK:

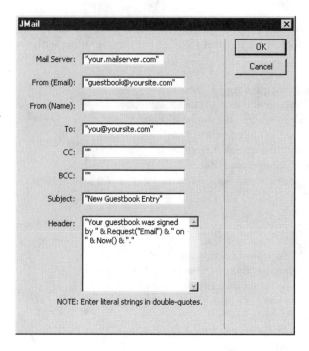

This sends a message to your e-mail address, notifying you that someone has signed the guestbook. Click the JMail button again. This time, send an e-mail to the visitor, thanking him for signing:

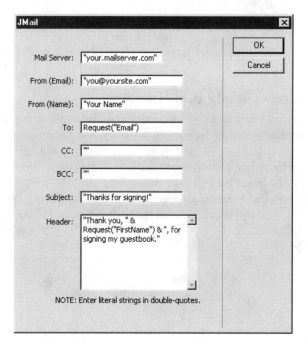

The JMail code blocks can be consolidated by removing the `If` statements and `For-Next` loops. The final code should look like this (replace the sample values with your own e-mail address, mail server, etc.):

```
<% '**** Send JMail to guestbook owner ****
Set JMail = Server.CreateObject("JMail.SMTPMail")
JMail.ServerAddress = "your.mailserver.com"
JMail.Sender = "guestbook@yoursite.com"
JMail.Subject = "New Guestbook Entry!"
JMail.AddRecipient "you@yoursite.com"
JMail.Body = "Your guestbook was signed by " & Request("Email") & ↵
" on " & Now() & "."
JMail.Execute
Set JMail = Nothing
%>
<% '**** Send JMail to guestbook signer ****
Set JMail = Server.CreateObject("JMail.SMTPMail")
JMail.ServerAddress = "your.mailserver.com"
JMail.Sender = "you@yoursite.com"
JMail.SenderName = "Your Name"
JMail.Subject = "Thanks for signing!"
JMail.AddRecipient Request("Email")
JMail.Body = "Thank you, " & Request("FirstName") & ↵
", for signing my guestbook."
JMail.Execute
Set JMail = Nothing
%>
```

Don't preview the page just yet. We still have to apply the Insert Record SB and define the page's conditional regions.

Sending E-mail Using <cfmail> (ColdFusion)

Once again, we're going to use `<cfmail>` to send e-mail as the confirmation region loads. This time, we're going to send one e-mail to the guestbook owner, and a second e-mail to the visitor, thanking him for signing.

In the Document window, place your cursor to the left of the Thank You image. Select the CFML Advanced tab on the Insert bar and click the cfmail button. Enter your e-mail address in the To text box, and **guestbook@yoursite.com** in the From text box. Enter **New Guestbook Entry!** in the Subject text box and select the Message Body category. Fill out the Message text box as shown next and click OK:

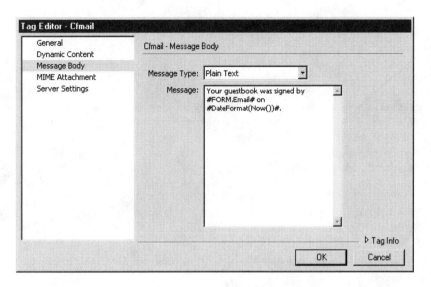

This sends a message to your e-mail address, notifying you that someone has signed the guestbook. Place your cursor after the closing `</cfmail>` tag and click the cfmail button again. This time, send an e-mail to the visitor, thanking him for signing. Enter **#FORM.Email#** in the To text box, and your e-mail address in the From text box. Enter **Thank you for signing!** in the Subject text box and select the Message Body category. Fill out the Message text box as shown here and click OK:

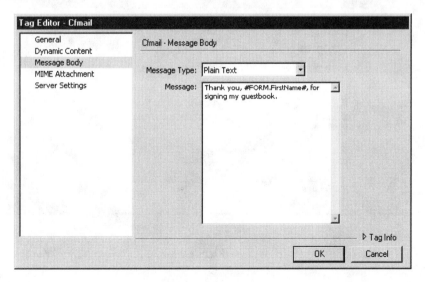

The completed `<cfmail>` code blocks should look like this (replace the sample values with your own e-mail address, etc.):

```
<cfmail to="you@yoursite.com" from="guestbook@yoursite.com"
subject="New Guestbook Entry!">
Your guestbook was signed by #FORM.Email# on #DateFormat(Now())#.
</cfmail>
<cfmail to="#FORM.Email#" from="you@yoursite.com"
subject="Thanks for signing!">
Thank you, #FORM.FirstName#, for signing my guestbook.
</cfmail>
```

Don't preview the page just yet. We still have to apply the Insert Record SB.

The Insert Record Server Behavior

To insert the new guestbook entry into the Newman Zone database, we'll use Dreamweaver's standard Insert Record SB.

From the Server Behaviors panel, choose Insert Record. Select the `previewGuestbook` form, and choose newmanzone from the Connection (or Data Source) drop-down menu. Select `Guestbook` as the destination table, and make sure all the form elements and database columns match up. Ignore the `GuestbookID`, `PostDate`, and `Active` columns (ASP users: ignore the `Mode` field). Leave the redirect text box empty and click OK to apply the SB.

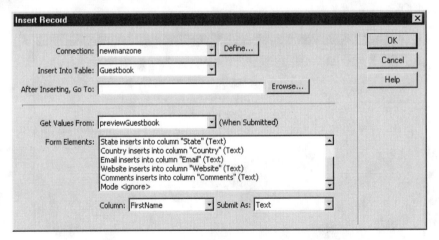

Notice that Dreamweaver MX adds a hidden field to the `previewGuestbook` form: `MM_insert` (or `MM_InsertRecord`). As we discussed in the previous chapter, the Insert Record code block will execute only if `MM_insert` (or `MM_InsertRecord`) contains a value.

Defining the Conditional Regions

We're going to use the same method to define the conditional regions that we used on the Contact Information page. In ASP, we'll use Waldo Smeets' Conditional Region extension. In ColdFusion, we'll use the isDefined extension.

The Conditional Region Extension (ASP)

Open `sign.asp` in Dreamweaver MX. In the Document window, select the Sign Guestbook image and the `signGuestbook` form below it. Switch to Code view to make sure you've selected the right elements. From the Server Behaviors panel, choose Conditional Region | Request And Script. Select Request.Form from the drop-down menu and enter **Mode** in the Name text box. Accept the default Condition, Equals, and enter two quotation marks ("") in the Script text box. Click OK.

Now select the `previewGuestbook` form by clicking <form> on the tag selector. Since we want to show this region only if Mode equals `preview`, choose Conditional Region | Request And Script from the SB panel. Select Request.Form from the drop-down menu and enter **Mode** in the Name text box. Accept the default Condition, Equals, and enter **"preview"** (including the quotation marks) in the Script text box:

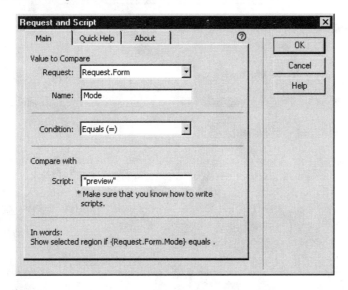

Finally, select everything in the Thank You region. Switch to Code view to ensure you've selected the JMail code blocks. Choose Conditional Region | Request And Script from the Server Behaviors panel. This time, we want to show the region only if Mode equals `sign`. Select Request.Form from the drop-down menu and enter **Mode** in the Name text box. Accept the default Condition, Equals, and enter **"sign"** (including the quotation marks) in the Script text box.

That's all there is to it! The beauty of this approach is that you can still go back and edit any of the three conditional regions in Design view, without having to wrestle with the underlying code. Save your work and preview the page in a browser (you may have to upload it to your remote server to test the e-mail functionality).

If you prefer, you can use an `If-Else If-Else` statement to show/hide the three conditional regions. In fact, the page's performance might improve slightly, because if the first condition is true, the other two statements (`Else If` and `Else`) are never evaluated. (That's why it's generally preferable to place the most likely condition first in a conditional statement.)

The IsDefined Extension (ColdFusion)

To create the conditional regions in ColdFusion, we'll use the IsDefined extension. Open `sign.cfm` in Dreamweaver MX.

In the Document window, select the Sign Guestbook image and the `signGuestbook` form below it. Switch to Code view to make sure you've selected the right elements. Select the CFML Flow tab on the Insert bar and click the isDefined button. Choose FORM from the drop-down menu, and enter **Mode** in the text box.

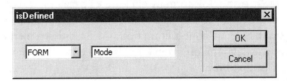

Click OK. Since we want to display the form only if `Mode` is *not* defined, revise the `<cfif>` statement as shown here (the new code is shaded):

```
<cfif NOT isDefined("FORM.Mode")>
```

Find the closing `</cfif>` tag (around line 149) and change it to the following:

```
<cfelseif (FORM.Mode IS "preview")>
```

Stay in Code view, and scroll down to the end of the `previewGuestbook` form (around line 185). Place your cursor to the left of the opening `<cfmail>` tag, and click the cfelse button on the Insert bar. Scroll down to the end of the Thank You region, and insert a closing `</cfif>` tag just before the library item (`navlinks.lbi`). Now, if neither of the first two conditions evaluates to true, the Thank You region is displayed.

Save your work and press F12 to preview the page in a browser.

Summary

We covered a lot of ground in this chapter, but hopefully it's starting to get a little easier. In case you didn't notice, you're well on your way to becoming a master chef. Here's what you learned to do:

◆ Create a DSN using Windows' ODBC Data Source Administrator
◆ Create a data source using ColdFusion Administrator

- ◆ Define a database connection in Dreamweaver MX
- ◆ Create a View Guestbook page to display guestbook entries
- ◆ Display alternative text if a database column is empty
- ◆ Create a Sign Guestbook page with three conditional regions
- ◆ Send e-mail to two recipients using JMail and `<cfmail>`

I'd like to see Martha do that! If you're still raring to go, try validating the `signGuestbook` form using JavaScript or a server-side validation extension.

In the next recipe, we'll delve into one of the underused features of Microsoft Access: parameter queries.

Chapter 7

Filtering Recordsets Using Parameter Queries

INGREDIENTS

File	Type	Server Model(s)	Source
newmanzone.mdb	Access database	ASP/CF	*Sample Code*
index.asp	Active Server Page	ASP	*Sample Code*
index.cfm	ColdFusion template	CF	*Sample Code*
Alternate Row Colour	Server Behavior	ASP	Owen Palmer

 from the desk of Paul Newman

I n Chapters 7 and 8, we're going to use parameters to filter Dreamweaver MX recordsets. In SQL Server, this means creating a stored procedure with an input parameter. In Microsoft Access, we'll create a parameter query. If you haven't done this before, don't worry: using parameterized queries in Dreamweaver MX is similar to filtering recordsets with run-time variables.

To demonstrate parameter queries and stored procedures in action, we will create—or at least start—the Newman Zone Downloads section. Strictly speaking, Access doesn't support stored procedures. You *can* create a stored procedure in an Access project, but Access projects require SQL Server or MSDE (Microsoft Database Engine).

 Note

 Access projects, which have an .adp extension, allow you to manage MSDE and SQL Server databases using Microsoft Access. For more on Access projects, see Chapter 3.

In this recipe, we will emulate the behavior of a SQL Server stored procedure by creating a parameter query in Access 2000. We will then use Dreamweaver MX to call the "stored procedure" on the default Downloads page.

The Downloads Table

If you open newmanzone.mdb in Access 2000, you'll find two tables that pertain to this chapter: Downloads and DownloadCats (see Figure 7-1).

Note

The Newman Zone database is included among the supporting files you downloaded earlier. If you haven't downloaded the supporting files for this book, please visit **www.newmanzone.com** or **www.osborne.com/downloads/downloads.shtml**.

The Downloads table stores information about the downloads in 13 fields or columns. The actual downloadable files reside in a folder above the site root (e.g., C:\Inetpub\wwwroot\newmanzone_asp_empty\downloads\exts). If you open the Downloads table in Microsoft Access, you'll see that it consists of five sample Dreamweaver extensions.

Most of the Downloads fields are self-explanatory. They include Filename (e.g., JMail.mxp), FilePath (the relative path to the file), AuthLastName (the author's last name), and Description (see Table 7-1).

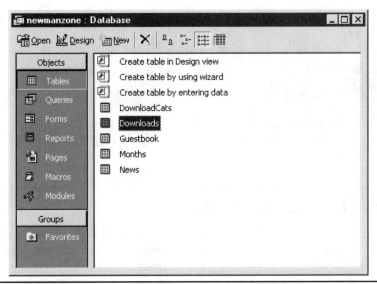

Figure 7-1   *The Newman Zone database consists of five tables:* DownloadCats, Downloads, Guestbook, Months, *and* News.

Field Name	Data Type	Field Size	Description
DownloadID	AutoNumber		Primary Key
DownloadCatID	Number		Foreign Key to DownloadCats
DateAdded	Date/Time		Default value: Date()
FileTitle	Text	50	
Filename	Text	50	
FilePath	Text	150	Relative path to file
FileSize	Text	10	File size in kilobytes
FileExt	Text	3	Three-digit extension
AuthFirstName	Text	20	
AuthLastName	Text	30	
DownloadNo	Text	10	Default value: 0
Active	Yes/No		Default value: −1
Description	Memo		

Table 7-1   *The* Downloads *Table Consists of 13 Fields or Columns*

In addition, several fields merit explanation:

◆ `DateAdded`   A timestamp indicating when the file was uploaded

◆ `DownloadNo`   The number of times the file has been downloaded

◆ `Active`   A Boolean field to show/hide the item

What's missing from the `Downloads` table is the file's MIME type (Word document, MP3 audio file, etc.). We could add a column to `Downloads` called `FileType`, but this functionality is better handled by creating another table altogether—in this case, `DownloadCats`.

The DownloadCats Table

The `DownloadCats` table was created to *normalize* the database by eliminating duplicate entries in the `FileType` column. In an Access 2000 database, without a lot of entries, a few duplicates aren't a big concern. But when you're running a web site with thousands of downloads, the redundant data can quickly add up to a lot of wasted space. This, in turn, can adversely affect the speed and performance of the database.

Note

Normalization is a process whereby database designers eliminate duplicate data by refining tables, columns, and relationships to create an optimized relational database. The process of normalization is accomplished by ensuring the database conforms to different "normal forms."

The purpose of `DownloadCats` is to provide different categories for the downloads. Since the `Downloads` table consists of Dreamweaver extensions, the categories have names like ASP, CF, JSP, and PHP. We'll also use the `DownloadCats` table to populate a drop-down menu, so visitors can sort extensions by category (not unlike the Macromedia Exchange).

By now, you've probably noticed that `Downloads.DownloadCatID` is a foreign key to the `DownloadCats` table. We'll use this database relationship to perform an *inner join* of the two tables when we create the parameter query in Access. For a visual understanding of this one-to-many relationship, see Figure 7-2. (Alternatively, you can open `newmanzone.mdb` in Microsoft Access and choose Tools | Relationships.)

For more on the nature of relational databases, see Chapter 3, "The Care and Feeding of Databases." You should also invest in a good reference book on SQL programming, such as *SQL: The Complete Reference* (McGraw-Hill/Osborne, 1999), or *Sams Teach Yourself SQL in 10 Minutes* (Sams Publishing, 2001) by Ben Forta.

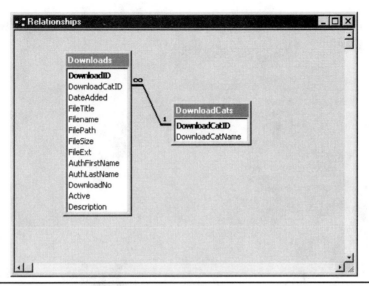

Figure 7-2   *The Relationships diagram for the Newman Zone database*

Creating the Parameter Query

Before we can create the Downloads page in Dreamweaver MX, we need to create the parameter query it will use to return a recordset. So fire up Microsoft Access and open `newmanzone.mdb`.

To create the query, click Queries (under Objects) and double-click Create Query In Design View. (The Newman Zone database already contains the queries we'll be designing in this chapter: `qDownloads` and `qDownloadCats`. Feel free to refer to them if you get stuck.)

Since this query will be an inner join of the `Downloads` and `DownloadCats` tables, use the CTRL key to select both tables and click Add. Click Close. Notice that Access automatically creates a "join line" between the two tables, illustrating the relationship between `Downloads.DownloadCatID` and `DownloadCats.DownloadCatID` (see Figure 7-3).

We want to select all of the columns from the `Downloads` table, and the `DownloadCatName` column from the `DownloadCats` table. An easy way to do this is to SHIFT-select all of the column names in the `Downloads` field list, and drag them onto the design grid below. Now you can select the `DownloadCatName` field from the `DownloadCats` table and drag and drop it over the `DateAdded` column (Access always inserts a new column to the left of the current column).

Now we have to create the parameter that will be passed by the Downloads page into Microsoft Access. Enter the following text in the Criteria cell of the `DownloadCatName` column: **LIKE "*"+[category]+"*"**. Using the LIKE operator in the WHERE clause enables us to search using *wildcard* characters.

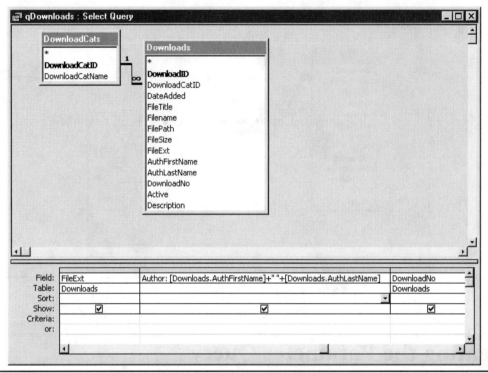

Figure 7-3 *Access creates a "join line" to illustrate the relationship between primary key and foreign key columns in two tables:* DownloadCats *and* Downloads.

Note

The wildcard character in Structured Query Language is the percent sign (%). The wildcard character in Microsoft Access, however, is the asterisk (*). Many database developers paid the ultimate price for this information, so you might want to make a mental note of it.

The square brackets ([ ]) tell Access to prompt us for the value of the category parameter. The asterisk (*) tells Access to accept any characters in its place as a match. For instance, to find the extension authors whose last names begin with M, we can write the following statement:

```
SELECT * FROM Downloads WHERE AuthLastName LIKE "M*" (Access)
SELECT * FROM Downloads WHERE AuthLastName LIKE 'M%' (SQL Server)
```

This query returns one result: the extension written by Tom Muck. Here's another example, using wildcard characters on both sides of the search string:

```
SELECT * FROM Downloads WHERE FileTitle LIKE "*z*" (Access)
SELECT * FROM Downloads WHERE FileTitle LIKE '%z%' (SQL Server)
```

This query returns one result, Horizontal Looper 2, because it's the only extension with the letter Z in the `FileTitle` column. Now that you've mastered the wildcard character, you can use `pam*` to search your hard drive for that Pamela Anderson photo you downloaded, and `*.doc` to find your boss's termination letter.

Tip The preceding examples do not adhere to SQL best practices. In general, you should avoid using asterisks (*) in `SELECT` statements (e.g., `SELECT * FROM Downloads`). Even if you add all the column names to the `SELECT` statement, the query is more efficient because the database doesn't have to generate a list of the table's columns. For more on SQL best practices, see **http://www.sql-server-performance.com/ vk_sql_best_practices.asp**.

Let's finish the `qDownloads` query. From the Access menu bar, choose Query | Parameters. Enter **category** in the Parameter column, and choose Text from the Data Type drop-down menu (see Figure 7-4). Click OK.

Now let's try it out. Click the red exclamation point to run the query, or choose Query | Run from the menu bar. A dialog box appears, prompting you to enter the value of the `category`

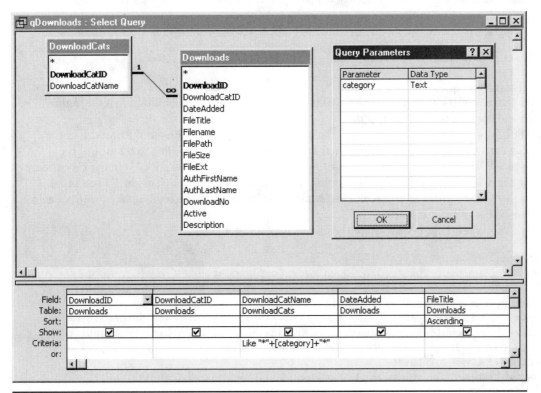

Figure 7-4   *The Microsoft Access parameter query,* `qDownloads`, *in Design view*

parameter. Type **cf** in the text box and click OK. A datasheet appears, displaying the results of the query. In this case, there are three matches because three extensions are ColdFusion-compatible.

As you can see, Access filters the query based on the run-time value of the `category` parameter (e.g., if you had entered php, no matches would have been found). If all of this isn't clear right now, don't worry: it will become clearer in a moment.

Note

If you're wondering why we didn't use `DownloadCatID` as the parameter, good eye! Generally, it's preferable to use a number—rather than a text data type—as a query or stored procedure parameter because databases can search through numbers faster than text.

Let's make a few more refinements to the `qDownloads` query. Choose View | Design View to return to the design grid, and scroll over to the `Active` column. Type **<>0** in the Criteria cell. This tells Access to return only those rows where the `Active` column is not false (`0`), or unchecked. This way, we can quickly show/hide an item by checking/unchecking the `Active` check box.

Now select the `AuthLastName` column. To do this, place your cursor above the column name. When the cursor changes to a downward-pointing arrow, click to select the column. Press DELETE on your keyboard.

Replace the text in the `AuthFirstName` Field cell with the following:

```
Author: [Downloads.AuthFirstName]+" "+[Downloads.AuthLastName]
```

This creates a column alias called `Author` that concatenates the values of `AuthFirstName` and `AuthLastName`. The alias also adds a space between the two columns so that the author's first and last names don't run together.

Finally, add an `ORDER BY` clause to the query by choosing Ascending in the Sort cell of the `FileTitle` column. This sorts the query results alphabetically according to the title of the download. When you're finished, choose Query | Run and enter an asterisk (*) in the `category` text box. Click OK. Notice that the extensions are now sorted alphabetically by `FileTitle`, and that the `AuthFirstName` and `AuthLastName` columns have been replaced with a single column alias called `Author`.

Choose View | SQL View to see the underlying SQL statement:

```
PARAMETERS category Text ( 255 );
SELECT Downloads.DownloadID, Downloads.DownloadCatID,
DownloadCats.DownloadCatName, Downloads.DateAdded, Downloads.FileTitle,
Downloads.Filename, Downloads.FileLocation, Downloads.FileSize,
Downloads.FileExt, [Downloads.AuthFirstName]+" "+[Downloads.AuthLastName]
AS Author, Downloads.DownloadNo, Downloads.Active, Downloads.Description
FROM DownloadCats INNER JOIN Downloads ON DownloadCats.DownloadCatID =
Downloads.DownloadCatID
WHERE (((DownloadCats.DownloadCatName) Like "*"+[category]+"*")
AND ((Downloads.Active)<>0))
ORDER BY Downloads.FileTitle;
```

The ability of Access to generate SQL code makes it a convenient way to create queries for other applications, including Dreamweaver MX and SQL Server. All you have to do is copy and paste the code from Access to the destination program. In fact, this is often the only way to get Access queries into SQL Server, since Data Transformation Services (DTS) and the Access Upsizing Wizard seem unable convert them. As you will see, we will be using the qDownloads query in Chapter 8 as the basis of a SQL Server stored procedure.

Close the Query window and click No when prompted to save it.

The qDownloadCats Query

Since we want visitors to the Downloads page to be able sort extensions by category, we need to create a query to populate the drop-down menu.

In Access, click Queries and double-click Create Query In Design View. Add the Downloads and DownloadCats tables and click Close. This time, the only fields we need are DownloadCats.DownloadCatID, DownloadCats.DownloadCatName, and Downloads.Active. Drag and drop these fields onto the design grid below. Type **<>0** in the Criteria cell of the Downloads.Active column. This will prevent the drop-down from displaying the categories of extensions that are "unpublished" or still being evaluated. Your grid should now look like this:

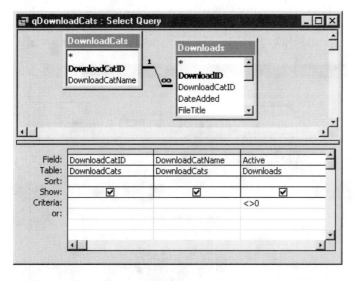

When you run the query, the ASP category appears twice. That's *not* what we want. Fortunately, there's an easy way to correct this. Choose View | SQL View. After SELECT type the word **DISTINCT**. The final SQL statement should look like this:

```
SELECT DISTINCT DownloadCats.DownloadCatID, DownloadCats.DownloadCatName,
Downloads.Active
FROM DownloadCats INNER JOIN Downloads ON DownloadCats.DownloadCatID =
```

```
Downloads.DownloadCatID
WHERE (((Downloads.Active)<> 0));
```

If you run the query again, the duplicate ASP category disappears. Good. Adding the DISTINCT keyword to the SELECT statement tells Access to omit duplicate rows from the results.

Close the Query window and exit Microsoft Access.

Building the Downloads Page

Now the fun begins. Launch Dreamweaver MX and expand the downloads folder in the Site panel. Open the default Downloads page (index.asp or index.cfm, depending on your server model). If you haven't defined the Newman Zone site in Dreamweaver MX, refer to Chapter 5 for details on setting it up.

The Dynamic Drop-Down Menu

Remember that query we created earlier, qDownloadCats? We're going to use it to allow visitors to sort downloads by category. Follow these steps to create the dynamic drop-down menu:

1. Create a new recordset called rsDownloadCats. Select newmanzone from the Connection (or Data Source) drop-down menu, and choose qDownloadCats from the Table drop-down menu. Make sure the All Columns radio button is selected. Test the recordset and click OK. Click OK again to apply the Recordset SB.

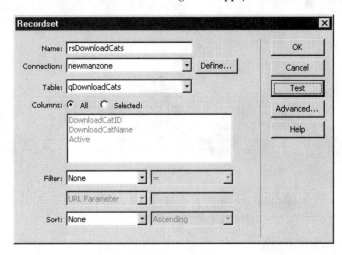

2. From the Bindings panel, choose Request Variable (URL Variable in ColdFusion). Enter **category** in the Name text box and click OK.

3. In the Document window, place your cursor below the "Dreamweaver Extensions" heading. Select Forms on the Insert bar and click the List/Menu button. When prompted to add a form tag, click Yes.

4. Select the drop-down menu in the Document window and use the Property inspector to change its name from `select` to `category`.

5. Now we're going to populate the drop-down menu with the results of the `qDownloadCats` query. From the Server Behaviors panel, choose Dynamic Form Elements | Dynamic List/Menu. The `category` menu is selected automatically.

6. Choose `rsDownloadCats` from the Recordset drop-down menu, and select `DownloadCatName` as the menu's Values and Labels.

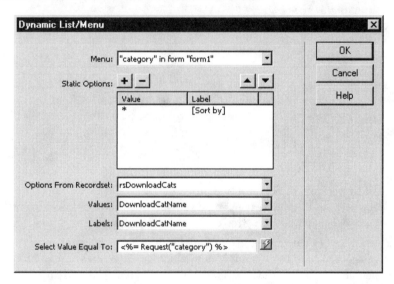

7. Click the lightning bolt icon beside the last text box to open the Dynamic Data dialog box. Choose the `category` variable we created in step 2, and click OK.

8. Finally, click the plus (+) button to add a Static Option to the menu. Enter an asterisk (*) in the Value column, and **[Sort by]** in the Label column. Click OK to apply the Dynamic List/Menu SB.

Save your work and press F12 to preview the page in a browser. The `category` drop-down menu should contain the static option and the four records returned by the `qDownloadCats` query.

Calling the Parameter Query

To display the downloads, we'll create a Dreamweaver MX recordset that calls the Access parameter query. This is the same approach we'll use to call the SQL Server stored procedure in the next chapter. This recordset can also be created by choosing Stored Procedure from the

Bindings panel, but the Stored Procedure dialog box is better suited to INSERT, UPDATE, and DELETE stored procedures, or to stored procedures that return a value, such as @@IDENTITY. For stored procedures and queries that use a parameter to create a SELECT statement, it's best to use Dreamweaver's Recordset dialog box.

Follow these steps to create the rsDownloads recordset:

1. From the Bindings panel, choose Recordset and click Advanced.
2. Name the recordset rsDownloads and choose the newmanzone connection or data source.
3. In the SQL area, enter the following:

```
{call qDownloads('category')}   (ASP)
{call qDownloads('#category#')}  (ColdFusion)
```

Tip

If it makes more sense to you, the ColdFusion statement can also be written like this: EXEC qDownloads @category='#category#'. The ASP statement can be written EXEC qDownloads @category='*variable*' (where *variable* is the name of the variable you create in step 4).

If qDownloads were a SQL Server stored procedure, we could simply select it in the Database Items area, and Dreamweaver would generate the necessary code. However, since this is an Access parameter query, we have to enter it manually.

4. **ASP**: Click the plus (+) button next to Variables. In the Name column, enter the Access parameter, **category**. Tab to the Default Value column and type an asterisk (*), the Access wildcard symbol. Finally, tab to the Run-Time Value column and enter **Request("category")**.

ColdFusion: Click the plus (+) button next to Page Parameters. In the Add Parameter dialog box, enter **category** in the Name text box, and an asterisk (*) in the Default Value text box. Click OK.

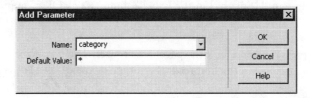

5. Click Test. If all five records are returned, click OK to close the Recordset dialog box (the ASP version is shown here).

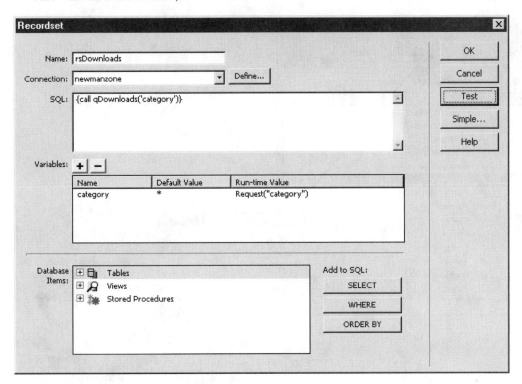

You can now work with `rsDownloads` as you would any other recordset.

Displaying the Downloads

Now for the easy part (mostly). In the Document window, create a two-row, five-column table beneath the `category` drop-down menu. Set the width to 500 pixels and the cellpadding to 5. Set the border and cellspacing to 0.

Use the tag selector to select the first table row (`<tr>`) and choose a green background color (I chose `#99CC99`). From left to right, name the column headings Extension, Author, Date, Type, and Count. You can make the column headings bold, if you like.

Drag and drop the respective `rsDownloads` columns from the Bindings panel into the table's second row: `FileTitle`, `Author`, `DateAdded`, `DownloadCatName`, and `DownloadNo`.

Select {rsDownloads.DateAdded} in the Document window. From the Bindings panel, choose an appropriate Date/Time format.

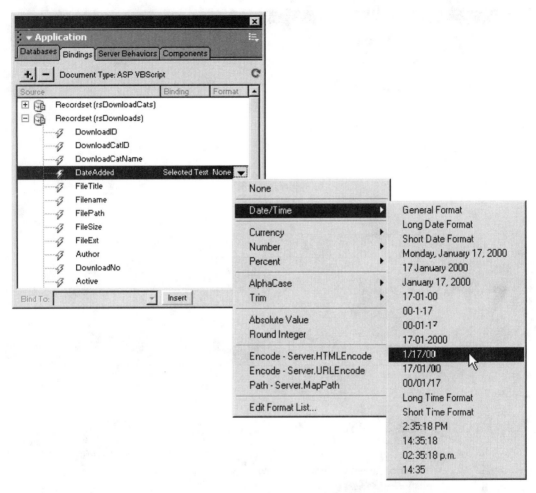

The Document window should now look something like the one that follows.

Use the tag selector to select the second table row. From the Server Behaviors panel, choose Repeat Region. Select the `rsDownloads` recordset and the All Records radio button. Click OK to apply the server behavior to the page.

Choose View | Live Data or click the Live Data View button on the Document toolbar. Enter the following URL parameter in the text box: `category=cf`. Click the Refresh Live Data icon or press CTRL-SHIFT-R. The Downloads page should resemble Figure 7-5.

Instead of five results, you should now see three (the ColdFusion-compatible extensions). Delete the URL parameter and click Live Data View or press CTRL-SHIFT-R to turn off Live Data view. Save your work.

Creating Alternately Colored Rows

To create alternately colored rows in ASP, we'll apply Owen Palmer's Alternate Row Colour extension. In ColdFusion, we'll hand-code this feature using the `IIF` function. First, open the Downloads page in Dreamweaver MX (`downloads/index.asp` or `downloads/index.cfm`).

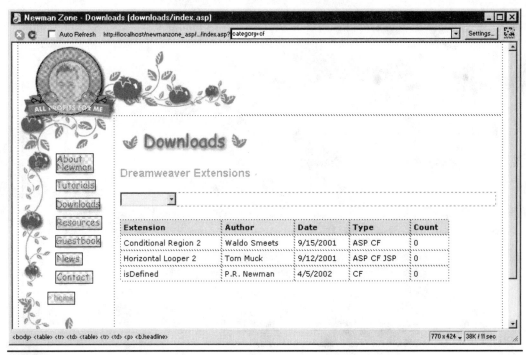

Figure 7-5   *The Downloads page in Live Data view. Notice the URL parameter text box to the right of the local server address.*

The Alternate Row Colour Extension (ASP)

In the Document window, place your cursor inside the first column of the Repeat Region. From the Server Behaviors panel, choose UltraDeviant | To Be Repeated | UltraDeviant - Alt Row Colour. Enter **#FFFFFF** in the Normal Row Colour text box, and **#E8E8E8** in the Alternative Row Colour text box. Click OK.

Save your work and press F12 to preview the page in a browser. The table rows should now alternate between gray and white.

The IIF Function (ColdFusion)

In the Document window, select the repeated region (the gray `<cfoutput>` icon) and switch to Code view. Replace the opening `<tr>` tag with the following code:

```
<tr bgcolor="###IIF(CurrentRow MOD 2, DE('FFFFFF'), DE('E8E8E8'))#">
```

The ColdFusion `IIF` function is essentially a shortcut for writing an `If-Else` statement. This code also uses the modulus operator (`MOD`), the delayed evaluation function (`DE`), and the `CurrentRow` variable. For more information, consult Macromedia's *CFML Reference*.

Revising the Drop-Down Menu

If you previewed the Downloads page in a browser, you probably noticed that the drop-down menu doesn't sort the extensions. That's what we're going to do next.

In the Document window, select the `category` drop-down menu and press CTRL-T to open Quick Tag Editor. At the end of the line, just before the closing > bracket, type the following:

```
onChange="document.forms[0].submit();"
```

Press ENTER to close Quick Tag Editor.

```
Edit Tag: <select name="category"
          onChange="document.forms[0].submit();
          ">
```

Now select `<form>` on the tag selector. Using the Property inspector, enter `index.asp` (or `index.cfm`) in the Action text box, and change the Method to GET. Save your work and press F12 to preview the page in a browser. Try using the drop-down menu to filter the extensions by category. Pretty groovy, huh?

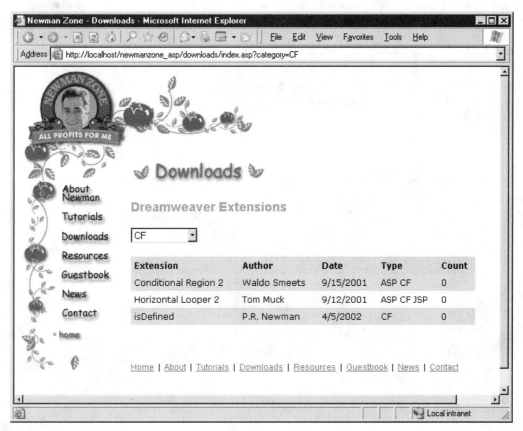

Let's make one more refinement to the page. Right now, visitors can filter downloads according to four categories: ASP, CF, ASP CF, or ASP CF JSP. Wouldn't it make more sense if they could select ASP, CF, JSP, or PHP?

In the Bindings panel, double-click the `rsDownloadCats` recordset and click Advanced. In the SQL area, replace this text

```
SELECT * FROM qDownloadCats
```

with the following:

```
SELECT DISTINCT Left(DownloadCatName, 3) AS CatName FROM DownloadCats
```

Click Test. The Test SQL Statement window returns four records: ASP, CF, JSP, PHP. Click OK. (Keep in mind, this is a bit of a hack. If you add a main category to the `DownloadCats` table that exceeds three characters—e.g., ASP.NET—you'll have to edit this recordset accordingly.) Click OK to close the Recordset dialog box.

In the Server Behaviors panel, double-click the broken Dynamic List/Menu SB (notice the red exclamation point). You should receive an error message: "The column 'DownloadCatName' was not found. Please select a new column." Click OK. The new column alias, `CatName`, is automatically selected in the Values and Labels menus. Click OK to close the Dynamic List/Menu dialog box.

Save your work and press F12 to preview the page. Try selecting a category from the drop-down menu. That's better, isn't it?

Still one problem: if you choose PHP from the drop-down, no results are returned. In the Document window, place your cursor in the empty space above the library item (`navlinks.lbi`) and type **No extensions found**. Select this paragraph and choose Show Region | Show Region If Recordset Is Empty from the Server Behaviors panel. Choose the `rsDownloads` recordset and click OK. Dreamweaver places a thin gray border around the conditional region.

Save your work and test the page in a browser. Now, if you select PHP from the drop-down menu, the alternative text is shown.

That's it—you're done. What's that? You can't actually download anything yet? (Picky, picky.) Don't worry: we'll get to that in Chapter 9, plus a lot more cool stuff.

Summary

You really flexed your culinary muscles in this chapter. Here's what you learned to do:

◆ Create a parameter query in Microsoft Access

◆ Relate two tables using an `INNER JOIN` clause

◆ Search a database column using wildcard characters

◆ Eliminate duplicate rows using the `DISTINCT` keyword

◆ Create a column alias using the `AS` keyword

◆ Populate a dynamic drop-down menu

◆ Call a parameter query to generate a recordset

◆ Preview a Dreamweaver MX page using Live Data view

◆ Create alternately colored table rows

In the next recipe, we'll use a SQL Server stored procedure to generate a Dreamweaver MX recordset. If you have SQL Server or Microsoft Data Engine (MSDE) installed on your machine, proceed to the next chapter. Otherwise, feel free to skip to Chapter 9.

Chapter 8

Filtering Recordsets Using Stored Procedures

INGREDIENTS

File	Type	Server Models	Source
newmanzone	SQL Server database	ASP/CF	*Sample Code*
newmanzone.mdb	Access database	ASP/CF	*Sample Code*

 from the desk of *Paul Newman*

One of the many advantages of SQL Server over Microsoft Access is the ability to use stored procedures. I know, I know—there's that term again.

What the hell is a *stored procedure*?

When I first started dabbling with SQL Server, stored procedures were baffling. I was used to queries in Microsoft Access. So I posted a question to a newsgroup: "What is the difference between stored procedures in SQL Server, and queries in Access?" The response? Two words: "Books Online." Of course, I had no idea what "Books Online" meant either. (Needless to say, this cryptic answer did nothing to allay my fears that database developers are members of an elite club whose membership is sworn to secrecy.) I searched Google for the phrase "books online," thinking it was an online library.

In the end, I figured out that *Books Online* is the rather uninspired title of the help system that comes installed with SQL Server. (To access BOL, as the "cultists" call it, choose Start | Programs | Microsoft SQL Server | Books Online.) Don't let the lackluster name fool you: BOL contains answers to almost every question you could have about SQL Server, and includes a searchable index. Try it out for yourself. Launch BOL, select the Search tab, and enter the term "stored procedure." Click List Topics.

My search returned 500 topics! Double-click one of the topics to read the article. BOL highlights your search terms and links to other topics at the end of the article. You can also bookmark articles by selecting the Favorites tab and clicking Add.

Tip

If you don't want search terms highlighted, choose Options | Search Highlight Off.

According to BOL, stored procedures are a "precompiled collection of SQL statements and optional control-of-flow statements stored under a name and processed as a unit. Stored procedures are stored within a database; can be executed with one call from an application; and allow user-declared variables, conditional execution, and other powerful programming features. Stored procedures can contain program flow, logic, and queries against the database. They can accept parameters, output parameters, return single or multiple result sets, and return values."

If that seems like too much information, here are a few simple things to remember about stored procedures:

◆ Stored procedures (SPs), in their simplest form, are similar to Access queries.

◆ SPs can accept input parameters and return output parameters and values.

◆ SPs are precompiled and stored on the server, so they generally run faster than embedded SQL statements.

◆ SPs can enhance security by restricting access to the database.

- ◆ SPs can call other SPs or views.
- ◆ SPs confine complex business logic to the database.

In addition, stored procedures can launch SQL Server Agent jobs, create DTS packages, replicate databases, send e-mail using SQL Mail, and much more. SQL Server also includes dozens of system stored procedures, which can perform countless administrative tasks. In fact, SQL Server uses Structured Query Language—behind the scenes—to perform virtually every task in Enterprise Manager. For more information, see *Books Online*.

In this recipe, we'll spend a little time examining the differences between Access queries, and SQL Server views and stored procedures. Then we'll use SQL Server Query Analyzer to create a stored procedure with an input parameter. Finally, we'll call a stored procedure to generate a Dreamweaver MX recordset. Once again, we'll be working on the Newman Zone Downloads section. If you haven't installed the newmanzone database on SQL Server, now would be a good time to do it. Refer to "The SQL Server Database" in Chapter 6 for details.

Queries, Views, and Stored Procedures

In making the transition from Microsoft Access to SQL Server, the first question many people ask is: How do you know when to create a stored procedure, and when to create a view? The simple answer is: SQL Server views are similar to Access queries, and SQL Server stored procedures are similar to Access *parameter* queries.

However, there is one important distinction: the ORDER BY clause can be used in a SQL Server view only when the TOP keyword is specified. For example:

```
CREATE VIEW dbo.vwTest
AS
SELECT TOP 3 *
FROM dbo.Downloads
WHERE (Active <> 0)
ORDER BY FileTitle
```

What if you want to return all of the rows? Use the TOP PERCENT clause:

```
CREATE VIEW dbo.vwTest
AS
SELECT TOP 100 PERCENT dbo.Downloads.*
FROM dbo.Downloads
WHERE (Active <> 0)
ORDER BY FileTitle
```

In addition, views are not precompiled like stored procedures. Practically speaking, this means that most of the time you'll be creating stored procedures. Think of SQL Server views as virtual tables. You can use views to filter and sort data from one or more tables, and to perform simple calculations, but you can't pass parameters to views. For this, we need a stored procedure.

Your First Stored Procedure

If, like most Dreamweaver MX users, you cut your teeth on Microsoft Access, SQL Server can be a little intimidating. For starters, it doesn't have the same warm and cuddly interface as Access. You may even feel a strong resistance to learning it. That's okay. When I first started tinkering with SQL Server, I found the whole interface unintuitive. Frankly, it's still a little byzantine at times. But don't let SQL Server intimidate you (and trust me, it will try). Having said that, take a deep breath and launch SQL Server Enterprise Manager (Start | Programs | Microsoft SQL Server | Enterprise Manager).

Note
If you don't have SQL Server, you can install Microsoft Data Engine (MSDE) from an Office 2000 CD-ROM. The setup file, `Setupsql.exe`, can be found in the `\Sql\x86\Setup` folder. Although MSDE is a fully SQL Server–compatible database engine, it doesn't include the visual tools, such as Query Analyzer and Enterprise Manager, that we'll be using in this chapter. However, you can still develop MSDE databases in a graphical environment using Access 2000 projects. (For more information, see "Using Access Projects" in Chapter 3. MSDE is also included with Microsoft Visual Studio.

The first thing you notice is that Enterprise Manager is not Microsoft Access (see Figure 8-1). If anything, it looks more like Windows Explorer. In a sense that's true: just as Windows Explorer is a graphical way to manipulate files, Enterprise Manager is a graphical way to manipulate SQL Server databases.

Before you start to panic, take heart. As daunting as Enterprise Manager may seem, some database applications don't even include a graphical user interface (sometimes called a "GUI client"). In fact, until MyCC came along, the only way to manage MySQL—the popular open-source relational database management system (RDBMS) on Linux—was from a command line.

Fortunately, SQL Server offers several visual methods for querying databases. Expand the console tree in Enterprise Manager until you locate the newmanzone database. Select the `Downloads` table and choose Action | Open Table | Query. This opens Query Designer.

Using Query Designer

Query Designer, one of SQL Server's Visual Database Tools, is arranged into four panes, each of which has a counterpart in Microsoft Access. Right now, all four panes should be visible. From top to bottom, they are

◆ **Diagram pane**   Allows you to add input sources (tables or views) and drag columns to the Grid pane below it (similar to field lists in Access).

◆ **Grid pane**   Specifies which database columns to output, sorting options, aliases, and filtering criteria (similar to the design grid in Access).

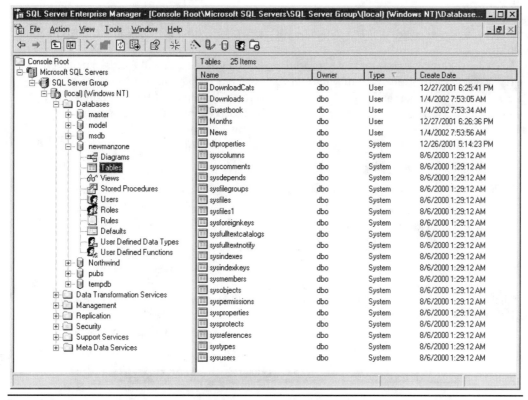

Figure 8-1   *The newmanzone database in SQL Server Enterprise Manager*

◆ **SQL pane**   Displays the SQL statement used to query the database (similar to SQL view in Access).

◆ **Results pane**   Shows the results of the executed query (similar to Datasheet view in Access).

You can toggle the different panes by clicking the Show/Hide buttons on the toolbar, or by holding down the CTRL key and pressing 1–4, respectively.

Unlike Microsoft Access, SQL Server Query Designer does not permit you to save your queries (that's what Query Analyzer is for). Think of it as a development tool—a place to test your view or stored procedure before creating it in Query Analyzer. (When you're more comfortable with Structured Query Language, you can skip this step and create your views and stored procedures directly from Query Analyzer.)

Click the Add Table button or right-click in the Diagram pane and choose Add Table. Select `DownloadCats` and click Add. Query Designer adds the table to the Diagram pane. Like Microsoft Access, Query Designer automatically creates a "join line" to illustrate the relationship between `Downloads.DownloadCatID` and `DownloadCats.DownloadCatID`. If you mouse over the icon at the center of the join line, you'll see the following tool tip: INNER JOIN Downloads.DownloadCatID = DownloadCats.DownloadCatID. Close the Add Table dialog box.

To create the spDownloads stored procedure, we'll revise the original Access parameter query. Open newmanzone.mdb in Microsoft Access and open qDownloads in Design view. Choose View | SQL View and copy the SQL statement to the clipboard (choose Edit | Copy or press CTRL-C). Exit Microsoft Access and return to SQL Server. Paste the SQL statement from Microsoft Access into the SQL pane in Query Designer by pressing CTRL-V.

Don't hit the Run button just yet. We have to make a few revisions:

◆ Delete the first line of the original parameter query:

PARAMETERS category Text (255)

◆ Change the quotation marks in the WHERE clause to single quotes (SQL Server interprets double quotes as database object delimiters, unless Quoted Identifiers is off).

◆ Replace the Access wildcard characters (*) with percent signs (%).

◆ Replace the parameter, [category], with 'cf'.

Click the Verify SQL button on the toolbar. You should receive a confirmation message: "The SQL syntax has been verified against the data source." Click OK. Notice that Query Designer automatically reformats the SQL statement and updates the Diagram and Grid panes. Now click the Run button (the exclamation point). Oops. What happened?

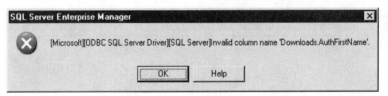

SQL Server doesn't like the brackets around [Downloads.AuthFirstName] and [Downloads.AuthLastName]. Click OK to dismiss the dialog box.

Change the code that creates the column alias,

[Downloads.AuthFirstName] + [ ] + [Downloads.AuthLastName] AS Author

to the following:

Downloads.AuthFirstName + ' ' + Downloads.AuthLastName AS Author

Click Run again. Eureka. It works!

If you see three records in the Results pane (see Figure 8-2), this means you successfully revised qDownloads to run in SQL Server. Now you can use this SQL statement as the basis for the stored procedure.

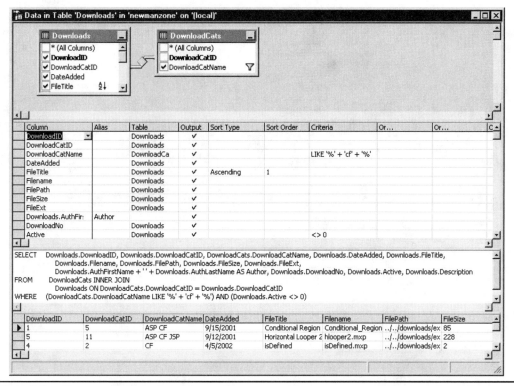

Figure 8-2 *The revised Microsoft Access parameter query,* `qDownloads`*, in SQL Server Query Designer*

Select the code in the SQL pane and copy it to the clipboard (right-click and choose Copy, or press CTRL-C). Close Query Designer and launch Query Analyzer.

Using Query Analyzer

Before you do anything else, paste the code we copied from Query Designer into the Editor pane (or Query window) of Query Analyzer. Make sure newmanzone is selected in the Current Database drop-down menu and click the Execute Query button. The results are displayed in the Results pane below. If you click the Messages tab, you will see "3 row(s) affected." In the Editor pane, change `'cf'` to `'asp'` and press F5. Four records are returned. Query Analyzer should now resemble Figure 8-3.

Click the Save button or press CTRL-S. Query Analyzer prompts you to save the SQL statement as a Query File. Save it as `downloads.sql` and close Query Analyzer.

Before we proceed, let's review the steps so far. First, we copied the original Access parameter query and pasted it into the SQL pane of Query Designer. Then we revised the SQL statement to make it compatible with SQL Server. Next, we copied the statement from Query Designer and pasted it into the Editor pane of Query Analyzer. Finally, we executed the query and saved it as `downloads.sql`.

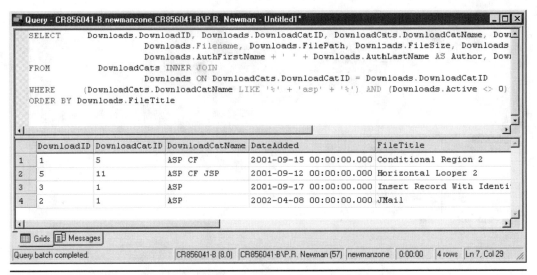

Figure 8-3   *The revised SQL statement after executing it in Query Analyzer*

The SQL script we saved is simply a text file. If you open `downloads.sql` in a text editor, such as Notepad, you'll see the following SQL statement:

```
SELECT     Downloads.DownloadID, Downloads.DownloadCatID,
DownloadCats.DownloadCatName, Downloads.DateAdded, Downloads.FileTitle,
Downloads.Filename, Downloads.FilePath, Downloads.FileSize,
Downloads.FileExt, Downloads.AuthFirstName + ' ' + Downloads.AuthLastName
AS Author, Downloads.DownloadNo, Downloads.Active, Downloads.Description
FROM          DownloadCats INNER JOIN
Downloads ON DownloadCats.DownloadCatID = Downloads.DownloadCatID
WHERE      (DownloadCats.DownloadCatName LIKE '%' + 'asp' + '%') AND
(Downloads.Active <> 0)
ORDER BY Downloads.FileTitle
```

The next step is revising this SQL statement to create a stored procedure using Query Analyzer.

Understanding Structured Query Language

If you've used Microsoft Access up until now, you probably haven't had much use for Structured Query Language. This is about to change.

Query Analyzer is a powerful tool for interacting with SQL Server. With it, you can create tables, views, and other commonly used database objects; execute and debug stored procedures;

locate, view, and work with objects; insert, update, and delete table rows; replicate, back up, and restore databases; and much, much more.

In order to use Query Analyzer effectively, however, you need a solid understanding of Structured Query Language. Not surprisingly, Structured Query Language is at the core of SQL Server and other ANSI-SQL databases such as Access, Oracle, Sybase, and MySQL. In fact, all applications that communicate with SQL Server use SQL statements, regardless of the interface.

While a full discussion of SQL is beyond the scope of this book, suffice it to say, if you're serious about using SQL Server, it's something you can't avoid learning. True, SQL Server has Create View and Create Stored Procedure wizards, and Visual Database Tools such as Query Designer and View Designer, but they'll get you only so far. To take full advantage of SQL Server's features, you have to speak its language. So do yourself a favor and pick up a good reference book on Structured Query Language.

Note

Microsoft's implementation of Structured Query Language is called Transact-SQL, or T-SQL. The main difference between T-SQL and the ANSI-SQL standard is that T-SQL includes additional features and enhancements exclusive to SQL Server.

For a glimpse of what Query Analyzer can do, open Object Browser (Tools | Object Browser | Show/Hide) and select the Templates tab. Each folder contains templates for common tasks such as creating tables, procedures, views, and triggers. If you examine the templates, you'll see that they all use SQL to perform the requested operations. Refer to these templates, or the stored procedures in the sample pubs and Northwind databases, when you need a little help getting started.

Creating a Stored Procedure

In Query Analyzer, database objects are created using a specific SQL syntax. For example, to create a new table in the newmanzone database, we could enter the following statement into the Editor pane:

```
CREATE TABLE TestTable
(TestID int,
TestName varchar (25),
TestAddress varchar (50),
TestPhone varchar (10)
);
```

If you were to execute this SQL statement in Query Analyzer, `TestTable` would be added to the newmanzone database. Let's give it a try. Launch Query Analyzer and make sure newmanzone is selected in the Current Database drop-down menu. Enter the preceding statement into the Editor pane and press F5. The following message appears in the Results pane: "The command(s) completed successfully."

Open Object Browser and expand the newmanzone database. Expand the User Tables folder. If `TestTable` isn't listed, right-click User Tables and choose Refresh. Expand the Columns folder under `dbo.TestTable`. The table's four columns are listed, along with each column's data type and size.

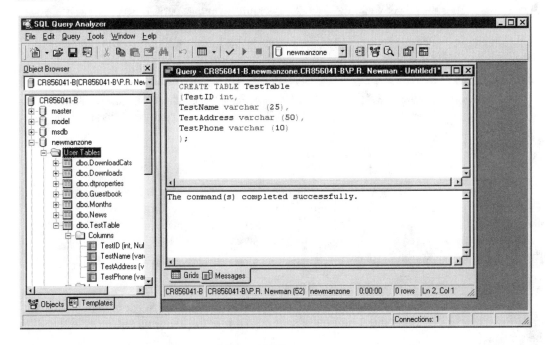

To remove `TestTable`, we use a different SQL statement:

```
DROP TABLE TestTable;
```

Enter the preceding statement into the Editor pane and press F5. `TestTable` is removed from the newmanzone database. This gives you a sense of how powerful Structured Query Language can be.

The following syntax is used to create a stored procedure in SQL Server:

```
CREATE PROCEDURE spProcedure_Name
@parameter_name data_type(size) [= default_value]
AS
[SQL statement]
```

In SQL Server, stored procedure parameters and variables must begin with the @ character. The data type and size must also be declared, but the default value of the parameter is optional.

Choose File | Open and load `downloads.sql` into Query Analyzer. Click No when prompted to save the `DROP TABLE` query. Add the following lines to the beginning of the SQL statement:

```
CREATE PROCEDURE spTest
@category varchar(15)
AS
```

In the `WHERE` clause, change `'asp'` to `@category` (the new code is shaded):

```
WHERE (DownloadCats.DownloadCatName LIKE '%' + @category + '%') AND
(Downloads.Active <> 0)
```

That's it! Click the Parse Query button to make sure the syntax is correct. You should receive a message in the Results pane: "The command(s) completed successfully." The completed code looks like this:

```
CREATE PROCEDURE spTest
@category varchar(15)
AS
SELECT      Downloads.DownloadID, Downloads.DownloadCatID,
DownloadCats.DownloadCatName, Downloads.DateAdded, Downloads.FileTitle,
Downloads.Filename, Downloads.FilePath, Downloads.FileSize,
Downloads.FileExt, Downloads.AuthFirstName + ' ' + Downloads.AuthLastName
AS Author, Downloads.DownloadNo, Downloads.Active, Downloads.Description
FROM        DownloadCats INNER JOIN
Downloads ON DownloadCats.DownloadCatID = Downloads.DownloadCatID
WHERE       (DownloadCats.DownloadCatName LIKE '%' + @category + '%') AND
(Downloads.Active <> 0)
ORDER BY Downloads.FileTitle
```

Click the Execute Query button. The new stored procedure, `spTest`, is added to the newmanzone database. Look for it in Object Browser under Stored Procedures (you may have to refresh Object Browser to reveal it).

Save `downloads.sql` and choose File | New to open a blank Query window. Enter the following statement in the Editor pane:

```
EXECUTE spTest @category = 'cf'
```

The EXECUTE statement calls the spTest stored procedure we just created and passes it a parameter ('cf'). Choose newmanzone from the Current Database drop-down menu and click Execute Query. Three records are returned: Conditional Region 2, Horizontal Looper 2, and isDefined:

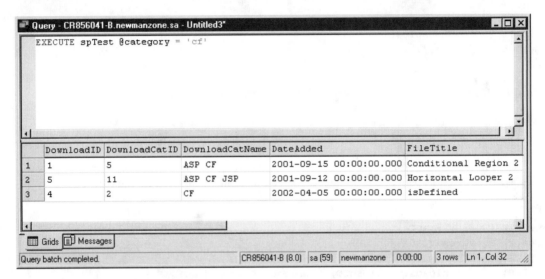

Pretty sweet. Now try changing 'cf' to '%' (as you may recall, the percent sign is the wildcard character in Structured Query Language). Click Execute Query. All five records are returned. We'll make the percent sign the default value of the parameter when we call spDownloads in Dreamweaver MX.

You can delete spTest using Object Browser, if you like, but there's no real harm in leaving it in the newmanzone database. Close Query Analyzer and click No when prompted to save the EXECUTE statement. Take a break. You've earned it.

Creating the ODBC Data Source

Before we can revise the Downloads page, we need to create a new System DSN that connects to the newmanzone database on SQL Server. Follow these steps to create the ODBC data source:

1. Launch Windows' ODBC Data Source Administrator and click the System DSN tab. Click Add and select SQL Server from the list of available drivers. Click Finish. Enter **sqlNewmanZone** in the Name text box, and an optional description. Choose your local SQL Server from the drop-down menu and click Next.

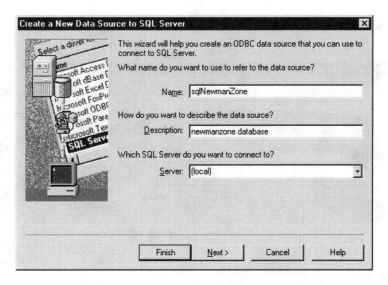

2. On the next screen, choose your desired authentication method and enter your SQL Server Login ID and Password. Click Next.

3. Check the first check box and select newmanzone from the database drop-down menu. Click Next.

4. Accept the default settings on the last screen and click Finish.

5. Confirm your selections in the ODBC Microsoft SQL Server Setup dialog box and click Test Data Source. A message appears: "TESTS COMPLETED SUCCESSFULLY!" Click OK.

6. Click OK again to close the ODBC Microsoft SQL Server Setup dialog box.

The new DSN, sqlNewmanZone, appears in the ODBC Data Source Administrator. Click OK.

Creating the ColdFusion Data Source

Follow these steps to create the ColdFusion data source:

1. Log in to ColdFusion Administrator and select Data Sources from the table of contents.

2. In the Add New Data Source region, enter **sqlNewmanZone** in the Data Source Name text box, and choose ODBC Socket from the Driver drop-down menu. Click Add.

3. On the next page, sqlNewmanZone is automatically selected in the ODBC DSN drop-down menu. Enter an optional description and click Show Advanced Settings.

4. Enter your SQL Server authentication information in the Username and Password text boxes, and click Submit.

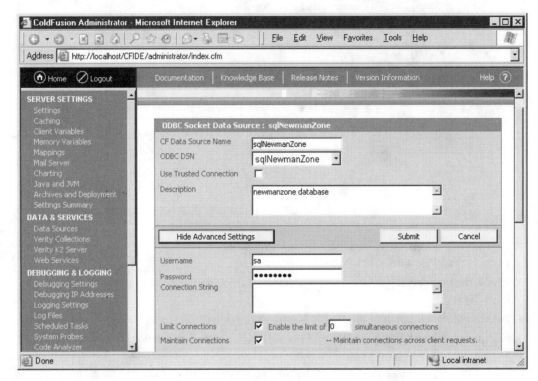

You should receive a confirmation message: "datasource updated successfully." The new data source, sqlNewmanZone, is now available to Dreamweaver MX and other programs that support RDS.

Revising the Downloads Page

In this section, we'll adapt the original Downloads page to pull the data from SQL Server. Launch Dreamweaver MX and open the Downloads page (`index.asp` or `index.cfm`, depending on your server model). Save the file as `index_sql.asp` or `index_sql.cfm`.

In the Document window, select the `category` drop-down menu and click `<form>` on the tag selector. Using the Property inspector, change the Action text box to the following:

```
<%= CStr(Request.ServerVariables("SCRIPT_NAME")) %> (ASP)
<cfoutput>#GetFileFromPath(GetTemplatePath())#</cfoutput> (ColdFusion)
```

This ensures that the new Downloads page posts to itself, rather than `index.asp` or `index.cfm`.

Revising rsDownloadCats

To change the source of the drop-down menu to the `DownloadCats` table on SQL Server, double-click `rsDownloadCats` in the Bindings panel. Change the connection (or data source) to sqlNewmanZone.

> **Note**
>
> If you're using ASP, you need to define a new connection to the database on SQL Server. To do this, click Define and choose New | Data Source Name (DSN). Enter **sqlNewmanZone** in the Connection Name text box, and choose sqlNewmanZone from the DSN drop-down menu. Enter your SQL Server authentication information in the User Name and Password text boxes and click Test. Click OK to close the dialog boxes. Click Done.

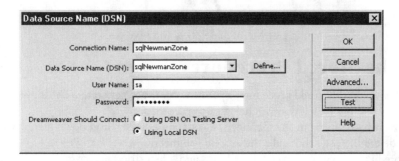

In the Recordset dialog box change the statement in the SQL area to the following:

```
SELECT TOP 4 *
FROM DownloadCats
```

Click Test. If you receive an error, you may need to change `DownloadCats` to `dbo.DownloadCats`. Click OK to close the Recordset dialog box.

> **Note**
>
> You may be wondering what "dbo" means. When objects, such as tables and stored procedures, are created in SQL Server, they are mapped to the user who created them. Any objects created by a member of the sysadmin fixed server role belong to dbo ("database owner"). If you're logged in as another user, SQL Server prepends that username to every object you create (e.g., `ringo.DownloadCats`). For more information, see "Administering SQL Server" in *Books Online*.

In the Server Behaviors panel, double-click Dynamic List/Menu (category). The column alias, `CatName`, no longer exists, so click OK to dismiss the error messages. Choose `DownloadCatName` from the Values and Labels drop-down menus. While you're at it, change the asterisk (`*`) in the Value column of Static Options to a percent sign (`%`).

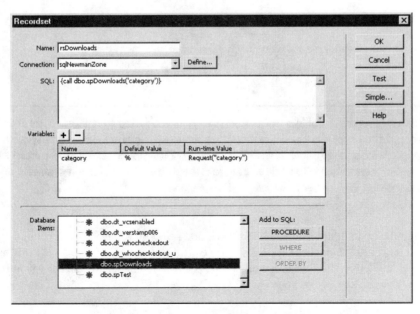

Click OK to close the Dynamic List/Menu dialog box and save your work.

Calling the Stored Procedure

Now we're going to use the stored procedure, `spDownloads`, to generate a Dreamweaver MX recordset. In the Bindings panel, double-click `rsDownloads`.

Choose sqlNewmanZone from the Connection (or Data Source) drop-down menu. Tab to the SQL area and delete the code that calls the Access parameter query.

Expand Stored Procedures under Database Items and select `dbo.spDownloads`. Click the PROCEDURE button. Notice that Dreamweaver parses the stored procedure and supplies the values for the SQL area and the variable name.

ASP Users: In the Variables area, enter a percent sign (%) in the Default Value column, and Request("category") in the Run-Time Value column.

ColdFusion Users: Click the Edit button next to Page Parameters and change the Default Value from an asterisk (*) to a percent sign (%). Click OK.

Test the SQL statement and click OK to close the Recordset dialog box. Save your work and press F12 to preview the page in a browser.

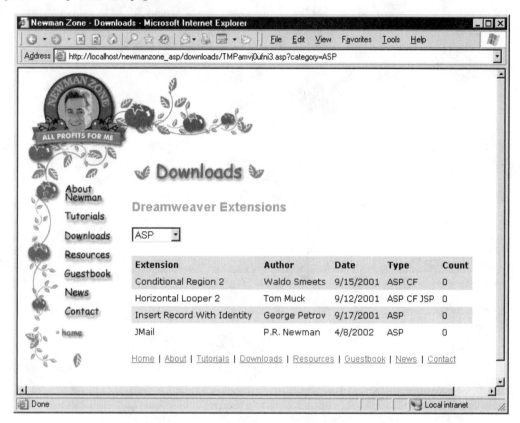

You did it! You created a Dreamweaver MX recordset using a SQL Server stored procedure!

Summary

That wasn't so hard, right? You breezed right through this recipe. Martha would be proud.

In case your loved ones are wondering what you've been doing on the computer all this time, here's your excuse. In Chapter 8 you learned to

◆ Revise an Access query in SQL Server Query Designer

◆ Save and load SQL scripts in Query Analyzer

- Create and drop tables using Query Analyzer
- Create a SQL Server stored procedure
- Define Dreamweaver MX connections to SQL Server
- Call a stored procedure to create a Dreamweaver MX recordset

In the next recipe, "Download Counter," you'll complete the Newman Zone Downloads section (finally!). Along the way, you'll learn how to stream files to a browser using the ADO Stream object (ASP) and the `<cfcontent>` tag (ColdFusion).

Chapter 9

Download Counter

INGREDIENTS

File	Type	Server Model(s)	Source
newmanzone.mdb	Access database	ASP/CF	*Sample Code*
BUD Force Download	Server Behavior	ASP	Tom Muck

 from the desk of *Paul Newman*

The original need for this recipe arose when a client asked to restrict file download access to authorized users. The client—we'll call him Voiceover Dude—wanted to ensure that only registered users could download MP3 and WAV files. Obviously, the first step was to require visitors to register and log in (see Chapter 19) before they could download files. But once visitors gained access to the Downloads area, how could we prevent them from sharing links with unauthorized users?

The solution was to place the files outside the site root, and to stream them to the browser using the ADO Stream object (ASP) or the `<cfcontent>` tag (ColdFusion). The advantage of serving files this way is that it discourages unauthorized users from "leeching" downloads. Even if a link is published—on a search engine or a message board, for instance—the file cannot be downloaded if the visitor is not logged in.

In this chapter, we're going to complete the Newman Zone Downloads section by implementing the features just described. To do this, we will

- ◆ Create a Downloads response page to stream the requested file
- ◆ Link to the Downloads response page and pass it a URL parameter
- ◆ Extract the requested filename from the `Downloads` table
- ◆ Increment a download counter using a SQL `UPDATE` statement

To complete this recipe, you'll need the Newman Zone database (`newmanzone.mdb`) and the Downloads page we created in Chapter 7. If you're using ASP, you'll also need to download and install the BUD Force Download extension from **www.basic-ultradev.com**.

Revising the Downloads Page

Before we can create the Downloads response page, we need to know which file to stream to the browser. To do this, we'll extract the `Downloads.DownloadID` column from the Newman Zone database, and pass it to the Downloads response page as a URL parameter. On the response page, we'll filter the recordset using the value of the URL parameter. Let's get started.

Launch Dreamweaver MX and open the Downloads page (`downloads/index.asp` or `downloads/index.cfm`, depending on your server model). In the Document window, right-click {rsDownloads.FileTitle} and choose Make Link. Enter `download.asp` (or `download.cfm`) in the URL text box and click Parameters. Enter `DownloadID` in the Name column, and click the lightning bolt icon in the Value column.

Expand `rsDownloads` in the Dynamic Data dialog box and select the `DownloadID` column. Click OK.

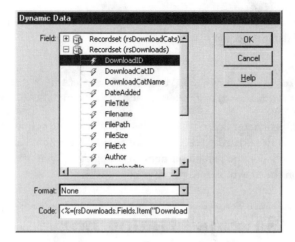

Click OK again to close the Parameters dialog box. Notice that the URL parameter is appended to `download.asp` (or `download.cfm`). Click OK.

Save your work and press F12 to preview the page in a browser. The extensions are now hyperlinks. Mouse over the JMail extension and look at the browser's status bar:

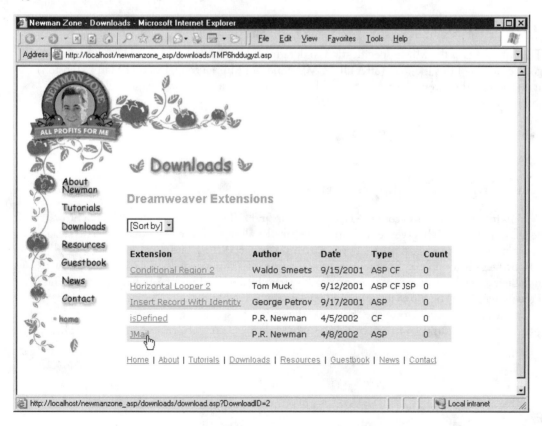

If you switch to Code view, you'll see that the anchor tag concatenates the parameter name and the value of the selected database column:

```
<a href="download.asp?DownloadID=  ⏎
<%=(rsDownloads.Fields.Item("DownloadID").Value)%>"> (ASP)
<a href="download.cfm?DownloadID=#rsDownloads.DownloadID#"> (ColdFusion)
```

Incidentally, the URL parameter doesn't have to be the same as the column name. In this case, we chose to accept the default (`DownloadID`), but we could have entered any value we wanted. Just make sure that if you change the parameter name to "asparagus," you use the same name when you filter the recordset on the Downloads response page.

Forcing the "Save As" Dialog Box

At the peak of Napster and MP3-mania, Voiceover Dude's clients began to complain that every time they tried to download an MP3, their default media player would launch. Voiceover Dude wanted to find a way to force the "Save As" dialog box in Netscape and Internet Explorer. Easier said than done.

The Content-Type Header Field

The Internet uses the MIME specification to determine how information should be displayed. A good example of this is e-mail (after all, MIME stands for Multipurpose Internet Mail Extension). If you look at the Internet headers of an HTML-formatted e-mail message, you might see the following:

```
Content-Type: multipart/mixed;
```

A plain text message might contain this line:

```
Content-Type: text/plain; charset= "iso-8859-1"
```

This information is also conveyed to browsers in an HTTP response-header. When a browser requests a file, the web server returns an HTTP header along with the requested file. This header contains fields such as `Content-Type`, `Cache-Control`, `Expires`, or `Transfer-Encoding`. The browser, or user agent, uses this information to determine how to handle the file. For instance, if the `Content-Type` header field is `application/pdf`, the browser hands off the file to its associated application (Acrobat Reader).

In the past, you could force the "Save As" dialog box by specifying `Content-Type: application/unknown`, or `Content-Type: application/octet-stream`. Then came Internet Explorer 4. Apparently, Microsoft's new browser had such keenly developed olfactory senses, it could "sniff" the data sent by the server and detect the file type (see Microsoft Knowledge Base Article Q182315). This is why Voiceover Dude's clients weren't prompted to save the requested files. Instead, Internet Explorer detected that the "unknown" file was an MP3 and handed it off to the registered application (e.g., WinAmp).

A method had to be devised to tell the browser what to do with the requested file. Enter the `Content-Disposition` header field.

The Content-Disposition Header Field

Although not strictly part of the HTTP standard, the `Content-Disposition` header field is now implemented by most browsers. Here's a sample `Content-Disposition` header:

```
Content-Disposition: attachment; filename="manual.pdf"
```

According to the Internet Engineering Task Force (IETF), "If this header is used in a response with the application/octet-stream content-type, the implied suggestion is that the user agent should not display the response, but directly enter a 'save response as...' dialog" (see **www.ietf.org/rfc/rfc2616.txt**). In theory this was true, but in practice Internet Explorer often behaved unexpectedly. For instance, even when the `attachment` parameter was specified, Internet Explorer displayed known MIME types, such as Microsoft Word documents, inline.

Unfortunately, subsequent versions of Internet Explorer made it even more difficult to force the "Save As" dialog box (see Microsoft Knowledge Base Article Q279667). In the end, Microsoft admitted that "there is no completely reliable way to force the File Download dialog box to appear when downloading a file to Internet Explorer."

The only safe prediction, at this point, is that browsers will continue to behave unpredictably. As a result, it's always a good idea to alert visitors to potential pitfalls. I usually add the following disclaimer to any download page: "To download a file without launching its associated application, right-click the link and choose 'Save Link/Target As' from the pop-up menu."

Incidentally, Netscape is much better about respecting HTTP response-headers. In my own informal tests, Netscape 3, 4, and 6 all prompt the user to open or save files when the `application/unknown` or `application/octet-stream` content-type is specified.

Is your head spinning from all this technical mumbo-jumbo? Then let's get on with it.

Creating the Downloads Response Page

As you probably guessed, the Downloads response page doesn't actually display any content to the visitor. Instead, it streams the requested file to the browser. In ASP, this is done using the ADO Stream object. In ColdFusion, we'll use the `<cfheader>` and `<cfcontent>` tags.

Using the ADO Stream Object (ASP)

Tom Muck's extension, BUD Force Download, uses the ADO Stream object to send the requested file to the browser. In addition, it uses the `Response.ContentType` and `Response.AddHeader` methods to define the `Content-Type` and `Content-Disposition` headers.

> **Note**
>
> The BUD Force Download extension requires MDAC 2.5 or higher. To obtain the latest version of MDAC, go to **www.microsoft.com/data/download.htm**.

Launch Dreamweaver MX and create a new file in the `downloads` folder called `download.asp`. This is the file we linked to from the default Downloads page. Follow these steps to complete the Downloads response page:

1. Open `download.asp` in Dreamweaver MX and choose Basic-UltraDev | BUD Force Download from the Server Behaviors panel.

2. Enter `strFullpath` in the first text box, and **strFilename** in the second. Enter `../home.asp` in the Error Page text box and click OK.

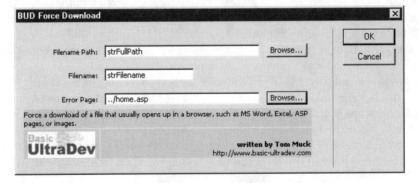

FYI: `strFullpath` and `strFilename` are variables that we will define in a moment.

3. Since the filename and path are stored in the Newman Zone database, we need to extract them using a Dreamweaver MX recordset. From the Bindings panel, create a new recordset called `rsGetDownload`. Choose newmanzone from the Connection drop-down menu and select the `Downloads` table (make sure you're in Simple mode). From the Columns list, select `Filename` and `FilePath`. Choose `DownloadID` from the Filter drop-down menu.

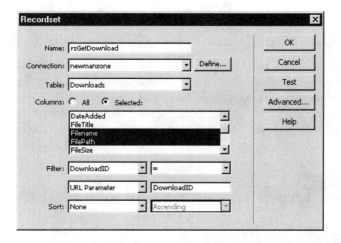

4. Click Test and enter **1** in the Test Value text box. The SQL statement should return one record: the Conditional Region extension. Notice that the `FilePath` column contains a relative link to the `exts` directory above the site root. The `Server.Mappath` function (see step 7) converts this value to the complete path to the `exts` folder (e.g., `C:\Inetpub\wwwroot\newmanzone_asp_empty\downloads\exts`). Click OK to close the dialog boxes.

5. Switch to Code view and select the BUD Force Download code block (lines 2–26). Cut and paste it *after* the `rsGetDownload` code (just before the opening `<html>` tag). This changes the execution order of the code blocks, but you can still access them from the Server Behaviors panel.

6. Now we have to stuff the recordset results into variables. Insert the following code between the `rsGetDownload` and BUD Force Download code blocks:

```
<% 'Stuff recordset results into variables
Dim strFilename, strFilepath, strFullpath
strFilename = rsGetDownload("Filename")
strFilepath = rsGetDownload("FilePath")
strFullpath = strFilepath & strFilename
%>
```

7. We have to make two changes to the BUD Force Download code block because we're using variables, rather than literal strings, as the filename and path values. In Code view, locate the line

```
tfm_downloadStream.LoadFromFile Server.Mappath("strFullpath")
```

and remove the quotation marks from the `strFullpath` variable:

```
tfm_downloadStream.LoadFromFile Server.Mappath(strFullpath)
```

Now locate the `Content-Disposition` line

```
"Content-Disposition", "attachment; filename=strFilename"
```

and change it to the following (the new code is shaded):

```
"Content-Disposition", "attachment; filename=" & strFilename
```

When you save these changes, BUD Force Download no longer appears in the Server Behaviors panel. Browse to the default Downloads page on your local server (e.g., **http://localhost/ newmanzone_asp/downloads/**) and click the JMail link. If you're redirected to the "error" page (`home.asp`), make sure you've got the latest version of MDAC (the Stream object was introduced in MDAC 2.5). Also, verify that the folder that `strFilepath` points to (`exts`) actually contains the requested extension. Last of all, make sure the `exts` folder has the proper NTFS permissions.

Using <cfheader> and <cfcontent> (ColdFusion)

In order to stream the requested file to the visitor in ColdFusion, we'll use the `<cfheader>` and `<cfcontent>` tags. Once again, ColdFusion makes quick work of what is a fairly complicated task in ASP.

Launch Dreamweaver MX and create a new ColdFusion template in the `downloads` folder called `download.cfm`. This is the file we linked to from the default Downloads page.

Follow these steps to complete the Downloads response page:

1. Open `download.cfm` and choose Recordset from the Bindings panel.

2. Enter **rsGetDownload** in the Name text box, and choose newmanzone from the Data Source drop-down menu. Choose `Downloads` from the Table drop-down menu and select `Filename` and `FilePath` from the Columns list (make sure you're in Simple mode). Finally, choose `DownloadID` from the Filter drop-down menu.

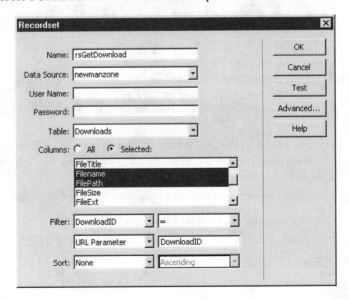

3. Click Test and enter **1** in the Test Value text box. The SQL statement should return one record: the Conditional Region extension. Notice that the `FilePath` column contains a relative link to the `exts` directory above the site root. The `ExpandPath` function (see step 6) converts this value to the complete path to the `exts` folder (e.g., `C:\Inetpub\ wwwroot\newmanzone_cf_empty\downloads\exts`). Click OK to close the dialog boxes.

4. Switch to Code view and insert a new line after the closing `</cfquery>` tag.

5. Select the CFML Advanced tab on the Insert bar and click the cfheader button. Enter **Content-Disposition** in the Name text box, and the following code in the Value text box:

```
attachment; filename=#rsGetDownload.Filename#
```

Click OK.

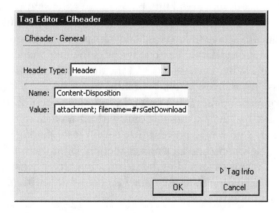

6. Insert a new line after the closing `</cfheader>` tag and click cfcontent on the Insert bar. Enter **application/unknown** in the MIME Type text box, and the following code in the Return File text box:

```
#ExpandPath(rsGetDownload.FilePath & rsGetDownload.Filename)#
```

Click OK.

Save your work and browse to the default Downloads page on your local server (e.g., **http://localhost/newmanzone_cf/downloads/**). Click the JMail link to download the extension. If it doesn't work, verify that the folder `rsGetDownload.Filepath` points to (`exts`) actually contains the requested extension. Also, if you're running Windows NT/2000/XP, make sure the `exts` folder has the proper NTFS permissions.

Restricting File Download Access

The advantage of streaming files to the browser is that at no time are the downloads directly accessible to the visitor. In other words, there is no way for the visitor to figure out where the files are located. A curious web surfer might think the extensions reside in the same folder, and enter the following URL in the address bar: **http://www.newmanzone.com/downloads/JMail.mxp**. If he was persistent, he might try several variations on this before giving up. The point is, the `downloads` folder is outside of the site root, so it can't be accessed via HTTP.

Now imagine our persistent web surfer paid fifty bucks for an extension you developed. You issue him a username and password to enter your site and download the file. He likes your extension so much, he decides to send a link to his buddy: **http://www.newmanzone.com/downloads/download.asp?DownloadID=2**. The buddy clicks the link and what happens? He's redirected to a login page. Why? Because you had the foresight to restrict access to `download.asp` using session variables. Voilà. Your killer app is safe.

Of course, no method for securing files is foolproof. In fact, developers of commercial Dreamweaver extensions have had quite a difficult time with this. Once someone pays for and downloads an extension, there's no way to prevent that person from sharing it with others. The same holds true for the Newman Zone Downloads section. Even if you restrict access to the Downloads pages using Dreamweaver's User Authentication server behaviors, you can't prevent registered visitors from sharing their usernames and passwords with others.

Incrementing the Download Counter

To increment the `Downloads.DownloadNo` column in the Newman Zone database, we'll create an Update command on the Downloads response page. In ColdFusion, we'll create an Update recordset.

Creating the Update Command (ASP)

If you haven't created a command in Dreamweaver MX before, don't worry—it's not that different than creating a recordset in Advanced mode. The main difference is that you're writing a SQL `UPDATE` statement, rather than a `SELECT` statement.

Follow these steps to add the command:

1. Open `download.asp` in Dreamweaver MX and choose Command from the Server Behaviors panel.
2. Enter `cmdCounter` in the Name text box, and choose the newmanzone connection. Choose Update from the Type drop-down menu and leave the Return Recordset check box unchecked. Dreamweaver inserts a sample SQL statement to demonstrate the proper syntax.

3. Expand Tables under Database Items and select the `Downloads` table. Click the SET button. Dreamweaver adds `Downloads` to the SQL statement.

4. Expand the `Downloads` table under Database Items and select `DownloadNo`. Click SET. The `DownloadNo` column is added to the SQL statement.

5. Select `DownloadID` and click the WHERE button. Once again, Dreamweaver updates the SQL statement.

6. Click the plus (+) button to add a variable. In the Name column, enter **intDownloadID**. In the Run-Time Value column, enter **Request("DownloadID")**. This sets the value of the variable, `intDownloadID`, to the incoming URL parameter. (For the record, I'm using the variable-naming convention that prefixes numbers with *int*, strings with *str*, and so forth.)

7. Now we need to revise the SQL statement to increment the `DownloadNo` column by 1. Change the second line to the following:

   ```
   SET DownloadNo = DownloadNo + 1
   ```

8. Finally, edit the `WHERE` clause to filter the recordset based on the value of the `intDownloadID` variable we just created:

   ```
   WHERE DownloadID = intDownloadID
   ```

9. Since this is an `UPDATE` statement, Dreamweaver MX won't let us test it against the database. Click OK to close the Command dialog box.

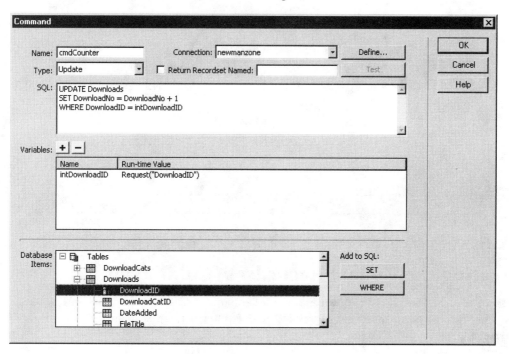

Switch to Code view to see where Dreamweaver placed the command. How do you like that? Dreamweaver inserted the command after the `rsGetDownload` recordset, which is exactly what we wanted.

Save your work and browse to the default Downloads page on your local server (**http://localhost/newmanzone_asp/downloads/**). Download the JMail extension. Click the Refresh button on your browser (or press CTRL-R).

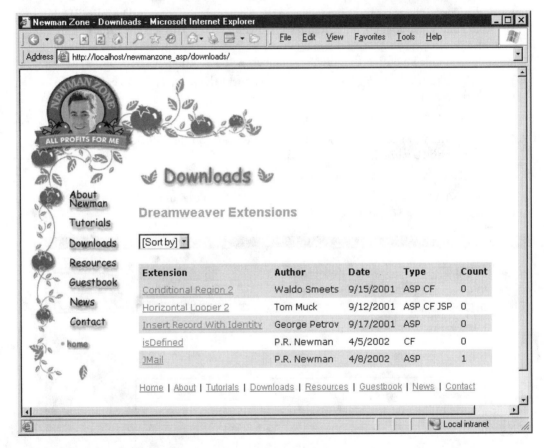

Lo and behold, the download counter actually counts! It's a good thing.

Creating the Update Recordset (ColdFusion)

To increment the `Downloads.DownloadNo` column in ColdFusion, we'll create an Update recordset. This recordset will consist of a SQL `UPDATE` statement, rather than a `SELECT` statement.

Open `download.cfm` in Dreamweaver MX. From the Server Behaviors panel, choose Recordset (Query) and click Advanced. Enter `rsCounter` in the Name text box and choose the newmanzone data source. Enter the following `UPDATE` statement in the SQL area:

```
UPDATE Downloads
SET DownloadNo = DownloadNo + 1
WHERE DownloadID = #URL.DownloadID#
```

The SET command increments DownloadNo by 1, and the WHERE clause filters the UPDATE statement according to the value of the URL parameter. The default value of #URL.DownloadID# is set by the <cfparam> tag that was added when we created the rsGetDownload recordset. Notice that Dreamweaver automatically adds URL.DownloadID to the list of Page Parameters.

 New Feature

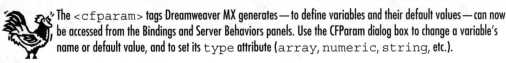 The <cfparam> tags Dreamweaver MX generates—to define variables and their default values—can now be accessed from the Bindings and Server Behaviors panels. Use the CFParam dialog box to change a variable's name or default value, and to set its type attribute (array, numeric, string, etc.).

Since this is a SQL UPDATE statement, Dreamweaver MX won't let us test it against the database. Click OK to close the Recordset dialog box.

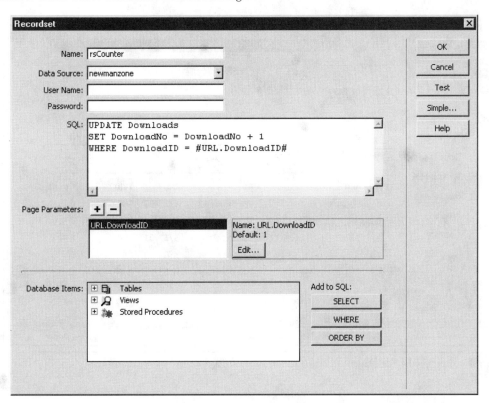

Save your work and browse to the default Downloads page on your local server (**http://localhost/newmanzone_cf/downloads/**). Download the JMail extension. Click the Refresh button on your browser (or press CTRL-R). Did the "Count" column increment? Congratulations, the Newman Zone Downloads section is now complete.

Cleaning Up

None of the following changes are necessary to make the Downloads section work. In fact, most of them are workarounds to address different browser issues that have cropped up over the years.

Internet Explorer Issues

For starters, delete all of the HTML at the end of the Downloads response page (`download.asp` or `download.cfm`). Now that we know how adept Internet Explorer is at "sniffing" files, there's no reason to give it a head start (see Figure 9-1).

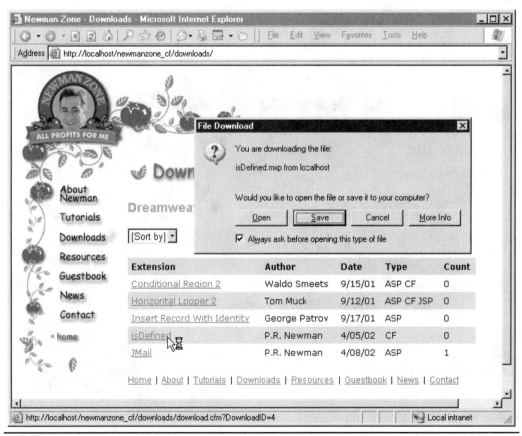

Figure 9-1 *Forcing the File Download dialog box in Internet Explorer 6*

In addition, there are some issues concerning Internet Explorer 4.01 and 5.5 (SP1) that you should be aware of. According to Microsoft Knowledge Base Article Q182315, IE 4.01 doesn't always prompt the user "when a file is returned to Explorer with a Content-Disposition header with type 'attachment.'" Although this is a confirmed bug, Microsoft doesn't offer a workaround. Some developers, however, recommend adding the following response-header:

```
Response.CacheControl = "public" (ASP)
<cfheader name="Cache-Control" value="public"> (ColdFusion)
```

The Internet Explorer 5.5 issue is documented in Knowledge Base Article Q281119. Afflicted browsers generate the filename and HTML content of the referrer document instead of the requested file. The problem "can occur if Internet Explorer does not correctly process the Content-Disposition header and the data that this header is defining." One established workaround is to test for Internet Explorer 5.5 and, if it is detected, dynamically generate a different Content-Disposition header. Here's an example that uses ASP:

```
<%
Dim strUA, strVersion, strContent
strUA = Request.ServerVariables("HTTP_USER_AGENT")
strVersion = Mid(strUA, InStr(strUA, "MSIE") + 5, 3)
    if strVersion = "5.5" then
        strContent = "inline; filename="
    else
        strContent = "attachment; filename="
    end if
%>
```

This revised BUD Force Download code incorporates the strContent variable:

```
Response.AddHeader "Content-Disposition", strContent & strFilename
```

When you visit the Microsoft Knowledge Base, you'll see there are dozens of articles relating to browser issues. It's impossible to accommodate all of them. The best you can do is to keep abreast of new issues and test your pages in every browser and platform you can get your hands on.

Security Issues

If you decide to implement the download counter using SQL Server, make sure to take security into consideration. For example, an unscrupulous user could append a SQL statement to the end of the query string:

```
downloads.asp?DownloadID=3;DROP%20TABLE%20Downloads
```

Depending on your SQL Server settings, this statement could potentially delete the Downloads table. One way to address this is to verify that the query string is the expected data type—in this case, an integer—before executing the SQL statement.

If you want to try this out, open the Downloads response page (download.asp or download.cfm) in Dreamweaver MX and switch to Code view. Locate this line

```
rsGetDownload__MMColParam = Request.QueryString("DownloadID") (ASP)
SELECT Filename, FilePath FROM Downloads WHERE DownloadID = ⤸
#URL.DownloadID# (ColdFusion)
```

and change it to the following (the new code is shaded):

```
rsGetDownload__MMColParam = CInt(Request.QueryString("DownloadID")) (ASP)
SELECT Filename, FilePath FROM Downloads WHERE DownloadID = ⤸
#Val(URL.DownloadID)# (ColdFusion)
```

In ASP, the CInt function converts the query string to an integer. In ColdFusion, the Val function returns a zero if the variable is not a number. If the user appends a non-numeric value to the end of the query string, an error will result. ColdFusion users can also take advantage of the <cfqueryparam> tag (consult the *CFML Reference* for details):

```
<cfquery name="rsGetDownload" datasource="newmanzone">
SELECT Filename, FilePath FROM Downloads WHERE DownloadID = ⤸
<cfqueryparam value="#URL.DownloadID#" cfsqltype="CF_SQL_INTEGER">
</cfquery>
```

If you want to display a custom error message, you can use the Response.End method (ASP) or the <cfabort> tag (ColdFusion) to stop processing the page if the query string is an inappropriate data type:

ASP Version

```
If not IsNumeric(Request.QueryString("DownloadID")) Then
Response.Write("Error: invalid query string")
Response.End
End If
```

ColdFusion Version

```
<cfif #Val(URL.DownloadID)# EQ 0>
<cfoutput>Error: invalid query string</cfoutput>
<cfabort>
</cfif>
```

This particular issue doesn't apply to Microsoft Access because Access doesn't support batch SQL commands. For more information, read Macromedia Security Bulletin ASB99-04: "Multiple SQL Statements in Dynamic Queries" (**http://www.macromedia.com/v1/handlers/index.cfm?ID=8728**).

Summary

I'm sure this has happened to you. You're at a party, and somebody asks what you do for a living. You tell him you're a web designer. "You actually get paid for that?" he says. "My nephew Skippy can do it, and he's only twelve."

The next time someone boasts about his twelve-year-old nephew, ask him if Skippy can do this:

- Stream files using the ADO stream object (ASP)
- Stream files using the `<cfcontent>` tag (ColdFusion)
- Force the "Save As" dialog box in Netscape and Internet Explorer
- Create an Update command (ASP)
- Create an Update recordset (ColdFusion)

I hope you'll find some practical uses for the techniques we covered in this chapter. (If nothing else, you can keep Skippy from stealing your files!)

In the next recipe, we'll create the Newman Zone News section, and link to articles from a DHTML scroller on the home page.

Chapter 10

News Section

INGREDIENTS

Ingredient(s)	Type	Server Model(s)	Source
`newmanzone.mdb`	Access database	ASP/CF	*Sample Code*
`news.asp`, `home.asp`, `home_scroller.asp`	Active Server Pages	ASP	*Sample Code*
`news.cfm`, `home.cfm`, `home_scroller.cfm`	ColdFusion templates	CF	*Sample Code*
Fading Text Scroller	DHTML script		Nicholas Poh

from the desk of Paul Newman

The need for this recipe also resulted from a client request. In this case, the client had dozens of news articles on his web site, spanning several years, but each article was a static HTML page. Any changes to the site's design or structure meant updating dozens of individual HTML pages. I proposed moving the news content into a database. This would permit us to do the following:

◆ Dynamically list current articles on the home page

◆ Allow visitors to sort articles by year

◆ Flag articles that were added in the last 30 days

◆ Allow the client to add and remove articles himself

In this chapter, we'll create the Newman Zone News page, and link to it from the home page. The source of the articles is the News table in the Newman Zone database (newmanzone.mdb). In addition, we'll create an alternate version of the home page that populates a DHTML scroller.

The News Table

Open newmanzone.mdb in Microsoft Access. Select the News table and click Design. As you can see, the News table consists of ten fields or columns (see Table 10-1). I've added four sample news articles for the purposes of this tutorial.

Field Name	Data Type	Size	Description
NewsID	AutoNumber		Primary Key
MonthID	Number		FK to Months table Default value: Month(Now())
NewsDay	Number		Default value: Day(Now())
NewsYear	Number		Default value: Year(Now())
DateAdded	Date/Time		Default value: Date()
NewsPic	Text	50	Optional image field
PicWidth	Text	3	
PicHeight	Text	3	
NewsHeadline	Text	100	
NewsDesc	Memo		

Table 10-1 *The News Table Consists of Ten Fields or Columns*

As you probably noticed, MonthID is a foreign key to the Months table. The Months table was added largely for administrative purposes and won't come into play in this chapter. However, you may find the Months table useful if you create an admin section to add/remove news items (you can use the Months table to populate a Dynamic List/Menu). The other optional fields are NewsPic, PicWidth, and PicHeight. If a news item requires a photograph, you can use these fields with an extension such as Show Image If Available, part of the suite of extensions offered on **www.robgt.com**.

Building the News Page

Launch Dreamweaver MX and open the News page (news.asp or news.cfm, depending on your server model). Once again, I've created placeholders for the data so you can visualize what the final page will look like.

Tip

I used Matt Lerner's Insert Corporate MumboJumbo extension to create the filler text for many of the Newman Zone pages. You can download it from the Macromedia Exchange (**www.macromedia.com/exchange**).

Since we'll be creating a Repeat Region later, go ahead and delete the second headline and article in the Document window. From the Bindings panel, choose Recordset and name it **rsNews**. Choose newmanzone from the Connection (or Data Source) drop-down menu, and select the News table (make sure you're in Simple mode). Select the following database columns: NewsID, NewsYear, DateAdded, NewsHeadline, NewsDesc. Choose NewsYear from the Filter drop-down and accept the defaults.

Note

If you decide to adapt this recipe for full-length news stories or press releases, you should filter the recordset using the NewsID column—one record per page—rather than the NewsYear column.

Finally, sort the recordset by the `DateAdded` column in descending order (this displays the latest news articles first).

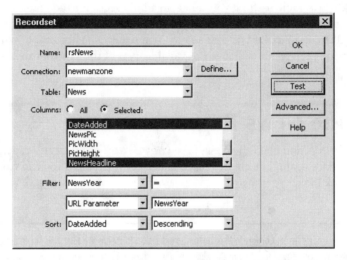

Click Advanced and enter **2002** in the Default Value column (ColdFusion users: click Edit and enter **2002** as the default parameter). Click Test. The query should return three results, because three news items were added in 2002. Click OK to close the dialog boxes.

Now that we've created the recordset, follow these steps to complete the News page:

1. In the Document window, select the date placeholder: *February 3, 2002.* In the Bindings panel, select `DateAdded` and click Insert.

2. Now select the filler paragraph that follows the date in the Document window. Select `NewsDesc` in the Bindings panel and click Insert.

3. To preserve paragraph formatting, select {rsNews.NewsDesc} in the Document window and switch to Code view:

   ```
   <%=(rsNews.Fields.Item("NewsDesc").Value)%> (ASP)
   <cfoutput>#rsNews.NewsDesc#</cfoutput> (ColdFusion)
   ```

   Replace this code with the following:

   ```
   <%=Replace((rsNews.Fields.Item("NewsDesc").Value), ↵
   vbNewLine, "<br>")%> (ASP)
   <cfoutput>#ParagraphFormat(rsNews.NewsDesc)#</cfoutput> (ColdFusion)
   ```

4. Switch back to Design view and select {rsNews.DateAdded} in the Document window. From the Format column of the Bindings panel, choose Date/Time | January 17, 2000. Dreamweaver MX inserts a `DoDateTime` (or `LSDateFormat`) function to format the `DateAdded` column.

5. In the Document window, select "This is a Headline" and bind it to `NewsHeadline` in the Bindings panel.

6. Now select the headline, date and article in the Document window. Switch to Code view to ensure you've made a clean selection, and apply the Repeat Region SB (Server Behaviors | Repeat Region).

Select the All Records radio button and click OK.

Save your work and press F12 to preview the page in a browser. You should now be looking at three news items. Add the parameter `?NewsYear=2001` to the end of the URL and press ENTER. Your browser should look something like this:

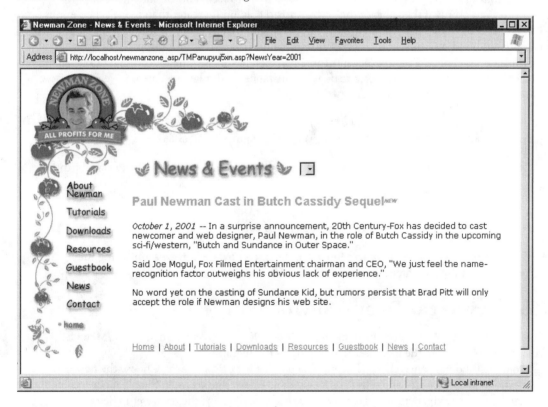

So far, so good. But why is an article from October 2001 identified as new? Let's revise the page so that the "NEW" image only appears next to articles posted in the last 30 days.

Flagging the Latest Articles

To identify the latest articles, we'll create a conditional region using an `If` statement and a date function.

In the Document window, select the "NEW" image (`new-red.gif`) and switch to Code view. If you're using ASP, place your cursor to the left of the `<img>` tag and click the If button on the Insert bar. If you're using ColdFusion, select the CFML Basic tab and click the cfif button. Complete the `If` statement as follows:

```
<% If rsNews("DateAdded") > (DateAdd("d", -30, Date)) Then %> (ASP)
<cfif rsNews.DateAdded GT (DateAdd("d", -30, Now() ))> (ColdFusion)
```

ASP users: Insert an `<% End If %>` statement at the end of the `<img>` tag by placing your cursor after the closing `>` bracket and clicking the End button on the Insert bar.

Save your work and press F12 to preview the page in a browser. The `If` statement displays `new-red.gif` only if the value of the `DateAdded` column is greater than today's date minus 30 days. (If the "NEW" image does not appear, make sure that at least one article is dated less than a month ago.)

The date function, `DateAdd`, accepts three parameters and uses the following syntax: `DateAdd(datepart, number, date)`. For instance, to display the date one year from now, you can write the following statement:

```
<%= DateAdd("yyyy", 1, Date) %> (ASP)
<cfoutput>#DateAdd("yyyy", 1, Now() )#</cfoutput> (ColdFusion)
```

To find out what day of the week your birthday falls on, try this (substitute your own birthday, of course):

```
<%= WeekdayName(DatePart("w", #1/1/02#)) %> (ASP)
<cfoutput>#DayOfWeekAsString(DayOfWeek("1/1/02"))#</cfoutput> (ColdFusion)
```

Since there is no `DateSubtract` function, we extract a date in the past by using the `DateAdd` function and entering a negative value (i.e., `-30`).

The NewsYear Drop-Down Menu

To create the `NewsYear` drop-down menu, we'll use Dreamweaver's Dynamic List/Menu SB. First, we need to create the recordset that populates the menu.

From the Bindings panel, choose Recordset and name it `rsNewsYear`. Choose the newmanzone connection (or data source) and select the `News` table (make sure you're in Simple mode). Click the Selected Columns radio button and select `NewsYear`. Finally, sort the recordset in descending order according to the `NewsYear` column. Click Test.

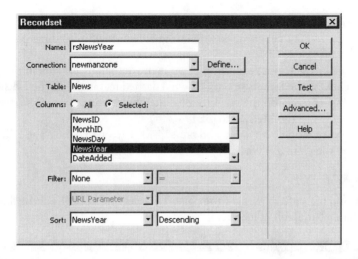

Oops! The current year, 2002, appears three times. To fix this, we need to be in Advanced mode, so click Advanced. In the SQL area, type **DISTINCT** after SELECT and click Test again. (As you may recall, the DISTINCT keyword omits duplicate rows from the results.) The query should return two records: 2002 and 2001. Click OK to close the dialog boxes.

Let's stuff the data into the menu. In the Document window, select the drop-down menu and use the Property inspector to change its name to NewsYear. From the Server Behaviors panel, choose Dynamic Form Elements | Dynamic List/Menu. Choose rsNewsYear from the Recordset drop-down menu. The Values and Labels menus are selected automatically.

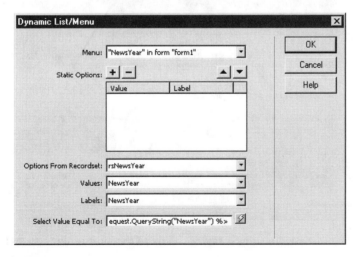

In the last text box, Select Value Equal To, enter the following code:

```
<%= Request.QueryString("NewsYear") %> (ASP)
<cfoutput>#URL.NewsYear#</cfoutput> (ColdFusion)
```

As you become more comfortable with writing code, you'll find it easier to enter this information directly into text boxes, rather than create additional variables using the Bindings panel. Click OK to apply the Dynamic List/Menu SB.

Now we need to make the `NewsYear` drop-down menu automatically submit the page's form. Select the form by clicking the form boundary (the red dashed rectangle) in the Document window, or by clicking `<form>` on the tag selector. Enter `news.asp` (or `news.cfm`) in the Action text box, and change the Method to GET.

Select the `NewsYear` drop-down menu and press CTRL-T to open Quick Tag Editor. Enter the following code before the closing `>` bracket:

```
onChange="this.form.submit();"
```

Save your work and press F12 to preview the page. Try selecting a year from the drop-down menu. More fun than a barrel full of monkeys!

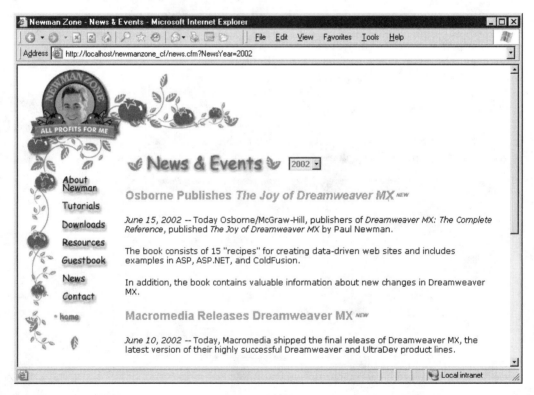

That wraps up the News page. Our next task is to link to the most recent articles from the home page.

Revising the Home Page

Launch Dreamweaver MX and open the Newman Zone home page (`home.asp` or `home.cfm`, depending on your server model). As you can see, I've created placeholders for the latest headlines. If we were to link these placeholders to the News page, we would have to revise the home page every time a new article is added. Instead, let's populate the bulleted list with the results of a Dreamweaver MX recordset.

Creating a Dynamic Bulleted List

From the Bindings panel, choose Recordset and name it rsHeadlines. Choose the newmanzone connection (or data source) and select News from the Table drop-down menu (make sure you're in Simple mode). Select NewsYear, DateAdded, and NewsHeadline from the database columns list, and sort the results in descending order according to the DateAdded column.

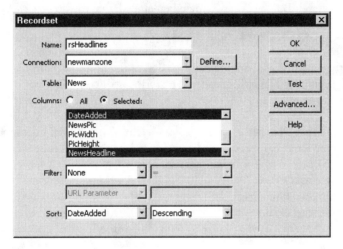

Click Test to verify the query (it should return all four records in the News table). Click OK to close the dialog boxes.

In the Document window, select the first headline. In the Bindings panel, select NewsHeadline and click Insert.

Since we're going to create a Repeat Region, switch to Code view and delete the last three <li> tags. Select the remaining list item by clicking <li> on the tag selector. From the Server Behaviors panel, choose Repeat Region and set it to display four records. Click OK.

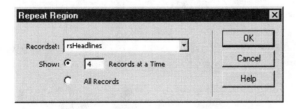

Whenever news items are added to the database, the home page will always display the four most recent articles. Save your work and press F12. You should be looking at a page that is virtually identical to the one we started out with, only now the headlines are pulled from the database.

Let's link the bulleted items to the News page. In the Document window, right-click {rsHeadlines.NewsHeadline} and choose Make Link. In the Select File dialog box, choose `news.asp` (or `news.cfm`). Click Parameters and enter **NewsYear** in the Name column. Tab to the Value column and click the lightning bolt icon. Select `NewsYear` in the Dynamic Data dialog box and click OK. Click OK again to close the Parameters dialog box. Dreamweaver MX appends the URL parameter to the end of `news.asp` (or `news.cfm`).

Click OK to close the Select File dialog box. Save your work and preview the page in a browser. Notice the URL parameters at the end of the links. Click the first and last headlines to make sure they work.

If you were to add another news item to the Newman Zone database, it would occupy the top spot in the bulleted list, and "Butch Cassidy" would be bumped from the home page (sorry, Butch).

Populating a DHTML Scroller

In this section, we're going to create an alternate version of the home page. Instead of populating a bulleted list, we'll populate a DHTML scroller. The script we'll be using, Fading Text Scroller, was written by Nicholas Poh. I chose this script because it's the only news scroller I've come across that works in Internet Explorer 4+, Netscape 4, and Netscape 6. You can download the latest version, and dozens of other DHTML scripts, from **www.dhtmlshock.com**. Instructions on how to install and configure the script can be found at **www.dhtmlshock.com/scrollers/NewsScroller**.

Open `home_scroller.asp` (or `home_scroller.cfm`) in Dreamweaver MX and press F12 to preview the page in a browser. Pretty slick, Nick. The DHTML script makes several modifications to the original home page. The code we need to adapt is contained in the `<SCRIPT>` block that starts on line 27:

```
<SCRIPT LANGUAGE="JavaScript1.2">
      function runMe()
      {
            // create fader
            var myFader = new DynFader();

            // add text
            myFader.addText('Welcome to Newman Zone!<br><br> ⌁
Here is the latest news...');
            myFader.addText('<font size=2>6/15/02</font><br> ⌁
<a href="#" class="scroller">Osborne Publishes The Joy of ⌁
Dreamweaver MX</a>');
            myFader.addText('<font size=2>6/10/02</font><br> ⌁
<a href="#" class="scroller">Macromedia Releases Dreamweaver MX</a>');

            // initialize fader
            myFader.attachPlaceHolder("PlaceHolderName");
            myFader.setFont('Arial,Helvetica,sans-serif', 'normal', 'left');
            myFader.setTextColor('#008000');
            // additional methods below
            myFader.setBackground('images/scroller-bg.gif');
            myFader.setDirection(1);
```

```
    myFader.setPauseMidInterval(80);
    myFader.setPauseTextInterval(10);
    myFader.setFontSize(12);
    // end additional methods
    myFader.beginFade();
  }
}
</SCRIPT>
```

The JavaScript runMe() function initializes Fading Text Scroller and invokes its various methods, including addText and setDirection. Right now, the script uses the myFader.addText method to create three scrolling messages. We're going to leave the greeting intact and replace the other two messages with data from a Dreamweaver MX recordset.

Before we do anything else, copy up the recordset from home.asp (or home.cfm). If you haven't done this before, open the home page in Dreamweaver MX. Right-click Recordset (rsHeadlines) in the Bindings panel and choose Copy. Close the home page and return to home_scroller.asp (or home_scroller.cfm). Right-click inside the Bindings panel and choose Paste. Voilà. Instant recordset.

In order to create a Repeat Region within the JavaScript code block, we're going to insert some adapted Dreamweaver MX code. Switch to Code view and locate the JavaScript runMe() function. About seven or eight lines into the <SCRIPT> block, three messages are defined using the myFader.addText method. Delete the second and third messages and replace them with the following code:

ASP Version

```
<%
'*** Scrolling Text Fader - adapted for ASP ***

dim intCount, strHeadline
intCount = 1

While (NOT rsHeadlines.EOF) AND (intCount <= 4)

'Escape apostrophes
strHeadline = Replace(rsHeadlines("NewsHeadline"), chr(39), "\'")

Response.Write "myFader.addText('<font size=""2"">" & _
rsHeadlines("DateAdded") & "</font><br><a href=""news.asp?NewsYear=" & _
rsHeadlines("NewsYear") & """ class=""scroller"">" & _
strHeadline & "</a>');" & chr(13) & chr(9) & chr(9)

intCount = intCount + 1
rsHeadlines.MoveNext()
Wend

'*** End of dynamic content ***
%>
```

ColdFusion Version

```
<!--- Scrolling Text Fader - adapted for ColdFusion --->

<cfoutput query="rsHeadlines" maxrows="4">
<cfset strNewsLink="news.cfm?NewsYear=" & rsHeadlines.NewsYear>
myFader.addText('<font size="2">#DateFormat(rsHeadlines.DateAdded)#</font>
<br><a href="#strNewsLink#" class="scroller">
#Replace(rsHeadlines.NewsHeadline, chr(39), "\'")#</a>');
</cfoutput>


<!--- End of dynamic content --->
```

To avoid JavaScript errors, make sure the `myFader.addText` method appears on a single line in ColdFusion (i.e., no carriage returns).

The JavaScript `myFader.addText` method uses single quotes to delimit the scrolling message. This means that any apostrophes in the `NewsHeadline` column will raise a JavaScript error. To avoid this, we use the `Replace` function to search for any occurrence of the ASCII single-quote character, `chr(39)`, and add a backslash to escape the apostrophe (`\'`).

Press F12 to preview the revised home page in a browser.

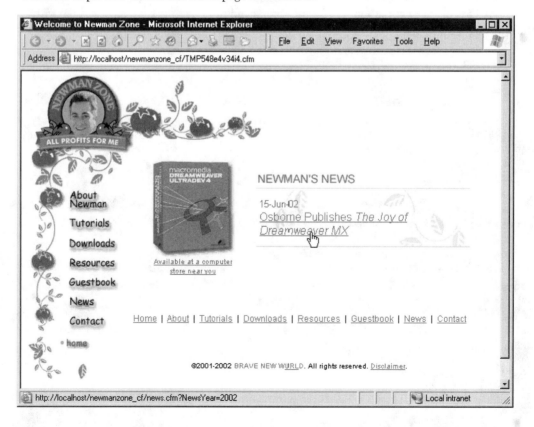

If you receive the following JavaScript error—'DynFader' is undefined—make sure that `dynfader.js` exists in the site's www directory. The easiest way to debug other errors is to view the source code in a browser. Look at the formatting of the `myFader.addText` lines. If the syntax doesn't match the hard-coded version, this is the most likely culprit.

How the ASP Code Works

There's a lot going on here, so let's examine it line-by-line. The fourth line of the inserted ASP code declares, or *dimensions*, two variables: `intCount` and `strHeadline`. On the next line, `intCount` is assigned a numeric value of 1. The seventh line is similar to the code that Dreamweaver MX generates for a Repeat Region. The main difference is that we use our own variable as a counter. The `While-Wend` statement loops through the `rsHeadlines` recordset until `intCount` reaches 4:

```
While (NOT rsHeadlines.EOF) AND (intCount <= 4)
```

Line 10 sets the value of `strHeadline` to

```
Replace(rsHeadlines("NewsHeadline"), chr(39), "\'")
```

The `Response.Write` line concatenates literal strings, database columns, and the `strHeadline` variable to compose the scrolling message. Since the `Response.Write` method uses quotation marks as delimiters, we have to escape them by using two double quotes (e.g., `class=""scroller""`). This is similar to using two single quotes to escape an apostrophe in a SQL statement:

```
INSERT INTO Guestbook (Comments) VALUES ('It''s great to see you!')
```

If we didn't escape the delimiter character, the scripting engine would think the string had ended, and an error would result.

On line 17, we increment the `intCounter` variable by 1. On the following line, we use the `MoveNext` method to move to the next record of the `rsHeadlines` recordset. As long as the specified condition remains true—`(NOT rsHeadlines.EOF) AND (intCount <= 4)`—the statement within the `While-Wend` loop executes. This code could also be written as a `Do While-Loop`:

```
Do While (condition)
statement
Loop
```

However, since Dreamweaver MX uses `While-Wend` loops to create Repeat Regions, I thought this code might seem more familiar to you.

How the ColdFusion Code Works

As usual, the ColdFusion code is shorter than its ASP counterpart. The entire statement consists of only four lines:

```
<cfoutput query="rsHeadlines" maxrows="4">
<cfset strNewsLink="news.cfm?NewsYear=" & rsHeadlines.NewsYear>
myFader.addText('<font size="2">#DateFormat(rsHeadlines.DateAdded)#</font> ↵
<br><a href="#strNewsLink#" class="scroller"> ↵
#Replace(rsHeadlines.NewsHeadline, chr(39), "\'")#</a>');
</cfoutput>
```

The `<cfoutput>` tag on the first line uses the `query` attribute to output the results of the `<cfquery>` tag at the top of the page. The `maxrows` attribute does exactly what it says—returns a maximum of four rows from the `rsHeadlines` recordset.

The second line uses the `<cfset>` tag to declare a variable, `strNewsLink`, and assign it a value. The value concatenates a literal string and a database column.

The third line is the scrolling message. Anything that appears within the `<cfoutput>` tags is repeated for every row the `rsHeadlines` recordset returns. This is why `strNewsLink` is declared *inside* the `<cfoutput>` tags. If it were declared before the output code block, `rsHeadlines.NewsYear` would always return the same value. Try it out: move the `<cfset>` tag above the opening `<cfoutput>` tag and press F12. The date and headline columns are valid, but the hyperlink—the value of `strNewsLink`—is always the same.

Also notice the `Replace` function. We use this to replace the ASCII single-quote character, `chr(39)`, with a literal string (`"\'"`). The backslash is the JavaScript escape character—used here to escape an apostrophe—just as the pound sign (#) is the escape character in ColdFusion. (This chapter has more escaped characters than Folsom Prison!)

Summary

In this chapter, you learned one of the truisms of computer programming: "Don't reinvent the wheel." If a client requests a feature you haven't implemented before, chances are, somebody else has. Let's face it: it's easier to adapt another programmer's code than it is to "reinvent the wheel" every time you start a project (provided you have the author's permission, of course). In this recipe, you converted Nicholas Poh's first-rate DHTML script into a data-driven news scroller. Along the way, you learned to do the following:

♦ Sort news articles by year

♦ Flag articles less than 30 days old

♦ Apply server formats

♦ Create a dynamic bulleted list

That wraps up Part II of *The Joy of Dreamweaver MX*. I hope you enjoyed hand-coding the changes to Fading Text Scroller, because we're going to be doing a lot more hand-coding from now on. In Part III, we're going to create a realty site for a fictitious realtor named Chip Havilmyer. Chip is a demanding client, so we're going to have to pull out all the stops to satisfy him. Some of the features Chip has requested include:

- File uploading
- Batch deletes
- Batch updates
- Nested repeat regions
- Content management
- User authentication

Congratulations on completing Part II. You are now an official Dreamweaver MX Sous Chef. By the time you complete Part III, you will be a Master Chef.

Part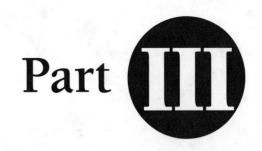

Entrees: Building a Data-Driven Web Application

Chapter

Preparation and Planning

INGREDIENTS			
File	**Type**	**Server Model(s)**	**Source**
sitemap.png	Fireworks file		*Sample Code*
home.png	Fireworks file		*Sample Code*
chip.jpg	JPG file		*Sample Code*
movies.mdb	Access database	ASP/CF	*Sample Code*

 from the desk of *Paul Newman*

Here's the pitch: your old college buddy Chip Havilmyer is now a moderately successful realtor in Seattle, Washington. Business is good, but some of his clients want their listings to appear on the Internet. Chip thinks it's time he got his own web site. And since you're his old college buddy, he's turned to you. In exchange for a discount, he's going to recommend you to every realtor he knows. "Once you finish my site," he says, "it'll be a snap for you to create the others."

Let's assume, for the sake of argument, that Chip is right. This could be an excellent opportunity for you to acquire new business. The challenge is to plan the site in such a way that it *will* be a snap for you to create others like it. This means doing your homework. Let's face it: it's much easier to go off and create the site and hope the client will be dazzled by the finished product. Don't bet on it. The ultimate success of the site is largely determined by how much preparation and planning go into the project before you ever touch Dreamweaver MX. That will be the focus of this chapter.

Every business has its own way of doing things. In the film industry, for example, there are three distinct stages of the production process: preproduction, production, and postproduction. Each stage consists of many different steps. For instance, preproduction involves budgeting the film, hiring the cast and crew, scouting locations, building sets, purchasing supplies, renting equipment, and so forth. During this stage, each crew member has clearly defined responsibilities. The production manager creates a shooting schedule. The director and cinematographer collaborate on shot lists. The production designer generates sketches for sets and locations. There are rehearsals, story conferences, wardrobe fittings—you name it. And all of this occurs long before a single frame of film is exposed.

On a slightly more modest scale, we're going to develop a production process—a six-step plan—for creating Chip Havilmyer's web site:

Preproduction

1. Define the Site's Goals
2. Define the Site's Structure

Production

3. Design the Front End
4. Design the Back End

Postproduction

5. Test Usability
6. Publish and Maintain

Of course, this plan is by no means definitive. You'll have to develop your own methodology based on what works for you. The point of this chapter is to get you thinking about the development process so that you can avoid mistakes and use your time more efficiently.

Defining the Site's Goals

The first step in creating a new web site is to define its goals. The *client's* goals. I know this seems obvious, but it's easy to impose your own objectives on a project. It doesn't matter how brilliant you are at designing Flash intros if your client hates Flash. Save those ideas for another project.

Frequently, the client doesn't have clearly defined goals for his site. He's relying on your expertise—after all, that's why he hired you—so it's up to you to draw the information out of him. What are Chip's goals for the site? Does he want to impress his customers? His boss? His wife Bunny? How will he measure the site's success? What are the metrics? Hits? Referrals? Annual sales? His checking account balance?

Ask the client for links to his competitors' sites (preferably, successful ones). Chances are, Chip has already bookmarked his favorites. What is it about those sites that appeals to him. The content? The user interface? The "eye candy"? Spend a little time browsing the Internet with him. Notice his surfing habits. Does he like widgets and thingamabobs? Or is he more of a cut-to-the-chase guy? Brainstorm. Suggest features that might enhance the site. Mention any potential stumbling blocks.

These initial meetings are critical. Take notes. Make sketches. E-mail the client frequently. Listen. And ask a lot of questions. The more information you have, the less chance for misunderstandings later. The Internet is a communications medium. You are communicating Chip's "message." Make sure you and Chip are on the same web page, so to speak.

Understanding the Client's Expectations

After two face-to-face meetings, several phone calls, and a dozen e-mails, you and Chip have finally hammered out the site's goals. Not surprisingly, he wants the site to promote his current real estate listings, raise his profile as a Seattle realtor, and generate new business. Since most of Chip's business comes from referrals, he also wants to use the site to maintain and nurture relationships with existing customers. Visually, the site should be a reflection of Chip himself: confident, friendly, professional. The interface should be straightforward and easy to navigate.

Now you know what Chip wants, but what does he *expect*? For instance, does he expect the site to look identical on all browsers and platforms? Does he expect unlimited technical support by phone? Does he expect free hosting and stats? Where is the content coming from? Does he expect you to photograph his listings and write his newsletters? Better to get these questions answered up front, or you'll rue the day you ever met Chip Havilmyer.

Delivering the Goods

Now that you and Chip have established the site's goals, what is the most efficient way to make them a reality? Since Chip wants to be able to add listings himself, the site will require a database. But should it be an Access database, or a SQL Server database? Does Chip's hosting provider offer SQL Server? If so, how much does it cost? Have you budgeted for this in your estimate?

Another feature Chip wants is the ability to upload photos. Does the hosting provider offer an upload component like FileUp, or will you have to purchase a commercial Dreamweaver extension like Pure ASP File Upload? If you're using ColdFusion, has the hosting provider enabled the `<cffile>` tag?

Eventually, Chip wants to be able to compose his monthly newsletters online, complete with custom fonts, colors, and images. In order to implement this feature, you'll have to buy an online HTML editor, such as ActivEdit or Xpad. Who's going to pay for this?

All of a sudden, Chip's "vanity site" is more than you bargained for. If you want to remain old college buddies, now would be a good time to draw up a simple contract or agreement. Make sure the client knows exactly what he's getting for his money—especially if he's paying you a flat rate—and make sure he understands that any work over and above the terms spelled out in the contract will require additional charges. You can find sample web design contracts on the Internet. Adapt one of them to suit your needs, and make sure to get the client's approval (i.e., signature) before you do any work.

Defining the Site's Structure

Drawing on your initial meetings and conversations, you have determined that Chip's site will consist of seven sections:

♦ **Home**   Sets the tone for the site and links to its main sections

♦ **Listings**   Displays Chip's most recent listings and links to detail pages

♦ **Links**   Offers online resources for home buyers and sellers

♦ **Biography**   Tells the visitor about Chip Havilmyer

♦ **News**   Displays Chip's most recent newsletter, and links to previous issues

♦ **Contact**   Allows visitors to contact Chip by submitting a form

♦ **Admin**   Allows Chip to add, edit, and delete listings, newsletters, links, and contacts

To understand the big picture, it may be helpful to create a preliminary site map (see Figure 11-1). You can use Illustrator, Freehand, or diagramming software such as Visio. Ideally, you want to use a vector drawing program so you can print high-resolution copies for the client.

The site map in Figure 11-1 doesn't include every page in the site. What the diagram does give you is a reference point—something tangible to work with. You can e-mail it to Chip and he'll be able to tell you, at a glance, if you've overlooked something.

Designing the Front End

Now that we understand what Chip wants, it's time to design the "front end." In web design parlance, this is often referred to as the graphical user interface, or GUI (pronounced "gooey"). By

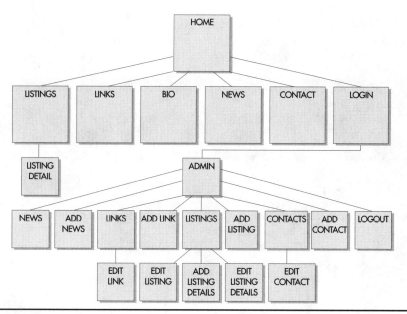

Figure 11-1   *Preliminary site map created in Fireworks MX*

now, you've made printouts of Chip's favorite web sites, and notes about what appeals to him. You might even have a few rough sketches ("paper prototypes"). Refer to these in the next step.

"Comping" in Fireworks MX

The process we are about to embark on is called "comping." Comps are merely mock-ups of one or more proposed pages for the site.

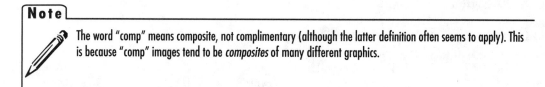

Note

The word "comp" means composite, not complimentary (although the latter definition often seems to apply). This is because "comp" images tend to be *composites* of many different graphics.

Sometimes you'll hear comps referred to as prototypes. On large-scale web projects, there may be many different kinds of prototypes: paper prototypes, horizontal and vertical prototypes, HTML prototypes, and so forth. Here is an early HTML prototype I created for Chip:

Unfortunately, Bunny thought it was too informal. She wants Chip's site to project a more professional attitude. So now it's back to the drawing board. Let's see if we can create a slick, corporate "front end" for Chip's web site. To create the comp, we'll use Macromedia Fireworks MX. If you prefer to use Illustrator, Freehand, or Flash, that's fine. I like Fireworks because it can export the design as HTML in addition to image formats like TIF and JPG.

Launch Fireworks MX and choose File | New (or press CTRL-N) to create a new document. In the New Document dialog box, set the canvas size to 760 × 400, and the resolution to 72. (Later, you can change the resolution to 150 or 300 pixels/inch if you need to make high-quality prints for the client.) Make the canvas color white and click OK.

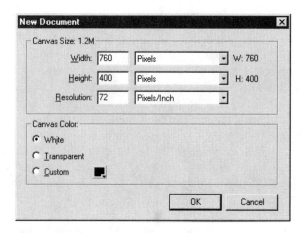

The reason we're making the canvas size 760×400 is that these dimensions roughly correspond to the browser window (minus the "chrome") on computer monitors with an 800×600 screen resolution. If you've already defined the Realty site in Dreamweaver MX, you can preview the completed version of Chip's template:

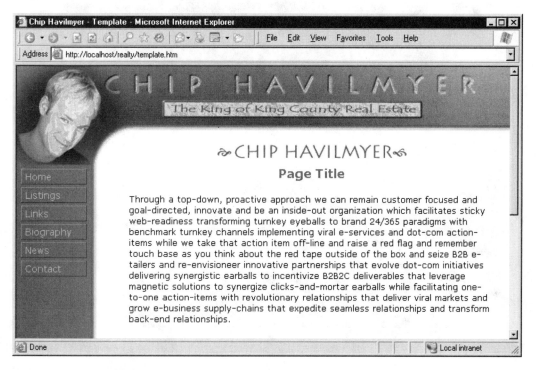

Now we'll review the steps to build it in Fireworks MX. Unfortunately, Chip hasn't given us a lot to work with. We've got a slogan, "The King of King County Real Estate," and a black-and-white photograph. You'll find Chip's photograph among the supporting files you downloaded earlier, in a folder called `Chapter11`. This folder also contains the site map (see Figure 11-1) and the completed Fireworks source file (`home.png`).

First, let's create the main "boomerang" interface. Click the Fill Color box on the Tools panel and change the color to dark blue (I chose #336699). Now select the Rectangle tool and draw a blue rectangle that covers the entire canvas (if you need more screen space, press TAB to show/hide the panels). Deselect the blue rectangle (CTRL-D) and change the Fill Color to white. Select the Rectangle tool again and draw a white rectangle over the blue rectangle. Since we want the left TOC to be 110 pixels wide, and the top header to be 90 pixels high, use the Info panel (Window | Info) to place your cursor at the proper starting point (X: 110, Y: 90). From this starting point, click and drag down and to the right to create a white rectangle that covers the blue rectangle. Make sure the white rectangle extends well beyond the bottom and right margins of the canvas. While the white rectangle is still selected, use the Properties panel (Window | Properties) to change the Rectangle Roundness to 30. This creates a rounded rectangle. At this stage, the Fireworks document should look something like this:

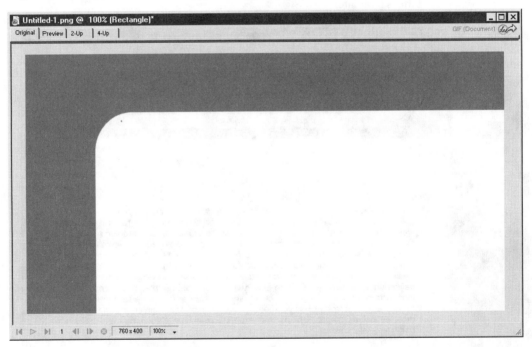

Press CTRL-S and save the document as home.png. Now we're going to "punch out" a portion of the blue rectangle. Select the white rectangle, hold down the SHIFT key, and select the blue rectangle. Choose Modify | Combine Paths | Punch. Examine the Layers panel (Window | Layers): instead of two rectangle objects on Layer 1, we now have one path. Give it a name you'll remember, such as "blue."

Note To name a layer or object in the Layers panel, double-click the layer or object, type its name, and press ENTER.

Notice that the "blue" object consists of Bézier points and handles that you can manipulate using the Subselection tool. While "blue" is still selected, click the plus (+) button next to Effects on the Properties panel and choose Shadow and Glow | Drop Shadow.

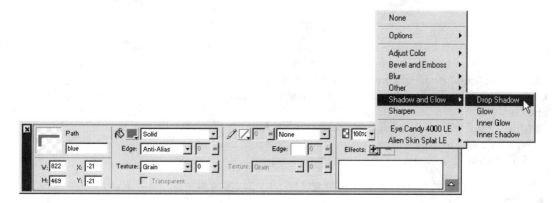

Voilà—instant interface! Save your work.

Now let's add Chip's photo. Choose File | Open and browse to chip.jpg on your hard drive. Double-click the file to open it in a new Document window. On the Tools panel, click and hold the Marquee tool to select the Oval Marquee tool. On the Properties panel, choose Feather from the Edge drop-down menu and set the feather amount to 30. Use the Oval Marquee tool to select Chip's head and left shoulder.

Press CTRL-C to copy the selection to the clipboard, and paste it into the home.png document. This creates a new bitmap object on Layer 1. Name it "chip." (You can close chip.jpg now, if you like.) While "chip" is still selected, resize it by choosing Modify | Transform | Numeric Transform. Choose Scale from the drop-down menu and enter **65**. Make sure Constrain Proportions is checked and click OK.

Move "chip" to the upper left-hand corner of the document and save your work.

Now let's use Fireworks to create a gradient. Select the "blue" object and choose Radial from the Fill Options drop-down menu on the Properties panel.

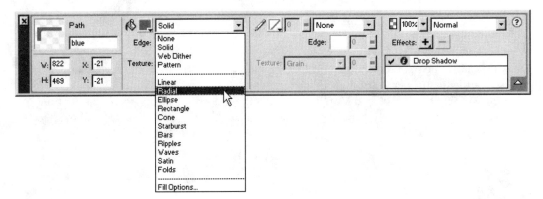

Click the Fill Color box on the Properties panel to open the Edit Gradient pop-up window. Select the color swatch on the left and change it to white (#FFFFFF). Click the color swatch on the right and make it dark blue (#1E3A48).

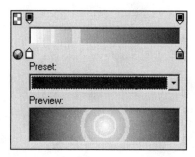

To add texture to the "blue" object, choose Plaid Tight from the Texture drop-down menu on the Properties panel and set the percentage to 20.

Now let's add Chip's slogan to the top header. Deselect all objects on the Layers panel (CTRL-D) and select the Rectangle tool. Change the Fill category from Radial back to Solid and set the fill color to #A8B4B8. Draw a rectangle that's about 350 pixels wide and 20 pixels high (you can change the rectangle's dimensions using the W and H text boxes on the Properties panel).

Use the Layers panel to name the rectangle "box." On the Properties panel, click the plus (+) button next to Effects and choose Bevel and Emboss I Outer Bevel. Choose Frame 1 from the Bevel Edge Shape drop-down, and change the color to #2E4955. Complete the remaining values as shown to the right.

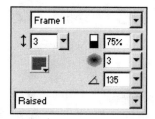

Let's give this beveled frame some texture, too. Make sure "box" is still selected and use the Texture drop-down menu on the Properties panel to change the texture to Parchment (50%). Select the Text tool and use the Properties panel to choose a sans-serif font (I chose Tempus Sans ITC 14-point bold). Sample Chip's shoulder for the font color, then click in the Document window and type Chip's slogan: **The King of King County Real Estate**.

Position the slogan over the "box" object—you can name the text object "slogan," if you like—and use the Properties panel to change its Horizontal scale to 150%.

Tip

To move a selected text block, hold down the CTRL key. Your cursor changes to the Pointer tool.

Group "slogan" and "box" by selecting both objects and choosing Modify I Group (CTRL-G). Move the "slogan" group into the top header (X: 225, Y: 55) and save your work.

Now we're going to place Chip Havilmyer's name above the slogan. Click the Text tool again and type **CHIP HAVILMYER** in the Document window. Change the font to Lithograph Light 34-point bold, or something similar. Change the font color to gray (#BCBCBC) and the kerning to 50.

Position the "CHIP HAVILMYER" text object above the "slogan" group. While "CHIP HAVILMYER" is still selected, click the Effects (+) button on the Properties panel and choose Bevel and Emboss | Raised Emboss. Change the softness to 1 and press ENTER. Save your work.

At this point, we could export the "comp" as a JPG image and e-mail it to Chip for his approval. However, it's almost as easy to export it as HTML.

Slicing and Dicing

In order to export home.png as HTML, we need to define four slice objects in Fireworks MX. Starting from the upper left-hand corner of the document (0,0), use the Slice tool to define a slice that that is 670 pixels wide and 105 pixels high. Use the Properties panel to name it "top" (the default name is "home_r1_c1").

Tip   If you can't see the slice, click the Show Slices And Hotspots button on the Tools panel. You can also toggle the visibility of slices by clicking the eye icon in the Web layer of the Layers panel.

Make sure Snap To Guides is selected (View | Guides | Snap To Guides) and create three more slice objects called "top-bg," "chin," and "left-bg" (see Figure 11-2). The small slices, "top-bg" and "left-bg," will be used as tiled backgrounds in the completed HTML page.

To export the document as HTML, choose File | Export Preview. Select JPEG from the Format drop-down menu and set the Quality to 70. Click Export to open the Export dialog box. Uncheck Include Areas Without Slices, and check Put Images In Subfolder. If you don't browse to a specific folder, Fireworks automatically creates a folder named images and places the JPG files inside it. The HTML filename is derived from the name of the Fireworks document (i.e., since our Fireworks document is home.png, the HTML document is home.htm). Click Save to export the images and HTML.

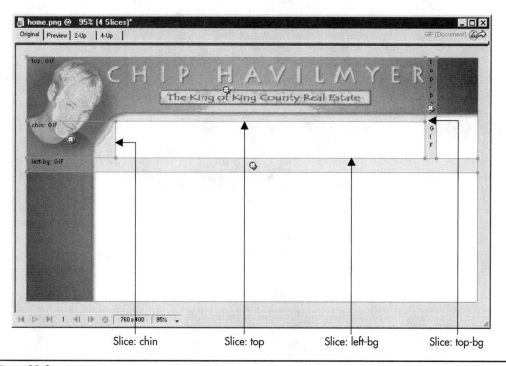

Slice: chin   Slice: top   Slice: left-bg   Slice: top-bg

Figure 11-2 *Create four slice objects called "top," "top-bg," "chin," and "left-bg."*

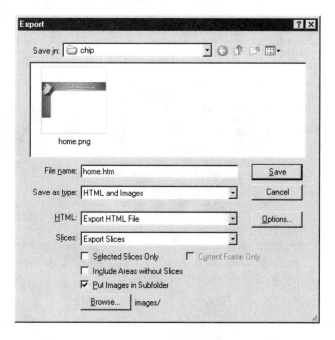

Save home.png and exit Fireworks MX. Now open home.htm in Dreamweaver MX. The easiest way to do this is to right-click home.htm in Windows Explorer and choose Edit with Dreamweaver MX. The Fireworks HTML reassembles the image slices using a table and spacer GIFs.

Press CTRL-J to open the Page Properties dialog box, and enter 0 in the Left Margin, Top Margin, Margin Width, and Margin Height text boxes. Click OK.

Select the Fireworks table by clicking <table> on the tag selector. Use the Property inspector to change its width from 760 pixels to 100%. To remove unnecessary table cells, enter 3 in the Rows text box, and 2 in the Cols text box.

Switch to Code view and delete the first table row (<tr>). This leaves us with one table cell in the first row, and two table cells in the second row. Switch back to Design view and use the tag selector to select the first table row. On the Property inspector, click the folder icon next to the Bg text box and select top-bg.jpg from the images folder.

Delete the spacer.gif in the second column of the second row, and enter some placeholder text. Place your cursor inside the first column of the second row and choose Top from the Vert drop-down menu on the Property inspector. To add the background image, click the folder icon next to the Bg text box on the Property inspector, and select left-bg.jpg from the images folder.

Save your work.

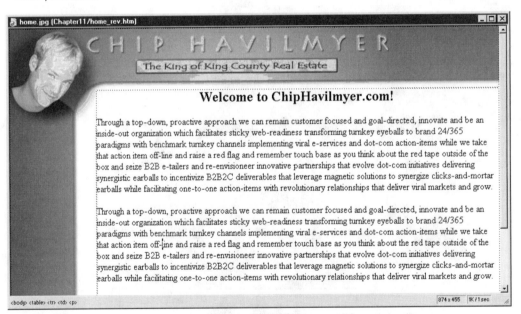

Your HTML comp, or prototype, is ready to show to the client. What's great about comping in Fireworks MX is that all the vector objects in the PNG source file remain fully editable. This way, if the client wants to change the color of the interface, transform a gradient, or make the TOC wider, you can produce a new comp in a matter of minutes.

Once everyone signs off on the comp, you can place a copy called `template.htm` in the root of your web site and use it as the basis of every new page. You can also use it to create a Dreamweaver MX template.

Designing the Back End

Now that our "front end" has been approved, it's time to create the database, or "back end." Returning to our hypothetical situation, let's assume that shortly after your first meeting, Chip faxed you the spec sheets for his three current listings. Your job is to take this information and convert it to database tables and columns.

Break out a yellow legal pad and start jotting down the names of tables and columns. Try to think of all the data your application will require, now and down the road. For instance, Chip said that he wants to use his site to maintain relationships with existing customers. Currently, he mails them a monthly newsletter. What if he could send the newsletter via e-mail, every time he posts a new issue to his site? Good idea, but how do you implement it? Simple. Add a Yes/No (or bit) column to the `Contacts` table. When a customer subscribes to the newsletter, you change the value of the `Contacts.Newsletter` column to true (checked).

The Realty Database Tables

You're about to design the database in Microsoft Access, and you have an epiphany. Since you plan to create similar realty sites for Chip's colleagues, why not design the database to hold *all* the realtors' information—not just Chip's. This means redesigning the database. Fortunately, since your design is still on paper, you can easily adapt it. At this point, the Realty database consists of 18 tables (see Table 11-1).

Note
If the Realty database seems a little overwhelming, don't worry. It's not essential to understand the particulars of every table and column. You'll have plenty of time to become familiar with them over the course of Part III.

The first change we need to make, now that we've decided to store more than one realtor's listings, is to add a foreign key column (`RealtorID`) to tables such as `Listings`, `News`, `Contacts`, and `Links`. This way, when we query the database, we can filter the results to display a specific realtor's data (e.g., `WHERE RealtorID = 1`).

Hopefully, the logic behind most of the Realty tables is clear. However, several tables were created with a special purpose in mind. For instance, `PropertyRegion` and `PropertyTown` will be used to populate two dependent drop-down menus on the Add Listing page. When a county is selected in the `PropertyRegion` drop-down, the content of the `PropertyTown` drop-down dynamically changes.

Table	Description
AccGrp	Login access levels (Admin, Realtor, Other)
Bathrooms	Bathroom count (None, 1, 2, 3, 4, 5 or more)
Bedrooms	Bedroom count (None, 1, 2, 3, 4, 5 or more)
Brokers	Real estate companies (RE/MAX, Century 21, etc.)
Contacts	Customer names and addresses
ContactCats	Customer categories (Buyer, Seller, etc.)
Links	Resources for home buyers and sellers
LinkCats	Link categories (News, Schools, Shopping, etc.)
Listings	Listing price, photo, address, description, and other details
ListingRooms	Additional listing photos and descriptions
Logins	Usernames, passwords, and access levels
News	Monthly newsletters
PropertyRegion	Washington counties (e.g., King County)
PropertyTown	Washington towns (e.g., Seattle, Tacoma)
PropertyType	Type of property for sale (house, apartment, etc.)
Realtors	Realtor names and addresses
RoomCats	Room categories (Main Floor, Upstairs, etc.)
RoomNames	Room names (kitchen, den, etc.)

Table 11-1   *The First Draft of the Realty Database Consists of 18 Tables*

Three other tables—Bathrooms, Bedrooms, and PropertyType—will also populate drop-down menus.

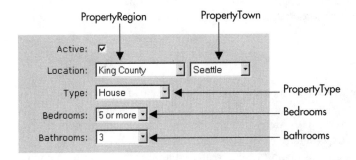

The ListingRealtors Table

You've got your "front end," you've got your "back end," you're ready to build Chip's site. Then, at two in the morning, it hits you: *What if a listing has more than one realtor?*

This is a classic database design problem: the many-to-many relationship. To illustrate this, imagine we've created a movie database with two tables: Movies and Directors. In the Movies table, Movies.DirectorID is a foreign key to Directors.DirectorID. Every time you add a film to the Movies table, you enter the director's DirectorID number. This works fine until you get to *Gone with the Wind*, which has three directors. What do you do? You could add two new columns to the Movies table—Director2, Director3—but this isn't very practical or efficient, in terms of database normalization.

The solution is to create a linking table (sometimes called an intersection, junction, or associative table): FilmDirectors. This linking table represents a many-to-many relationship between Films and Directors by creating a pair of one-to-many relationships:

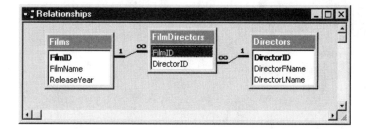

When you query the database, you *join* the three tables based on their relationships (hence the term *relational database*). If you're having trouble picturing this, open the sample Movies database (movies.mdb) in the Chapter11 folder and run the qFilmDirectors query:

DirectorID	DirectorFName	DirectorLName	FilmName	ReleaseYear
1	George Roy	Hill	Butch Cassidy and the Sundance Kid	1969
1	George Roy	Hill	Butch and Sundance in Outer Space	2003
2	George	Cukor	Gone with the Wind	1939
3	Victor	Fleming	Gone with the Wind	1939
4	Sam	Wood	Gone with the Wind	1939

Record: 1 of 5

We'll use the same technique to represent a many-to-many relationship in the Realty database. The linking table, ListingRealtors, consists of two columns: ListingID and RealtorID. These columns, as you might have guessed, are foreign keys to the Listings and

`Realtors` tables. Now we can handle the scenario that woke you up at two in the morning: realtors with multiple listings and, more to the point, listings with multiple realtors.

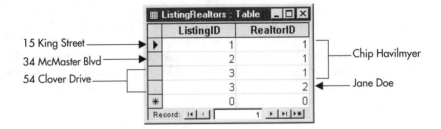

The only drawback to this approach is that it requires making inserts into two tables every time a listing is added. But let's not worry about that right now: we'll address that in the next chapter.

Testing Usability

Before a site is published, it should be tested. On large-scale web projects, this is the responsibility of the quality assurance (QA) technicians. However, since Chip can't afford to hire professional consultants, he's volunteered his friends and colleagues.

Note

We're the jumping the gun here, since we haven't actually created Chip's site yet. If this disrupts your sense of continuity, you may want to return to this section after completing Chapter 20.

The first step is to make the site accessible to Chip's "beta testers." One way to do this is to create a subdomain—e.g., **http://chip.yourdomain.com**—and send the URL to the client. If that isn't possible, you can upload the site to a "hidden" folder (e.g., **http://www.yourdomain.com/ mybuddychip**).

Cross-Browser and Cross-Platform Compatibility

If you do nothing else, test new sites on every browser and platform you can get your hands on. I guarantee you'll be shocked when you see what your site looks like in Netscape 3, or Opera 6, or Internet Explorer for the Mac. If you don't have access to a Mac, find a Kinko's or an Internet cafe that rents computers by the hour. Alternatively, you can use a web-based service that approximates your site's display on different browsers and platforms. For example, according to **www.anybrowser.com**, here's what Chip's site would look like on MSN TV (formerly WebTV):

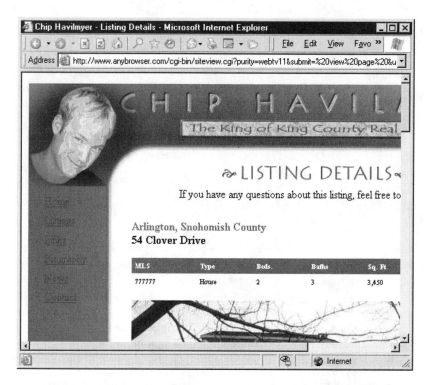

Gives you chills, doesn't it? Of course, this doesn't mean that you should redesign the site for MSN TV viewers (MSN TV's resolution is 560×420). Even the MSN TV home page doesn't fit in the WebTV Viewer without scrolling.

> **Note**
>
> Depending on whom you believe, MSN TV browsers account for less than 2 percent of North American Internet users, compared to AOL's 5–6 percent. If you're still concerned about your MSN TV audience, you can download the WebTV Viewer from **http://developer.msntv.com/Tools/WebTVVwr.asp**.

Be realistic: if you expect 95 percent of your site's visitors to use Netscape 4+ or Internet Explorer 4+, it's not practical to redirect Opera and MSN TV users to alternate versions of your site. Try to design your site for the broadest possible audience and, if possible, accommodate earlier browsers by writing code that degrades gracefully.

On the other hand, there will be times when you are forced to use a specific browser to take advantage of its special features. For instance, the online HTML editors I mentioned earlier, ActivEdit and Xpad, work only on PCs with Internet Explorer 5 or higher. In these cases, make sure the client's browser meets the application's minimum requirements.

Other compatibility issues to consider are:

◆ **Accessibility**   How accessible is your site to people with disabilities?

◆ **HTML Validation**   Does your site validate as HTML 4.01 Transitional?

◆ **CSS Validation**   Does your site conform to the CSS2 Specification?

◆ **XHTML Validation**   Are you ready for the next generation of HTML?

The World Wide Web Consortium (W3C) offers extensive information on Internet standards, and validators for HTML, CSS, and XHTML (**http://validator.w3.org**). Another good resource is **W3Schools.com.**

Error-Handling and Debugging

Once you start dealing with numerous scripting languages—JavaScript, VBScript, SQL, ASP, ColdFusion, etc.—errors are inevitable. Hopefully, you've managed to identify and debug most of them during the course of building your application. However, visitors to the site won't have your thorough understanding of how the application works. They'll make mistakes, they'll hit the wrong buttons, they'll enter the wrong information—in short, expect them to do the unexpected.

Since it's impossible to anticipate every possible error that can occur in your application, try to implement some kind of error-handling routine, especially in your data-driven pages. We touched briefly on this topic in Chapter 5, but I'm still astonished by how many high-profile web sites don't employ any error-handling whatsoever:

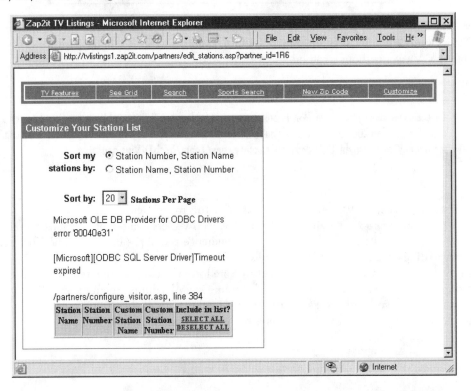

If you don't have an error-handling routine, don't worry. There are plenty of good resources on the Internet to help you develop one (**15seconds.com** and **4guysfromrolla.com** spring to mind). You can even implement a notification system that e-mails you every time an error occurs.

Publishing and Maintaining the Site

Once the client has signed off on the site, you're ready to publish it to the Internet. If you're using an Access database, you can simply upload it with your files and images. If you're using SQL Server, transferring the database to a remote SQL Server is a little more complicated. Essentially, you have three options: you can upload the `.mdf` and `.ldf` files and reattach them to the remote SQL server; you can use Data Transformation Services (DTS) to transfer the database from the local to the remote SQL server; or you can generate a SQL script (e.g., `realty.sql`) and run it on the remote SQL server. For more on this, see "How to Deploy and Manage Remote Databases" in Chapter 3.

Now that the site is published, you and the client must decide how to evaluate its success. To calculate hits and other statistics, you need a log file analysis tool. Most hosting providers offer a service such as WebTrends (**www.webtrends.com**) free of charge. In addition to hits, referrers, and visitor demographics, WebTrends reports useful debugging information such as browser errors, server errors, and form errors. For more precise user tracking, check out 2eNetWorx's free statistics reporting application, StatCounteX (**www.2enetworx.com**). StatCounteX uses invisible GIF files, or "web bugs," to monitor click paths.

Some of the other "metrics" we discussed at the beginning of the chapter cannot be gleaned from log files. For instance, has the site raised Chip's profile as a Seattle realtor? Has it resulted in any new referrals? Has he received any feedback from customers and coworkers? If so, what sort of improvements would they like to see?

In short, site maintenance is an ongoing process. Use a site reporting service such as NetMechanic (**www.netmechanic.com**) to check for broken links and other errors. Solicit feedback from the site's visitors. Armed with this information, it will be easier for you and the client to make informed decisions about updates and revisions.

Summary

In this chapter, we talked about the importance of planning a complex site like Chip Havilmyer's. We also developed a methodology to help us create data-driven web sites:

◆ Define the Site's Goals
◆ Define the Site's Structure
◆ Design the Front End

- Design the Back End
- Test Usability
- Publish and Maintain

In Chapter 12, the real fun begins, as we push Dreamweaver MX to its limits to construct Chip Havilmyer's realty site. By the time we finish, it will incorporate all of the advanced features he requested.

Chapter

Insert Record and Retrieve Identity

File	Type	Server Model(s)	Source
realty.mdb	Access database	ASP/CF	*Sample Code*
addListing.asp	Active Server Page	ASP	*Sample Code*
addListing.cfm	ColdFusion template	CF	*Sample Code*
DynaList	Code Snippets	ASP	*Sample Code*
TwoSelectsRelated.cfm	Custom tag	CF	Nate Weiss
Insert Record With Identity	Server Behavior	ASP	George Petrov

 from the desk of Paul Newman

239

I n this chapter, we begin Chip Havilmyer's realty site in earnest. Your mission, if you choose to accept it, is to create the Add Listing page. This page poses several unique challenges:

◆ Creating dynamic dependent drop-down menus

◆ Retrieving the value of the AutoNumber (or Identity) column

◆ Inserting records into two tables with one form

In order to complete this chapter, and the remainder of Part III, you need to define a new site named Realty in Dreamweaver MX. The source files and database (`realty.mdb`) for the site can be downloaded from **www.newmanzone.com** or **www.osborne.com/downloads/downloads.shtml**. If you downloaded the files earlier, there are four folders that pertain to Part III: `realty_asp`, `realty_asp_empty`, `realty_cf`, and `realty_cf_empty`. Unless you want to preview the completed site, copy the empty version to the root of your web server, and create a virtual directory called `realty_asp` (or `realty_cf`) that points to the www folder (e.g., `C:\Inetpub\wwwroot\realty_asp_empty\www`). For more on defining sites in Dreamweaver MX, see Chapter 5.

Retrieving the Identity Column

As you know, when you create an AutoNumber column in Microsoft Access, it automatically increments every time you insert a new record into the table. In SQL Server, an AutoNumber column is called an Identity column.

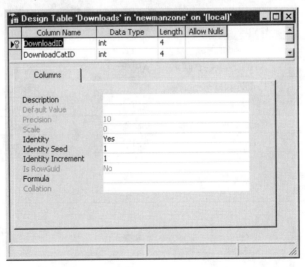

Every time you insert a record into a table with an Identity column, SQL Server holds the new value of the Identity column in a global variable called @@IDENTITY. For example, the Listings table in the Realty database contains three records. If we were to add another record to it, the Identity column would automatically increment by 1. So the value of @@IDENTITY, in this example, would be 4.

SQL Server users often use the @@IDENTITY variable to make inserts into multiple, related tables, returning its value in a stored procedure as an output parameter. Starting with Access 2000, Microsoft makes the @@IDENTITY variable available to Access users as well.

Why Do I Need to Know This?

Now that you know what @@IDENTITY is, you may be wondering why you'd need to use it. The short answer: to make inserts into two related tables. To illustrate this, let's take a look at the two tables we'll be working with in this chapter: Listings and ListingRealtors.

Open realty.mdb in Microsoft Access. Select the Listings table and click Design. As you can see, the Listings table consists of 22 fields or columns (see Table 12-1). I've added three sample listings for the purposes of this tutorial.

Field Name	Data Type	Size	Description
ListingID	AutoNumber		Primary Key
DateAdded	Date/Time		Default: Date()
ListingPrice	Currency		Default: 0
ListingAddress	Text	250	
MLSNumber	Text	10	Unique Multiple Listing Service (MLS) number
PropertyRegionID	Number		FK to PropertyRegion
PropertyTownID	Number		FK to PropertyTown
PropertyAge	Number		
PropertyTypeID	Number		FK to PropertyType
BedroomID	Number		FK to Bedrooms
BathroomID	Number		FK to Bathrooms
ListingPic	Text	50	Default: "nopic.gif"
ListingThumb	Text	50	Optional thumbnail photo
ListingSqFt	Text	50	
ListingLotSize	Text	50	
Amenities	Text	250	(e.g., alarm system)
Basement	Yes/No		
Active	Yes/No		Listing status
Sold	Yes/No		
Equipment	Text	250	(e.g., washer/dryer)
Remarks	Text	250	internal remarks
ListingDesc	Memo		

Table 12-1   *The Listings Table Consists of 22 Fields or Columns*

In an effort to normalize the database, repeating data has been moved into its own table. This is best demonstrated by examining the `qListings` query in Design view.

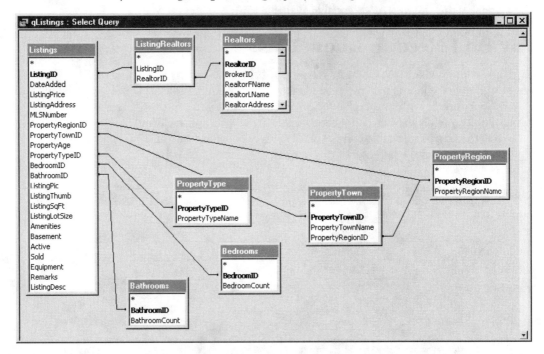

As this diagram illustrates, the `qListings` query uses joins—in this case, *inner joins*—to relate tables based on common values (primary key–foreign key relationships). The bold columns are primary keys; the columns they're joined to are foreign keys. This allows us to return the related values of foreign key columns like `Listings.PropertyTownID` (e.g., "Seattle") and `Listings.PropertyTypeID` (e.g., "House"). Otherwise, the default Listings page would consist of a bunch of numbers nobody understands. Are you with me so far?

In the last chapter, as you may recall, we added a "linking" table to the Realty database: `ListingRealtors`.

Note

A linking table—sometimes called an intersection, junction, or associative table—allows us to represent a many-to-many relationship between two tables by creating a pair of one-to-many relationships.

This was done to accommodate listings with more than one realtor. As you can see, `ListingRealtors` consists of two columns:

ListingID is a foreign key to Listings.ListingID, and RealtorID is a foreign key to Realtors.RealtorID. Even though the Realty database contains three listings, ListingRealtors returns four records. This is because the third listing is shared by two realtors: Chip Havilmyer and Jane Doe. What's more, since ListingRealtors is part of qListings, the query also returns four records:

ListingID	Region	Town	RealtorID	Realtor	MLSNumber	ListingPrice	ListingAddress
1	King County	Bellevue	1	Chip Havilmyer	123456	$500,000.00	15 King Street
2	Pierce County	Ashford	1	Chip Havilmyer	678910	$600,000.00	34 McMaster Blvd.
3	Snohomish Count	Arlington	1	Chip Havilmyer	777777	$740,000.00	54 Clover Drive
3	Snohomish Count	Arlington	2	Jane Doe	777777	$740,000.00	54 Clover Drive

Adding the ListingRealtors table to the database solves an important problem: accommodating listings with multiple realtors. However, it does make adding new listings a little more difficult. Now, instead of making inserts into one table (Listings), we have to make inserts into two tables (Listings and ListingRealtors). How do we make inserts into two related tables with Dreamweaver MX?

This is where @@IDENTITY comes in. We insert a record into the Listings table, retrieve the new value of the Identity column (Listings.ListingID), and redirect to a second page to insert a record into the ListingRealtors table.

Available Extensions

As of this writing, there are three Dreamweaver insert-retrieve identity extensions: two for ASP, and one for ColdFusion. All three retrieve the new value of the Identity (or AutoNumber) column and stuff it into a local variable.

◆ **Insert Record With Identity (ASP)** Written by George Petrov, this free extension is available from **www.udzone.com**. It works with SQL Server and—with a little tweaking—Microsoft Access.

◆ **Insert-Retrieve ID (ASP)** This commercial extension, written by Tom Muck, only works with Access databases. The extension is part of the UltraSuite 4000 Extensions package (**www.ultrasuite.com**).

◆ **CF Insert-Retrieve ID (ColdFusion)** Also written by Tom Muck, this extension is only compatible with Dreamweaver UltraDev 4 pages. Future versions are likely to support Dreamweaver MX. Visit **www.basic-ultradev.com** for details.

Before we can build the Add Listing page, we need to define an ODBC data source that connects to `realty.mdb`.

Setting Up the Realty Database

If you downloaded the supporting files earlier, you'll find `realty.mdb` in the `databases` folder. The Realty database contains the sample data that will be referenced—in screenshots and code listings—throughout Part III. You'll also find `realty.mdb` in the `db` directory of the Realty site (e.g., `C:\Inetpub\wwwroot\newmanzone_asp_empty\db`).

Creating the ODBC Data Source

To connect to the Access 2000 database, `realty.mdb`, we'll create a new System DSN (Data Source Name) using Windows' ODBC Data Source Administrator.

Open the Windows Control Panel and launch ODBC Data Source Administrator. Select the System DSN tab and click Add. From the list of available drivers, choose Microsoft Access Driver (*.mdb) and click Finish.

Enter **realty** in the Data Source Name text box, and an optional description. Click Select and browse to the location of `realty.mdb` on your hard drive. Click OK to close the Select Database dialog box.

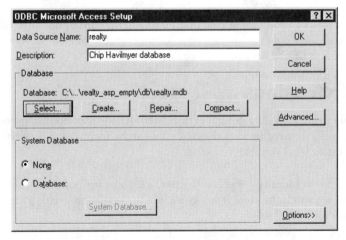

Click OK again to close the ODBC Microsoft Access Setup dialog box.

Creating the ColdFusion Data Source

To create the ColdFusion data source for the realty site, log in to ColdFusion Administrator (e.g., **http://localhost/cfide/administrator**) and choose Data Sources from the table of contents.

In the Add New Data Source region, enter **realty** in the Data Source Name text box, and choose ODBC Socket from the Driver drop-down menu. Click Add.

On the next page, the DSN we created with Windows' ODBC Data Source Administrator is automatically selected in the drop-down menu. Enter an optional description and click the Show Advanced Settings button.

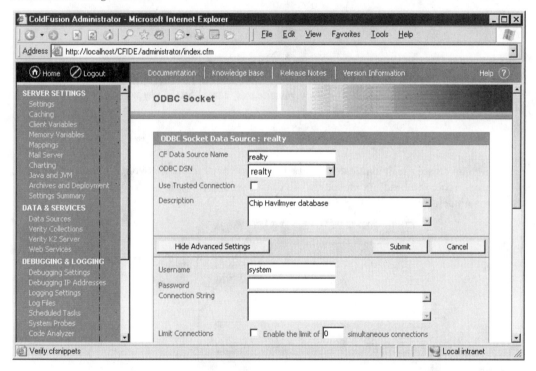

In the Advanced Settings, make sure Enable Long Text Retrieval (CLOB) is checked (CLOB is required for Microsoft Access Memo fields). Click Submit.

The realty data source is added to ColdFusion Administrator, and "ok" appears in the Status column. This data source is now available to Dreamweaver MX and other programs that support Remote Development Services (RDS).

Building the Add Listing Page

To ensure that accurate data is inserted into the `PropertyRegion` and `PropertyTown` tables, we need to create two dynamic dependent menus on the Add Listing page. In ColdFusion, this is a snap, thanks to Nate Weiss's excellent tag, `<CF_TwoSelectsRelated>`. In ASP, we'll use the DynaList extension, a collection of four Macromedia code snippets.

Dynamic Dependent Menus (ASP)

Expand the `adminch` folder in the Site panel and open `addListing.asp` in Dreamweaver MX.

> **Note**
>
>
>
> *Adminch?* I renamed Chip's `admin` folder for two reasons. First, many hosting providers map the `admin` folder to an online control panel (e.g., **www.yoursite.com/admin**). Second, why make the hacker's job easier?

Before we can create the dynamic dependent menus, we need to create two recordsets to populate them. From the Bindings panel, choose Recordset and name it `rsPropertyRegion`. Click Define and choose New | Data Source Name (DSN).

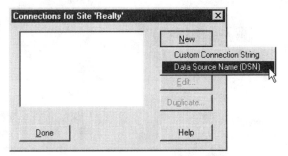

Enter **realty** in the Connection Name text box, and choose realty from the DSN drop-down menu. Make sure the second radio button is selected (Using Local DSN). Click Test to verify the connection and click OK to close the dialog boxes.

In the Recordset dialog box, choose realty from the Connection drop-down menu and select the `PropertyRegion` table. The All Columns radio button should be selected by default. Click OK.

Create a second recordset and name it `rsPropertyTown`. Select `PropertyTown` from the Table drop-down menu and click OK.

The code snippets we'll be using to create the dynamic dependent menus come from Macromedia Tech Note 14924: "Creating client-side dynamic dependent list boxes" (**www.macromedia.com/support/ultradev/ts/documents/client_dynamic_listbox.htm**).

First, we'll create the "parent" menu. From the Server Behaviors panel, choose Dynamic Form Elements | Dynamic List/Menu. Choose `PropertyRegionID` from the Menu drop-down, and rsPropertyRegion from the Recordset drop-down. Set the Values to PropertyRegionID, and the Labels to PropertyRegionName. Ignore the Static Options and click OK to apply the Dynamic List/Menu SB.

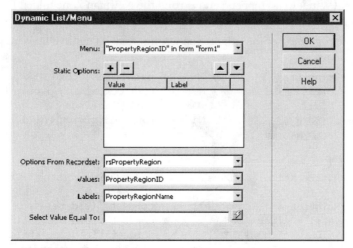

Macromedia's dynamic dependent code consists of four snippets: the main code, which is pasted into the <head> of the document; the onChange event, which is applied to the parent menu; the onLoad event, which is applied to the <body> tag; and the "Netscape 4 Modification." To speed up the process, the DynaList extension collects these snippets into one folder in the Snippets panel.

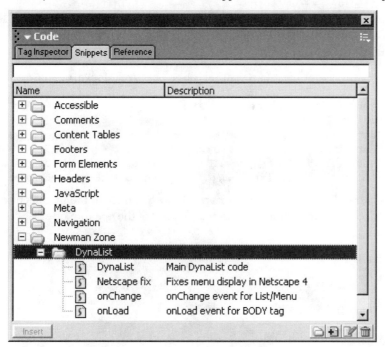

Follow these steps to complete the dynamic dependent menus:

1. Switch to Code view and place your cursor before the closing `</head>` tag. Open the Snippets panel (Window | Snippets) and expand the Newman Zone folder. Expand the DynaList folder and select `DynaList`. Click Insert.

2. Scroll up to the beginning of the snippet you just inserted. About five lines in, you'll find the following code:

```
arrDL1[1] = "[selList1]";      // Name of parent list box
arrDL1[2] = "[form1]";         // Name of form containing parent list box
arrDL1[3] = "[selList2]";      // Name of child list box
arrDL1[4] = "[form2]";         // Name of form containing child list box
arrDL1[5] = arrDynaList;

<%
Dim txtDynaListRelation, txtDynaListLabel, txtDynaListValue, oDynaListRS

txtDynaListRelation = "[Relation]"  ' recordset field relating to parent
txtDynaListLabel = "[Labels]"       ' recordset field for child Item Labels
txtDynaListValue = "[Values]"       ' recordset field for child Values
Set oDynaListRS = [rsList2]         ' child list box recordset
```

   Change the preceding shaded values to the actual form names and database columns:

```
arrDL1[1] = "PropertyRegionID";  // Name of parent list box
arrDL1[2] = "form1";             // Name of form containing parent list box
arrDL1[3] = "PropertyTownID";    // Name of child list box
arrDL1[4] = "form1";             // Name of form containing child list box
arrDL1[5] = arrDynaList;

<%
Dim txtDynaListRelation, txtDynaListLabel, txtDynaListValue, oDynaListRS

txtDynaListRelation = "PropertyRegionID" ↵
' recordset field relating to parent
txtDynaListLabel = "PropertyTownName" ↵
' recordset field for child Item Labels
txtDynaListValue = "PropertyTownID"      ' recordset field for child Values
Set oDynaListRS = rsPropertyTown         ' child list box recordset
```

3. Select the "parent" drop-down menu, `PropertyRegionID`, in the Document window. Switch to Code view and place your cursor at the end of the opening `<select>` tag. Insert the onChange snippet:

```
onChange="setDynaList(arrDL1)"
```

4. Place your cursor at the end of the page's opening `<body>` tag and insert the `onLoad` snippet:

   ```
   onLoad="setDynaList(arrDL1)"
   ```

5. Optionally, you can replace the "child" menu, `PropertyTownID`, with the "Netscape 4 Modification." Select the child menu in the Document window and delete it in Code view. Select `Netscape fix` in the Snippets panel and click Insert.

6. Change the child menu name from `[selList2]` back to `PropertyTownID`.

That should do it. Save your work and press F12 to preview the page in a browser. Select "Pierce County" from the drop-down menu. The contents of the right drop-down menu should change dynamically. Pretty sweet, huh?

New   Feature

 If you're a ColdFusion Studio or HomeSite user, you already know about Snippets. Snippets are little pieces of reusable code that you can create, edit, insert, and delete via the Snippets panel. You can preview the code or rendered HTML by expanding the preview area above the Snippets folders. What's great about Snippets is that, unlike library items, Snippets are available to every site you define in Dreamweaver MX. For more information, see *Using Dreamweaver MX.*

Now that you're so adept at creating dynamic menus, I need you to create one more: `PropertyTypeID`. To do this, create a new recordset, `rsPropertyType`, and use Dreamweaver's Dynamic List/Menu SB to populate the `PropertyTypeID` menu. If you get stuck, you can find the completed version of `addListing.asp` in the `realty_asp` folder you downloaded earlier.

Dynamic Dependent Menus (ColdFusion)

Creating dynamic dependent menus in ColdFusion is a cakewalk compared to ASP. That's because Nate Weiss, co-author of *The Macromedia ColdFusion 5 Web Application Construction Kit,* has created a custom ColdFusion tag called `<CF_TwoSelectsRelated>`. For more information about the tag, and its author, visit **www.nateweiss.com**.

Typically, before you can use a custom tag, you must first install it by placing it in ColdFusion's `CustomTags` directory (e.g., `C:\CFusionMX\CustomTags`). Chances are, however, you won't have access to this folder on your remote server. In this case, you can use a special ColdFusion tag, `<cfmodule>`, to specify a different location for the custom tag. Confused? Don't worry: it's going to make perfect sense in a moment.

Launch Dreamweaver MX and expand the `CustomTags` folder in the Site panel. You should see a copy of Nate Weiss's tag, `TwoSelectsRelated.cfm`. This is the ColdFusion template that you would ordinarily place into ColdFusion's `CustomTags` directory. Now expand the `adminch` folder and open `addListing.cfm`.

Before we can create the dynamic dependent menus, we need to create a recordset to populate them. From the Bindings panel, choose Recordset.

Name the recordset **rsLocation** and choose realty from the Data Source drop-down menu. Select the query, `qTwoSelectsRelated`, from the Table drop-down menu and choose the All Columns radio button. Click OK to close the Recordset dialog box.

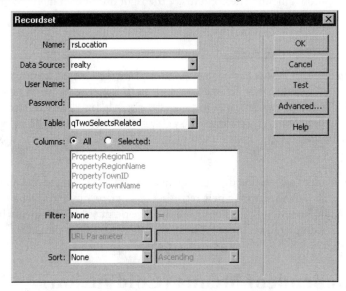

To reiterate, if you have access to ColdFusion's `CustomTags` directory on your remote server, you can use the `<CF_TwoSelectsRelated>` tag. Otherwise, you have to use the `<cfmodule>` tag. In the Document window, place your cursor in the table cell to the right of "Location". Switch to Code view and insert the following code between the `<td>` tags:

```
<cfmodule template="../CustomTags/TwoSelectsRelated.cfm"
QUERY="rsLocation"
NAME1="PropertyRegionID"
NAME2="PropertyTownID"
DISPLAY1="PropertyRegionName"
DISPLAY2="PropertyTownName"
DEFAULT1="1"
DEFAULT2="1"
VALUE1="PropertyRegionID"
```

```
VALUE2="PropertyTownID"
FORCEWIDTH1="10"
FORCEWIDTH2="10"
SIZE1="1"
SIZE2="1"
HTMLBETWEEN=" "
AUTOSELECTFIRST="Yes">
```

Switch back to Design view. Save your work and press F12 to preview the page in a browser. Choose "Snohomish County" from the drop-down menu. The contents of the right drop-down should change dynamically. Hallelujah!

Note

For more information about `<CF_TwoSelectsRelated>`, read the help file, `CF_TwoSelectsRelated.html`, in the `CustomTags` folder.

Now that you're so adept at creating dynamic menus, I need you to create one more: `PropertyTypeID`. To do this, create a new recordset, `rsPropertyType`, and use Dreamweaver's Dynamic List/Menu SB to populate the `PropertyTypeID` menu. If you get stuck, you can find the completed version of `addListing.cfm` in the `realty_cf` folder you downloaded earlier.

Insert Record With Identity (ASP)

The extension we're going to use for the ASP version of the Add Listing page is Insert Record With Identity. This free extension, written by George Petrov, is available from **www.udzone.com/go?195**. You need to download and install it, using Extension Manager, before we proceed. (Make sure to download the latest version, because version 1.0.0 is not compatible with Dreamweaver MX.)

Launch Dreamweaver MX and open `addListing.asp`. George's extension looks and functions just like Dreamweaver's standard Insert Record server behavior, but it also stuffs the new value of the Identity (or AutoNumber) column into a local variable called `LastIdent`. The extension works flawlessly with SQL Server, but it needs a little tweaking to get along with Access 2000. Let's get started.

From the Server Behaviors panel, choose InsertRecordWithIdent. Select the realty connection and choose `Listings` from the Table drop-down menu. In the redirect text box, enter **addListing-response.asp** (we'll construct this page later in the chapter). Most of the form elements should sync up nicely with the database columns. Select the Yes/No columns, `Active` and

Basement, and change their Submit As values to Checkbox –1, 0. Ignore the `File1` form field for now. Click OK to apply the server behavior.

If you were to preview the page now—and submit the form—you would receive the following error:

Invalid SQL statement; expected 'DELETE', 'INSERT', 'PROCEDURE', 'SELECT', or 'UPDATE'.

Switch to Code view and locate the following block of code (it should start at about line 86):

```
' execute the insert
Set MM_editCmd = Server.CreateObject("ADODB.Command")
MM_editCmd.ActiveConnection = MM_editConnection
MM_editCmd.CommandText = "SET NOCOUNT ON;" & MM_editQuery & ⤶
";SELECT @" & "@IDENTITY AS Ident"
Set rsLastIdent = MM_editCmd.Execute
if NOT rsLastIdent.EOF then
    LastIdent = rsLastIdent.Fields.Item("Ident").Value
end if
MM_editCmd.ActiveConnection.Close
```

To the best of my knowledge, this code doesn't work with Access 2000 for two reasons: Access doesn't support batch command processing, and it doesn't support the SQL Server SET NOCOUNT ON statement. Fortunately, this is easy to fix. Replace the preceding code with the following:

```
' execute the insert
Set MM_editCmd = Server.CreateObject("ADODB.Command")
MM_editCmd.ActiveConnection = MM_editConnection
MM_editCmd.CommandText = MM_editQuery
```

```
MM_editCmd.Execute
MM_editCmd.CommandText = "SELECT @" & "@IDENTITY"
Set rsLastIdent = MM_editCmd.Execute
if NOT rsLastIdent.EOF then
    LastIdent = rsLastIdent(0).Value
end if
MM_editCmd.ActiveConnection.Close
```

Now the insert will occur without raising an error. Before we move on, let's append the value of `LastIdent` to the redirect page as a URL parameter. In Code view, locate the `Response.Redirect` method (around line 99):

```
Response.Redirect(MM_editRedirectUrl)
```

Change it to the following:

```
Response.Redirect(MM_editRedirectUrl & "?ListingID=" & LastIdent)
```

Save your work. Don't test the page in a browser just yet: we still have to build the response page (see "Building the Response Page," later in this chapter).

Insert-Retrieve ID (ColdFusion)

Prior to Dreamweaver MX, you could use Tom Muck's extension, CF Insert-Retrieve ID, to insert a record and retrieve the new value of the Identity (or AutoNumber) column. But as you know, ColdFusion server behaviors created prior to Dreamweaver MX are only compatible with UltraDev 4 pages. Until Tom releases a new version of the extension, we'll have to use Dreamweaver's standard Insert Record SB, and hand-code the rest.

Launch Dreamweaver MX and open `addListing.cfm`. From the Server Behaviors panel, choose Insert Record. Choose the realty data source and select `Listings` from the Table drop-down menu.

Most of the form elements should sync up nicely with the database columns. Select the Yes/No columns, `Active` and `Basement`, and change their Submit As values to Checkbox –1, 0. Ignore the `ListingPic` column for now.

Notice that `PropertyRegionID` and `PropertyTownID` are not assigned values. This is because `TwoSelectsRelated.cfm` generates the drop-down menus dynamically. To work around this, we have to cheat a little. Select the `PropertyRegionID` and `PropertyTownID` columns, and choose FORM.PropertyTypeID from the Value drop-down menu. We'll correct this as soon as the Insert Record SB is applied.

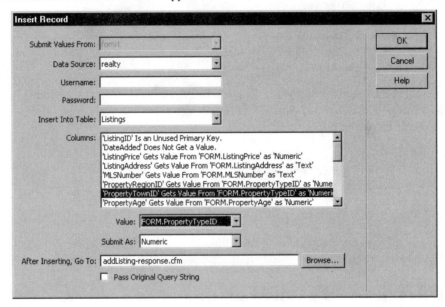

Finally, in the redirect text box, enter addListing-response.cfm (we'll build this page later in the chapter). Click OK and save your work.

Before we do anything else, let's revise the INSERT statement. Switch to Code view and locate the following code (lines 26–36):

```
<cfif IsDefined("FORM.PropertyTypeID") AND #FORM.PropertyTypeID# NEQ "">
#FORM.PropertyTypeID#
<cfelse>
NULL
</cfif>
,
<cfif IsDefined("FORM.PropertyTypeID") AND #FORM.PropertyTypeID# NEQ "">
#FORM.PropertyTypeID#
<cfelse>
NULL
</cfif>
```

Replace FORM.PropertyTypeID with FORM.PropertyRegionID and FORM.PropertyTownID (the new code is shaded):

```
<cfif IsDefined("FORM.PropertyRegionID") AND #FORM.PropertyRegionID# NEQ "">
#FORM.PropertyRegionID#
<cfelse>
NULL
</cfif>
,
<cfif IsDefined("FORM.PropertyTownID") AND #FORM.PropertyTownID# NEQ "">
#FORM.PropertyTownID#
<cfelse>
NULL
</cfif>
```

Now we have to retrieve the new value of the AutoNumber column, and stuff it into a variable. In Code view, insert a new line after the closing `</cfquery>` tag (line 110) and add the following code:

```
<cfquery name="rsLastIdent" datasource="realty">
SELECT @@IDENTITY AS LastIdent FROM Listings
</cfquery>
<cfset intLastIdent = rsLastIdent.LastIdent>
```

Notice that, even though we added the SELECT statement in Code view, the `rsLastIdent` recordset appears in the Bindings panel.

Let's append the value of `intLastIdent` to the redirect page as a URL parameter. Change the `<cflocation>` tag (around line 115) to the following:

```
<cflocation url="addListing-response.cfm?ListingID=#intLastIdent#"
addtoken="no">
```

The response page, `addListing-response.cfm`, will use the value of the URL parameter to insert a related record into the `ListingRealtors` table. That's what we'll do next.

Building the Response Page

As you've probably guessed by now, the Add Listing response page doesn't display any content to the visitor. Its only purpose is to make an insert into the "linking" table, `ListingRealtors`, and redirect to the default Listings page.

This page is similar in concept to the Downloads response page we created in Chapter 9. Instead of updating an existing record, however, it will insert a new record. To do this, we'll create an Insert command (ColdFusion users will create an Insert recordset).

Creating the Insert Command (ASP)

Launch Dreamweaver MX and create a new file in the adminch folder called addListing-response.asp. Double-click the file in the Site panel to open it.

From the Server Behaviors panel, choose Command. Enter **cmdListingRealtors** in the Name text box, and choose Insert from the Type drop-down menu. Leave Return Recordset unchecked. Notice Dreamweaver MX generates a sample SQL statement to guide us. In the Database Items area, expand Tables and ListingRealtors. Select ListingID and click the COLUMN button. Select RealtorID and click the COLUMN button again. Dreamweaver MX automatically adds the database columns to the SQL INSERT statement.

Now we have to specify the values to insert. Click the plus (+) button next to Variables and enter **intListingID** in the Name column. Tab to the Run-Time Value column and enter **Request.QueryString("ListingID")**.

Finally, revise the VALUES clause:

```
VALUES (intListingID, 1)
```

In case you're wondering, the second value (1) is Chip Havilmyer's RealtorID number. Ordinarily, this value would be a session variable (e.g., Session("svRealtorID")). However, since we don't cover sessions until Chapter 19, we're entering a hard-coded value. The completed command should look like this:

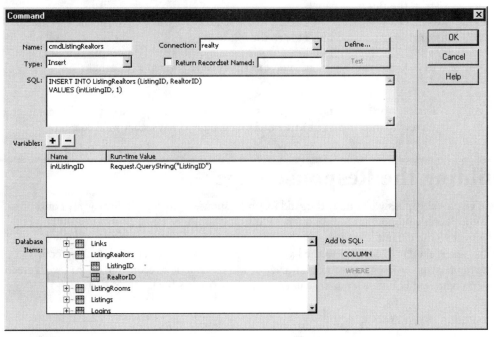

Click OK to close the Command dialog box. Switch to Code view and insert the following code before the opening <html> tag:

```
<% Response.Redirect("../listings.asp") %>
```

This redirects the visitor to Chip's Current Listings page after making the insert. Later, you can change this statement to redirect to the admin Listings page.

That's it! Save your work and browse to the Add Listing page on your local server (e.g., **http://localhost/realty_asp/adminch/addListing.asp**). Enter some data and click the Add Listing button. The Current Listings page should look something like this:

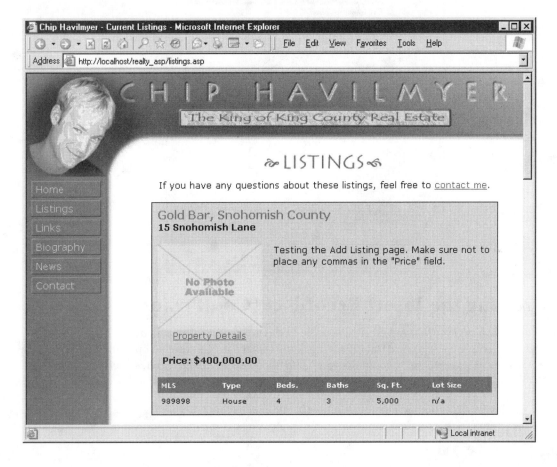

The reason the placeholder image appears is that "nopic.gif" is the default value of the ListingPic column (see Table 12-1).

If you receive an error—such as "Operation must use an updateable query"—it's probably a permissions issue. To change the security settings, right-click on `realty.mdb` in Windows Explorer and choose Properties.

On the Security tab, make sure the Internet Guest Account has Write access to the database.

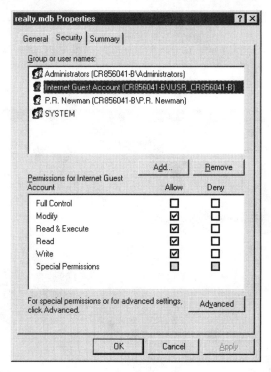

Creating the Insert Recordset (ColdFusion)

Launch Dreamweaver MX and create a new file in the `adminch` folder called `addListing-response.cfm`. Double-click the file in the Site panel to open it.

From the Bindings panel, choose Recordset and click Advanced. Enter **rsListingRealtors** in the Name text box and choose the realty data source. In the SQL area, enter the following code:

```
INSERT INTO ListingRealtors (ListingID, RealtorID)
VALUES (#URL.ListingID#, 1)
```

In case you're wondering, the second value (`1`) is Chip Havilmyer's `RealtorID` number. Ordinarily, this would be a session variable—e.g., `#SESSION.RealtorID#`—but since we don't cover sessions until later in the book, we're entering a hard-coded value.

Now we have to set the default value of `#URL.ListingID#`. Click the plus (+) button next to Page Parameters. The URL variable, `#URL.ListingID#`, appears in the Add Parameters dialog box. Enter **0** in the Default Value column and click OK.

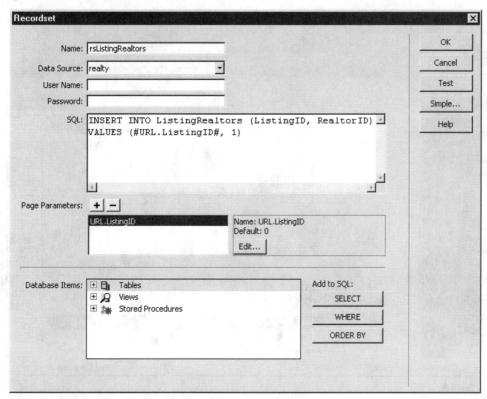

Click OK to close the Recordset dialog box. Switch to Code view and enter the following code before the opening `<html>` tag:

```
<cflocation url="../listings.cfm" addtoken="no">
```

This redirects the browser to Chip's Current Listings page after making the insert. Later, you can change the `url` attribute to point to the admin Listings page.

That's it. Save your work and browse to the Add Listing page on your local server (e.g., **http://localhost/realty_cf/adminch/addListing.cfm**). Enter some data and click the Add Listing button. The Current Listings page should look something like this:

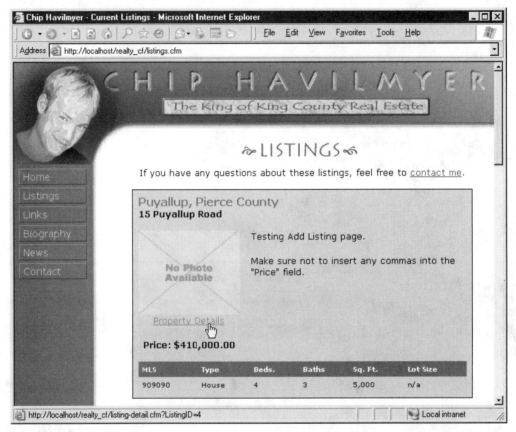

Congratulations! You inserted, you retrieved, you conquered.

Summary

In this chapter, we broke ground on Chip Havilmyer's realty site by creating the Add Listing page. This page posed several unique challenges, but we were able to use Dreamweaver extensions to overcome most of them. This demonstrates why Dreamweaver's extensibility makes it such a formidable web design tool.

To recap, here's what you learned to do in this chapter:

◆ Create dynamic dependent drop-down menus

◆ Invoke a custom ColdFusion tag using `<cfmodule>`

◆ Insert a record and retrieve the value of the Identity (or AutoNumber) column

◆ Create an Insert command (ASP)

◆ Create an Insert recordset (ColdFusion)

In the next chapter, we'll edit the Add Listing page so that Chip can browse to an image on his computer and upload it using the same form.

Chapter 13

Uploads Made Simple

INGREDIENTS

File(s)	Type	Server Model(s)	Source
realty.mdb	Access database	ASP/CF	*Sample Code*
addListing.asp, addDetails.asp	Active Server Pages	ASP	*Sample Code*
addListing.cfm, addDetails.cfm	ColdFusion templates	CF	*Sample Code*
Pure ASP File Upload 2.0.8	Server Behavior	ASP	George Petrov
isDefined	Object	CF	*Sample Code*
Check Form 4.66	Behavior		Jaro von Flocken
Check Image Upload 2.1	Behavior		Massimo Foti

 from the desk of *Paul Newman*

I n this chapter, we're going to revise the Add Listing page to allow Chip Havilmyer to upload an image along with a new realty listing. We'll also revise the Insert Record server behavior to insert the image's filename into the database.

As you probably know, implementing a file upload feature can be difficult. Often it requires the installation of a third-party component, such as AspUpload or FileUp, and a thorough knowledge of how to script that component. In addition, your hosting provider may not offer the same component on your remote server (if they offer one at all).

The goal of this recipe is to make file uploading as simple as possible. Thanks to new support for the `<cffile>` tag, and a first-rate ASP extension by George Petrov, implementing file uploads with Dreamweaver MX has never been easier. But before we start cookin', it may be useful to understand what has traditionally made file uploading such a downer.

The Trouble with Multipart/Form-Data

Before someone can upload a file from a web page, it must contain a file field. In Dreamweaver MX, you add a file field to an existing form by choosing Insert | Form Objects | File Field. In Code view, here's what the file field looks like:

```
<input type="file" name="file">
```

Not much to it, is there? If only it were that simple! Because HTML forms were originally designed to submit text data, the W3C (World Wide Web Consortium) had to come up with a standard for handling binary, or non-ASCII, form data. The solution? The HTML 3.2 Specification introduced a new form attribute: `enctype="multipart/form-data"`. Including this attribute in an HTML `<form>` tag instructs the browser that the contents of the submitted form will be encoded as binary data (the default content type is `"text/html"`):

```
<form name="upload" method="post" enctype="multipart/form-data">
```

Here's where the trouble begins. Once you add `enctype="multipart/form-data"` to an HTML form, the ASP Form collection cannot process the binary data. In plain English, this means that you can't use `Request.Form` on the action page to retrieve the values of the form fields. If you do, you'll receive an error message like this: "Cannot call BinaryRead after using Request.Form collection."

As a workaround, most ASP upload components offer an alternative Form collection to give you access to the form variables. Then what's the big deal? Dreamweaver's Insert Record server behavior uses the `Request.Form` collection. This means that if you script an upload using FileUp, and then apply the standard Insert Record SB, your ASP page won't work. This leaves you with two options: revise the standard Insert Record SB, or obtain a Dreamweaver MX upload extension that revises it for you.

Uploading files with ColdFusion, on the other hand, is much easier. This is because ColdFusion's FORM variables are still intact when the `enctype="multipart/form-data"` attribute is specified. In addition, upload support is built right into ColdFusion with the `<cffile>` tag. Whereas ASP requires you to instantiate an object, ColdFusion only requires a special tag. Here's an ASP example that uses Soft Artisans FileUp to upload an image:

```
<%
'*** Create an instance of the FileUp object ***
Set upl = Server.CreateObject("SoftArtisans.FileUp")

'*** Set the path to store uploaded file ***
upl.Path = Server.MapPath("/images/")

'*** Instruct FileUp to generate a unique filename
'if the file already exists on the server ***
upl.CreateNewFile = TRUE

'*** Save the file ***
upl.Save
%>
```

Here's a ColdFusion example that performs the same task:

```
<cffile action="upload" filefield="File1"
destination="#ExpandPath("images")#" nameconflict="makeunique">
```

Of course, there are other issues to keep in mind—for instance, many hosting providers disable the `<cffile>` tag for security reasons—but as you can see, ColdFusion gets the job done with a single line of code.

ASP Upload Components

There are literally dozens of ASP file upload components available on the Internet. Some are free, but most of the components that enjoy wide support require costly per-server or per-site licenses. Here are four of the most popular ASP upload components:

◆ **Soft Artisans FileUp** ($179)   Arguably the most popular ASP component, FileUp offers upload and download capabilities, and also comes bundled with FileManager and SMTPmail. Installation registers `safileup.dll` on your server. To use the progress indicator, you must manually register `saprgres.dll`. A 14-day trial is available from **www.softartisans.com**.

◆ **Persits AspUpload** ($149)   AspUpload offers many of the same features as FileUp and also includes a nifty HTML progress bar. The setup program automatically registers `aspupload.dll` on your server. For more information, and to download the 30-day trial, visit **www.persits.com**.

◆ **w3 Upload** ($49)   From the makers of the popular mail component, JMail, comes w3 Upload. Although the site license is relatively inexpensive, the trade-off is skimpy documentation. A free trial is available from **www.dimac.net**.

◆ **ASP Simple Upload** (free)   Because it's free, ASP Simple Upload is a favorite of discount NT hosting providers. The setup program automatically registers the component on your server. For more information, visit **www.asphelp.com**.

Before you run out and buy one of these components, check with your hosting provider. Chances are, they've already installed one of them on your remote server. If that's the case, visit the manufacturer's web site to view and download documentation and sample code.

Dreamweaver Upload Extensions

Of the four components just listed, only FileUp and AspUpload are supported by Dreamweaver extensions. ColdFusion users have two extensions to choose from: CF Upload and CFFILE. At the time of this writing, CFFILE is compatible only with UltraDev 4 pages.

◆ **CF Upload 1.2** (ColdFusion)   Written by Massimo Foti, CF Upload offers the same features as many commercial upload extensions at a very uncommercial price (i.e., free). Make sure to download the latest, Dreamweaver MX–compatible version from Massimo's web site: **www.massimocorner.com**.

◆ **CFFILE** (ColdFusion)   Tom Muck's CFFILE extension is like nine extensions in one. This is because the `<cffile>` tag supports many different actions, including `upload`, `move`, `rename`, `delete`, etc. Future versions will probably offer Dreamweaver MX support. For more information, visit **www.basic-ultradev.com**.

◆ **UltraUploads** (ASP)   The UltraSuite 4000 Extensions Package ($69.99) includes no fewer than 16 upload extensions: eight each for FileUp and AspUpload. Written by Jag S. Sidhu, these extensions are great time-savers. For more information, visit **www.ultrasuite.com**.

◆ **WA FileUp Integration Kit** (ASP)   WebAssist.com's FileUp Integration Kit extension ($29.99) is *not* compatible with Dreamweaver's standard Insert Record SB. In practical terms, this means you cannot use it with forms that contain non-binary data (i.e., text fields). For more information, visit **www.webassist.com**.

◆ **Pure ASP File Upload** (ASP)   George Petrov offers free and commercial versions of his popular Pure ASP File Upload extension on his web site, **www.udzone.com**. The commercial version, Pure ASP File Upload 2.0.8 ($49), comes with lots of extras, including the ability to save an image's dimensions to a database.

In fairness to WebAssist.com, Pure ASP File Upload is the only ASP upload extension that is compatible with Dreamweaver's standard Insert Record server behavior. So that's what we're going to use to revise the Add Listing page.

Revising the Add Listing Page

Now that we understand some of the advantages, and potential pitfalls, of implementing a file upload feature, let's revise Chip Havilmyer's Add Listing page. To do this, we'll use George Petrov's Pure ASP File Upload 2.0.8 extension (ASP) and the `<cffile>` tag (ColdFusion).

Using Pure ASP File Upload (ASP)

As you may recall, when you add the `enctype="multipart/form-data"` attribute to a `<form>` tag, the ASP Form collection is unable to process the binary data. To get around this, many ASP upload components offer their own Form collection to extract the values of the form fields (e.g., `upl.Form("FileDescription")`). But these collections aren't compatible with Dreamweaver's standard Insert Record SB. What's a developer to do?

One solution is to find every occurrence of `Request.Form` and `Request.QueryString` on your ASP page, and replace them with the new form object (e.g., `upLoad.Form`). This is easy enough to do using Dreamweaver's Find and Replace feature (Edit | Find And Replace). After applying these changes, however, the Insert Record SB can no longer be edited using the Server Behaviors panel.

The Pure ASP File Upload extension, on the other hand, detects the Insert Record SB, parses its code, and replaces `Request.Form` and `Request.QueryString` with `UploadFormRequest` and `UploadQueryString`, respectively.

Launch Dreamweaver MX and open `addListing.asp`. In the last chapter, we used George Petrov's Insert Record With Identity extension in place of Dreamweaver's standard Insert Record SB. Fortunately, since George is also the author of Pure ASP File Upload, the two extensions are compatible.

This recipe uses the commercial version of Pure ASP File Upload (version 2.0.8), and not Pure ASP File Upload 1.5. At the time of this writing, the free version is not compatible with Dreamweaver MX.

Follow these steps to apply Pure ASP File Upload to the Add Listing page:

1. From the Server Behaviors panel, choose UDzone | Pure ASP Upload 2.08. On the Main tab, click Browse and select the "`../images/listings`" directory.
2. Click the Images Only radio button and select MakeUnique from the Conflict Handling drop-down menu. Since there is only one form on the page, it should be selected automatically.

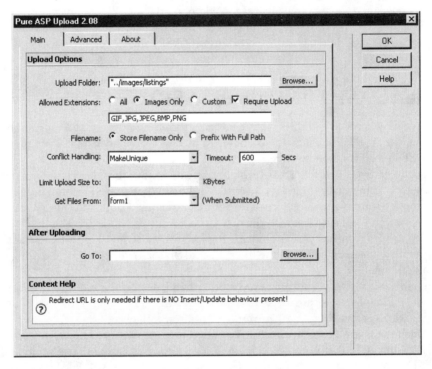

3. Ignore the remaining text boxes and click OK to apply Pure ASP File Upload.
4. A dialog box informs you that a new folder, `ScriptLibrary`, has been created in the site root. This folder and the file it contains—`incPureUpload.asp`—must be uploaded to your remote site for Pure ASP File Upload to work.

Now let's add the filename of the image to the database insert. Double-click Insert Record in the Server Behaviors panel. In the Form Elements area, select `File1` and choose `ListingPic` from the Column drop-down menu.

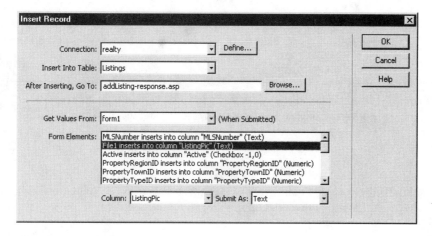

That's it! If you've installed MDAC 2.5 or higher, and you've set the NTFS permissions correctly, you should be able to test the upload feature on your local server. Save your work and press F12 to preview the page in a browser. Fill out all of the form fields and browse to an image on your hard drive. Click the Add Listing button. Your new listing should look something like this:

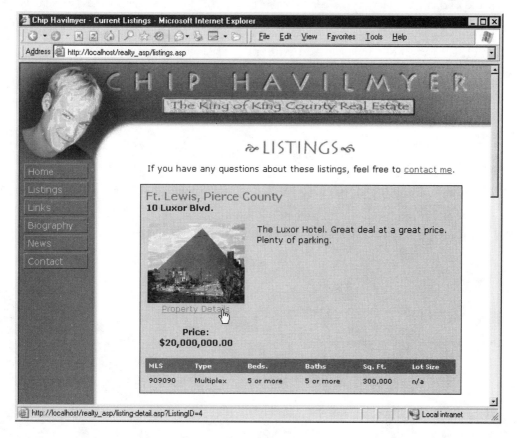

If you receive an error—e.g., "Syntax error in INSERT INTO statement"—verify that you completed all of the form fields. In particular, make sure *not* to insert any commas in the Price field.

Note

Pure ASP File Upload uses JavaScript to validate the file field. While this reduces the strain on the server, keep in mind that users can circumvent client-side code by disabling JavaScript in the browser.

If you're still having trouble, you may want to skip ahead to the "Form Validation" section. This will ensure that all of the form fields contain properly formatted data.

Using <cffile> (ColdFusion)

Uploading files with <cffile> is fairly straightforward. This is largely because ColdFusion's FORM variables are still intact when the enctype="multipart/form-data" attribute is added to the <form> tag. However, we do have one minor wrinkle to consider. Because we edited the Insert Record SB by hand in Chapter 12, we won't be able to use the Server Behaviors panel to revise the INSERT INTO statement. We're not going to let that stop us, are we?

Launch Dreamweaver MX and open addListing.cfm. Follow these steps to apply the <cffile> tag:

1. Switch to Code view and insert a new line after the opening <cfif> tag on line 2.

2. Select the CFML Advanced tab on the Insert bar and click the cffile button. This launches the Cffile tag editor.

3. Make sure Upload is selected from the Action drop-down menu and enter **File1** in the File Field text box.

4. Type **#ExpandPath("../images/listings")#** in the Destination Path text box.

5. In the Accept Files text box, enter **image/***.

6. Choose Makeunique from the Filename Resolution drop-down and leave the other text boxes blank. Click OK.

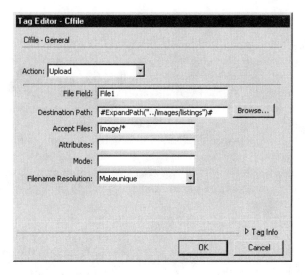

7. Now we're going to add some code to confirm that the image was uploaded. Insert a new line after the `<cffile>` tag and select the CFML Flow tab on the Insert bar. Hold down the CTRL key and click the isDefined button (holding down the CTRL key bypasses the dialog box).

8. Type **FILE**, followed by a period (`.`). Code Hints pops up with a list of available FILE parameters. Choose `FileWasSaved` and press ENTER.

9. Place your cursor between the opening and closing `<cfif>` tags and select the CFML Basic tab on the Insert bar. Click the cfset button. Complete the `<cfset>` tag as follows: `<cfset FORM.File1 = FILE.ServerFile>`.

   Save your work. The completed code should look like this:

```
<cffile action="upload" filefield="File1"
destination="#ExpandPath("../images/listings")#"
nameconflict="makeunique" accept="image/*">
<cfif isDefined("FILE.FileWasSaved")>
<cfset FORM.File1 = FILE.ServerFile></cfif>
```

For some reason, Code Hints doesn't appear when you type CFFILE, even though FILE is deprecated in ColdFusion MX. In any case, let's take a closer look at the code we just inserted.

How the Code Works

The `<cffile>` tag has three required attributes: `action`, `filefield`, and `destination`. Possible values for the `action` attribute include `upload`, `rename`, `move`, and `delete`. The `filefield` attribute expects the name of the form's file field (e.g., `File1`). The `destination` attribute requires the absolute path to the file or directory on the server. In order to extract this value from a relative path, we use the ColdFusion `ExpandPath` function. The `nameconflict` attribute, which is optional, accepts four possible values: `error`, `skip`, `overwrite`, and `makeunique`. If `makeunique` is specified, ColdFusion creates a unique filename for the upload and stores it in the `FILE` parameter, `ServerFile`. The `accept` attribute, also optional, allows you to require specific MIME types (e.g., `accept="application/pdf"`). You can also use wildcard characters (e.g., `accept="image/*"`) or a comma-delimited list (e.g., `accept="*.gif,*.jpg,*.png"`).

If the file upload is successful—i.e., if the `FILE.FileWasSaved` status parameter evaluates to true—we set the `FORM.File1` variable to `FILE.ServerFile`. This way, if ColdFusion changes the filename to make it unique, the new filename is inserted into the database. For more information about `<cffile>`, consult the *CFML Reference*.

Revising the INSERT INTO Statement

Before we can test the upload feature, we need to revise the SQL statement. Switch to Code view and locate the `<cfquery>` tag on line 6. Carefully add the `ListingPic` column to the beginning of `INSERT INTO` statement (the new code is shaded):

```
INSERT INTO Listings (ListingPic, ListingPrice, ListingAddress...
```

Now we have to add the form field, `File1`, to the `VALUES` clause. Insert a new line after `VALUES` (line 10) and enter the following code:

```
<cfif IsDefined("FORM.File1") AND #FORM.File1# NEQ "">
'#FORM.File1#'
<cfelse>
NULL
</cfif>
,
```

That should do it. Save your work and press F12 to preview the page in a browser. Browse to an image, fill out the form, and click the Add Listing button. Make sure *not* to place any commas in the Price field. Your new listing should look something like the following:

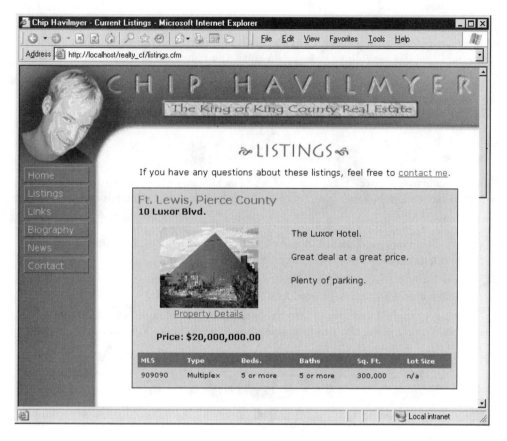

If you run into problems, make sure to complete all of the form fields on the page. Also check the NTFS permissions on the `images/listings` folder. The Internet Guest Account should have Read and Write permissions.

Form Validation

If you had trouble getting the Add Listing page to work, you can appreciate the importance of form validation: it protects the user from himself. To validate the Add Listing page, we'll use Jaro von Flocken's trusty Check Form extension. If you didn't install Check Form 4.66 in Chapter 5, you can download it from the Dreamweaver Exchange: **http://www.macromedia.com/exchange/ dreamweaver**. Of course, the usual admonitions about client-side validation apply.

Open the Add Listing page in Dreamweaver MX (`addListing.asp` or `addListing.cfm`, depending on your server model). Click `<form>` on the tag selector and choose yaromat | Check Form from the Behaviors panel. If you receive the following error message

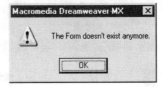

there is a conflict between Check Form and Pure ASP File Upload's `checkFileUpload` function. To use both behaviors on the same page, try the following workaround (ColdFusion users can skip steps 1, 7, and 8):

1. Open the Behaviors panel and change the Event trigger for `checkFileUpload` from `onSubmit` to `onReset`. Now choose yaromat | Check Form.

2. Using the list box, select each form element in turn and make sure it's required. (Select the Any radio button for the check boxes, `Active` and `Basement`.)

3. When you get to the `ListingPrice` field, select the second radio button to require a number. Enter **1** in the first text box, and **10000000** in the second text box.

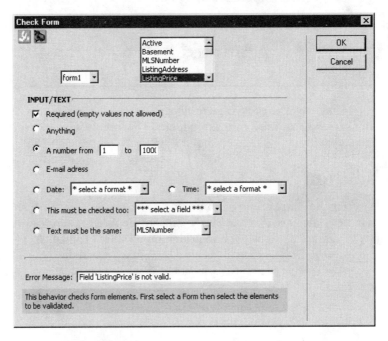

4. Do the same with `PropertyAge`, but specify a number from **1** to **200**.

5. On the last four fields—ListingDesc, Remarks, Equipment, Amenities— click the second radio button and enter **1** to make them required.

6. Click OK to apply the Check Form behavior.

> **Note**
>
> The workaround in steps 1, 7, and 8 is required only for ASP users.

7. Select the checkFileUpload function in the Behaviors panel and change its Event back to onSubmit.

8. If this changes the execution order of the scripts, select checkFileUpload in the Behaviors panel and click the Up arrow to make it first.

Now both behaviors are triggered by the form's onSubmit event.

> **Caution**
>
> Reapplying one of the behaviors may change the execution order of the scripts.

Save your work and press F12 to preview the page in a browser. Try submitting the page without completing all of the required fields. If you're able to foil the JavaScript validation routine, you may need to return to the Behaviors panel and tweak Check Form until you get it just right.

ColdFusion users may have noticed that the file field, `File1`, is not validated by the Check Form behavior. To address this, you can insert the following function into the `<head>` of the document (within the existing `<script>` tags):

```
function File_Validator(theFile){
  if (theFile.value == ''){
  alert('Please select an image.');
  theFile.focus();
  }
}
```

Call the function by adding it to the form's `onSubmit` event (*before* Jaro von Flocken's `YY_checkform` function):

```
onSubmit="File_Validator(File1); YY_checkform...
```

If you have any trouble getting this to work, take a look at the completed version of `addListing.cfm` in the `realty_cf` folder you downloaded earlier.

The Add Listing Details Page

Now that we've got the hang of file uploading, let's apply what we've learned to another admin page: Add Listing Details. Expand the `adminch` folder in the Site panel and open `addDetails.asp` (or `addDetails.cfm`). The purpose of this page is to allow Chip Havilmyer to add additional photos and descriptions to a selected listing. These photos are displayed on the Listing Details page (see Chapter 17).

The Add Listing Details page presents an interesting challenge. The dimensions of the uploaded image have to be saved to the `PicWidth` and `PicHeight` columns of the `ListingRooms` table. Why? Because Chip wants visitors to be able to click on thumbnail photos of the rooms to make full-size photos appear in pop-up windows. In order to open pop-up windows sized to the exact dimensions of the image, we need to store the width and height of the image in the database.

How do we do this? Fortunately, Pure ASP File Upload already includes this feature in its advanced options. ColdFusion users can take advantage of Massimo Foti's Check Image Upload behavior. Both of these extensions allow you to store an image's dimensions in hidden form fields.

Before we can apply these extensions, we need to create the hidden form fields. In the Document window, place your cursor inside the `addDetails` form and select the Forms tab on the Insert bar. Click the Hidden Field button twice. Using the Property inspector, name the hidden fields `PicWidth` and `PicHeight`.

Storing Image Dimensions in Hidden Fields (ASP)

Follow these steps to complete the Add Listing Details page:

1. From the Server Behaviors panel, choose Insert Record. Choose the realty connection and select `ListingRooms` from the Insert Into Table drop-down menu.

2. Most of the form fields and database columns should sync up nicely. Select `File1` in the Form Elements area and choose `ListingRoomPic` from the Column drop-down.

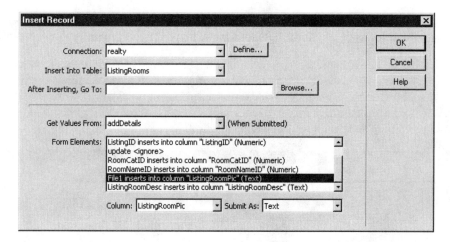

Click OK to apply the Insert Record SB.

3. Now we can upload the image. From the Server Behaviors panel, choose UDzone | Pure ASP Upload 2.08.

4. On the Main tab, click Browse and select the `"../images/listings/details"` folder.

5. Click the Images Only radio button and select MakeUnique from the Conflict Handling drop-down menu.

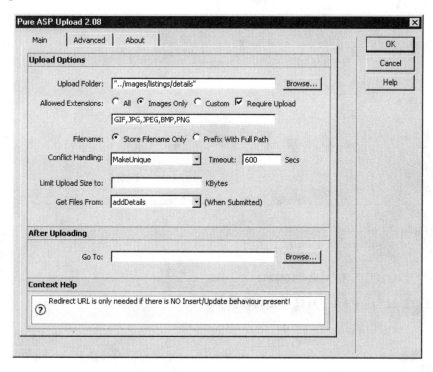

6. Click the Advanced tab and select `PicWidth` from the Save Width In drop-down. Select `PicHeight` from the Save Height In drop-down. Click OK to apply Pure ASP File Upload.

Save your work and press F12 to preview the page in a browser. The first listing, 15 King Street, appears by default. To work with a different listing, add a URL parameter to the page (e.g., **http://localhost/realty_asp/adminch/addDetails.asp?ListingID=3**).

Select an image and submit the form. If all goes well, the image is uploaded to `images/listings/details`, and the conditional region is displayed:

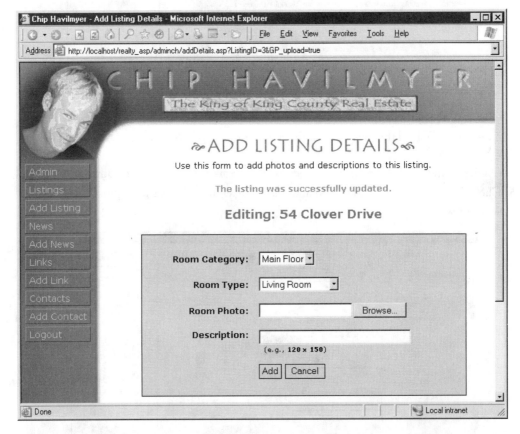

You can open the `ListingRooms` table in Microsoft Access to confirm that the image's width and height were saved to the `PicWidth` and `PicHeight` columns.

Storing Image Dimensions in Hidden Fields (ColdFusion)

Follow these steps to complete the Add Listing Details page:

1. Click `<form>` on the tag selector and choose Massimocorner | Check Image Upload from the Behaviors panel. The file field, `File1`, should be selected automatically.

2. On the Main tab, enter **1** as the minimum file size in the From text box.

3. Click the Advanced tab. From the first drop-down menu, Store Image's Width In Form Field, choose the `PicWidth` field. From the second drop-down, choose the `PicHeight` field.

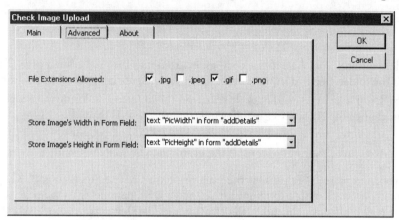

Click OK to apply Check Image Upload.

4. Now we can make the database insert. From the Server Behaviors panel, choose Insert Record. Choose realty from the Data Source drop-down menu, and `ListingRooms` from the Insert Into Table drop-down.

5. Most of the database columns and form fields should sync up nicely. Select `ListingRoomPic` in the Columns area and choose `FORM.File1` from the Value drop-down menu.

6. Leave the redirect text box empty and click OK to apply the Insert Record SB.

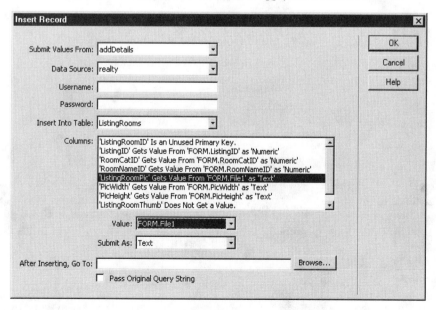

7. To upload the image, switch to Code view and enter the following code after the opening `<cfif>` tag on line 3.

```
<cffile action="upload" filefield="File1"
destination="#ExpandPath("../images/listings/details")#"
nameconflict="makeunique" accept="image/*">
<cfif isDefined("FILE.FileWasSaved")>
<cfset FORM.File1 = FILE.ServerFile></cfif>
```

This code is virtually identical to the code we inserted into the Add Listing page. The only change is the folder specified in the `destination` attribute of the `<cffile>` tag.

8. Switch back to Design view and click `<form>` on the tag selector. Using the Property inspector, change the Action to the following (the new code is shaded):

```
<cfoutput>#CurrentPage#?#CGI.QUERY_STRING#</cfoutput>
```

This way, the correct listing is selected if the visitor decides to make another insert.

Save your work and press F12 to preview the page in a browser. The first listing, 15 King Street, appears by default. To work with a different listing, add a URL parameter to the page (e.g., **http://localhost/realty_cf/adminch/addDetails.cfm?ListingID=3**).

Select an image and submit the form. If all goes well, the image is uploaded to images/ listings/details, and the conditional region is displayed:

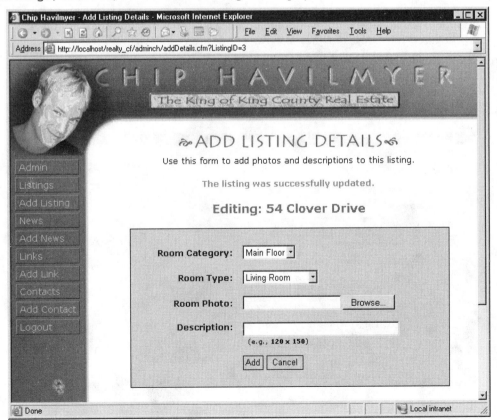

You can open the `ListingRooms` table in Microsoft Access to confirm that the image's width and height were saved to the `PicWidth` and `PicHeight` columns.

> **Note**
>
> Massimo's extension uses cutting-edge JavaScript to obtain the image's dimensions. So cutting-edge, in fact, that this feature—storing the image's dimensions in hidden fields—works only on PCs with Netscape 6+ or Internet Explorer 5+.

If you run into any problems, take a look at the completed version of the Add Listing Details page in the `realty_cf` folder you downloaded earlier.

Summary

In this chapter, we learned how to overcome some of the obstacles to implementing a file upload feature using ASP and ColdFusion. We also discussed the dreaded `enctype` attribute, and the merits and limitations of popular ASP upload components. Finally, we reviewed the current crop of Dreamweaver upload extensions to select the best tools for the job.

To sum up, in this chapter you learned to

◆ Create an insert-upload page using Pure ASP File Upload

◆ Create an insert-upload page using `<cffile>`

◆ Use `FILE.FileWasSaved` and `FILE.ServerFile`

◆ Validate an upload page using Check Form

◆ Validate a file field using Check Image Upload

◆ Store an image's dimensions in hidden form fields

In the next chapter, we'll revise the Add Listing page once more, so that Chip can preview an image on his hard drive before uploading it to his web site.

Chapter 14

Preview Image Before Upload

INGREDIENTS

File(s)	Type	Server Model(s)	Source
realty.mdb	Access database	ASP/CF	*Sample Code*
addListing.asp, preview.asp	Active Server Pages	ASP	*Sample Code*
addListing.cfm, preview.cfm	ColdFusion templates	CF	*Sample Code*
preview_iframe.htm	HTML page		*Sample Code*

from the desk of *Paul Newman*

C hip Havilmyer may be a successful realtor, but when it comes to computers, he's technologically challenged. Here's the dilemma: When Chip Havilmyer gets a new listing, he borrows the office camera, snaps a few pics, and turns them over to Jennifer, the in-house computer geek. Jennifer resizes the photos and e-mails them to Chip.

When Chip receives the photos as e-mail attachments, he saves them to his desktop. But because the photos were taken with a digital camera, they all have sequential names like `R0010023.jpg`, `R0010037.jpg`, `R0010044.jpg`, etc. "How do I know which file is the kitchen, and which file is the master bedroom?" he asks.

What can we do to help Chip out? You guessed it: an image preview feature.

Instead of creating an image preview feature from scratch, however, we're going to adapt a solution by extension developer Tom Steeper: "Preview File Before Uploading." (If you're curious, you can download the original code from Tom's web site: **www.webuality.com/t-cubed/sample_details.asp?SampleID=1**.)

Our revisions will focus on three areas:

1. Making the code cross-browser compatible

2. Customizing the image preview page

3. Scripting a version for ColdFusion

In addition, we're going to make the code reusable, so we can easily incorporate this feature into sites for other clients.

Revising the Add Listing Page

Tom Steeper's original code consists of two main components: a preview page written in ASP (`preview.asp`), and a JavaScript function that opens the preview page in a pop-up window. To make Tom's code reusable, we're going to revise the JavaScript to pass a single parameter to a function called `nz_PreviewImage`. This function will loop through the page's form elements to find the file field and extract its value. Then it will format the local file path for different browsers. Finally, it will open `preview.asp` (or `preview.cfm`) in a new window using Macromedia's `MM_openBrWindow` function.

If all of this doesn't make sense right now, don't worry: we'll take it step-by-step.

Adding the Preview Button

Before we create the `nz_PreviewImage` function, let's call it from the Add Listing page. Open `addListing.asp` (or `addListing.cfm`) in Dreamweaver MX. Place your cursor to the right of the file field (`File1`) and select the Forms tab on the Insert bar. Click Button. Using the Properties inspector, change the button's name and label to **Preview**, and its Action to None:

In the Document window, select the Preview button and press CTRL-T to open Quick Tag Editor. Enter the following code at the end of the tag, just before the closing > bracket:

```
onClick="nz_PreviewImage(this);"
```

This calls the `nz_PreviewImage` function and passes it the clicked button object as a parameter.

> **Note**
>
> The keyword `this` refers to the object that calls the script. Since the object, in this example, is the `Preview` button, `this` evaluates to `document.form1.Preview`.

If you click the Preview button now, nothing happens. That's because it calls a function that doesn't exist. So let's write it.

Writing the JavaScript Function

Before we start, let's agree on what we need the `nz_PreviewImage` function to do:

◆ Find the file field.

◆ Alert the visitor if the file field is empty.

◆ Construct the local file path for different browsers.

◆ Open the preview page in a pop-up window.

To open the pop-up window, we'll use a tried-and-true Macromedia function, `MM_openBrWindow`. The rest we'll have to script ourselves.

The first step is to place the functions within the `<head>` tags of the Add Listing page (`addListing.asp` or `addListing.cfm`). You may prefer to do this using your favorite text editor:

```
<SCRIPT Language="JavaScript" type="text/javascript">
<!--

function MM_openBrWindow(theURL,winName,features, ⤸
myWidth, myHeight, isCenter) { //v3.0
  if(window.screen)if(isCenter)if(isCenter=="true"){
    var myLeft = (screen.width-myWidth)/2;
    var myTop = (screen.height-myHeight)/2;
    features+=(features!='')?',':'';
    features+=',left='+myLeft+',top='+myTop;
  }
window.open(theURL,winName,features+((features!='')?',':'')Ã
+'width='+myWidth+',height='+myHeight);
```

```
}

function nz_PreviewImage(previewBtn){ //v 1.0
  var theform = previewBtn.form;  //find form object
}
//-->
</SCRIPT>
```

Where you place this code doesn't really matter, as long as it's between the `<head>` tags. However, you may want to place it just before the closing `</head>` tag to make it easier to find.

Looping Through Form Elements

As you can see, the `nz_PreviewImage` function isn't quite finished. All it does is declare a variable, `theform`, and set its value to the `Preview` button's form object (`form1`). What we want to do now is use the variable to find the file field. So insert the following `for` loop after the line where `theform` is declared (and before the closing `}` curly brace):

```
for (var i=0; i<theform.elements.length; i++){  //find file field
  var field = theform.elements[i];
  if (field.type.toUpperCase() == 'FILE'){var filefield = field; break;}
}
```

What this does is loop through all of the form elements in `form1` until the file field is located.

Note

If you plan to use more than one file field on the page, you'll have to revise this code accordingly.

Next, we declare a new variable, `filefield`, and set its value to the file field object. Finally, we use the JavaScript `break` keyword to terminate the loop and move to the next part of our script.

The Document Object Model (DOM)

A common JavaScript debugging technique is to use `alert` messages to return the values of objects, variables, and functions. You can try this by adding the following code after the `for` loop: `alert(filefield.name)`. Now browse to the Add Listing page on your local server and click the Preview button. You should receive the following JavaScript `alert` message:

Notice we specified `filefield.name`. If we remove the `name` parameter—
`alert(filefield)`—the message looks like this:

This is an important distinction to understand. JavaScript uses the browser's Document Object Model (DOM) to refer to elements of an HTML page. When you reference one of these elements—e.g., a form, a text field, an image—you are referencing an *object*. To obtain the name, value, or other properties and methods of an object, you use JavaScript dot notation to identify it. For example, `document.form1.elements[1].name` evaluates to `File1` because the file field is the second element of the Add Listing form (JavaScript starts counting from zero).

Now add the following `If-Else` statement after the `for` loop to validate the file field:

```
if (filefield.value == '') {alert('Please select an image.'); 
filefield.focus(); return false;}
  else {var thepath = filefield.value;}
```

If the file field is empty, the user is prompted to select an image. Otherwise, the value of the file field is stored in a new variable, `thepath`. Save your work and refresh the Add Listing page. Click the Preview button without browsing to an image. You should receive the following `alert` message, and a blinking cursor should appear in the file field:

Experiment with adding, and commenting out, `alert` messages throughout the script to see if the variables return the expected values.

Local File Paths

The reason Tom Steeper's original code doesn't work in Netscape and Opera is that these browsers use different local file paths than Internet Explorer (see Figure 14-1).

As you can see, Netscape and Opera place forward slashes in the path to a local file. What's more, Netscape prefixes the path with `file:///` and Opera prefixes it with `file://localhost/`.

Figure 14-1   *The local file path to* `luxor.jpg` *in Internet Explorer 6 (top), Netscape 6 (middle), and Opera 6 (bottom)*

So let's add an `If-Else If` statement to the function that reformats the path for Netscape and Opera:

```
if (thepath.indexOf('"') != -1){thepath = "file://" + ⤶
thepath.replace(/\"/g,"");} //make Opera path
  else if (navigator.appVersion.indexOf("MSIE") == -1)⤶
{thepath = "file:///" + thepath.replace(/\\/g,"/"); ⤶
thepath = thepath.replace(/\s/g,"%20");} //make NS path
  var thelink = "preview.asp?FILE=" + thepath;
```

The first line checks for double quotes in the file path (Opera places file field paths in quotation marks). If the `filepath` variable contains double quotes—e.g., `"C:\images\luxor.jpg"`—we use the string `replace` method to remove them. (The reason we don't change the backslashes to forward slashes is that Opera does this automatically.)

If the file path *doesn't* contain double quotes, we know the browser is either Netscape or Internet Explorer (or some other, unknown browser). So on the second line, we check the `appVersion` property of the `navigator` object. If it does *not* contain the string `"MSIE"`, then we know the browser is probably Netscape. To construct the Netscape path, we concatenate `"file:///"` and `thepath`. We also URL-encode any blank spaces by replacing them with `%20`. (Netscape 6, Opera, and Internet Explorer URL-encode spaces automatically, but Netscape 4 does not.)

Note

In case you're wondering, those *are* regular expressions. The string `replace` method takes two arguments: a regular expression, and the replacement string. In the following example, the regular expression searches for every occurrence of a backslash in `thepath` and replaces it with a forward slash:

`thepath.replace(/\\/g,"/")`.

Finally, we create a new variable, `thelink`, and set its value to `"preview.asp?FILE="` + `thepath`. This appends the value of `thepath` to the preview page as a URL parameter. Here's what `thelink` will look like in different browsers:

```
preview.asp?FILE=C:\images\luxor.jpg (Internet Explorer)
preview.asp?FILE=file:///C:/images/luxor.jpg (Netscape)
preview.asp?FILE=file://C:\images\luxor.jpg (Opera)
```

Now all we have to do is pass `thelink` to the `MM_OpenBrWindow` function as a parameter. So insert the following line at the end of our function, just before the closing } curly brace:

```
MM_openBrWindow(thelink,'preview',↵
'scrollbars=auto,resizable=yes','450','470','true')
```

The final code for the `nz_PreviewImage` function should look like this:

```
function nz_PreviewImage(previewBtn){ //v 1.0
  var theform = previewBtn.form;                    //find form object
  for (var i=0; i<theform.elements.length; i++){  //find file field
    var field = theform.elements[i];
    if (field.type.toUpperCase() == 'FILE'){var filefield = field; break;}
  }
  if (filefield.value == ''){alert('Please select an image.');↵
filefield.focus(); return false;}
  else {var thepath = filefield.value;}
  if (thepath.indexOf('"') != -1) ↵
{thepath = "file://" + thepath.replace(/\"/g,"");} //make Opera path
  else if (navigator.appVersion.indexOf("MSIE") == -1) ↵
{thepath = "file:///" + thepath.replace(/\\/g,"/"); ↵
thepath = thepath.replace(/\s/g,"%20");} //make NS path
  var thelink = "../preview/preview.asp?FILE=" + thepath;
  MM_openBrWindow(thelink,'preview',↵
'scrollbars=auto,resizable=yes','450','470','true')
}
```

Notice anything different? I changed the path to the preview page to `../preview/preview.asp`. This is because the template for the preview page resides in the `preview` folder. (If you're using ColdFusion, change the path to `../preview/preview.cfm`.)

Save your work and close the Add Listings page. In the next section, we're going to edit the preview page to display the selected image in an embedded IFRAME.

Creating the Preview Page

Launch Dreamweaver MX and expand the `preview` folder in the Site panel. Open the preview page (`preview.asp` or `preview.cfm`, depending on your server model). The Document window should look something like this:

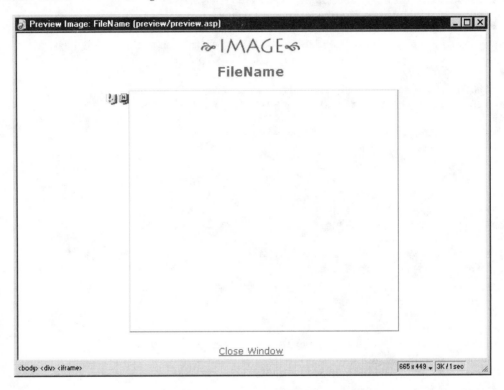

Press F12 to preview the page in a browser. This is what we want the completed page to look like. The image—in this case, `luxor.jpg`—is displayed in an `<iframe>` tag. The source of the `<iframe>` tag is `preview_iframe.htm`, which is also located in the `preview` folder.

If you haven't used IFRAMES before, an IFRAME is a floating frame object that can be placed anywhere on an HTML page. Its width, height, and border are determined by tag attributes:

```
<iframe width="380" height="330" frameborder="0" ↵
style="border: 1px solid gray;" src="preview_iframe.htm"></iframe>
```

The `<iframe>` tag is supported by Internet Explorer 3+, Netscape 6+, and Opera 5+. Since we don't know the dimensions of the image the user will select, an IFRAME is the ideal solution. This way, if the image is larger than the pop-up window, the user can scroll to see all of it.

Tip

Dreamweaver MX doesn't have an IFRAME Property inspector, but you can download one from **www.massimocorner.com** or the Macromedia Exchange. In addition, you can right-click the `<iframe>` tag in Code view and edit its attributes using tag editor.

If you switch to Code view, you'll see that the path to the image is contained in a JavaScript variable near the top of the page:

```
strFullPath = ↵
"C:\\Inetpub\\wwwroot\\realty_asp_empty\\www\\images\\luxor.jpg" (ASP)
strFullPath = ↵
"C:\\Inetpub\\wwwroot\\realty_cf_empty\\www\\images\\luxor.jpg" (CF)
```

The IFRAME source page, `preview_iframe.htm`, uses the value of the `strFullPath` variable to display the selected image. Right now, the value is hard-coded. We want it to be dynamic, so set the value of `strFullPath` to the URL parameter we passed from the Add Listing page:

```
strFullPath = "<%= Replace(Request("FILE"),"\","\\") %>" (ASP)
strFullPath = "<cfoutput>#Replace(URL.FILE,"\","\\","ALL")#</cfoutput>" (CF)
```

Save your work and browse to the Add Listing page on your local server. Use the Browse button to select an image and click Preview. The pop-up window should look something like this:

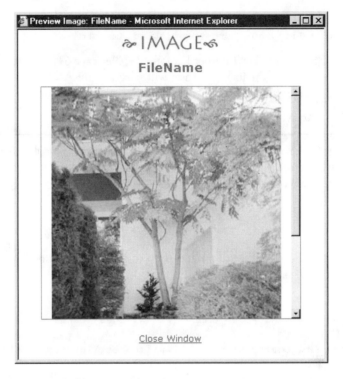

We could leave the preview page as it is, but wouldn't it be cool to display the name of the selected file? (I was hoping you'd feel that way.)

Revising the Preview Page (ASP)

Tom Steeper's original code extracts the filename and extension of the selected image to redirect the page if the user doesn't select a GIF or JPG file. In the sections that follow, most of Tom's code is intact. All I've done is add some comments to make it easier to follow.

Extracting the Filename and Extension

Open `preview.asp` in Dreamweaver MX and switch to Code view. At the top of the page, before the opening `<html>` tag, insert the following code:

```
<%@LANGUAGE="VBSCRIPT"%>
<% Response.Buffer = True %>
```

```
<%
' Preview Image - P.R. Newman - www.newmanzone.com
' (Based on code by Tom Steeper - www.webuality.com/t-cubed)

Dim FullPath, pathArray, FileName, FilenameArray, Extension

FullPath = Request.QueryString("FILE")
If InstrRev(FullPath, "\") Then    ' If FullPath is like C:\images\luxor.jpg
   pathArray=Split(FullPath,"\")   ' converts FullPath into array
Else
   pathArray=Split(FullPath,"/")   ' Netscape uses forward slashes
End If
FileName=UBound(pathArray)         ' returns upper bound of FullPath array ⤷
(e.g., 2)
FileName=pathArray(FileName)       ' returns luxor.jpg
filenameArray=Split(FileName,".")  ' converts FileName into array
Extension=UBound(filenameArray)    ' returns upper bound of FileName array ⤷
(e.g., 1)
Extension=filenameArray(Extension) ' returns jpg
%>
```

As you can see, there's a lot going on here, so let's review it line-by-line.

1. After the language declaration at the top of the page, we dimension our variables. Then we set FullPath to the value of the FILE query string (e.g., C:\images\luxor.jpg).

2. Next, we use an If-Else statement to check whether FullPath contains forward slashes or backslashes. (As you may recall, the nz_PreviewImage function formats the Netscape path using forward slashes.)

3. Next we create a one-dimensional array, pathArray, using the VBScript Split function. The Split function accepts up to four arguments, but we're using only the first two. The first argument is the string expression, FullPath, and the second argument is the delimiter. (If you omit the second argument, the default delimiter is an empty space.) For example, if the value of FullPath is C:\images\luxor.jpg, and the delimiter is a backslash, the array would consist of three elements: C:, images, and luxor.jpg. To access the second element of the array, you would use pathArray(1), which returns images.

4. Next, we use another VBScript function, UBound, to obtain the "upper bound" of the array. In the previous example, the array contains three elements, so the value of Ubound(pathArray) would be 2 (VBScript starts counting from zero). This allows us to extract the filename from the path: FileName = pathArray(Filename).

5. Now that we know the filename, we can use the Split function again to retrieve the file's extension. This time, a period (.) is the delimiter. Since FileName evaluates to luxor.jpg, filenameArray contains two elements: luxor and jpg. (If the file were named luxor.hotel.jpg, the array would contain three elements.)

6. We use same technique to obtain the upper bound of `filenameArray`—the `UBound` function—and set the value of `Extension` to `filenameArray(Extension)`. In our example, this would return `jpg`.

Now that we've got our `FileName` variable, we can use it in the preview page. In the Title text box of the Document toolbar (View | Toolbars | Document), replace "FileName" with `<%= FileName %>`. In the Document window, select "FileName" and select the ASP tab on the Insert bar. Click the Output button. Finally, change the JavaScript variable on line 32 to the following:

```
strFullPath = "<%= Replace(FullPath,"\","\\") %>"
```

Save your work and browse to the Add Listing page on your local server. Give it a test-drive.

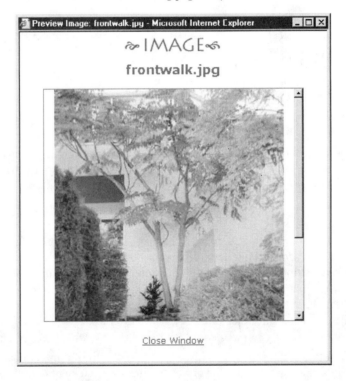

Pretty sweet, huh? But what happens if the visitor selects a text file or a QuickTime movie? Read on, kimosabe.

Server-Side Validation

In order to redirect the page if the user doesn't select a GIF or JPG image, we're going to create an `If-Else` statement that checks the value of the `Extension` variable.

Switch to Code view and locate the opening <html> tag. Enter the following code above it:

```
<%
If (UCase(Extension) = "JPG") OR (UCase(Extension) = "GIF") Then
%>
```

Now scroll to the end of the document and place the following code after the closing </html> tag:

```
<%
Else
Response.Redirect(FullPath)
End If
%>
```

First, we use the VBScript UCase string function to convert the Extension variable to uppercase format. Then we check if Extension equals "GIF" or "JPG". If it does, the preview page is displayed. Otherwise, the visitor is redirected to the unknown file.

Note

The Redirect method may not work in Netscape, resulting in an "Object Moved" error. Even though we set Response.Buffer to true, the content has already been sent to the browser. Opera and Internet Explorer should handle the redirect properly. (Incidentally, buffering is set to true by default in IIS 5.0 and later.)

Now browse to the Add Listing page and click the Preview button. If you browse to a file with a different extension, such as an MP3, the page should redirect. Alternatively, you can replace Response.Redirect(FullPath) with a Response.Write statement instructing the user to choose a GIF or JPG file. If you want to take this a step further, you can use a Select Case statement to dynamically render different tags according to the value of Extension.

Revising the Preview Page (ColdFusion)

Tom Steeper's original code extracts the filename and extension of the selected image to redirect the page if the user doesn't select a GIF or JPG file. We're going to adapt this code for ColdFusion using CFScript.

Using CFScript

CFScript implements the same functions, variables, and operators you're accustomed to using in ColdFusion tags. The main difference is that functions and variables between <cfscript> tags do not have to be delimited by the pound sign (#). For example, to define the `FullPath` variable using ColdFusion tags, you would do this:

```
<cfset FullPath="#URL.FILE#">
```

In CFScript, the code would look like this:

```
<cfscript>FullPath = URL.FILE;</cfscript>
```

CFScript syntax is similar to JavaScript in the sense that it encloses control statements in curly braces:

```
If (FullPath CONTAINS "\") {
  pathArray = ListToArray(FullPath,"\");
}
Else {
  pathArray = ListToArray(FullPath,"/");
}
```

Although CFScript is based on JavaScript, there are some important differences to keep in mind:

◆ You cannot use CFML tags in CFScript.

◆ You cannot create user-defined functions.

◆ CFScript is case-insensitive.

◆ All statements must end with a semicolon.

The last point is important: if you omit the semicolon (;) at the end of a statement, the script will "bomb."

Extracting the Filename and Extension

Open `preview.cfm` in Dreamweaver MX and switch to Code view. At the top of the page, before the opening `<html>` tag, insert the following code:

```
<cfscript>
// Preview Image - P.R. Newman - www.newmanzone.com
// (Based on code by Tom Steeper - www.webuality.com/t-cubed)
FullPath = URL.FILE;
```

```
If (FullPath CONTAINS "\") { //If FullPath is like C:\images\luxor.jpg
  pathArray = ListToArray(FullPath,"\"); //converts FullPath into array
}
Else {
  pathArray = ListToArray(FullPath,"/"); //Netscape uses forward slashes
}

FileName = ArrayLen(pathArray); //returns length of FullPath array ⏎
(e.g., 3)
FileName = pathArray[FileName];           //returns luxor.jpg
filenameArray = ListToArray(FileName,"."); //converts FileName into array
Extension = ArrayLen(filenameArray);      //returns length of FileName ⏎
array (e.g., 2)
Extension = filenameArray[Extension];     //returns jpg
</cfscript>
```

Since CFScript is still new to many ColdFusion users, let's review the code line-by-line:

1. After the opening <cfscript> tag, we set the variable FullPath to the value of the FILE query string (e.g., C:\images\luxor.jpg).

2. Next, we use an If-Else statement to check whether FullPath contains forward slashes or backslashes. (As you may recall, the nz_PreviewImage function formats the Netscape path using forward slashes.) CONTAINS is a ColdFusion decision operator, like IS and NEQ.

3. Next we create a one-dimensional array, pathArray, using the ColdFusion ListToArray function. The ListToArray function takes two arguments: the list (FullPath) and the delimiter ("\"). For example, if the value of FullPath is C:\images\luxor.jpg, the array consists of three elements: C:, images, and luxor.jpg. To access the second element of the array, we would use pathArray[2], which returns images. (In ColdFusion, array indexes start with 1. This may seem counterintuitive, since the index number in JavaScript arrays starts with 0.)

4. Next, we use another ColdFusion function, ArrayLen, to obtain the length of the array. In the previous example, the array contains three elements, so the value of ArrayLen(pathArray) would be 3. This allows us to extract the filename from the path: FileName = pathArray[Filename].

5. Now that we know the filename, we can use the ListToArray function again to retrieve the file's extension. This time, a period (.) is the delimiter. Since FileName evaluates to luxor.jpg, filenameArray contains two elements: luxor and jpg. (If the file were named luxor.hotel.jpg, the array would contain three elements.)

6. Finally, we use `ArrayLen` again to determine the length of `filenameArray`. Then we set the value of `Extension` to `filenameArray[Extension]`. In our example, this would return `jpg`.

Now that we've got our `FileName` variable, we can use it in the preview page. In the Title text box of the Document toolbar (View | Toolbars | Document), replace "FileName" with `<cfoutput>#FileName#</cfoutput>`. In the Document window, select "FileName" and select the CFML Basic tab on the Insert bar. Click the Surround with # button. This wraps `FileName` with ColdFusion pound signs. Now click the cfoutput button to wrap `#FileName#` with `<cfoutput>` tags.

Finally, change the JavaScript variable on line 28 to the following:

```
strFullPath = "<cfoutput>#Replace(FullPath,"\","\\","ALL")#</cfoutput>"
```

At this point, the Document window should look like this:

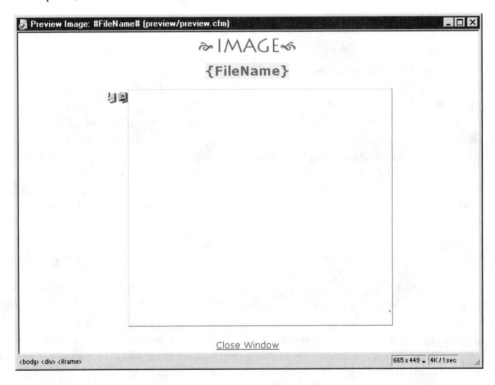

Save your work and browse to the Add Listing page on your local server. Try out the image preview feature.

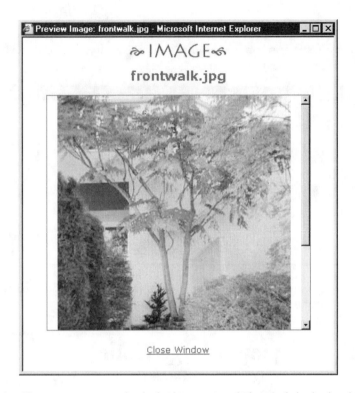

Notice that the filename appears in both the browser's title bar and the body of the page.

Server-Side Validation

Now that the image preview feature is working, what happens if Chip selects a Microsoft Word document? To display an error message if the user doesn't select a GIF or JPG image, we'll create an If-Else statement that checks the value of the Extension variable.

Switch to Code view and locate the preview image (`preview.gif`). Enter the following code after the `<img>` tag:

```
<cfif (#UCase(Extension)# IS "JPG") OR (#UCase(Extension)# IS "GIF")>
```

Now scroll to the end of the document and place the following code after the closing `</iframe>` tag:

```
<cfelse>
<p class="hline">Please select a GIF or JPG image.</p>
</cfif>
```

First, we use the ColdFusion UCase function to convert the Extension variable to uppercase format. Then we check if Extension equals "GIF" or "JPG". If it does, the preview page is displayed. Otherwise, the visitor sees an error message.

If you want to take this a step further, you can use <cfswitch> and <cfcase> to dynamically render different tags according to the value of Extension.

Reusing the Preview Image Code

In the beginning of this recipe, we decided to write reusable code so that we can employ this feature on other web sites. One way to do this is to write a Dreamweaver extension. Another solution is to add the JavaScript functions, MM_openBrWindow and nz_PreviewImage, to the Snippets panel so that you can easily insert them into the <head> of other documents.

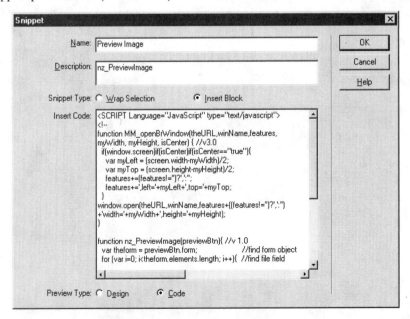

Of course, you'll have to copy the `preview` folder to the root of your new site. In addition, you'll need to edit the image tag and style sheet link. Alternatively, you can make the preview page more generic—and therefore more reusable—by removing the references to external files.

Summary

In this chapter, we created an image preview feature for Chip Havilmyer's site by adapting Tom Steeper's ASP code. Hopefully, this recipe helped you master some fundamental "cooking" techniques in Dreamweaver MX (not to mention JavaScript, VBScript, and CFScript). Some of the new skills you acquired include

- Creating a custom JavaScript function
- Calling the function from a button's `onClick` event
- Embedding an IFRAME in an HTML page
- Creating an array using the VBScript `Split` function (ASP)
- Creating an array using the `ListToArray` function (ColdFusion)
- Writing reusable code

In the next chapter, "Batch Deletes," we'll create a page that allows Chip to remove listings from his web site. In addition to deleting the database entries, we'll delete the associated image files from the server.

Chapter ⬤15

Batch Deletes

INGREDIENTS

File(s)	Type	Server Model(s)	Source
realty.mdb	Access database	ASP/CF	*Sample Code*
links.asp, listings.asp	Active Server Pages	ASP	*Sample Code*
links.cfm, listings.cfm	ColdFusion templates	CF	*Sample Code*
Popup Confirm Message	Behavior		George Petrov

from the desk of *Paul Newman*

I n this chapter, we're going to work on two of Chip Havilmyer's admin pages: Links and Current Listings. Each of these pages deletes multiple records from the Realty database. Since the Links page is relatively easy, we'll tackle it first. The admin Listings page, on the other hand, poses a number of challenges.

Every time a new listing is added to Chip's site, the Add Listing page makes inserts into two tables: `Listings` and `ListingRealtors`. (`ListingRealtors`, as you may recall, is the "linking" table we created to accommodate listings with multiple realtors.) If the user adds additional photos to the listing, the Add Details page makes inserts into a third table: `ListingRooms`. Practically speaking, this means that in order to delete a single listing from Chip's site, we have to do the following:

◆ Delete record(s) from `ListingRooms`.

◆ Delete associated image(s) from the server.

◆ Delete record from `Listings`.

◆ Delete associated image from the server.

◆ Delete record(s) from `ListingRealtors`.

That's a pretty tall order. But we're going to deliver it with a single click of a button. Behind the scenes, the Delete Listing page performs all the necessary deletes according to the value of a single URL parameter (e.g., `delete-listing.asp?ListingID=3`).

The Dangers of DELETE Statements

How many times have you deleted a file from your computer, only to scavenge through the Recycle Bin a week or two later, like an electronic dumpster-diver? Databases don't have recycle bins: once you delete a record, it's gone forever. This is why many database management systems restrict `DELETE` permission to the database owner and administrator.

The SQL syntax for deleting a record from a database is simple. For example, to delete a record from the `Listings` table in the Realty database, we could write the following statement:

```
DELETE FROM Listings
WHERE ListingID = 3
```

As you would expect, this deletes one row from the `Listings` table—the row in which the primary key, `ListingID`, equals 3. If you omit the `WHERE` clause, *all* of the rows in the `Listings` table are deleted. Fortunately, Dreamweaver MX won't let you create a `DELETE` statement without a `WHERE` clause using the standard Delete Record SB. But you *can* create a `WHERE`-less `DELETE` statement using a command. Therefore, as a precaution, you should run your `DELETE` statement as a `SELECT` statement first, to ensure it returns the right data:

```
SELECT * FROM Listings
WHERE ListingID = 3
```

Let's look at another example using the `Links` table. To return two records from the table, we could write the following SQL statement:

```
SELECT * FROM Links
WHERE LinkID = 2 OR LinkID = 5
```

Here's a shorthand method that returns the same results:

```
SELECT * FROM Links
WHERE LinkID IN (2,5)
```

The `IN` operator accepts a comma-delimited list or subquery as an argument. In this example, the `IN` operator is followed by a list of values. If any of the values in parentheses match the criteria, they are returned in the results of the `SELECT` statement.

The `IN` operator can also be used in `DELETE` statements. To delete two records from the `Links` table, we could write the following statement:

```
DELETE FROM Links
WHERE LinkID IN (2,5)
```

If the very idea of using `DELETE` statements gives you the willies, there is an alternative. As you probably noticed, the `Listings` table has a Yes/No (or bit) column called `Active`. Instead of permanently deleting a listing, Chip can change its status to inactive by unchecking the `Active` column.

If you open `realty.mdb` in Microsoft Access, you'll notice that several of the queries exist in two versions. Open the `Listings` table and uncheck the `Active` column in the third listing. Run the `qListings` query. It returns only two records. Now run the `qListingsAdmin` query. Voilà: the third listing is back. If you examine `qListings` in Design view, you'll see that the Criteria cell of the `Active` column contains the following value: `<>0`. (Don't forget to change the `Active` column in the `Listings` table back to its original value.)

The Links Page

The admin Links page allows Chip Havilmyer to delete multiple records using check boxes. Without further ado, open the Links page in Dreamweaver MX (`adminch/links.asp` or `adminch/links.cfm`, depending on your server model).

To save time, I've already applied a recordset and repeat region to the page. If you open the recordset, `rsLinks`, you'll see that it displays only records in which the `RealtorID` column equals `1`. This is a hard-coded value, rather than a session variable, because sessions aren't covered until later in the book.

Also notice the Delete button above the check box. This button submits the form if one or more check boxes are checked (a JavaScript in the `<head>` of the document validates the form). Right now, submitting the form has no effect because we haven't applied a Delete Record SB. So let's do that.

The Delete Record SB (ASP)

From the Server Behaviors panel, choose Delete Record. Choose the realty connection and select Links from the Delete From Table drop-down menu. Since rsLinks is the only recordset on the page, it should be selected automatically. Choose LinkID from the Unique Key Column drop-down, and make sure Numeric is checked. Leave the redirect text box empty. Click OK to apply the SB.

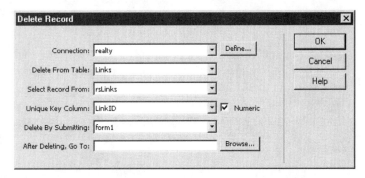

Notice that the Delete Record SB adds two hidden fields to the end of the form: MM_delete and MM_recordId.

Tip If you can't see the hidden form fields in the Document window, choose View | Visual Aids | Invisible Elements.

The hidden form fields determine whether the Delete Record code block is executed:

```
if (CStr(Request("MM_delete")) <> "" ↵
And CStr(Request("MM_recordId")) <> "") Then
```

MM_recordId holds the value of rsLinks.LinkID and appears in the SQL DELETE statement (around line 67):

```
MM_editQuery = "delete from " & MM_editTable & ↵
" where " & MM_editColumn & " = " & MM_recordId
```

The Delete Record SB is designed to delete a single record according to the value of MM_recordId. We want to delete multiple records. So right-click the MM_recordId icon in the Document window and choose Value. Press CTRL-X to cut the value and click OK. Now right-click the check box and choose Value. Press CTRL-V to paste the value and click OK. Repeat these steps with the Name attribute, cutting it from the hidden field and pasting it into the check box. (You can delete the empty hidden field now.)

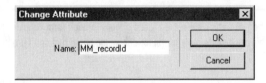

Save your work and press F12 to preview the page. View the browser's source. Notice that each check box has a different value. These values correspond to the primary key (`Links.LinkID`) of each record. Return to the Document window and click `<form>` on the tag selector. Using the Property inspector, click the folder icon and choose `form-tester.asp` in the site's root folder. Save your work and preview the page in a browser. Check off two or three links and click Delete. Your browser should look something like this:

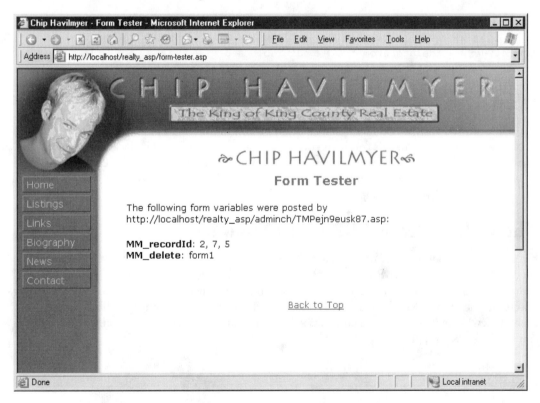

Notice the `MM_recordId` form variable: its value is a comma-delimited list. Look familiar? Return to Dreamweaver MX and choose Edit | Undo Set Attribute, or press CTRL-Z to restore the form's action page.

> **Note**
>
> In case you're wondering, `form-tester.asp` loops through form variables posted by *any* page — not just the Links page. This can be extremely useful for debugging pages that don't produce the expected results.

Remember the `IN` operator we discussed earlier? Let's add it to the SQL `DELETE` statement. Switch to Code view and find the `DELETE` statement:

```
MM_editQuery = "delete from " & MM_editTable & ⏎
" where " & MM_editColumn & " = " & MM_recordId
```

Change this code to the following (the new code is shaded):

```
MM_editQuery = "delete from " & MM_editTable & ⏎
" where " & MM_editColumn & " IN (" & MM_recordId & ")"
```

That's it. The Links page is done. (You were expecting hollandaise sauce?)

Save your work and test the page (needless to say, make a backup of the Realty database before you delete any records). Works like a charm, doesn't it?

Now you can implement this feature on other pages and sites. In fact, if you want some more practice, try applying the same feature to the admin Contacts page (`adminch/contacts.asp`).

We were lucky this time: the Links page doesn't require deleting associated images. If only the admin Listings page were this simple!

The Delete Record SB (ColdFusion)

If it's not open already, open `links.cfm` in Dreamweaver MX. From the Server Behaviors panel, choose Delete Record. Select Primary Key Value from the first drop-down menu, and select the realty data source. Choose `Links` from the Table drop-down menu. By default, `LinkID` is selected as the Primary Key Column, and Numeric is checked. Choose Form Variable from the Primary Key Value drop-down and enter **LinkID** in the text box. Leave the redirect text box empty. Click OK to apply the Delete Record SB.

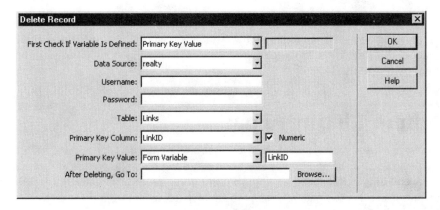

Switch to Code view and examine the code Dreamweaver MX generates to delete the record:

```
<cfif IsDefined("FORM.LinkID") AND #FORM.LinkID# NEQ "">
<cfquery datasource="realty">
DELETE FROM Links WHERE LinkID=#FORM.LinkID#
</cfquery>
</cfif>
```

The SQL statement is almost identical to the one we discussed earlier in the chapter. Since we want to delete multiple records, change the SQL statement to the following:

```
DELETE FROM Links WHERE LinkID IN (#FORM.LinkID#)
```

Now we need to create the form variable that appears in the SQL statement. Switch back to Design view and select the check box. Using the Property inspector, name it **LinkID**. In the Checked Value text box, enter **#rsLinks.LinkID#**.

> **Note**
>
> The reason `#rsLinks.LinksID#` is not wrapped in `<cfoutput>` tags is that the repeat region already uses `<cfoutput>` to loop through the `rsLinks` recordset.

Save your work and press F12 to preview the page. View the browser's source. Notice that each check box has a different value. Try checking off a couple rows and clicking Delete (needless to say, make a backup of the Realty database first). It doesn't get much easier, does it?

Now you can implement this feature on other pages and sites. In fact, if you want some more practice, try applying the same steps to the admin Contacts page (`adminch/contacts.cfm`).

We were lucky this time: the Links page doesn't require deleting associated images. If only the admin Listings page were this simple!

The Admin Listings Page

In order to remove a listing from Chip Havilmyer's web site, we have to delete records from three tables—`ListingRooms`, `Listings`, and `ListingRealtors`—as well as any associated images. If we were using SQL Server, we could write a stored procedure to delete entries from three tables, but that still doesn't address the problem of deleting files from the server.

Open the admin Listings page in Dreamweaver MX (`adminch/listings.asp` or `adminch/listings.cfm`, depending on your server model). As you can see, the Listings page links to four other pages using button images: Edit Listing, Add Listing Details, Edit Listing Details, and Delete Listing. It's the last page that concerns us right now. We're going to link to the Delete Listing page and pass it the current value of `Listings.ListingID` as a URL parameter. On the Delete Listing page, we'll use the value of the URL parameter to query the `ListingRooms` and `Listings` tables for associated images, and make the required deletes.

First, let's create a recordset to display the current listings. From the Bindings panel, choose Recordset and name it `rsListings`. Choose the realty connection (or data source) and select `qListingsAdmin` from the Table drop-down menu. This query returns all of the current listings, even if the value of the `Active` column is false. Choose the Selected Columns radio button and select the following columns: `ListingID`, `MLSNumber`, `ListingAddress`, and `Active`.

Click Test. The SQL statement returns four records. This is because Chip Havilmyer and Jane Doe share the third listing. So choose `RealtorID` from the Filter drop-down, and set the Entered Value to `1` (later, you can change Entered Value to Session Variable). Finally, sort the records by `ListingID` in descending order (this displays the most recent listing first). Click OK to apply the Recordset.

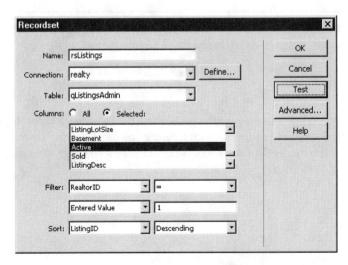

Use the Bindings panel to bind `rsListings.MLSNumber` and `rsListings.ListingAddress` to the text placeholders in the Document window ("MLS Number" and "Address," respectively).

Displaying the Active Column (ASP)

Place your cursor to the left of the word "Active" in the Document window. Select the ASP tab on the Insert bar and click the If button. Dreamweaver MX switches to Split view. Complete the `If` statement as follows:

```
<% If rsListings("Active") <> 0 Then %>Active
```

This displays the word "Active" if the `Active` column is checked in the `Listings` table. Let's add an `Else` statement to display "Inactive" if the column is unchecked. Place your cursor at the end of the preceding line and click Else on the Insert bar. Type **Inactive**. Click the End button on the Insert bar. The completed code should look like this:

```
<% If rsListings("Active") <> 0 Then %>Active<% Else %>Inactive<% End If %>
```

Save your work.

Displaying the Active Column (ColdFusion)

Select the word "Active" in the Document window. Choose the CFML Flow tab on the Insert bar and click the cfif button. Dreamweaver MX switches to Split view. Complete the `<cfif>` statement as follows:

```
<cfif rsListings.Active NEQ 0>Active</cfif>
```

This displays the word "Active" if the `Active` column is checked in the `Listings` table. Let's add a `<cfelse>` tag to display "Inactive" if the column is unchecked. Place your cursor before the closing `</cfif>` tag and click cfelse on the Insert bar. Type **Inactive**. The completed code should look like this:

```
<cfif rsListings.Active NEQ 0>Active<cfelse>Inactive</cfif>
```

Save your work.

Creating the Repeat Region

Switch back to Design view and use the tag selector to select the table row (`<tr>`) we've been working on. From the Server Behaviors panel, choose Repeat Region. Select the Show All Records radio button and click OK.

Now we need to link to the Delete Listing page. Select the delete button (the Recycle Bin icon) in the Document window. Using the Property inspector, enter the following code in the Link text box:

```
delete-listing.asp?ListingID=<%= rsListings("ListingID") %> (ASP)
delete-listing.cfm?ListingID=#rsListings.ListingID# (ColdFusion)
```

Since deleting a listing is an irreversible action, let's give Chip a warning in case he changes his mind. Select the delete button in the Document window and click its anchor tag `<a>` using the tag selector (we want to apply the behavior to the link, not the image). From the Behaviors panel, choose Popup Confirm Message.

Note

If you haven't installed the Popup Confirm Message extension, you can download it from **www.udzone.com/go?16**.

Enter **Are you sure you want to delete this listing?** in the Message text box and click OK. Make sure the behavior is applied to the anchor's `onClick` event.

Save your work and press F12 to preview the page in a browser. Click one of the delete buttons. You should receive a JavaScript `confirm` message, displaying the phrase we just entered. Click Cancel. This gives Chip one last chance to change his mind. If he clicks OK, the browser continues to the Delete Listing page, which performs the requested operations.

Creating the Delete Listing Page

Now for the hard part. Create a new file in the `adminch` folder and name it **delete-listing.asp** (or **delete-listing.cfm**). Double-click the file in the Site panel to open it.

Since we need to delete associated images from the `ListingRooms` and `Listings` tables, our first task is to create two recordsets: `rsListingRooms` and `rsListings`. These recordsets query the tables for the filenames of the images we want to delete.

From the Bindings panel, choose Recordset and name it **rsListingRooms**. Choose the realty connection (or data source) and select `ListingRooms` from the Table drop-down menu. Click the Selected Columns radio button and choose the `ListingRoomPic` column. Last of all, choose `ListingID` from the Filter drop-down menu, and URL Parameter from the menu below it (this should be selected by default).

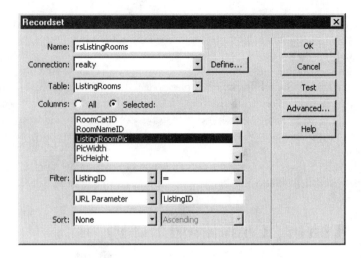

Click Advanced. Enter **1** in the Default Value column and click Test. (If you're using ColdFusion, click Edit and enter **1** in the Default Value text box.) The SQL statement should return eight records: the eight images associated with 15 King Street.

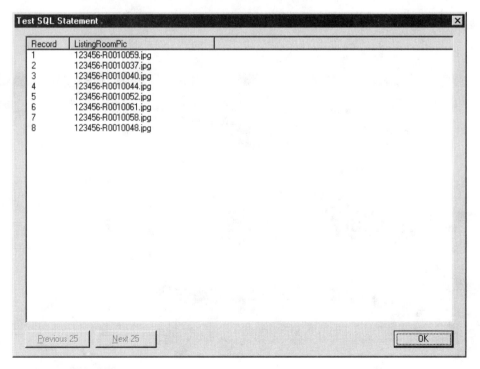

Close the Test SQL Statement window and change the Default Value to **0** (we don't want the Delete Listing page to automatically delete the first listing if no URL parameter is specified!). Click OK to close the Recordset dialog box.

Now let's create the second recordset. From the Bindings panel, choose Recordset and name it **rsListings** (you may have to switch back to Simple mode). Choose `Listings` from the Table drop-down menu and `ListingPic` from the list of Columns. Filter the recordset the same way you filtered `rsListingRooms`. You may have to switch to Advanced mode to enter **0** in the Default Value column (Dreamweaver MX enters **1** by default). Click OK to apply the recordset and save your work.

There's no need to create a recordset for the `ListingRealtors` table, since it doesn't contain any image filenames. Instead, we'll create a delete command (or a ColdFusion delete recordset) to remove any related records.

The Delete Listing Command (ASP)

From the Server Behaviors panel, choose Command and name it **cmdListingRealtors**. Choose the realty connection and select Delete from the Type drop-down menu. Click the plus (+) button to add a new variable. Enter **intListingID** in the Name column, and **Request.QueryString("ListingID")** in the Run-Time Value column. Change the SQL statement to the following:

```
DELETE FROM ListingRealtors
WHERE ListingID = intListingID
```

The completed command should look like this:

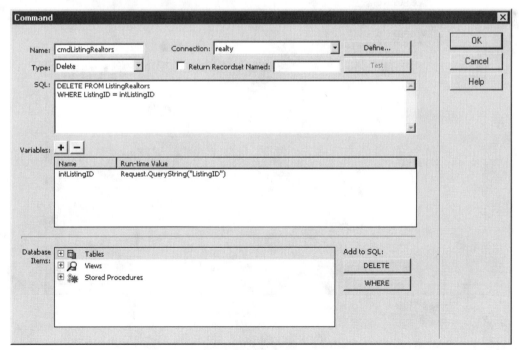

Click OK to close the Command dialog box.

Now we're going to make a few edits so that we can test the Delete Listing page without actually deleting anything. For starters, delete all of the HTML code at the bottom of the page (lines 61–69). Insert a carriage return after the `rsListingRooms` recordset (line 28) and enter the following code:

```
<%
While NOT rsListingRooms.EOF
Response.Write "ListingRooms image: " & ↵
rsListingRooms("ListingRoomPic") & "<br>"
rsListingRooms.MoveNext
Wend
%>
```

Scroll to the end of the `rsListings` recordset and enter the following code after line 56:

```
<%
Response.Write "<br>Listings image: " & rsListings("ListingPic")
%>
```

Finally, scroll down to the `cmdListingRealtors` command and place an apostrophe (') at the beginning of each line to comment it out (we don't want the delete command to execute during this test). You'll know the code is inactive when the text color changes to gray. You may also get an alert message, warning you that the command was only partially deleted. Click OK to dismiss it and save your work.

Browse to the admin Listings page on your local server and click one of the delete buttons. Your browser should look something like this:

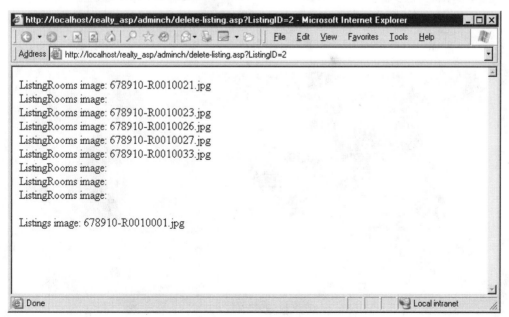

Notice the second listing returns filenames with empty values. These are the rooms for which no images exist. We'll address this in the next section when we use the File System Object to delete associated images (see "Deleting Files Using FSO (ASP)," later in this chapter).

The Delete Listing Recordset (ColdFusion)

ColdFusion doesn't support commands, but we can enter any valid SQL statement in the Recordset dialog box. If it's not open already, open `delete-listing.cfm` in Dreamweaver MX. From the Bindings panel, choose Recordset and name it **rsListingRealtors**. Choose the realty data source and enter the following code in the SQL area:

```
SELECT * FROM ListingRealtors
WHERE ListingID = #URL.ListingID#
```

Click the plus (+) button next to Page Parameters and enter **3** in the Default Value text box (`#URL.ListingID#` should appear in the Name text box automatically). Click OK.

Click Test. The SQL statement should return two records. Now that we know the SELECT statement works, change it to a DELETE statement by replacing the first line with the following:

```
DELETE FROM ListingRealtors
```

Also change the default value of the parameter to **0** (we don't want to delete the third record if no URL parameter is specified!). The DELETE recordset should now look like this:

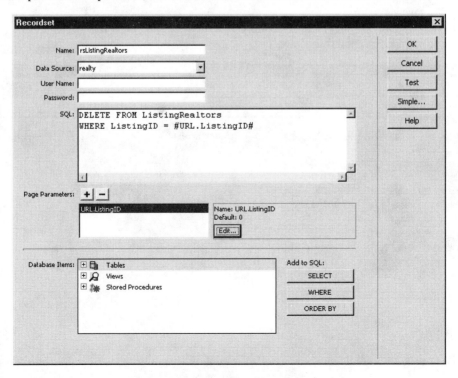

Click OK to close the Recordset dialog box.

> **Tip**
>
> The delete recordset doesn't appear in the Bindings panel, but you can edit it by double-clicking `CFQuery(rsListingRealtors)` in the Server Behaviors panel.

Now we're going to make a few edits so that we can test the Delete Listing page without actually deleting anything. For starters, go ahead and delete all of the HTML code at the bottom of the page (lines 12–20). Insert a carriage return after the `rsListingRooms` query and enter the following code on line 6:

```
<cfoutput query="rsListingRooms">ListingRooms image: ⤶
#rsListingRooms.ListingRoomPic#<br></cfoutput>
```

Insert a carriage return after the `rsListings` query and enter the following code on line 10:

```
<cfoutput><br>Listings image: #rsListings.ListingPic#</cfoutput>
```

Finally, select the `rsListingRealtors` query (lines 11–13) and select the CFML Basic tab on the Insert bar. Click the Comment button to wrap the selection with ColdFusion `<!--- comment --->` tags. (You'll know it's commented out if `rsListingRealtors` no longer appears in the Server Behaviors panel.)

Save your work. Browse to the admin Listings page on your local server and click one of the delete buttons. Your browser should look something like this:

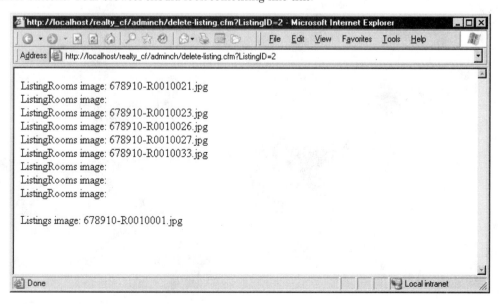

ListingRooms image: 678910-R0010021.jpg
ListingRooms image:
ListingRooms image: 678910-R0010023.jpg
ListingRooms image: 678910-R0010026.jpg
ListingRooms image: 678910-R0010027.jpg
ListingRooms image: 678910-R0010033.jpg
ListingRooms image:
ListingRooms image:
ListingRooms image:

Listings image: 678910-R0010001.jpg

Notice the second listing returns filenames with empty values. These are the rooms for which no images exist. We'll address this in the next section when we use the <cffile> tag to delete associated images (see "Deleting Files Using <cffile> (ColdFusion)," later in this chapter).

Deleting Files Using FSO (ASP)

Now that we've successfully queried the database for the image filenames, we can use ASP's File System Object (FSO) to delete them. If it's not already open, open delete-listing.asp in Dreamweaver MX and switch to Code view. Find the code block on lines 29–34 and change it to the following:

```
<%
Dim strFilePath, FSO

' Set strFilePath variable to details folder
strFilePath = Server.MapPath("../images/listings/details/") & "\"

' Instantiate the FSO
Set FSO = CreateObject("Scripting.FileSystemObject")

While NOT rsListingRooms.EOF
Response.Write "ListingRooms image: " & rsListingRooms("ListingRoomPic")
  If FSO.FileExists(strFilePath & rsListingRooms("ListingRoomPic")) Then
  Response.Write " (File exists)"
  Else Response.Write " (File not found)"
  'FSO.DeleteFile (strFilePath & rsListingRooms("ListingRoomPic")), True
  End If

Response.Write "<br>"
'rsListingRooms.Delete
rsListingRooms.MoveNext
Wend
%>
```

This code uses the File System Object to determine if the file exists on the server. If it exists, the file is deleted using the DeleteFile method: FSO.DeleteFile. To delete the associated record, we use the Delete method of the ADO Recordset object: rsListingRooms.Delete. Right now, these two lines are commented out so that we can test the page without deleting anything.

Scroll down to the bottom of the page and find the code block on lines 71–73. Replace it with the following:

```
<%
Dim strFilePath2

' Set strFilePath2 variable to listings folder
```

```
strFilePath2 = Server.MapPath("../images/listings/") & "\"

Response.Write "<br>Listings image: " & rsListings("ListingPic")
If FSO.FileExists(strFilePath2 & rsListings("ListingPic")) Then
  Response.Write " (File exists)"
  Else Response.Write " (File not found)"
  'FSO.DeleteFile (strFilePath2 & rsListings("ListingPic")), True
End If

'rsListings.Delete

' Close the File System Object
Set FSO = Nothing
%>
```

Once again, the FSO `DeleteFile` method and the Recordset `Delete` method are commented out for testing purposes. Save your work and browse to the admin Listings page on your local server. Click the delete button next to "34 McMaster Blvd." Your browser should look something like this:

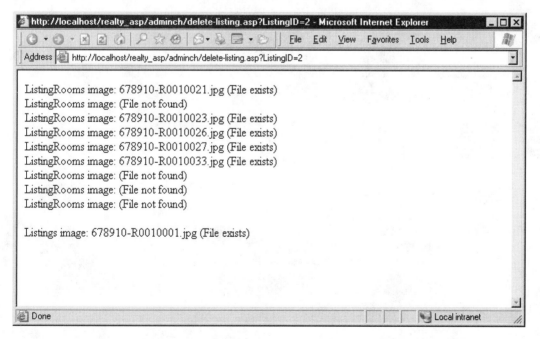

Of course, it's not always necessary to go to these lengths to test an application, but in this case, there are simply too many ways to make a mistake.

Now we're ready to test the Delete Listing page for real. In Code view, uncomment the commented lines, and delete (or comment) the lines that use `Response.Write` statements to test values. (Just be sure not to uncomment the real comments!) Also uncomment the `cmdListingRealtors` command at the bottom of the page. Finally, add the following `Response.Redirect` statement to the very end of the page:

```
<% Response.Redirect("listings.asp") %>
```

In order to use the Recordset `Delete` method, we have to change the `LockType` property to Optimistic, and the `CursorType` property to Static. In the Server Behaviors panel, select `rsListingRooms`. Using the Property inspector, choose Static from the Cursor Type drop-down, and Optimistic from the Lock Type drop-down. Now select `rsListings` in the Server Behaviors panel and change its Cursor Type to Static and its Lock Type to Optimistic.

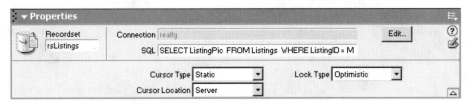

Save your work and browse to the admin Listings page on your local server. (Make sure to back up the database and images first, so you can restore them.) Click one of the delete buttons. You should now be looking at two listings—instead of three—on the admin Listings page.

If you receive a VBScript "Permission denied" error, change the NTFS permissions on the `images/listings` folder accordingly. If you run into any problems, take a look at the completed version of `delete-listing.asp` in the `realty_asp` folder you downloaded earlier.

Deleting Files Using <cffile> (ColdFusion)

Now that we've successfully queried the database for the image filenames, we can use ColdFusion's `<cffile>` tag to delete them. If it's not already open, open `delete-listing.cfm` in Dreamweaver MX and switch to Code view. Replace the `<cfoutput>` tag on line 6 with the following:

```
<cfset strFilePath = "#ExpandPath("../images/listings/details")#">
<cfoutput query="rsListingRooms">
<cfset strFileName = "#rsListingRooms.ListingRoomPic#">
<cfset strFullPath = "#strFilePath#\#strFileName#">
ListingRooms image: #strFullPath#
<cfif FileExists(strFullPath)> (File Exists)
<!--- cffile action="delete" file="#strFullPath#" --->
<cfelse> (File not found)
</cfif>
<br>
</cfoutput>
<!--- cfquery name="deleteListingRooms" datasource="realty">
DELETE FROM ListingRooms WHERE ListingID = #URL.ListingID#
</cfquery> --->
```

This code uses the `FileExists` method to determine if the file exists on the server. If it does, the file is deleted using CFFile's `action` parameter: `action="delete"`. To delete the associated records, we use `<cfquery>` tags and a SQL `DELETE` statement.

Right now, the `<cffile>` and `<cfquery>` tags are commented out so that we can test the page without deleting anything. Scroll down to line 23 and replace the `<cfoutput>` tag with the following code:

```
<cfset strFilePath2 = "#ExpandPath("../images/listings")#">
<cfoutput query="rsListings">
<cfset strFileName2 = "#rsListings.ListingPic#">
<cfset strFullPath2 = "#strFilePath2#\#strFileName2#">
<br>Listings image: #strFullPath2#
<cfif FileExists(strFullPath2)> (File Exists)
<!--- cffile action="delete" file="#strFullPath2#" --->
<cfelse> (File not found)
</cfif>
</cfoutput>
<!--- cfquery name="deleteListings" datasource="realty">
DELETE FROM Listings WHERE ListingID = #URL.ListingID#
</cfquery> --->
```

Once again, the `<cffile>` and `<cfquery>` tags are commented for testing purposes. Save your work and browse to the admin Listings page on your local server. Click the delete button next to "34 McMaster Blvd." Your browser should look something like this:

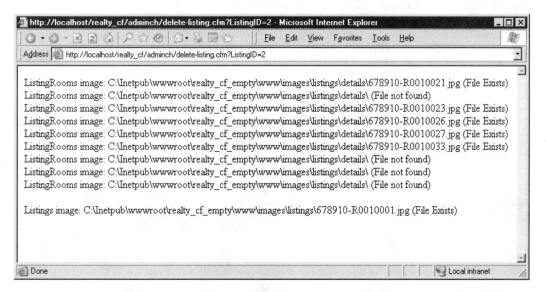

Now we're ready to test the Delete Listing page for real. In Code view, uncomment the `<cffile>` and `<cfquery>` tags, and delete (or comment) the lines that start with `<cfelse>` tags. Also uncomment the `rsListingRealtors` query. Finally, add the following `<cflocation>` tag to the very end of the page:

```
<cflocation url="listings.cfm" addtoken="no">
```

The output text on lines 11–12, 16, and 28–29 is now superfluous. Go ahead and delete it, too. The completed Delete Listing page should look like this:

```
<cfparam name="URL.ListingID" default="0">

<cfquery name="rsListingRooms" datasource="realty">
SELECT ListingRoomPic FROM ListingRooms WHERE ListingID = #URL.ListingID#
</cfquery>
<cfset strFilePath = "#ExpandPath("../images/listings/details")#">
<cfloop query="rsListingRooms">
<cfset strFileName = "#rsListingRooms.ListingRoomPic#">
<cfset strFullPath = "#strFilePath#\#strFileName#">
<cfif FileExists(strFullPath)>
<cffile action="delete" file="#strFullPath#">
</cfif>
</cfloop>
<cfquery name="deleteListingRooms" datasource="realty">
DELETE FROM ListingRooms WHERE ListingID = #URL.ListingID#
</cfquery>
<cfquery name="rsListings" datasource="realty">
SELECT ListingPic FROM Listings WHERE ListingID = #URL.ListingID#
</cfquery>
<cfset strFilePath2 = "#ExpandPath("../images/listings")#">
<cfloop query="rsListings">
<cfset strFileName2 = "#rsListings.ListingPic#">
<cfset strFullPath2 = "#strFilePath2#\#strFileName2#">
<cfif FileExists(strFullPath2)>
<cffile action="delete" file="#strFullPath2#">
</cfif>
</cfloop>
<cfquery name="deleteListings" datasource="realty">
DELETE FROM Listings WHERE ListingID = #URL.ListingID#
</cfquery>
<cfquery name="rsListingRealtors" datasource="realty">
DELETE FROM ListingRealtors WHERE ListingID = #URL.ListingID#
</cfquery>
<cflocation url="listings.cfm" addtoken="no">
```

Notice that the `<cfoutput>` tags have been replaced with `<cfloop>` tags. This is because we're no longer outputting any text to the page (although the code will work either way).

Save your work and browse to the admin Listings page on your local server. Click one of the delete buttons (make sure to back up the database and images first, so you can restore them). You should now be looking at two listings—rather than three—on the admin Listings page. If you run into any problems, take a look at the completed version of `delete-listing.cfm` in the `realty_cf` folder you downloaded earlier.

Summary

Congratulations: you can now batch-delete records and images with the best of them! Before you start trashing files and databases, however, there are a few points to consider. While the Delete Listing page does what it's supposed to do, it doesn't offer much in the way of error handling.

One place to start is checking for the existence of the URL parameter, `ListingID`, and redirecting the page if it isn't supplied. Right now, browsing to the Delete Listing page without specifying a URL parameter results in an error. Another good idea would be to use a session variable in the SQL `DELETE` statement:

```
DELETE FROM ListingRealtors
WHERE ListingID=#URL.ListingID# AND RealtorID=#SESSION.RealtorID#
```

This way, Chip can't delete his competitors' listings (he's been known to do that).

Having said that, let's review. In this recipe, you learned to do the following:

◆ Write a SQL `DELETE` statement

◆ Use the `IN` operator to select or delete records in a list

◆ Adapt the standard Delete Record SB to make batch deletes using check boxes

◆ Apply the Popup Confirm Message behavior

◆ Create a delete command (ASP)

◆ Create a delete recordset (ColdFusion)

◆ Delete files using the File System Object (ASP)

◆ Delete files using the `<cffile>` tag (ColdFusion)

◆ Test the Delete Listing page using `Response.Write` statements (ASP)

◆ Test the Delete Listing page using `<cfoutput>` statements (ColdFusion)

In the next chapter we'll create a new admin page: Edit Listing Details. This page allows Chip to update all of the details for a particular listing by submitting a single form.

Chapter **16**

Batch Updates

INGREDIENTS

File	Type	Server Model(s)	Source
realty.mdb	Access database	ASP/CF	*Sample Code*
edit-details.asp	Active Server Page	ASP	*Sample Code*
edit-details.cfm	ColdFusion template	CF	*Sample Code*

from the desk of *Paul Newman*

I n this recipe, we're going to create a batch update page for Chip Havilmyer's site. The Edit Listing Details page displays all of the photos and descriptions for the current listing and allows Chip to update them with a single click of a button. Behind the scenes, the form's action page dynamically constructs a SQL UPDATE statement for each record.

As you may recall, listing details are inserted into the ListingRooms table using the Add Listing Details page we completed in Chapter 13. Adding details one record at a time is easy. Updating all of them at once—that's another story. In order to pull this off, we have to do the following:

◆ Determine the total number of records to update

◆ Create and increment a counter variable

◆ Use the counter variable to uniquely identify form elements

◆ Loop through form variables on the action page

◆ Generate an UPDATE statement for each record

Dreamweaver MX doesn't ship with a Batch Update server behavior, so we're going to write our own batch update code. The inspiration and basis for this code is an article by Scott Mitchell called "Using Forms to Do Batch Database Updates" (**www.4guysfromrolla.com/webtech/ 100199-2.2.shtml**). Since Scott was kind enough to let us adapt his code for this recipe, please return the favor by visiting 4GuysFromRolla.com, an excellent source of information about ASP and ASP.NET.

Using UPDATE Statements

The SQL syntax for updating a database record is quite different than the SELECT and DELETE statements we've dealt with so far. Here's an example that updates the Links table in the Realty database:

```
UPDATE Links
SET LinkCatID = 13,
LinkTitle = 'Newman Calzone',
LinkURL = 'www.newmanzcalzone.com',
LinkDescription = 'Lots of spicy calzone recipes'
WHERE LinkID = 2
```

You can try this out yourself by opening realty.mdb in Microsoft Access. Click Queries under Objects and double-click Create Query In Design View. Close the Show Table dialog box and choose View | SQL View from the menu bar. Enter the preceding SQL statement and choose Query | Run (or click the red exclamation point). Microsoft Access warns you that you're about to update a record:

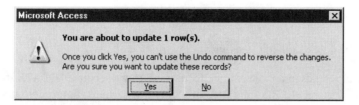

Click Yes to make the update. Save the query as qUpdateLinks and close the query window. Notice the update query has a different icon than the select queries: a pencil with an exclamation point. If you run the qLinks query, you'll see that the update to the Links table was applied.

Select qUpdateLinks and click Design. If the query opens in SQL view, choose View | Design View. As you can see, Microsoft Access also supports update queries:

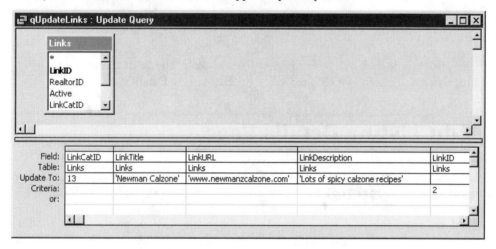

Change the columns in qUpdateLinks back to their original values—I won't be offended if you don't—and run the query. Notice that literal strings—as opposed to numeric values—are enclosed in single quotes. What happens if the string contains an apostrophe?

```
UPDATE Links
SET LinkCatID = 13,
LinkTitle = 'Newman Calzone',
LinkURL = 'www.newmanzcalzone.com',
LinkDescription = 'Newman's favorite calzone recipes'
WHERE LinkID = 2
```

The query doesn't run. Instead, an error message appears: "Syntax error (missing operator) in query expression 'Newman's favorite calzone recipes' WHERE LinkID = 2." To escape single quotes in SQL, you simply use another single quote:

```
LinkDescription = 'Newman''s favorite calzone recipes'
```

Dreamweaver's Update Record SB uses the same technique to escape single quotes:

```
MM_formVal = "'" & Replace(MM_formVal,"'","''") & "'"
```

To update several records in a table at once requires writing a separate UPDATE statement for each record. Unlike writing SELECT and DELETE statements, there are no shortcuts when it comes to updates:

```
UPDATE Links
SET LinkTitle = 'Newman Calzone'
WHERE LinkID = 2

UPDATE Links
SET LinkTitle = 'Ozzy Ozborne/McGraw-Hill'
WHERE LinkID = 1
```

In essence, this is how the batch update page will work, except the UPDATE statements will be generated dynamically—one for each record on the Edit Listing Details page.

The Edit Listing Details Page

Open the Edit Listing Details page in Dreamweaver MX (edit-details.asp or edit-details.cfm, depending on your server model). The Edit Listing Details page consists of three recordsets: rsListingRooms, rsRoomCats, and rsRoomNames. The last two recordsets populate dynamic drop-down menus (RoomCatID and RoomNameID, respectively).

The rsListingRooms recordset is filtered according to the URL parameter, ListingID (e.g., edit-details.asp?ListingID=1). Notice that the form also includes three hidden fields (see Figure 16-1).

If you click the Hidden Field markers—the yellow "H" icons—the values of the hidden fields are displayed in the Property inspector. Each of these hidden fields plays an important role on the batch update page.

◆ totalCount   The total number of records returned by the rsListingRooms recordset. This tells us how many SQL UPDATE statements to write.

◆ ListingID   The foreign key value of ListingRooms.ListingID. This is used in a Response.Redirect statement (ASP) or a <cflocation> tag (ColdFusion).

◆ ListingRoomID   The primary key value of ListingRooms. This is used in the WHERE clause of the UPDATE statements.

You may have noticed that totalCount doesn't have a value yet. Select the totalCount icon in the Document window and examine the Property inspector. If you're using ASP, click the lightning bolt icon and choose [total records] from the rsListingRooms recordset. Click OK.

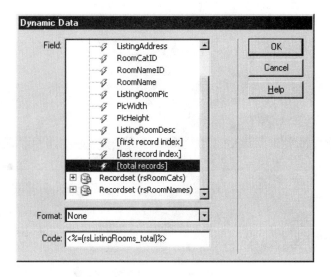

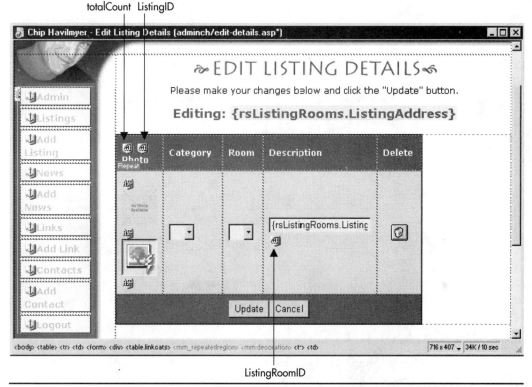

Figure 16-1 *The Edit Listing Details page includes three hidden form fields:* `totalCount`, `ListingID`, *and* `ListingRoomID`.

If you're using ColdFusion, enter the following code in the Value text box:

```
<cfoutput>#rsListingRooms.RecordCount#</cfoutput>
```

Let's test the page. Click `<form>` on the tag selector and use the Property inspector to change the Action to `../form-tester.asp` (or `../form-tester.cfm`). Save your work and press F12 to preview the page in a browser. Click Update to submit the form.

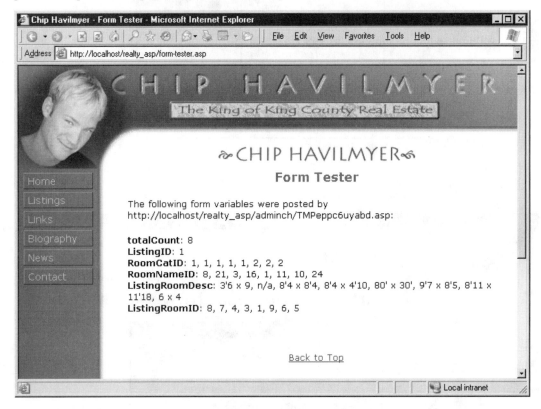

As you can see, the values of the form elements inside the Repeat Region are returned in a comma-delimited list. This would be useful if we were deleting records, but since we want to generate multiple UPDATE statements on the batch update page, we need to ensure that each form element has a unique name. To do this, we'll create a counter variable and append its value to the form elements inside the Repeat Region.

Creating the Counter Variable

Select the gray Repeat icon in the Document window and switch to Code view. (If you're using ColdFusion, select the gray `<cfloop>` icon.) We want to define the counter variable *before* the Repeat Region starts, and increment it by 1 every time it loops. So find the line that starts the Repeat Region.

ASP Version

```
<%
While ((Repeat1__numRows <> 0) AND (NOT rsListingRooms.EOF))
%>
```

ColdFusion Version

```
<cfloop query="rsListingRooms">
```

and insert the following code before and after it (the new code is shaded):

ASP Version

```
<% Counter = 0 %>
<%
While ((Repeat1__numRows <> 0) AND (NOT rsListingRooms.EOF))
%>
<% Counter = Counter + 1 %>
```

ColdFusion Version

```
<cfset Counter = 0>
<cfloop query="rsListingRooms">
<cfset Counter = Counter + 1>
```

Now we can use the value of the Counter variable to rename the form elements inside the Repeat Region.

Renaming the Form Elements

In the Document window, select the RoomCatID drop-down menu. Using the Property inspector, change its name from RoomCatID to the following:

```
RoomCatID_<%= Counter %>
```
(ASP)
```
RoomCatID_<cfoutput>#Counter#</cfoutput>
```
(ColdFusion)

Do the same with the other three form elements inside the Repeat Region: RoomNameID, ListingRoomDesc, and ListingRoomID.

Tip

If you prefer, you can make these changes using tag editor. To do this, select the form element in the Document window and press CTRL-F5.

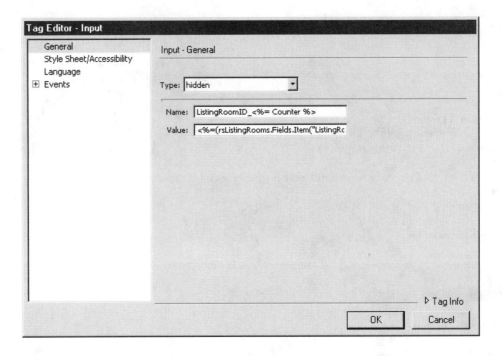

Make sure to change the form element's name attribute, not its value. The revised names are listed in the table below:

Name	Revised Name	Version
RoomCatID	RoomCatID_<%= Counter %>	ASP
RoomNameID	RoomNameID_<%= Counter %>	ASP
ListingRoomDesc	ListingRoomDesc_<%= Counter %>	ASP
ListingRoomID	ListingRoomID_<%= Counter %>	ASP
RoomCatID	RoomCatID_<cfoutput>#Counter#</cfoutput>	ColdFusion
RoomNameID	RoomNameID_<cfoutput>#Counter#</cfoutput>	ColdFusion
ListingRoomDesc	ListingRoomDesc_<cfoutput>#Counter#</cfoutput>	ColdFusion
ListingRoomID	ListingRoomID_<cfoutput>#Counter#</cfoutput>	ColdFusion

Let's test these changes to see if the name of each form element is, in fact, unique. Save your work and press F12 to preview the page in a browser. Click Update to submit the form. Your browser should look something like the following:

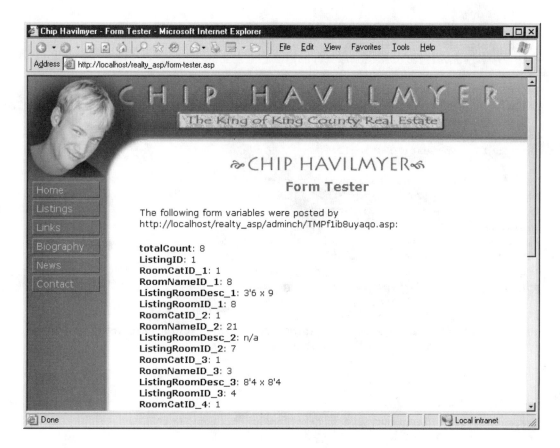

Each form element now has a unique name (RoomCatID_1, RoomCatID_2, etc.). We're ready to create the batch update page.

Creating the Batch Update Page (ASP)

Create a new file in the adminch folder of the Realty site and name it batch-update.asp. Double-click the file in the Site panel to open it. Switch to Code view and enter the following code above the opening <html> tag:

```
<!-- #include file="../Connections/realty.asp" -->
<%
Set rsListingRooms = Server.CreateObject("ADODB.Connection")
rsListingRooms.ConnectionString = MM_realty_STRING
rsListingRooms.Open()
%>
```

```
<%
' Batch update code adapted from
' http://www.4guysfromrolla.com/webtech/100199-2.2.shtml

' Get the total number of records to update
totalCount = Request("totalCount")

' Get ListingID for redirect
intListingID = Request("ListingID")

' Loop through form elements for each record
  For i = 1 to totalCount
  intRoomCatID = Request("RoomCatID_" & i)
  intRoomNameID = Request("RoomNameID_" & i)
  strListingRoomDesc = Request("ListingRoomDesc_" & i)
  intListingRoomID = Request("ListingRoomID_" & i)
  ' Escape single quotes
  strListingRoomDesc = Replace(strListingRoomDesc,"'","''")

  ' Create the SQL UPDATE statement
  strSQL = "UPDATE ListingRooms SET RoomCatID = " & CInt(intRoomCatID) & _
          ", RoomNameID = " & CInt(intRoomNameID) & _
          ", ListingRoomDesc = '" & strListingRoomDesc & "'" & _
          " WHERE ListingRoomID = " & CInt(intListingRoomID)

  ' Update the current record
  'rsListingRooms.Execute(strSQL) '**** Comment to test ****
  Response.Write strSQL & "<br><br>" '**** Uncomment to test ****

  Next 'record

' Clean up
rsListingRooms.Close

'Response.Redirect ("edit-details.asp?ListingID=" & intListingID) ⤶
'**** Comment to test ****
%>
```

The purpose of the batch update page is to write a separate SQL UPDATE statement for each record on the Edit Listing Details page. Let's see if it works. Open edit-details.asp and change the form's action page to batch-update.asp. Save your work and browse to **http://localhost/realty_asp/adminch/edit-details.asp?ListingID=2**. Click the Update button. Your browser should look something like the following:

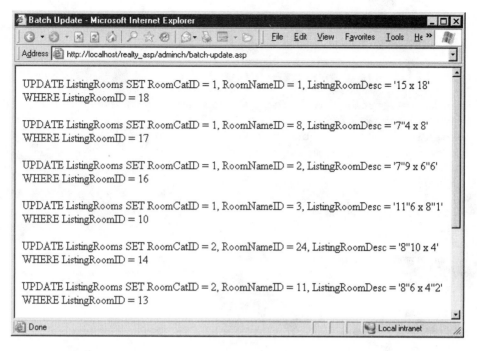

If you scroll down the page, you'll see that there are nine SQL UPDATE statements— one for each record on the Edit Listing Details page. If you change the URL parameter of edit-details.asp to ListingID=1, the batch update page generates eight UPDATE statements.

How It Works

Let's examine the batch update code in detail. At the top of batch-update.asp, we use the ADO Recordset Open method to establish a connection to the database.

```
<%
Set rsListingRooms = Server.CreateObject("ADODB.Connection")
rsListingRooms.ConnectionString = MM_realty_STRING
rsListingRooms.Open
%>
```

Notice that the ConnectionString property is set to MM_realty_STRING. This variable is defined in the realty.asp file in the Connections folder:

```
MM_realty_STRING = "dsn=realty;"
```

Next, we define two variables called `totalCount` and `intListingID`, and set their values to the hidden form fields on the Edit Listing Details page.

Looping Through Form Elements

The meat and potatoes of Scott Mitchell's code is the `For-Next` loop (lines 19–37). First, we define the index variable, `i`, and set its value to the number 1. Then we tell the code to loop until `i` reaches the value of `totalCount`. Assuming `totalCount` equals 9, here is what the *evaluated* code looks like during the second iteration of the loop:

```
' Loop through form elements for each record
  For 2 to 9
  intRoomCatID = Request("RoomCatID_2")
  intRoomNameID = Request("RoomNameID_2")
  strListingRoomDesc = Request("ListingRoomDesc_2")
  intListingRoomID = Request("ListingRoomID_2")
  ' Escape single quotes
  strListingRoomDesc = Replace("7'4 x 8","'","''")

  ' Create the SQL UPDATE statement
  strSQL = UPDATE ListingRooms SET RoomCatID = 1,
           RoomNameID = 8,
           ListingRoomDesc = '7''4 x 8'
           WHERE ListingRoomID = 17

  ' Update the current record
  rsListingRooms.Execute(strSQL) '**** Comment to test ****

  Next 'record
```

Toward the end of the loop, the ADO Connection `Execute` method is used to execute the SQL statement (`strSQL`).

On line 40, we close the `rsListingRooms` recordset, and on line 42, we redirect the user back to `edit-details.asp`. The value of the URL parameter, `ListingID`, is supplied by the `intListingID` variable that's defined on line 16.

Trying It Out

As you probably noticed, several lines in `batch-update.asp` are commented out to allow us to test the page. Now that we know it works, follow these steps to make `batch-update.asp` operational:

1. Uncomment the `rsListingRooms.Execute` statement on line 34.

2. Comment the `Response.Write` statement on line 35.

3. Uncomment the `Response.Redirect` statement on line 42.

Save your work and browse to the following URL: **http://localhost/realty_asp/adminch/ edit-details.asp?ListingID=2**. (Before you proceed, make a backup of `realty.mdb` so that you can restore it later.) Enter values with single quotes and double quotes in the description fields, and select new categories and rooms from the drop-down menus. When you're finished, click Update to submit the form. The Edit Listing Details page should look something like this:

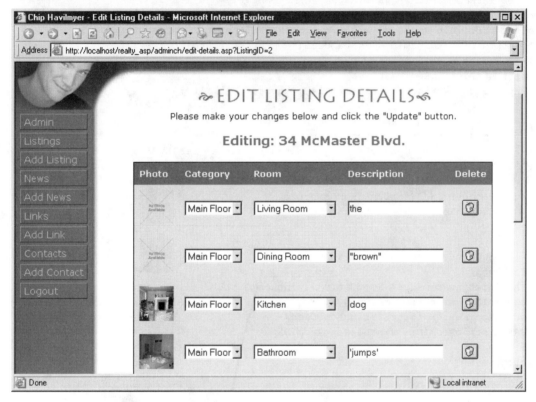

Congratulations. You're a batch-updater! Now you can modify and reuse this code on other pages and sites. Just be sure to edit the variables and database columns to correspond to your application.

Creating the Batch Update Page (ColdFusion)

Create a new file in the `adminch` folder of the Realty site and name it `batch-update.cfm`. Double-click the file in the Site panel to open it. Switch to Code view and enter the following code above the opening `<html>` tag:

```
<!--- Batch update code adapted from &
http://www.4guysfromrolla.com/webtech/100199-2.2.shtml --->

<!--- Get the total number of records to update --->
```

```
<cfset totalCount = FORM.totalCount>
<cfset intListingID = FORM.ListingID>

<!--- Loop through form elements for each record --->
<cfloop from="1" to="#totalCount#" index="i">
<cfset intRoomCatID = "#Evaluate("FORM.RoomCatID_" & i)#">
<cfset intRoomNameID = "#Evaluate("FORM.RoomNameID_" & i)#">
<cfset strListingRoomDesc = "#Evaluate("FORM.ListingRoomDesc_" & i)#">
<cfset intListingRoomID = "#Evaluate("FORM.ListingRoomID_" & i)#">
<!--- Escape double quotes --->
<cfset strListingRoomDesc = ⤸
"#Replace(strListingRoomDesc,chr(34),"&quot;","ALL")#">

<!--- Create the SQL UPDATE statement --->
<!--- Comment out cfquery tags to test --->
<!--- cfquery name="updateListingRooms" datasource="realty">
UPDATE ListingRooms SET RoomCatID = #intRoomCatID#,
RoomNameID = #intRoomNameID#,
ListingRoomDesc = '#strListingRoomDesc#'
WHERE ListingRoomID = #intListingRoomID#
</cfquery --->

<!--- Uncomment cfoutput tags to test --->
<cfoutput>
UPDATE ListingRooms SET RoomCatID = #intRoomCatID#,
RoomNameID = #intRoomNameID#,
ListingRoomDesc = '#strListingRoomDesc#'
WHERE ListingRoomID = #intListingRoomID#
<br><br>
</cfoutput>

</cfloop>

<!--- Comment out cflocation tag to test --->
<!--- cflocation url="edit-details.cfm?ListingID=#intListingID#" ⤸
addtoken="no" --->
```

The purpose of the batch update page is to write a separate SQL UPDATE statement for each record on the Edit Listing Details page. Let's see if it works. Open `edit-details.cfm` and change the form's action page to `batch-update.cfm`. Save your work and browse to **http://localhost/realty_cf/adminch/edit-details.cfm?ListingID=2**. Click the Update button. Your browser should look something like the following:

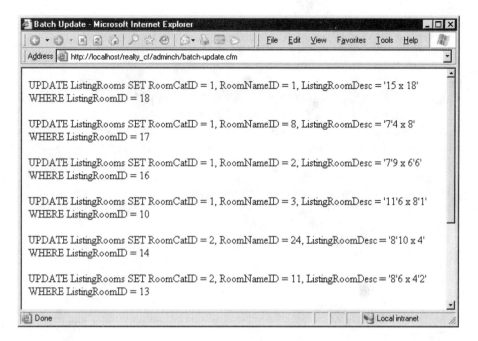

If you scroll down the page, you'll see that there are nine SQL UPDATE statements—one for each record on the Edit Listing Details page. If you change the URL parameter of edit-details.cfm to ListingID=1, the batch update page generates eight UPDATE statements.

How It Works

Let's examine the batch update code in detail. At the top of batch-update.cfm, we define two variables, totalCount and intListingID, and set their values to the hidden form fields on the Edit Listing Details page.

To loop through the remaining form elements, we create an index loop using the <cfloop> tag:

```
<cfloop from="1" to="#totalCount#" index="i">
```

The variable defined by the index attribute contains the loop's current increment value. In other words, during the third iteration of the loop, the value of i would be 3. The code within the <cfloop> tags repeats until i reaches the value of totalCount. When we tested the batch update page, the value of totalCount was 9, so the code looped nine times.

On lines 9–12, the ColdFusion Evaluate function is used to concatenate text-variable combinations:

```
<cfset intRoomCatID = "#Evaluate("FORM.RoomCatID_" & i)#">
<cfset intRoomNameID = "#Evaluate("FORM.RoomNameID_" & i)#">
```

```
<cfset strListingRoomDesc = "#Evaluate("FORM.ListingRoomDesc_" & i)#">
<cfset intListingRoomID = "#Evaluate("FORM.ListingRoomID_" & i)#">
```

Without the `Evaluate` function, ColdFusion would return a literal string (e.g., `"FORM.RoomCatID_1"`), rather than the value of the `FORM` variable (e.g., 3).

On line 14, we replace all occurrences of `chr(34)` with `&quot;`. This way, if Chip enters double quotes in the description field, the SQL statement will execute without a hitch.

On lines 18–23, a dynamically generated SQL UPDATE statement is wrapped in `<cfquery>` tags. Right now, the `<cfquery>` tags are commented out for testing purposes:

```
<!--- cfquery name="updateListingRooms" datasource="realty">
UPDATE ListingRooms SET RoomCatID = #intRoomCatID#,
RoomNameID = #intRoomNameID#,
ListingRoomDesc = '#strListingRoomDesc#'
WHERE ListingRoomID = #intListingRoomID#
</cfquery --->
```

The `datasource` attribute specifies the `"realty"` data source we've been using throughout Part III. Because the `<cfquery>` tags appear within `<cfloop>` tags, a separate SQL UPDATE statement is generated each time we loop.

Finally, the `<cflocation>` tag—also commented out—redirects the user back to the Edit Listing Details page.

> **Caution**
>
> Some ColdFusion users claim the `<cflocation>` tag occasionally redirects a page before all of its code is executed. Although I have yet to observe this behavior, it's something to keep in mind on templates that take a long time to process.

The value of the URL parameter, `ListingID`, is supplied by the `intListingID` variable that's defined on line 5.

Trying It Out

Several blocks of code in `batch-update.cfm` are commented out to allow us to test the page. Now that we know it works, follow these steps to make `batch-update.cfm` operational:

1. Uncomment the `<cfquery>` block on lines 18–23.
2. Comment the `<cfoutput>` block on line 26–32.
3. Uncomment the `<cflocation>` tag on line 38.

Save your work and browse to the following URL: **http://localhost/realty_cf/adminch/ edit-details.cfm?ListingID=2**. (Before you proceed, make a backup of `realty.mdb` so you can restore it later.) Enter values with single quotes and double quotes in the description fields, and select new categories and rooms from the drop-down menus. When you're finished, click Update to submit the form. The Edit Listing Details page should look something like this:

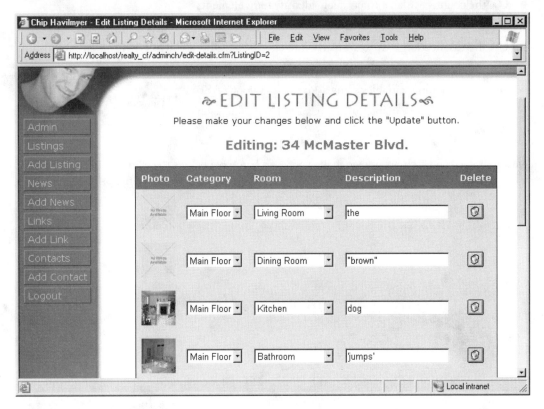

Congratulations. You're a batch-updater! Now you can modify and reuse this code on other pages and sites. Just be sure to edit the variables and database columns to correspond to your application.

Summary

This recipe illustrates the value of adapting existing code—provided you have the author's permission, of course—rather than designing a feature from scratch. We've done this three times now, with solutions by Nicholas Poh ("Fading Text Scroller"), Tom Steeper ("Preview File Before Uploading"), and Scott Mitchell ("Using Forms to Do Batch Database Updates").

Do you feel like a coder yet? You should, because in this recipe you learned to

◆ Write SQL UPDATE statements

◆ Create and increment a counter variable

◆ Use the counter variable to uniquely identify form elements

◆ Use the Recordset Open method to establish a database connection (ASP)

◆ Use the Connection Execute method to execute a SQL statement (ASP)

◆ Use the Evaluate function to concatenate text and variables (ColdFusion)

◆ Loop through form variables using a For-Next loop (ASP)

◆ Loop through form variables using <cfloop> (ColdFusion)

◆ Escape single quotes and double quotes

Now that you can batch update, go make yourself a batch of cookies to celebrate. In the next chapter we'll create the Listing Details page that displays the records we've been editing.

Chapter 17

Nested Repeat Regions

INGREDIENTS

File(s)	Type	Server Model(s)	Source
`realty.mdb`	Access database	ASP/CF	*Sample Code*
`links.asp,` `listing-detail.asp`	Active Server Pages	ASP	*Sample Code*
`links.cfm,` `listing-detail.cfm`	ColdFusion templates	CF	*Sample Code*
Nested Repeat	Server Behavior	ASP	Tom Muck
Horizontal Looper	Server Behavior	ASP	Tom Muck
JustSo Picture Window	Behavior		E. Michael Brandt

from the desk of Paul Newman

I n this recipe, we're going to use nested repeat regions to display Chip Havilmyer's Links and Listing Details pages. The goal is not only to display records by category, but to display *only those categories in which records exist*. In addition, we're going to loop records horizontally as well as vertically. On the Links page, we're going to nest a repeat region inside a horizontal looper. On the Listing Details page, we'll do the opposite: nest a horizontal looper inside a repeat region.

If you don't know what a nested repeat region is, don't worry. A nested repeat region is simply a repeat region that's *nested* inside another repeat region. Since you've already created repeat regions, it's only a matter of becoming familiar with the steps to insert one repeat region inside another:

- Create the appropriate table relationships
- Design queries for the outer and inner loops
- Use SELECT DISTINCT in the outer loop query
- Create the outer loop
- Create the inner loop

Nesting repeat regions can be a little tricky, but once you get the hang of it, you'll wonder how you ever got along without them. Thanks to first-rate server behaviors by Tom Muck—Nested Repeat and Horizontal Looper—most of the hard work has been automated.

The Nested Repeat extension doesn't support ColdFusion. The good news is, ColdFusion users don't really need it. We can create a nested repeat region using the <cfoutput> tag's group attribute. What's more, we can do it with a single recordset!

Understanding the Table Relationships

The completed Links page (see Figure 17-1) repeats the link categories using a horizontal looper. Even though there are 16 categories in the LinkCats table, the Links page displays only those categories in which records exist. To better understand this, open realty.mdb in Microsoft Access and double-click the Links table to open it.

The Links table consists of nine records in four categories ("Dreamweaver," "Extensions," "News," and "Shopping"). The Links.LinkCatID column is a foreign key to the LinkCats table. This allows us to represent the category name using an ID number (e.g., 9, 12, 15, 16), rather than entering the full category name for each record.

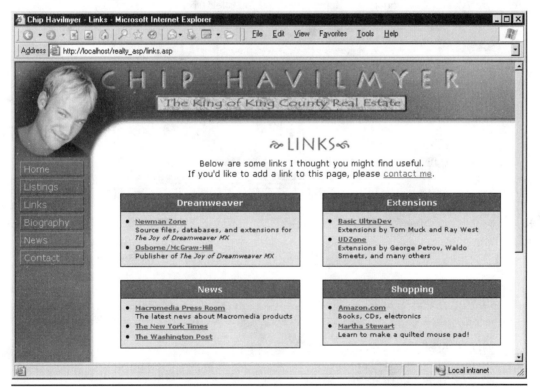

Figure 17-1 *The completed Links page nests repeat regions inside a horizontal looper.*

In terms of database normalization, this is the preferred method, since any typos in the category names would return inaccurate results. For instance, if someone misspelled "Shopping" in one of the records, Martha Stewart might find herself in a new category called "Shipping"! Or worse, the *New York Times* might appear in a category called "Newts."

Moving the link categories into a separate table has other advantages. For instance, if Chip Havilmyer decides to change the "Restaurants" category to "Dining," all we have to do is edit one record in the `LinkCats` table, rather than every affected record in the `Links` table.

The qLinkCats Query

In the introduction, I mentioned the importance of using `SELECT DISTINCT` in the outer loop query. Let's examine the outer loop queries for the Links and Listing Details pages: `qLinkCats` and `qRoomCats`.

Select the `qLinkCats` query in Microsoft Access and click Design.

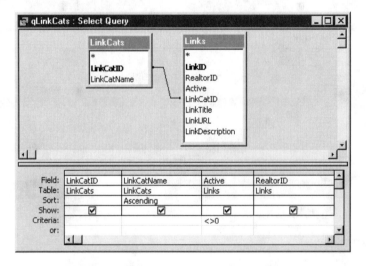

The `qLinkCats` query creates an `INNER JOIN` between the `Links` and `LinkCats` tables. If you run the `qLinkCats` query, you'll see that it returns only four categories, even though there are nine records in the `Links` table. Choose View | SQL View to access the underlying code:

```
SELECT DISTINCT LinkCats.LinkCatID, LinkCats.LinkCatName,
Links.Active, Links.RealtorID
FROM LinkCats INNER JOIN Links ON LinkCats.LinkCatID = Links.LinkCatID
WHERE (((Links.Active)<>0))
ORDER BY LinkCats.LinkCatName;
```

Notice the `DISTINCT` keyword in the `SELECT` clause. As you may recall, the `DISTINCT` keyword instructs the database to omit duplicate rows from the results. If you remove `DISTINCT` from the SQL statement, the `qLinkCats` query returns nine records, because there are nine items in the `Links` table.

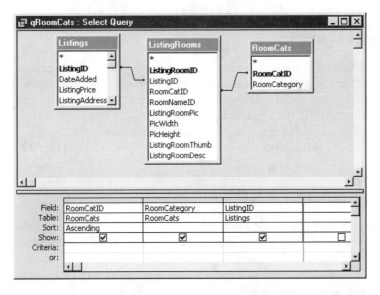

Starting to make sense? When we design the Links page, we'll use `qLinkCats` to retrieve the categories for the outer loop, and `qLinks` to retrieve the records for the inner loop.

The qRoomCats Query

Although the `qRoomCats` query doesn't come into play until later in this chapter ("The Listing Details Page"), let's take a quick look at it.

The `qRoomCats` query uses `INNER JOINS` to represent the relationships between the `Listings`, `ListingRooms`, and `RoomCats` tables. It also uses the `DISTINCT` keyword to omit duplicate rows:

```
SELECT DISTINCT RoomCats.RoomCatID, RoomCats.RoomCategory,
Listings.ListingID
```

```
FROM Listings INNER JOIN (RoomCats INNER JOIN ListingRooms
ON RoomCats.RoomCatID = ListingRooms.RoomCatID)
ON Listings.ListingID = ListingRooms.ListingID
ORDER BY RoomCats.RoomCatID;
```

If you run qRoomCats, however, it doesn't return the expected results:

The duplicate categories appear because the Listings table contains three records. Open qRoomCats in Design view and enter the number **3** in the Criteria cell of the ListingID column. Behind the scenes, this adds a WHERE clause to the SQL statement:

```
WHERE Listings.ListingID = 3
```

Now click the red exclamation point to run the query. Tada! No duplicate categories.

When we use qRoomCats to retrieve the categories for the Listing Details page, we'll filter the recordset according to the URL parameter, ListingID (e.g., listing-detail.asp?ListingID=3). To create the inner loop, we'll use the qListingRooms query, which will also be filtered at run time.

Don't forget to remove the number 3 from the Criteria cell of the ListingID column!

The Links Page (ASP)

In this section, we're going to create a nested repeat region in ASP using two of Tom Muck's extensions: Horizontal Looper and Nested Repeat. If you haven't already, please download the extensions from **www.basic-ultradev.com** and install them.

The rsLinkCats Recordset

Open the Links page (links.asp) in Dreamweaver MX. From the Bindings panel, choose Recordset and name it rsLinkCats. Choose the realty connection and select qLinkCats from the Table drop-down menu. Leave the All Columns radio button selected and choose RealtorID from the Filter drop-down menu. Change the second drop-down to Entered Value and enter **1** in the text box (Chip Havilmyer's RealtorID number). Click OK.

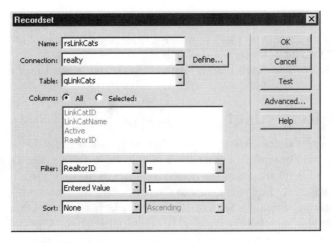

In the Document window, select "Link Category" and expand the `rsLinkCats` recordset in the Bindings panel. Select `LinkCatName` and click Insert.

The Horizontal Looper

To create the outer loop, we'll use Tom Muck's Horizontal Looper extension.

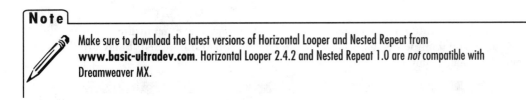

Note — Make sure to download the latest versions of Horizontal Looper and Nested Repeat from **www.basic-ultradev.com**. Horizontal Looper 2.4.2 and Nested Repeat 1.0 are *not* compatible with Dreamweaver MX.

In the Document window, select the links table (it's the second `<table>` tag from the left on the tag selector). Choose Horizontal Looper from the Server Behaviors panel. Enter **2** in the Columns text box and select the All Records radio button. Click OK.

Save your work and press F12 to preview the page in a browser. Looks pretty good, but the tables are flush left and there's not enough vertical space between them. Select the new table created by Tom's extension—the second `<table>` tag from the left on the tag selector—and press CTRL-ALT-SHIFT-C to center it. Now place your cursor to the right of the blue-and-gray links table and press SHIFT-ENTER to insert a `<br>` tag below it.

Save your work and preview the page again. Better? Good. That takes care of the outer loop. Now for the tricky part.

The Nested Recordset

The trick to nesting repeat regions is writing the proper SQL statement for the nested (or inner loop) recordset. No Dreamweaver extension can help you with that. But Tom Muck's RecordsetForNesting SB helps you insert the nested recordset in the right place.

In the Document window, place your cursor to the right of the dynamic text, {rsLinkCats.LinkCatName}. From the Server Behaviors panel, choose Basic-UltraDev | RecordsetForNesting. This launches the standard Recordset dialog box. What makes Tom's extension different is that it inserts the recordset at the cursor location, rather than at the top of the ASP page.

Name the recordset `rsLinks` and choose `qLinks` from the Table drop-down menu. Click the Selected Columns radio button and select `LinkCatID`, `LinkTitle`, `LinkURL`, and `LinkDescription`. Click Advanced.

In the SQL area, add the following `WHERE` clause:

```
WHERE LinkCatID = intLinkCatID
```

Click the plus (+) button to define the `intLinkCatID` variable. Enter **intLinkCatID** in the Name column, and **9** in the Default Value column. Finally, enter **rsLinkCats("LinkCatID")** in the Run-time Value column.

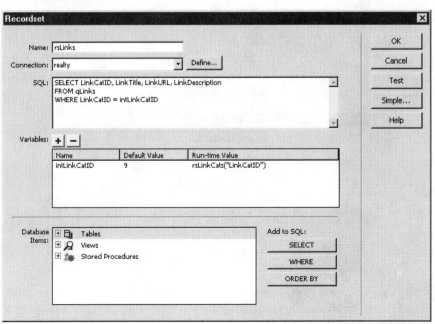

Click Test. The SQL statement should return three records in the "News" category: Macromedia Press Room, The New York Times, and The Washington Post. Change the Default Value to 0 and click OK to apply the rsLinks recordset. You should see two ASP Server Markup Tags in the Document window. If you click the second icon and examine the Property inspector, you'll see that the rsLinks recordset has been inserted *after* the start of the outer loop, instead of at the top of the ASP page.

The Inner Loop

Let's bind the rsLinks columns to their respective placeholders. In the Document window, select "Link Title." Expand the rsLinks recordset in the Bindings panel, select LinkTitle, and click Insert. Right-click {rsLinks.LinkTitle} and choose Change Link. Click the Data Sources radio button and select the LinkURL column. Enter **http://** at the beginning of the URL text box and click OK.

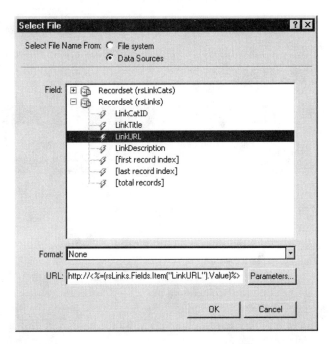

Select "This is the link description" and bind it to the LinkDescription column in the Bindings panel. Finally, select the bulleted list item by clicking <li.legal> on the tag selector. From the Server Behaviors panel, choose Basic-UltraDev | NestedRepeat, and choose rsLinks from the drop-down menu. Click OK.

Save your work and press F12 to preview the page in a browser. The Links page should look something like this:

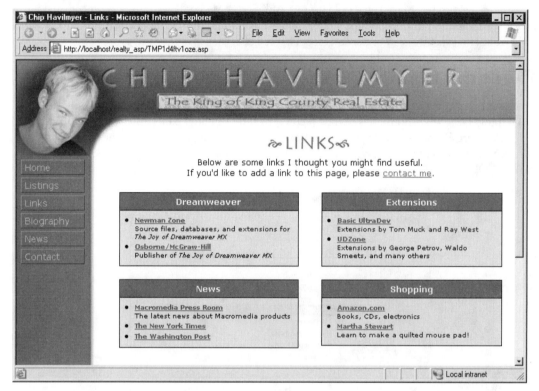

Whaddaya know—it works. But *how* does it work?

The SQL statement in `rsLinks` repeats the inner loop as long as `rsLinks("LinkCatID")` equals the run-time value of `rsLinkCats("LinkCatID")`. Once the logic of this SQL statement makes sense to you, the whole process will seem far less mysterious.

In case you're wondering, it's possible to create a nested repeat region using a standard Dreamweaver MX recordset. Tom's extension merely spares you the hassle of cutting and pasting the recordset into the proper location. In fact, this is how we'll create the ColdFusion version of the Listing Details page, later in this chapter.

The Links Page (ColdFusion)

In this section, we're going to create a nested repeat region in ColdFusion using a single recordset. The secret is adding the `group` attribute to the `<cfoutput>` tag.

The rsLinks Recordset

Open the Links page (`links.cfm`) in Dreamweaver MX. From the Bindings panel, choose Recordset and name it `rsLinks`. Choose the realty data source and select the `qLinks` query

from the Table drop-down menu. Click the Selected Columns radio button and select
`RealtorID`, `LinkCatID`, `LinkCatName`, `LinkTitle`, `LinkURL`, and
`LinkDescription`. Choose `RealtorID` from the Filter drop-down menu, and select Entered
Value from the drop-down below it. In the text box, enter the number **1** (Chip Havilmyer's
`RealtorID` number). Finally, sort the records in Ascending order by `LinkCatName`. Click OK
to close the Recordset dialog box.

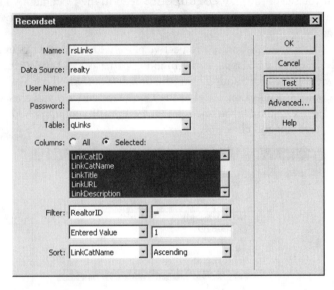

The records are sorted by the `LinkCatName` column because that's the column we'll specify
in the `group` attribute.

Using the group Attribute

Select the links table in the Document window (it's the second `<table>` tag from the left on the
tag selector). Select the CFML Basic tab on the Insert bar and click the cfoutput button. Enter
rsLinks in the Query Name text box, and **LinkCatName** in the Group Field text box. Click OK.

Dreamweaver MX switches to Split view to show you where the code was inserted. If you scroll up to line 54, you'll see the `group` attribute at work in the opening `<cfoutput>` tag:

```
<cfoutput query="rsLinks" group="LinkCatName">
```

Switch back to Design view. Notice that a thin gray border surrounds the region wrapped in `<cfoutput>` tags. If you select the gray `<cfoutput>` icon in the Document window and click the Attributes button on the Property inspector, you can edit the `query` and `group` attributes of the `<cfoutput>` tag.

Let's bind the `rsLinks` columns to their respective placeholders. In the Document window, select "Link Category." Expand `rsLinks` in the Bindings panel, select `LinkCatName`, and click Insert. Do the same with "Link Title" and "This is the link description." To make the anchor tag (`<a>`) dynamic, right-click {rsLinks.LinkTitle} in the Document window and choose Change Link. Click the Data Sources radio button and select the `LinkURL` column. Add **http://** to the beginning of the URL text box and click OK.

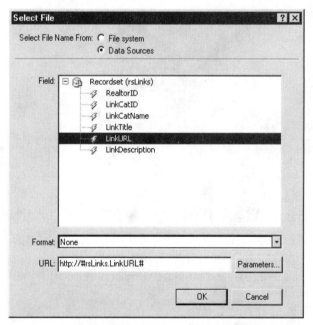

Finally, select the bulleted list item by clicking `<li.legal>` on the tag selector. This is the nested region. To make it repeat, we need to wrap it with `<cfoutput>` tags, so click the cfoutput button on the Insert bar and click OK to dismiss tag editor.

Save your work and press F12 to preview the page in a browser. How do you like them apples? Only one problem: the link categories don't loop horizontally.

Looping Horizontally

To create a horizontal looper in ColdFusion, we'll borrow the `Counter` variable from Chapter 16. Whenever `Counter` returns an even number, we'll start a new table row (`<tr>`).

Switch to Code view and find the opening `<cfoutput>` tag on line 54:

```
<cfoutput query="rsLinks" group="LinkCatName"><table>
    <tr valign="top">
      <td>
```

Replace this code with the following:

```
<table>
  <tr valign="top">
  <cfset Counter = 0>
  <cfoutput query="rsLinks" group="LinkCatName">
  <cfset Counter = Counter + 1>
    <td>
```

The new code moves the `<cfoutput>` tag down a couple lines, so the outside loop repeats the table cell (`<td>`), rather than the entire table. The `Counter` variable simply keeps track of how many times we've looped (see "Creating the Counter Variable" in Chapter 16).

Now locate the code on lines 73–75:

```
    </td>
  </tr>
</table></cfoutput>
```

Replace it with the following:

```
    </td>
    <cfif Counter MOD 2 EQ 0></tr><tr></cfif>
    </cfoutput>
  </tr>
</table>
```

To balance out the first code block, the closing `</cfoutput>` tag has been moved *up* a couple lines, to follow the closing `</td>` tag. The interesting part of this code is the `<cfif>` tag and the MOD (or modulus) operator.

Note

The MOD operator divides the number on its left by the number on its right and returns the remainder. For instance, 7 MOD 3 returns 1, whereas 6 MOD 3 returns 0. To create three columns on `links.cfm`, change the `<cfif>` tag to `<cfif Counter MOD 3 EQ 0>`.

If the `Counter` variable is an even number, we end the current table row and start a new table row: `</tr><tr>`. If `Counter` is *not* evenly divisible by 2, the looper returns to the opening `<cfoutput>` tag, increments the `Counter` variable, and creates another table cell (`<td>`).

Save your work and press F12 to preview the page in a browser.

Sweet. Still one problem: the links aren't sorted alphabetically. Open the `rsLinks` recordset in the Bindings panel and click Advanced. Add the `LinkTitle` column to the ORDER BY clause (the new code is shaded):

```
ORDER BY LinkCatName, LinkTitle ASC
```

Save your work and preview the page again:

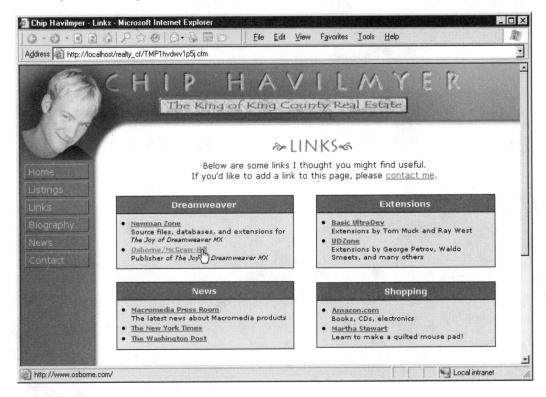

That's more like it. Notice the ORDER BY clause sorts the records in the same order as the repeat regions: `LinkCatName` (outer loop), `LinkTitle` (inner loop). This is required for the `group` attribute to produce the desired results. (Try transposing `LinkTitle` and `LinkCatName` in the ORDER BY clause and you'll see what I mean!)

That wraps up the Links page. If you have any trouble getting the horizontal looper to work, take a look at the completed Links page in the `realty_cf` folder you downloaded earlier.

The Listing Details Page

The primary purpose of the Listing Details page is to display additional listing photographs and descriptions. As you may recall, this information is stored in the `ListingRooms` table. To create the page's outer loop (room categories) and inner loop (room photos and descriptions), we'll use the qRoomCats and qListingRooms queries, respectively.

The Outer Loop

Open the Listing Details page in Dreamweaver MX (`listing-detail.asp` or `listing-detail.cfm`, depending on your server model). To save time, two recordsets have already been applied to the page: `rsListing` and `rsRoomCats`. Press F12 to preview the page in a browser.

To display the room categories for each listing—"Main Floor," "Upstairs," "Basement," etc.—we need to create a repeat region. In the Document window, select "Room Category." Expand `rsRoomCats` in the Bindings panel, select `RoomCategory`, and click Insert. Now select the blue-and-gray table in the Document window by clicking `<table.adminTbl>` on the tag selector.

> **Note**
>
> If a CSS style has been applied to an HTML element, Dreamweaver MX appends the style's name to the element on the tag selector.

From the Server Behaviors panel, choose Repeat Region. Select `rsRoomCats` from the Recordset drop-down menu, and click the All Records radio button. Click OK to apply the Repeat Region. Save your work and press F12 to preview the page.

Hmm. If your page looks like mine, the tables don't have any vertical space between them. Select `<table.adminTbl>` on the tag selector and switch to Code view. Add a `<br>` tag after the closing `</table>` tag. Save your work and preview the page again. Add the parameter `?ListingID=2` to the URL and press ENTER. You should see three categories: "Main Floor," "Upstairs," and "Basement."

That takes care of the outer loop. Now we're going to nest a horizontal looper inside of it.

The Inner Loop (ASP)

Before we can create the inner loop, we need to create its recordset. Place your cursor to the right of `{rsRoomCats.RoomCategory}` in the Document window and choose Basic-UltraDev | RecordsetForNesting from the Server Behaviors panel (make sure you're in Simple mode). Name the recordset `rsListingRooms` and choose the realty connection. Select `qListingRooms` from the Table drop-down menu and click the All Columns radio button.

Click Advanced and add the following WHERE clause to the end of the SQL statement:

```
WHERE ListingID = intListingID AND RoomCatID = intRoomCatID
```

Click the plus (+) button and add two variables named `intListingID` and `intRoomCatID`. The Default and Run-Time Values are listed in the table that follows:

Variable Name	Default Value	Run-Time Value
intListingID	1	Request.QueryString("ListingID")
intRoomCatID	1	rsRoomCats("RoomCatID")

The completed recordset should look like this:

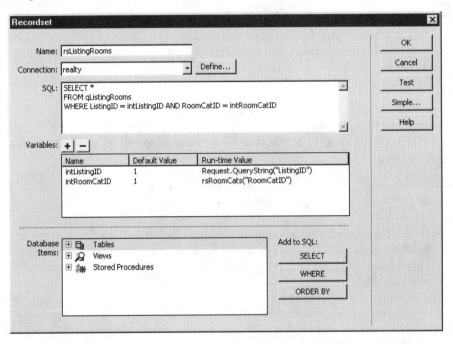

Click OK and save your work.

Binding the Data to the Page

Expand `rsListingRooms` in the Bindings panel and bind the following columns to their placeholders in the Document window: `RoomName`, `ListingRoomDesc`, `ListingRoomPic`. To bind the image, right-click `nopic.gif` in the Document window and choose Source File. Click the Data Sources radio button and select `ListingRoomPic` from the `rsListingRooms` recordset. Insert the path to `images/listings/details` in the beginning of the URL text box:

```
images/listings/details/ ↵
<%=(rsListingRooms.Fields.Item("ListingRoomPic").Value)%>
```

Click OK.

If the image dimensions change, use the Property inspector to set the width to 150 and the height to 120. Since we want to show the image only if its filename exists in the database, switch to Code view and place your cursor before the opening <img> tag. Select the ASP tab on the Insert bar and click the If button. Complete the If statement as follows:

```
<% If rsListingRooms("ListingRoomPic") <> "" Then %>
```

To display an alternate image if the ListingRoomPic column is empty, scroll to the end of the <img> tag and place your cursor after the <br> tag. Click the Else button on the Insert bar and add the following line after the <% Else %> statement:

```
<img src="images/nopic.gif" width="150" height="120" hspace="10"><br>
```

Click End on the Insert bar to end the If-Else statement (<% End If %>).

Creating the Horizontal Looper

Now we're ready to loop. In the Document window, select no-pic.gif and use the tag selector to select the <div> tag on its left. From the Server Behaviors panel, choose Horizontal Looper. Select rsListingRooms from the Recordset drop-down menu and click the All Records radio button. Enter 3 in the Columns text box and click OK.

Horizontal Looper wraps the selection in another HTML table. Save your work and press F12 to preview the page in a browser.

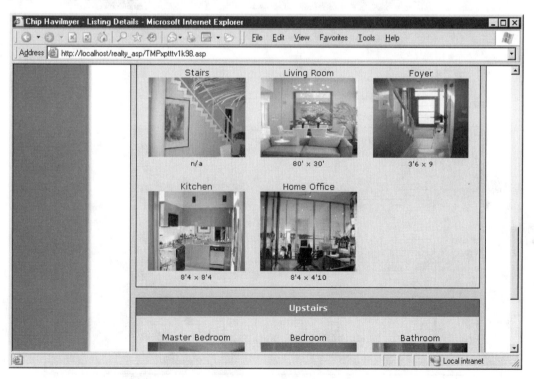

Congratulations, you've done it! You've nested a horizontal looper inside a repeat region. If you want to refine the page a little further, skip ahead to the section "JustSo Picture Window." If you're unable to get the Listing Details page to work, take a look at the completed page in the `realty_asp` folder you downloaded earlier.

The Inner Loop (ColdFusion)

Before we can create the inner loop, we need to create its recordset. From the Server Behaviors panel, choose Recordset and name it **rsListingRooms** (make sure you're in Simple mode). Choose the realty data source and select `qListingRooms` from the Table drop-down menu. Make sure the All Columns radio button is selected.

Click Advanced and add the following WHERE clause to the end of the SQL statement:

```
WHERE ListingID = #URL.ListingID#
AND RoomCatID = #rsRoomCats.RoomCatID#
```

Click Test. Dreamweaver MX prompts you to enter a Test Value for `rsRoomCats.RoomCatID`. Enter **1** in the Test Value text box and click OK. The SQL statement returns five records, because there are five photos in the "Main Floor" category.

The completed recordset should look like this:

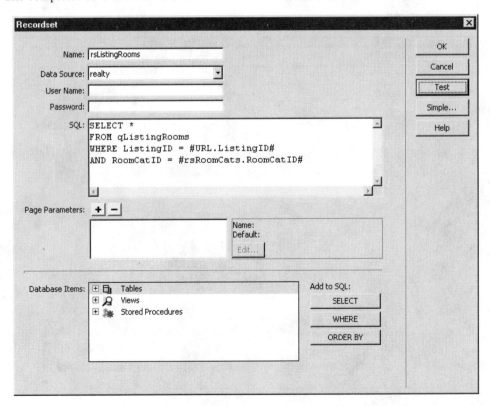

Click OK to close the Recordset dialog box.

The rsListingRooms Recordset

Because we used Dreamweaver's standard Recordset SB to create `rsListingRooms`, it was placed at the top of `listing-detail.cfm`. So switch to Code view and select the `rsListingRooms` query (lines 8–11):

```
<cfquery name="rsListingRooms" datasource="realty">
SELECT * FROM qListingRooms
WHERE ListingID = #URL.ListingID#
AND RoomCatID = #rsRoomCats.RoomCatID#
</cfquery>
```

Press CTRL-X to cut the selection. Scroll down to line 122 and press CTRL-V to paste the query before the opening `<div>` tag. Switch back to Design view and expand `rsListingRooms` in the Bindings panel. Bind the following columns to their placeholders in the Document window: `RoomName`, `ListingRoomDesc`, and `ListingRoomPic`. To bind the image, right-click `nopic.gif` in the Document window and choose Source File. Click the Data Sources radio button and select `ListingRoomPic` from the `rsListingRooms` recordset. Insert the path to `images/listings/details` in the beginning of the URL text box:

```
images/listings/details/#rsListingRooms.ListingRoomPic#
```

Click OK to close the dialog box. If the image dimensions change, use the Property inspector to set the width to `150` and the height to `120`. While the dynamic image is still selected, choose the CFML Flow tab on the Insert bar. We want to show the image only if its filename exists in the database, so click the cfif button. Dreamweaver MX switches to Split view to show you where the code was inserted. Complete the `<cfif>` tag as follows:

```
<cfif rsListingRooms.ListingRoomPic NEQ "">
```

To display an alternate image if the `ListingRoomPic` column is empty, scroll to the end of the `<img>` tag and place your cursor before the closing `</cfif>` tag. Enter a new line and click the cfelse button on the Insert bar. Insert the following code after the `<cfelse>` tag:

```
<img src="images/nopic.gif" width="150" height="120" hspace="10"><br>
```

Save your work.

Creating the Horizontal Looper

To loop the `rsListingRooms` recordset horizontally, we're going to use the same technique we employed on the Links page. The outer loop on the Listing Details page is defined by the `<cfoutput query="rsRoomCats">` tag on line 115. As you know, you can't nest `<cfoutput>` tags in ColdFusion (with one notable exception). But you *can* nest a `<cfloop>` tag inside a `<cfoutput>` tag. So that's exactly what we're going to do.

In the Document window, select the table cell (`<td>`) that contains the `rsListingRooms` data and switch to Code view. The code (lines 129–134, give or take a line or two) should look like this:

```
<td>
<div align="center"><br>
#rsListingRooms.RoomName#<br>
<cfif rsListingRooms.ListingRoomPic NEQ ""> ⏎
<img src="images/listings/details/#rsListingRooms.ListingRoomPic#" ⏎
width="150" height="120" hspace="10"><br>
<cfelse><img src="images/nopic.gif" ⏎
width="150" height="120" hspace="10"><br></cfif>
<font size="1">#rsListingRooms.ListingRoomDesc#</font>
</div></td>
```

Change it to the following (the new code is shaded):

```
<cfloop query="rsListingRooms"><td>
  <div align="center"><br>
    #rsListingRooms.RoomName#<br>
    <cfif rsListingRooms.ListingRoomPic NEQ "">
    <img src="images/listings/details/#rsListingRooms.ListingRoomPic#" ⏎
    width="150" height="120" hspace="10"><br>
    <cfelse>
    <img src="images/nopic.gif" hspace="10" width="150" height="120"><br>
    </cfif>
    <font size="1">#rsListingRooms.ListingRoomDesc#</font>
  </div>
</td><cfif rsListingRooms.CurrentRow MOD 3 EQ 0></tr><tr></cfif></cfloop>
```

Switch back to Design view. Save your work and press F12 to preview the page in a browser.

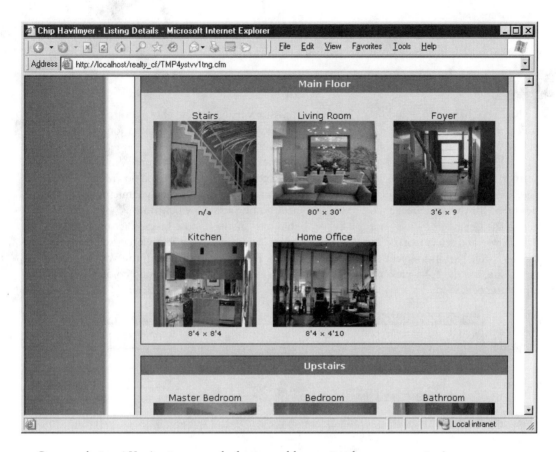

Congratulations! You've just nested a horizontal looper inside a repeat region!

Let's take a closer look at the code that creates the looper. It's almost identical to the code we used on the Links page, except for a few minor adjustments. For starters, we use `<cfloop>` to create the repeat region because ColdFusion doesn't permit nested `<cfoutput>` tags. Next, we use `rsListingRooms.CurrentRow` in lieu of a counter variable.

Note

`CurrentRow` is a built-in ColdFusion variable that, aptly enough, returns the query's current row number. This is merely a counter variable—it is *not* the value of the primary key column.

Finally, we generate three columns in the horizontal looper by entering **3**, rather than **2**, after the MOD operator.

If you were unable to get the Listing Details page to work, take a look at the completed page in the `realty_cf` folder you downloaded earlier.

JustSo Picture Window

Way back in Chapter 13, I said that Chip wants full-size versions of the photos on the Listing Details page to open in pop-up windows. That's why we saved the image's dimensions in the `PicWidth` and `PicHeight` columns of the `ListingRooms` table.

To deliver this feature, we're going to use E. Michael Brandt's JustSo Picture Window extension (you'll find JustSo Picture Window in the `extensions` folder you downloaded earlier). Open the Listing Details page in Dreamweaver MX and select the dynamic image in the inner loop (the dynamic image icon resembles a tree getting struck by lightning).

From the Behaviors panel—not the Server Behaviors panel—choose JustSo Picture Window. Click Browse and select `nopic.gif` in the `images` directory. Leave Autodetect selected and click the toggle button to select the hug image option. Finally, enter **Photo** in the Window Title text box and use the color picker to select white (#FFFFFF) as the background color. Click OK to apply the behavior.

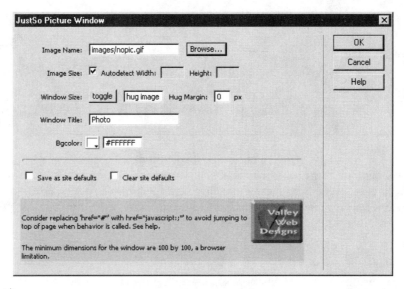

While the dynamic image is still selected, switch to Code view and locate the opening anchor (`<a>`) tag:

```
<a href="javascript:;" onClick="JustSoPicWindow ⤶
('images/nopic.gif','150','120','Photo','#FFFFFF','hug image','0'); ⤶
return document.MM_returnValue">
```

Replace it with the following (the new code is shaded):

ASP Version

```
<a href="javascript:;" onClick="JustSoPicWindow ⤸
('images/listings/details/<%= rsListingRooms("ListingRoomPic") %>', ⤸
'<%= rsListingRooms("PicWidth") %>', ⤸
'<%= rsListingRooms("PicHeight") %>', ⤸
'Photo','#FFFFFF','hug image','0');return document.MM_returnValue">
```

ColdFusion Version

```
<a href="javascript:;" onClick="JustSoPicWindow ⤸
('images/listings/details/#rsListingRooms.ListingRoomPic#', ⤸
'#rsListingRooms.PicWidth#','#rsListingRooms.PicHeight#', ⤸
'Photo','##FFFFFF','hug image','0');return document.MM_returnValue">
```

This code replaces the static image's path, width, and height with columns from the `rsListingRooms` recordset. In ColdFusion, we also add a pound sign (#) to escape the pound sign in #FFFFFF. Save your work and press F12 to preview the page in a browser.

Click on a thumbnail photo. The full-size image should appear in a pop-up window. If you're using ASP, you can download the dynamic version of JustSo Picture Window, or purchase Dynamic JustSo Picture Window Gold. The Gold version determines the image's dimensions on the server, so you don't have to store its width and height in the database. Visit **http://www.valleywebdesigns.com/vwd_gold.htm** for more information.

Summary

Now that you've gained some experience creating nested repeat regions and horizontal loopers, try putting these skills to use on other web sites. Don't be dismayed if it doesn't work on the first try. Refer to this chapter, and the sample code, until you master the basic principles. Eventually, it'll become second nature, and you'll be nesting and looping like the best of 'em.

Let's review. In this chapter, you learned to

◆ Use the DISTINCT keyword in a SELECT statement

◆ Nest a repeat region inside a horizontal looper

◆ Nest a horizontal looper inside a repeat region

- Use the `<cfoutput>` tag's `group` attribute (ColdFusion)
- Use the `MOD` operator to loop horizontally (ColdFusion)
- Apply the Nested Repeat and Horizontal Looper SBs (ASP)
- Use the `CurrentRow` variable to count records (ColdFusion)
- Adapt JustSo Picture Window to work with database columns

In the next chapter we'll create two admin pages for Chip Havilmyer's site: Add News and Edit News. The ASP version incorporates Public Domain's PD On-line HTML Editor extension. ColdFusion users will learn how to invoke `activedit.cfm`, a custom tag from CFDev.com.

Chapter 18

Online HTML Editors

INGREDIENTS

File(s)	Type	Server Model(s)	Source
realty.mdb	Access database	ASP/CF	*Sample Code*
addNews.asp, index.asp, preview.asp	Active Server Pages	ASP	*Sample Code*
preview_iframe.htm	HTML document		*Sample Code*
addNews.cfm	ColdFusion template	CF	*Sample Code*
Pure ASP File Upload 2.0.8	Server Behavior	ASP	George Petrov
PD On-Line HTML Editor	Object	ASP	Public Domain
ActivEdit 2.5	Custom tag	CF	CFDev.com

 from the desk of Paul Newman

I n this recipe, we're going to use two popular online HTML editors to create the Add News and Edit News pages of Chip Havilmyer's site. The purpose of these admin pages is to enable Chip to add and edit newsletters using a simple and familiar WYSIWYG interface. With an online HTML editor, Chip can insert links and images, create bulleted and numbered lists, and customize fonts and colors. He can even edit the HTML source code (you may want to disable this feature for some clients).

To create the ASP version of these pages, we'll use Public Domain's PD On-Line HTML Editor extension. At the time of this writing, PD On-Line HTML Editor doesn't support uploading and inserting images, so we're going to add this functionality ourselves.

ColdFusion users will invoke a custom tag, `activedit.cfm`, and learn how to make it compatible with Dreamweaver's standard Insert Record and Update Record server behaviors. Both of these online HTML editors take advantage of DHTML features exclusive to the PC version of Internet Explorer 5+ (future versions of ActivEdit may support Netscape and the Mac OS). Before you implement these editors, make sure your client's system meets the minimum requirements.

Using PD On-Line HTML Editor (ASP)

If you haven't done so already, download the PD On-Line HTML Editor extension from **www.publicdomain.to** or **www.udzone.com/go?578**. Once installed, PD On-Line HTML Editor appears on the Common tab of Dreamweaver's Insert bar.

The Add News Page

Launch Dreamweaver MX and open the Add News page (`adminch/ addNews.asp`). As you can see, I've already created a simple form with three fields: `NewsDate`, `RealtorID`, and `NewsHead`. If you open `realty.mdb` in Microsoft Access, you'll see that these form fields correspond to columns of the `News` table.

To apply the PD On-Line HTML Editor extension, place your cursor inside the last row of the `addNews` form and click the Public Domain Html Editor button on the Insert bar.

Note

 To view the Insert bar, choose Window | Insert. PD On-Line HTML Editor appears on the Common tab.

This launches the PD On-Line HTML Editor Wizard, which consists of four screens. On the first screen, Select Editor Toolbars, accept the defaults and click Next. On the second screen, Enter Editor Size, type **400** in the Width text box and leave the Height text box empty. Click Next. On the third screen, enter **#D0DCE0** in the Background Color text box, and leave the Border Color text box empty. Click Next.

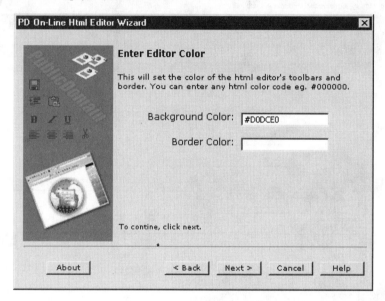

The last screen informs you that a folder called `editor_images`, and a file called `pd_edit.htm`, will be copied to your site. Click Finish.

For some reason, PD On-Line HTML Editor copies its supporting files to the site root, rather than the current folder. This is easy to fix. In Dreamweaver's Site panel, drag and drop the `editor_images` folder into the `adminch` folder. When prompted to update the files, click Don't Update. Do the same with `pd_edit.htm`, then close and reopen `addNews.asp`. The broken images in the Document window should be restored.

Notice that there's a new form field above PD Editor's toolbars: `EditorValue`. This is the field referred to in the last screen of the PD On-Line HTML Editor Wizard. When you click the Save button on PD Editor's toolbar, the contents of an `<iframe>` called `myEditor` are copied to this hidden text area. How is it hidden? This is what `EditorValue` looks like in Code view:

```
<textarea name="EditorValue" style="display: none;"></textarea>
```

Save the page and press F12 to preview it in a browser. If your browser doesn't resemble the screen shot below, make sure you're viewing the page in Internet Explorer 5 or later.

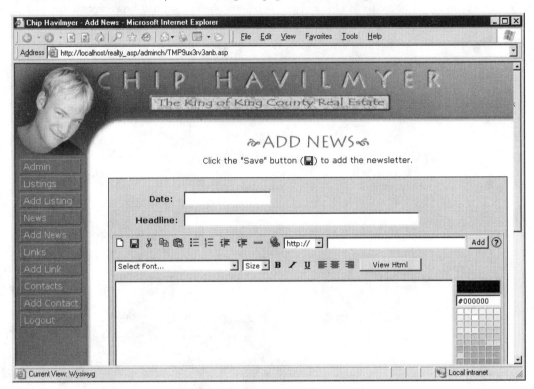

To remove the gray border around PD Editor, select PD Editor's outer table (it's the third `<table>` tag from the left on the tag selector). Use the Property inspector to change the Border attribute from 1 to 0. Now select the `url` text field—above the View Html button—and change its size (Char Width) from 35 to 19.

Save your work and press F12 again. That's better.

Before we apply the Insert Record server behavior, let's make one last change. Select the hidden text area, `EditorValue`, in the Document window. Using the Property inspector, enter the following instructions in the Init Val area: **Compose your newsletter here.**

Follow these steps to apply the Insert Record SB:

1. From the Server Behaviors panel, choose Insert Record.

2. Choose the realty connection and select `News` from the Table drop-down menu.

3. In the redirect text box, enter **../news.asp**.

4. Three form fields and database columns—`NewsDate`, `RealtorID`, and `NewsHead`—should already be matched up. Select `EditorValue` and choose `NewsItem` from the Column drop-down menu. Ignore the remaining form elements used by PD Editor.

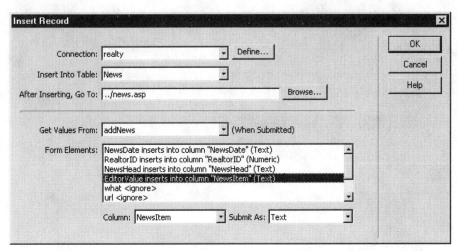

5. Click OK to apply the Insert Record SB.

Switch to Code view and locate the JavaScript statement that submits the form (around line 343):

```
document.fHtmlEditor.submit();
```

Since our form is called `addNews`, change this line to the following:

```
document.addNews.submit();
```

Save your work and press F12 to preview the page in a browser. Try pasting a selection from another web page into PD Editor's `<iframe>`. The links and formatting, even the images, should remain intact.

Click the Save button to insert the item into the Realty database. A JavaScript prompt appears: "This Document is about to be submitted. Are you sure you have finished editing?" Click OK.

You should be looking at your new entry on Chip's default Newsletter page, which now consists of three items. If the new entry doesn't appear first, make sure it's dated after March 4, 2002.

As you can see, PD Editor is an extremely useful content management tool. However, it doesn't support uploading and inserting images. We'll tackle this feature next.

The Insert Image Feature

To add the Insert Image feature to PD Editor, we'll adapt the Preview Image page we created in Chapter 14. First, however, we have to add an Insert Image button to PD Editor's toolbar.

Open addNews.asp in Dreamweaver MX and place your cursor to the right of the "HR" image (hr.gif). Choose Insert | Image (or press CTRL-ALT-I) and select image.gif from the images/news folder. Click OK.

While the image is still selected, choose Open Browser Window from the Behaviors panel (Window | Behaviors). The Insert Image files—index.asp, preview.asp, and preview_iframe.htm—are in a subfolder of adminch called Insert_Image. Use the Browse button to select Insert_Image/index.asp.

Enter **450** in the Width text box and **240** in the Height text box. Leave the Attributes unchecked and name the window **insertImage**. Click OK to apply the behavior.

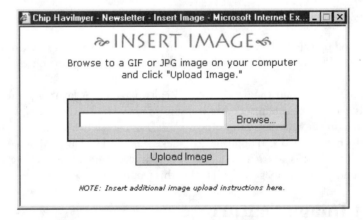

In the Behaviors panel, change Open Browser Window's trigger event from onLoad to onClick. Use the Property inspector to enter **Insert Image** in the Alt text box.

Save your work and press F12 to preview the page in a browser. Click the Insert Image button. This opens an image upload form in a pop-up window.

If you click the Upload Image button, nothing happens. That's our next step.

The Upload Page

In the Site panel, expand the adminch/Insert_Image folder and double-click index.asp to open it. This is the upload form that opens in the pop-up window.

From the Server Behaviors panel, choose UDzone | Pure ASP Upload 2.08. Click Browse and select **"../../images/news"** as the Upload Folder. Select the Images Only radio button, and choose Overwrite from the Conflict Handling drop-down menu. Finally, enter **preview.asp** in the Go To text box. Click OK to apply the server behavior.

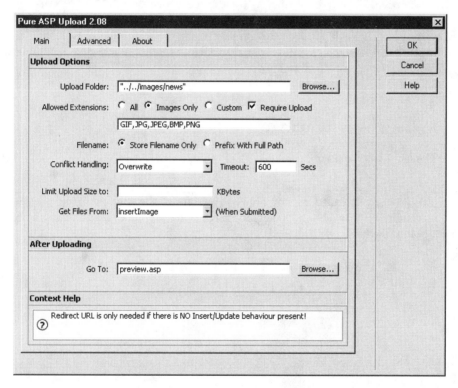

We need to make one revision to George Petrov's code. The response page previews the newly uploaded image and allows Chip to insert or delete it. In order to preview the image, we have to pass its filename to preview.asp as a URL parameter.

Switch to Code view and locate the Response.Redirect statement (around line 37):

```
Response.Redirect(GP_redirectPage)
```

Change it to the following:

```
Response.Redirect(GP_redirectPage & "?FILE=" & UploadFormRequest("FILE1"))
```

As you may recall, ASP's Form collection is unavailable when the `enctype="multipart/form-data"` attribute is added to a `<form>` tag. To get around this, George's code creates a new collection called `UploadFormRequest`. The revised redirect statement uses this collection to get the name of the image file—`UploadFormRequest("FILE1")`—and append it as a URL parameter to `preview.asp`.

The Preview Page

Open `preview.asp` in Dreamweaver MX. As you can see, it's virtually identical to the page we created in Chapter 14.

To preview the newly uploaded image, we have to stuff the value of the URL parameter (e.g., `preview.asp?FILE=luxor.jpg`) into a local variable. Switch to Code view and enter the following code above the opening `<html>` tag:

```
<%@LANGUAGE="VBSCRIPT"%>
<%
FileName=Request.QueryString("FILE")
FilePath="../../images/news/"
FullPath=FilePath & FileName
%>
```

Since the file is already uploaded, we don't have to go through the same rigmarole to extract its path. Scroll down to the first JavaScript code block and change the value of `strFullPath` (line 14) to the following (the new code is shaded):

```
strFullPath = "<%= Fullpath %>";
```

While we're at it, insert the `FileName` variable into lines 9 and 27 as well:

```
<title>Preview Image: <%= FileName %></title>     (line 9)
<span class=hline><%= FileName %></span><br>     (line 27)
```

Now we have to activate the Insert Image and Cancel buttons. Scroll down to line 35 and locate the Insert Image button:

```
<input type="button" class="button" value="Insert Image" ⤶
onMouseover="this.className='buttonover'" ⤶
onMouseout="this.className='button'">
```

Change this line to the following (the new code is shaded):

```
<input type="button" class="button" value="Insert Image" ⤶
onMouseover="this.className='buttonover'" ⤶
```

```
onMouseout="this.className='button'" ↵
onClick="window.opener.doFormat↵
('InsertImage', '../images/news/<%= FileName %>'); top.close();">
```

The preceding code adds an `onClick` event to the Insert Image button. When the user clicks the button, the event calls the `doFormat` function in `addNews.asp`, and passes it two parameters: the `InsertImage` command and the relative path to the image (`'../images/news/<%= FileName %>'`). Notice the image path is relative to `addNews.asp`, not to `preview.asp`.

> **Note**
>
> PD Editor takes advantage of the DHTML Object Model introduced in Internet Explorer 5. On the Add News page, the `doFormat` function invokes the JScript `execCommand` method and passes it two parameters: a command identifier (i.e., `InsertImage`) and an optional value. For more information, see **http://msdn.microsoft.com/library/default.asp?url=/workshop/author/dhtml/reference/methods/execcommand.asp**. A complete list of command identifiers can be found here: **http://msdn.microsoft.com/library/default.asp?url=/workshop/author/dhtml/reference/commandids.asp**.

Save your work and browse to the Add News page on your local server. Try uploading and inserting an image. When you click the Insert Image button, the newly uploaded image is inserted into PD Editor's `<iframe>` and the pop-up window closes.

What if Chip Havilmyer uploads the wrong image? We need to provide an option to cancel the current operation and delete the uploaded image.

In the Document window, select the Cancel button and press CTRL-T to open Quick Tag Editor. Add the following code before the closing > bracket:

```
onClick="window.location='deleteimage.asp?FILE=<%= FileName %>'"
```

Save your work and close `preview.asp`. Now we'll create the page that deletes the image.

The Delete Page

Create a new file in the `Insert_Image` folder and name it `deleteimage.asp`. Open the file and switch to Code view. Insert the following code above the opening `<html>` tag:

```
<% ' Delete uploaded news image

' Set path to image folder
strFilePath = Server.Mappath("../../images/news/") & "\"
strFileName = Request.QueryString("FILE")
```

```
' Instantiate the FSO
Set FSO = CreateObject("Scripting.FileSystemObject")

   If FSO.FileExists(strFilePath & strFileName) Then
      FSO.DeleteFile (strFilePath & strFileName), True
   End If

'Clean up
Set FSO = Nothing

%>
```

Scroll down to the `<body>` tag and add the following code before the closing > bracket:

```
<body onLoad="self.close();"
```

The `onLoad` event closes the pop-up window after the ASP code has executed. Save your work and browse to the Add News page on your local server. This time, upload an image and click Cancel on the preview page. The image is deleted and the pop-up window closes (you can open the `images/news` folder in the Site panel, or Windows Explorer, to verify that the image was deleted).

Congratulations! You've completed the Add News page. Now you can implement this content-management solution for other clients, or use it to manage your own web site. Just make sure to restrict access to your admin pages (see Chapter 19).

The Edit News Page

In this section, we're going to use the Add News page as the basis of the Edit News page. Since pages that insert and update records have a lot in common, it makes sense to modify the Add News page, rather than create the Edit News page from scratch.

Open `addNews.asp` in Dreamweaver MX and choose File | Save As to save it as `news.asp`. Use the Document toolbar (View | Toolbars | Document) to change the page's title from "Add News" to "Edit News." Select the "Add News" image (`add-news.gif`) in the Document window, and change its source to `edit-news.gif`. While we're at it, change the instructions to read: **Click the "Save" button to update the newsletter.** Save your work.

To change Edit News from an insert to an update page, we have to remove the Insert Record SB and apply Dreamweaver's Update Record SB. In the Server Behaviors panel, select Insert Record (form "addNews") and click the minus (–) button to delete it.

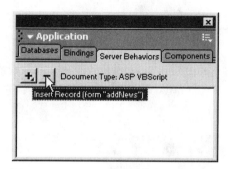

Before we can apply the Update Record SB, we have to create a recordset. From the Bindings panel, choose Recordset and name it **rsNews** (make sure you're in Simple mode). Choose the realty connection and select `News` from the Table drop-down menu. Leave the All Columns radio button selected and choose `RealtorID` from the Filter drop-down menu. Choose Entered Value from the drop-down below it and type **1** in the text box (Chip's `RealtorID` number). Finally, sort the records by `NewsDate` in Descending order (this displays the most recent newsletter first). Click OK to close the Recordset dialog box.

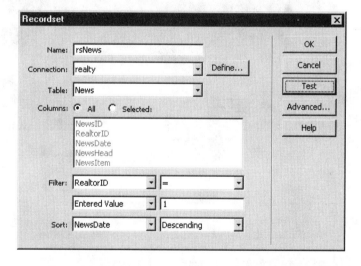

Now we need to bind the `rsNews` columns to the Edit News page. In the Bindings panel, expand the `rsNews` recordset and select the `NewsDate` column. Drag and drop it onto the

`NewsDate` text field in the Document window. (You'll see the cursor change to a plus (+) sign before you release the mouse button.) Do the same with the `NewsHead` column. Finally, drag and drop the `NewsItem` column onto the `EditorValue` text field. Save your work and press F12 to preview the page in a browser.

Unless you added another news item, you should be looking at the sample newsletter dated 3/4/2002. To allow Chip to edit previous issues of his newsletter, we have to add a navigation SB. You can use Dreamweaver's Recordset Navigation Bar (Insert | Application Objects | Recordset Navigation Bar), or one of the extensions in Tom Muck's Recordset Navigation Suite. I placed Pages List (Server Behaviors | Basic-UltraDev | Pages List) in a two-column table above the PD Editor interface.

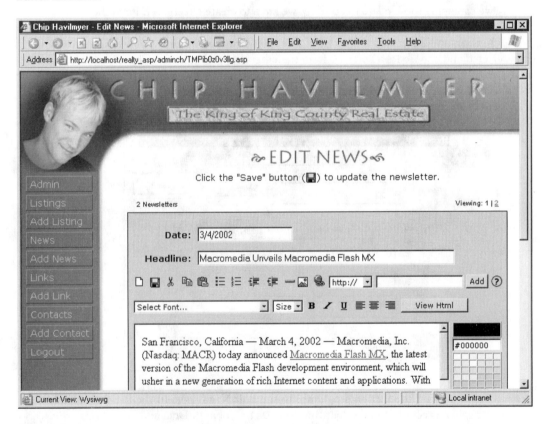

Now we can apply the Update Record SB. From the Server Behaviors panel, choose Update Record. Choose the realty connection and select `News` from the Table To Update drop-down menu. Select `NewsID` from the Unique Key Column drop-down and make sure Numeric is checked. Click Browse and select the default Newsletter page, or enter **../news.asp** in the redirect text box.

Most of the form elements are already matched up with their corresponding database columns. Select `RealtorID` and choose `<ignore>` from the Column drop-down menu. Make sure `EditorValue` updates the `NewsItem` column and click OK to apply the Update Record SB.

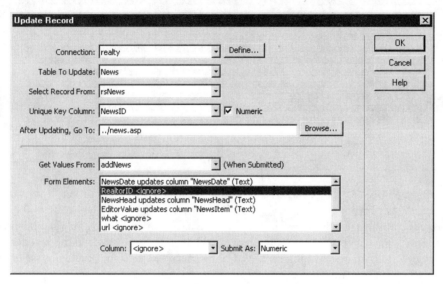

Save your work and press F12 to preview the page. Edit the first sample newsletter, dated 3/4/2002, and click Save. You should be redirected to the default Newsletter page, which now incorporates your changes.

That wraps up the recipes for PD On-Line HTML Editor. If you run into any problems, take a look at the completed pages in the `realty_asp` folder you downloaded earlier.

Using ActivEdit (ColdFusion)

The makers of ActivEdit 2.5 offer a free developer edition of `activedit.cfm` on their web site. Before we proceed, go to **http://www.cfdev.com/products/trial/index.cfm?product= ActivEdit&lang=CF** and download it. Once you've downloaded `ae25trial.zip`, extract the archive to a temporary folder on your hard drive. The ActivEdit trial consists of four folders: `cf40`, `docs`, `examples`, and `inc`. Copy `activedit.cfm` into the `CustomTags` folder of the Realty site, and copy the `inc` folder—ActivEdit's supporting files—into the `adminch/news` folder of the Realty site.

Expand the `CustomTags` folder in the Realty site and open `activedit.cfm` in a text editor. You'll find it contains nothing but gobbledygook. That's because `activedit.cfm` is encrypted.

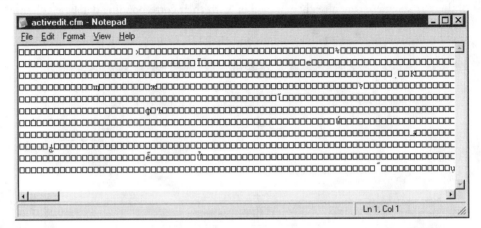

The developer edition of `activedit.cfm` is fully functional on a local server. If you attempt to use `activedit.cfm` on a remote server, you will receive a JavaScript alert message: "This is a trial version of ActivEdit 2.5. Please contact CFDev.com for a licensed version." The licensed version comes in two flavors: encrypted and unencrypted. If you want to remove the JavaScript alert, you can buy the encrypted version for $99. The unencrypted version, which allows you to edit the source code and remove the copyright notice, costs $400. Why the steep price tag? As you'll see, implementing ActivEdit is a great deal easier than using PD On-Line HTML Editor. For the most part, all you have to do is insert the custom tag, `<cf_activedit>`, into a ColdFusion page and supply the required attributes.

Tip

Don't feel like shelling out 99 bucks? Try Massimo Foti's CF XHMTL Editor, a Dreamweaver MX extension that implements a custom ColdFusion tag. Visit **www.massimocorner.com** for details.

Before we can invoke the ActivEdit tag, however, we have to install it.

Installing a Custom Tag

As you may recall, a custom tag is installed by placing it in ColdFusion's `CustomTags` directory (e.g., `C:\CFusionMX\CustomTags`). If you have access to this folder, copy `activedit.cfm` into it. If you don't have access to this folder, you can still invoke ActivEdit using the `<cfmodule>` tag.

Since most ISPs do not allow their customers to install custom ColdFusion tags, we're going to use `<cfmodule>` in the construction of the Add News and Edit News pages.

The Add News Page

Launch Dreamweaver MX and expand the `adminch/news` folder in the Site panel. Double-click `addNews.cfm` to open it.

As you can see, the Add News page consists of a simple form with three fields: `NewsDate`, `RealtorID`, and `NewsHead`. If you open `realty.mdb` in Microsoft Access, you'll see that these form fields correspond to columns of the `News` table.

In the Document window, select the Comment icon—the little yellow icon with the exclamation point—and switch to Code view. Insert the following code *after* the ColdFusion comment:

```
<cfset imgpath="C:\Inetpub\wwwroot\realty_cf_empty\www\images\news\">
<cfset imgurl="http://localhost/realty_cf/images/news/">
<cfmodule template="../../CustomTags/activedit.cfm" inc="inc" 
fieldname="NewsItem" imagepath="#imgpath#" imageurl="#imgurl#" 
upload="1" alloweditsource="1" tabview="1" width="580" border="0px">
Compose your newsletter here.</cfmodule>
```

Ordinarily, `<cfmodule>` isn't used with a closing tag. In this case, however, a closing tag is necessary because `<cf_activedit>` uses its opening and closing tags to delimit the editor area. Switch back to Design view.

Before you preview the page, there are a few things to be aware of:

1. The first `<cfset>` tag defines a variable called `imgpath`. This is simply the folder you wish to upload images to (you may need to edit this path to reflect the actual location of the news folder on your hard drive).

2. The second `<cfset>` tag defines a variable called `imgurl`. Edit this value to correspond to your local server, if necessary.

3. The third line of code is the opening `<cfmodule>` tag, used here as a means of invoking `activedit.cfm`. Notice the `inc` attribute. This points to the `inc` folder we copied earlier (the `inc` folder contains all of ActivEdit's supporting files and images). Without this folder, ActivEdit will not work.

If you're satisfied that the two `<cfset>` tags, and the `inc` attribute, point to valid locations, save your work and press F12 to preview the page in a browser.

Note

You don't have to use `<cfset>` tags with ActivEdit. I use them because I'm always changing the `imagepath` and `imageurl` attributes, and this makes them easier to find.

Click the Insert Image button. A pop-up window appears with a list of available images. Click the "New Image" link and upload an image to the news folder. If the upload succeeds, the new image is previewed in an `<iframe>`. Click the "Insert Image" link.

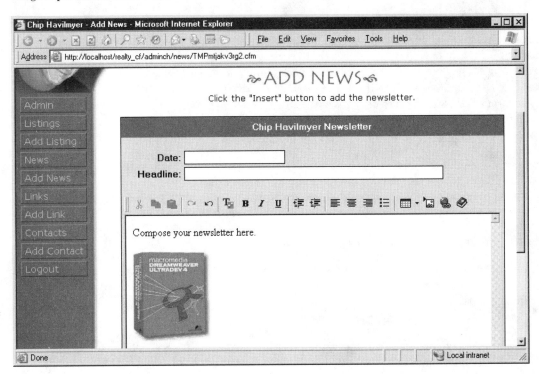

How do you like them apples? You created a full-blown HTML editor with three lines of code!

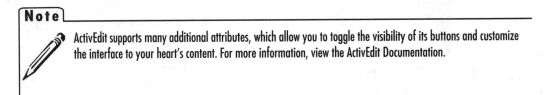

Note

ActivEdit supports many additional attributes, which allow you to toggle the visibility of its buttons and customize the interface to your heart's content. For more information, view the ActivEdit Documentation.

Now that we've got ActivEdit working, we have to teach it to play nice with Dreamweaver MX. From the Server Behaviors panel, choose Insert Record. Choose the realty data source and select News from the Table drop-down menu. Click Browse and select the default Newsletter page, or enter **../../news.cfm** in the redirect text box.

Notice that Dreamweaver MX doesn't assign a value to the `NewsItem` column. Even though we specified `"NewsItem"` in the `fieldname` attribute of the `<cfmodule>` tag, Dreamweaver doesn't recognize it because ActivEdit creates the form element at run time. As a workaround, select `NewsItem` in the Columns area and choose `FORM.NewsHead` from the Value drop-down menu. As soon as we apply the server behavior, we'll make this right. Click OK.

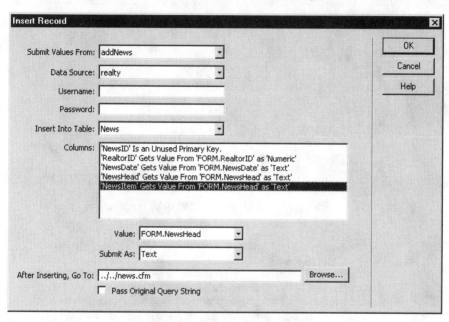

Switch to Code view and locate lines 23–24:

```
<cfif IsDefined("FORM.NewsHead") AND #FORM.NewsHead# NEQ "">
'#FORM.NewsHead#'
```

Replace the `FORM.NewsHead` variable with `FORM.NewsItem` (the new code is shaded):

```
<cfif IsDefined("FORM.NewsItem") AND #FORM.NewsItem# NEQ "">
'#FORM.NewsItem#'
```

Save your work and press F12 to preview the page. Try pasting some content from another web page into ActivEdit's `<iframe>`. The links and formatting, even the images, should remain intact.

Click the Insert button to add the item to the Realty database. You should be looking at your new entry on Chip's default Newsletter page, which now consists of three items.

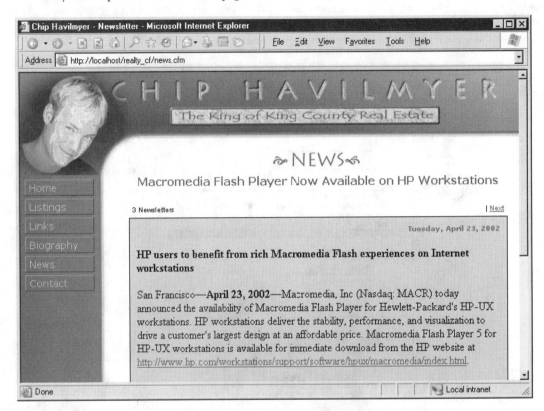

Congratulations! You've completed the Add News page (yes, it really is that simple). Now you can implement ActivEdit for other clients, or use it to manage your own web site. Just make sure to restrict access to your admin pages using Dreamweaver's User Authentication server behaviors (see Chapter 19).

The Edit News Page

Creating the Edit News page is mostly a matter of copying the Add News page and making some revisions (after all, insert and update pages have a lot in common). Open `addNews.cfm` in Dreamweaver MX and save it as `index.cfm`. Follow these steps to revise the page:

1. Using the Document toolbar (View | Toolbars | Document), change the page's title from "Add News" to "Edit News."

2. In the Document window, select the "Add News" image (`add-news.gif`) and change its source to `edit-news.gif`.

3. Change the instructions beneath the "Edit News" image to read: **Click the "Update" button to save your changes.**

4. Select the Insert button and change its Label from "Insert" to "Update."

5. Select Insert Record (form "addNews") in the Server Behaviors panel, and click the minus (–) button to delete it.

6. Click `<form>` on the tag selector and change the form's name from `addNews` to **editNews**.

7. From the Bindings panel, choose Recordset and name it **rsNews**.

8. Choose the realty data source and select `News` from the Table drop-down menu.

9. Leave the All Records radio button selected, and choose `RealtorID` from the Filter drop-down menu. Set the Entered Value to **1** (Chip Havilmyer's `RealtorID` number).

10. Sort the records by the `NewsDate` column in Descending order.

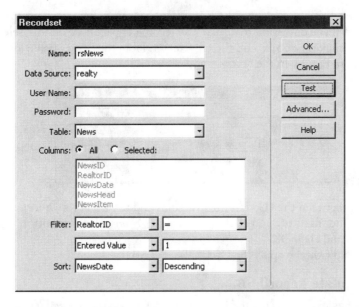

Click OK to apply the `rsNews` recordset.

11. Expand the `rsNews` recordset in the Bindings panel, and drag and drop `NewsDate` onto the `NewsDate` text field in the Document window.

12. Drag and drop the `NewsHead` column onto the `NewsHead` text field.

13. Select the hidden form field, `RealtorID`, and use the Property inspector to change its name to **NewsID**. Click the lightning bolt icon to set its value to `rsNews.NewsID`.

14. Select "Compose your newsletter here" in the Document window and switch to Code view. Make sure the closing `</cfmodule>` tag is *not* selected. Select `NewsItem` in the Bindings panel and click Insert.

Save your work and press F12 to preview the page in a browser.

So far, so good. But the date should appear in a more readable format. Select the `NewsDate` text field in the Document window and switch to Code view. Find the `<cfoutput>` statement

```
<cfoutput>#rsNews.NewsDate#</cfoutput>
```

and change it to the following:

```
<cfoutput>#DateFormat(rsNews.NewsDate, "m/d/yy")#</cfoutput>
```

To give Chip access to his previous newsletters, we'll apply Dreamweaver's Recordset Navigation Bar.

Applying the Recordset Navigation Bar

In ColdFusion sites, before you can apply the Recordset Navigation Bar, you have to create a Repeat Region (even if you only want to display one record per page). To do this, select the `editNews` form by clicking `<form>` on the tag selector. From the Server Behaviors panel, choose Repeat Region. Enter **1** in the text box and click OK.

Place your cursor between the "Update" instructions and the `editNews` form. Select the Application tab on the Insert bar and click the Recordset Navigation Bar button. Select the Images radio button and click OK.

Save your work. Now we can apply the Update Record SB.

Applying the Update Record SB

From the Server Behaviors panel, choose Update Record. Choose the realty data source and select `News` from the Update Table drop-down menu. Make sure the `NewsID` column is identified as the primary key. Select `NewsItem` in the Columns area and choose `FORM.NewsHead` from the Value drop-down menu. Select the Pass Original Query String check box and click OK to apply the Update Record SB.

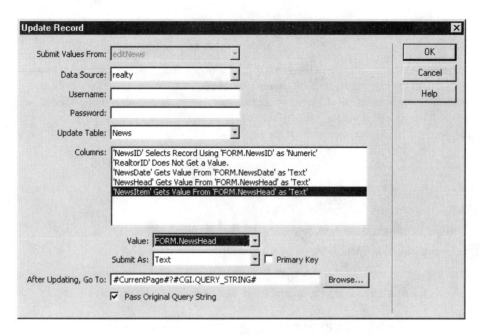

Once again, we employed a workaround to enter a value for the `NewsItem` column. To address this, switch to Code view and locate lines 17–19:

```
, NewsItem=
<cfif IsDefined("FORM.NewsHead") AND #FORM.NewsHead# NEQ "">
'#FORM.NewsHead#'
```

Replace the `FORM.NewsHead` variable with `FORM.NewsItem` (the new code is shaded):

```
, NewsItem=
<cfif IsDefined("FORM.NewsItem") AND #FORM.NewsItem# NEQ "">
'#FORM.NewsItem#'
```

That's it—you're done. Save your work and browse to the following URL on your local server: **http://localhost/realty_cf/adminch/news/**. Insert an image and revise the first news item. Click Update to save your changes. The Edit News page submits to itself, and your changes are reflected immediately. Good job!

If you run into any problems, view the completed Edit News page in the `realty_cf` folder you downloaded earlier.

Summary

As a homework assignment, consider customizing PD Editor or ActivEdit by adding and removing toolbar buttons, and tweaking the interface to suit your needs. In addition, you might want to apply a Dreamweaver behavior—such as Jaro von Flocken's Check Form, or Massimo Foti's Check Image Upload—to validate the pages before they're submitted.

Let's review. In this chapter, you learned to

◆ Insert PD On-Line HTML Editor into a Dreamweaver document (ASP)

◆ Revise PD Editor to support uploading and inserting images (ASP)

◆ Delete files using the File System Object (ASP)

◆ Install the developer edition of ActivEdit 2.5 (ColdFusion)

◆ Invoke a custom ColdFusion tag using `<cfmodule>` (ColdFusion)

◆ Revise Dreamweaver's server behaviors to work with ActivEdit (ColdFusion)

◆ Convert an insert record page to an update record page

In the next chapter you'll learn how to use session variables, and Dreamweaver's User Authentication server behaviors, to restrict access to Chip's admin section.

Chapter 19

User Authentication

I n this chapter, we're going to use Dreamweaver's User Authentication server behaviors to create a Login page for Chip Havilmyer's site. We'll also apply the Restrict Access To Page SB to an admin page, and use a session variable to filter its recordset. Finally, we'll create a Reminder page that e-mails users their login information.

Prior to Dreamweaver MX, the User Authentication server behaviors had a number of shortcomings. For instance, the password validation code in Dreamweaver UltraDev's Log In User server behavior allowed "entry of character strings which can modify the SQL statement used to query the validation table" (see **http://www.macromedia.com/support/ultradev/ts/documents/login_sb_security.htm**). According to the Macromedia TechNote, "a user with adequate coding knowledge can gain access without knowing either a username or [a] password."

In addition, the ColdFusion Log In User SB did not use `<cflock>` when accessing session variables, even though locking shared scope variables is essential in ColdFusion 4.x and 5.0 (see **http://www.macromedia.com/v1/handlers/index.cfm?ID=20370**). According to Macromedia, with the introduction of ColdFusion MX, it is no longer necessary to wrap statements that access session variables in `<cflock>` tags. However, since many applications created with Dreamweaver MX are still likely to be hosted on ColdFusion 4.x and 5.0 servers, the new-and-improved User Authentication SBs now incorporate `<cflock>` tags.

The good news is, most of the security issues concerning the User Authentication SBs have been addressed in Dreamweaver MX. Nevertheless, these server behaviors are not infallible. Malicious users can still (potentially) intercept login information that is sent across the Internet via HTTP. For greater security, consider using a secure socket layer (SSL) to encrypt the visitor's username and password during login. Visit VeriSign (**www.verisign.com/products/site**) for more information.

Understanding Sessions

One of the problems developers face when designing web applications is the "statelessness" of the Internet. Since every web page on the Internet exists as a separate entity, how do we track visitors and share data across multiple pages?

To "maintain state" across client requests, both ASP and ColdFusion offer application and session variables. Application variables, which are typically defined in a `global.asa` (ASP) or `Application.cfm` (ColdFusion) file, are non-user-specific variables that persist between page requests. A typical use of application variables is tracking and displaying the number of active visitors.

Note

In addition to application and session variables, ColdFusion offers client variables. While beyond the scope of this book, client variables offer the same functionality as cookies and can be stored in a database or the server's Registry.

Session variables, on the other hand, are per-user variables. For example, a session variable called `Username` is different for each user (e.g., "pnewman," "chavilmyer," etc.), whereas an application variable called `Sitename` is the same for all users (e.g., "Newman Zone"). Generally speaking, a session starts when a user first visits, or logs in to, an application, and persists until he clicks the Logout button, or the session times out.

Session variables, like cookies, have earned a bit of a bad reputation over the years. Because session variables are stored in the server's memory, overusing them—especially on shared servers—can adversely affect the server's performance. Some developers go to great lengths to avoid using session variables, preferring to maintain state by passing form variables or query strings from page to page. If used judiciously, however, session variables are an extremely effective way to store user-specific data for the duration of the visit (after all, that's why session variables were invented!).

Manipulating Session Variables

The syntax for defining a session variable is similar to that for defining a local variable. For example, to create a session variable called `Username`, we could write the following statement:

```
<% Session("Username") = "chavilmyer" %> (ASP)
<cfset SESSION.Username = "chavilmyer"> (ColdFusion)
```

The syntax for reading a session variable is similar to that for retrieving form variables:

```
<%= Session("Username") %> (ASP)
<cfoutput>#SESSION.Username#</cfoutput> (ColdFusion)
```

Sessions end when the user has not requested or refreshed the page for a specified period of time. The timeout interval is determined by the server's settings (the default timeout on IIS and ColdFusion Server is 20 minutes).

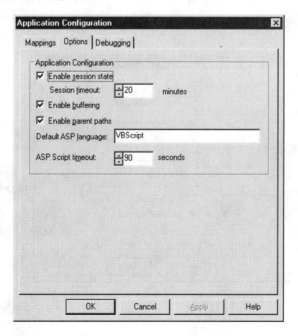

You can also change the timeout interval using a `global.asa` (ASP) or `Application.cfm` file (ColdFusion). In ASP, you can change the timeout interval on a page-by-page basis using the `Session.Timeout` property (e.g., `<% Session.Timeout = 10 %>`).

To remove session variables, you can either delete all of them at once:

`<% Session.Abandon %>` **(ASP)**
`<cfset StructClear(SESSION)>` **(ColdFusion)**

or delete them one at a time (the preferred method):

`<% Session.Contents.Remove("Username")%>` **(ASP)**
`<cfset SESSION.Username="">` **(ColdFusion)**

As you will see, Dreamweaver MX uses the second method to remove session variables in the Log Out User server behavior.

Revising Application.cfm (ColdFusion)

Before we can use session variables in ColdFusion, we have to enable session management in the `Application.cfm` page. (As you may recall, we used an `Application.cfm` file to define a site-wide errors template in the Newman Zone site.)

Launch Dreamweaver MX and open `Application.cfm` in the root folder of the Realty site. Switch to Code view. As you can see, the page already contains a `<cferror>` tag. Insert a new line at the top of the page and select the CFML Advanced tab on the Insert bar. Click the cfapplication button.

Enter **Chip** in the Application Name text box, and `#CreateTimeSpan(0,0,10,0)#` in the Session Timeout text box. Select the Enable Session Variables and Set Client Cookies check boxes and leave the other text boxes empty. Click OK.

Dreamweaver MX inserts the following code into `Application.cfm`:

```
<cfapplication name="Chip" clientmanagement="no" sessionmanagement="yes" ⅋
setclientcookies="yes" setdomaincookies="no" ⅋
sessiontimeout="#CreateTimeSpan(0,0,10,0)#">
```

The only required attribute in the `<cfapplication>` tag is name, which ColdFusion uses to identify the application. Avoid using generic names, like shop or store, to prevent the possibility of another application on a shared server using the same name. In the preceding example, the ColdFusion `CreateTimeSpan` function is used to change the default timeout value to 10 minutes. (The `CreateTimeSpan` function creates a special date/time object and accepts four parameters: days, hours, minutes, seconds.)

The `<cfapplication>` tag's remaining attributes are optional. If you decide to implement domain cookies, or client variables, you can enable them by changing the value of the attributes from `"no"` to `"yes"`. Save your work and close `Application.cfm`.

The User Login Page

Expand the `login` folder in the Site panel and open the Login page (`index.asp` or `index.cfm`, depending on your server model). As you can see, I've already created a simple login form. To complete the page, we have to apply the Log In User SB and define a third session variable (`svRealtorID`). In addition, we're going to modify the code to display an error message if the user enters the wrong username or password, rather than redirect to a separate error page.

The Log In User Server Behavior (ASP)

To apply Dreamweaver's Log In User SB, choose User Authentication | Log In User from the Server Behaviors panel. Dreamweaver MX automatically selects the login form (`loginform`) and its `Username` and `Password` fields. Choose realty from the Connection drop-down menu, and `Logins` from the Table drop-down. Select `LoginUsername` as the Username Column, and `LoginPassword` as the Password Column.

The next two text boxes redirect the browser depending on the success or failure of the login attempt. Click the Browse button next to If Login Succeeds and choose the default admin page (`../adminch/index.asp`). Check the Go To Previous URL check box. In the If Login Fails text box, enter **Invalid login. Please try again.** (instead of redirecting the browser to another page, we're going to display an error message).

The last section of the Log In User SB lets you decide how you want to restrict access to your site. Click the second radio button—Username, Password, and Access Level—and choose `AccGrpID` from the Get Level From drop-down menu. Click OK to apply the Log In User SB.

Switch to Code view and locate the line that redirects the browser if the login fails (line 37):

```
Response.Redirect(MM_redirectLoginFailed)
```

Change this line to the following:

```
strErrorMsg = MM_redirectLoginFailed
```

The value assigned to the `MM_redirectLoginFailed` variable is the string we entered in the Log In User SB: "Invalid login. Please try again." The preceding code merely reassigns the error message to a new variable: `strErrorMsg`.

Switch back to Design view and place your cursor in the fourth row of the login form. Press CTRL-M to insert a new table row (`<tr>`) above it. Select the new table row and use the Property inspector to merge its two cells (or press CTRL-ALT-M). Place your cursor inside the new table row and type **strErrorMsg**. Select "strErrorMsg" in the Document window and use the CSS Style drop-down menu on the Property inspector to apply the `red` class to the selection:

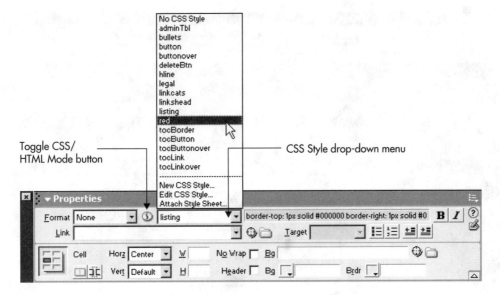

Toggle CSS/
HTML Mode button

CSS Style drop-down menu

To center the error message, choose Center from the Horz drop-down menu. This adds an `align="center"` attribute to the `<tr>` tag.

New Feature

When working with text in the Document window, the Property inspector now allows you to choose HTML or CSS mode. In CSS mode, any custom styles defined in the page, or in an external style sheet, appear in the drop-down menu. In HTML mode, menus related to the `<font>` tag appear. To change modes, click the Toggle CSS/HTML Mode button.

While "strErrorMsg" is still selected, click the ASP tab on the Insert bar and click the Output button. Dreamweaver MX switches to Split view to show you the inserted code: `<%= strErrorMsg %>`.

Save your work and press F12 to preview the page in a browser. Enter invalid values in the Username and Password fields and click Submit. The bold red error message appears.

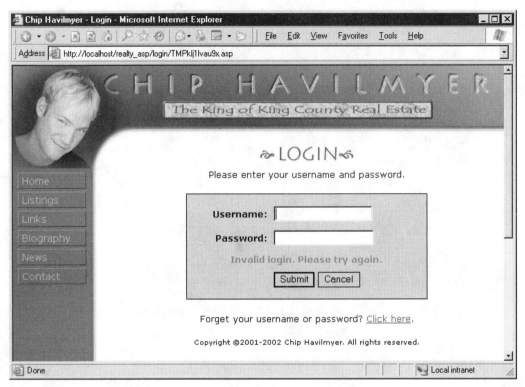

The Login User server behavior creates two session variables: `MM_Username` and `MM_UserAuthorization`. The first session variable stores the visitor's username (e.g., "chavilmyer"), and the second session variable stores the visitor's access level (e.g., 2). (If you open the `AccGrp` table in Microsoft Access, you'll see that levels 1, 2, and 3 correspond to Admin, Realtor, and Other.) To filter recordsets according to the realtor currently logged in, we have to add a third session variable: `svRealtorID`.

Switch to Code view and locate the statement that defines the `MM_Username` session variable (line 24):

```
Session("MM_Username") = MM_valUsername
```

Insert the following line below it:

```
Session("svRealtorID") = MM_rsUser("RealtorID")
```

Only one problem: the `MM_rsUser` recordset selects only the `LoginUsername`, `LoginPassword`, and `AccGrpID` columns. So scroll up to the SQL `SELECT` statement on line 15

```
MM_rsUser.Source = "SELECT LoginUsername, LoginPassword"
```

and change it to the following (the new code is shaded):

```
MM_rsUser.Source = "SELECT RealtorID, LoginUsername, LoginPassword"
```

Save your work and press F12 to preview the page in a browser. Enter **chavilmyer** in the Username field, and **realtyking** in the Password field. Click Submit. If all goes well, you should be redirected to Chip's admin section.

The Log In User Server Behavior (ColdFusion)

To apply Dreamweaver's Log In User SB, choose User Authentication | Log In User from the Server Behaviors panel. Dreamweaver MX automatically selects the login form (loginform) and its Username and Password fields. Choose realty from the Data Source drop-down menu, and the qLogins query from the Table drop-down. Select LoginUsername as the Username Column, and LoginPassword as the Password Column.

The next two text boxes redirect the browser depending on the success or failure of the login attempt. Click the Browse button next to If Login Succeeds and choose the default admin page (../adminch/index.cfm). Check the Go To Previous URL check box. In the If Login Fails text box, enter index.cfm?Error=1 (instead of redirecting the browser to another page, we're going to display an error message).

The last section of the Log In User SB lets you decide how you want to restrict access to your site. Click the second radio button—Username, Password, and Access Level—and choose AccessGroup from the Get Level From drop-down menu. Click OK to apply the Log In User SB.

Place your cursor in the fourth row of the login form, and press CTRL-M to insert a new table row (`<tr>`) above it. Select the new table row and use the Property inspector to merge its two cells (or press CTRL-ALT-M). Place your cursor inside the new table row and type **Invalid login. Please try again.** Select the error message in the Document window and use the CSS Style drop-down menu on the Property inspector to apply the `red` class to the selection (you may have to click the Toggle CSS/HTML Mode button to display the CSS Style drop-down menu).

While the error message is still selected, click the CFML Flow tab on the Insert bar and click the isDefined button. Choose URL from the drop-down menu and enter **Error** in the text box. Click OK. This displays the error message only if the URL parameter, `Error`, is defined (i.e., `index.cfm?Error=1`).

Switch to Code view and locate the `MM_redirectLoginFailed` variable (line 4):

```
<cfset MM_redirectLoginFailed="index.cfm?Error=1">
```

Insert a new line after the `<cfset>` tag and insert the following code:

```
<cfif CGI.QUERY_STRING NEQ "">
<cfset MM_redirectLoginFailed=MM_redirectLoginFailed & "&"
& CGI.QUERY_STRING>
</cfif>
```

This appends any existing URL parameters to the `MM_redirectLoginFailed` variable.

Save your work and press F12 to preview the page in a browser. Enter invalid values in the Username and Password fields and click Submit. The bold red error message appears.

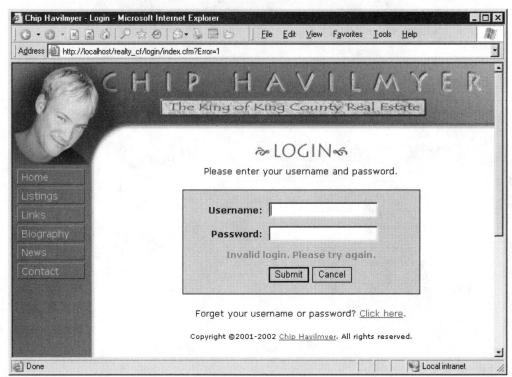

The Log In User server behavior creates two session variables: `MM_Username` and `MM_UserAuthorization`. The first session variable stores the visitor's username (e.g., "chavilmyer"), and the second session variable stores the visitor's access level (e.g., Realtor). To filter recordsets according to the realtor currently logged in, we have to add a third session variable: `svRealtorID`.

Switch to Code view and locate the statement that defines the `MM_Username` session variable (line 12):

```
<cfset Session.MM_Username=FORM.Username>
```

Insert the following line below it:

```
<cfset SESSION.svRealtorID=MM_rsUser.RealtorID>
```

Only one problem: the `MM_rsUser` recordset selects only the `LoginUsername`, `LoginPassword`, and `AccessGroup` columns. Scroll up to the `SELECT` statement on lines 6 and 7:

```
SELECT LoginUsername,LoginPassword,AccessGroup FROM qLogins
WHERE LoginUsername='#FORM.Username#' AND LoginPassword='#FORM.Password#'
```

and change it to the following (the new code is shaded):

```
SELECT RealtorID,LoginUsername,LoginPassword,AccessGroup FROM qLogins
WHERE LoginUsername='#FORM.Username#' AND LoginPassword='#FORM.Password#'
```

Unfortunately, this change makes Log In User vanish from the Server Behaviors panel. (You win some, you lose some.) Save your work and press F12 to preview the page in a browser. Enter **chavilmyer** in the Username field, and **realtyking** in the Password field. Click Submit. If all goes well, you should be redirected to Chip's admin section.

The Logout Page

Compared to creating the Login page, the Logout page is a snap. Create a new file in the `login` folder called `logout.asp` (or `logout.cfm`) and double-click the file in the Site panel to open it.

From the Server Behaviors panel, choose User Authentication | Log Out User. Select the second radio button to log out the user when the page loads. Click Browse and select Chip Havilmyer's home page (`../index.asp` or `../index.cfm`). Click OK to apply the Log Out User SB.

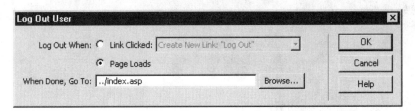

Since we added another session variable earlier, switch to Code view and insert the following code to remove it:

```
Session.Contents.Remove("svRealtorID") (ASP)
<cfset SESSION.svRealtorID = ""> (ColdFusion)
```

Save your work and close the Logout page.

Revising the Current Listings Page

Now that we can log in to and out of Chip Havilmyer's site, we can use session variables to restrict page access and filter recordsets. To illustrate this, expand the adminch folder in the Site panel and open the Current Listings page (listings.asp or listings.cfm, depending on your server model).

Restricting Page Access

To restrict access to the Current Listing page, choose User Authentication | Restrict Access To Page from the Server Behaviors panel. Select the second radio button to restrict access according to Username, Password, and Access Level. Click Define. In the Define Access Levels dialog box, create three access levels using the values shown here:

ASP	ColdFusion
1	Admin
2	Realtor
3	Other

The Define Access Levels interface can be a little confusing. To define an access level, click the plus (+) button and enter the value in the Name text box. Click the plus (+) button again to enter a second level. Click OK when you've added all three levels.

Now that we've defined three access levels, we can decide which levels are granted access to the admin section. Since we want only realtors and administrators to be able to add, edit, and remove listings, CTRL-click the first two access levels.

Finally, click the Browse button next to If Access Denied and select the Login page (.../login/index.asp or .../login/index.cfm). Click OK to apply the server behavior.

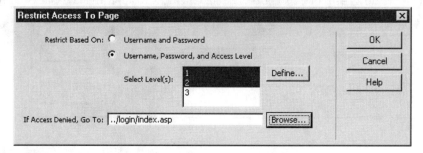

Save your work and press F12 to preview the page. The browser is redirected to the Login page, and the page you tried to access is passed as a URL parameter:

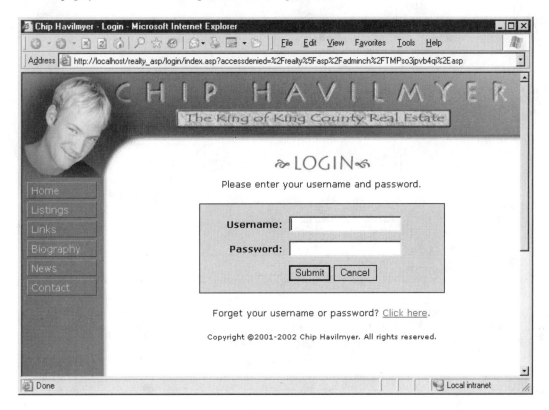

Enter **chavilmyer** in the Username field and **realtyking** in the Password field and click Submit. You should be redirected to the Current Listings page you first requested. Pretty cool, huh? Click the Logout button in the left TOC to log out. The session variables are deleted and the browser is redirected to Chip's home page.

Next, we'll filter the recordset on the Current Listings page using a session variable.

Revising the rsListings Recordset

As you may recall, Chip Havilmyer shares the third listing, 54 Clover Drive, with a realtor named Jane Doe. To avoid giving Jane access to all of Chip's listings, we're going to revise the `rsListings` recordset to filter the query using the `svRealtorID` session variable.

If it's not open already, open the Current Listings page in Dreamweaver MX (`adminch/ listings.asp` or `adminch/listings.cfm`). In the Bindings panel, double-click `rsListings`. Right now, the recordset is filtered according to Chip Havilmyer's `RealtorID` number (1). Select the drop-down menu under `RealtorID` and change Entered Value to Session Variable. Enter `svRealtorID` in the text box and click OK.

Save your work and press F12 to preview the page. The browser is redirected to the Login page. This time, enter Jane Doe's login information—username: **mejanedoe**; password: **abracadabra**— and click Submit. Instead of three listings, you should be looking at one. This is because Jane Doe is only associated with one listing. (You can verify this by opening `realty.mdb` in Microsoft Access and running the `qListings` or `qListingsAdmin` query.)

If you're feeling ambitious, you can repeat the preceding steps to restrict access to the remaining admin pages. You can also filter the recordsets on the following admin pages using the `svRealtorID` session variable:

♦ Add Listing response page

♦ Add News page

♦ Edit News page

♦ Contacts page

♦ Links page

Close the Current Listings page and log out of Chip's admin section.

The Reminder Page

The Reminder page is a courtesy for users like Chip Havilmyer, who always forgets his username and password. Fortunately, he's able to remember his e-mail address, so that's what we'll use to retrieve his login information.

Expand the `login` folder in the Site panel and open the Reminder page (`reminder.asp` or `reminder.cfm`, depending on your server model). As you can see, the Reminder page consists of a form with a single field: Email. The visitor (i.e., Chip) enters his e-mail address, and if he's a registered user, his login information is sent to him.

To search the database for Chip's login information, we have to create a new recordset. Choose Recordset from the Bindings panel and name it rsCheckEmail (make sure you're in Simple mode). Select the realty connection (or data source) and choose Logins from the Table drop-down menu. Click the Selected Columns radio button and choose FirstName , LastName, LoginUsername, LoginPassword, and Email. Finally, choose Email from the Filter drop-down menu and Form Variable from the menu below it. Click OK.

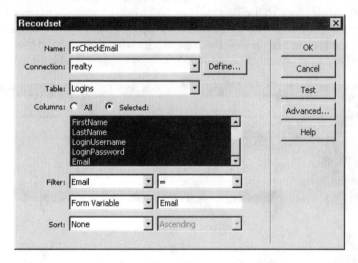

If the e-mail address is found in the Logins table, we display a confirmation message, informing Chip that his login information has been sent to him. If the e-mail address is not found—in other words, if the rsCheckEmail recordset is empty—we display an alternate message, asking the user to try again. To create the conditional regions, we'll use the ASP and CFML Flow tabs on the Insert bar.

Creating the Conditional Regions (ASP)

Switch to Code view and place your cursor *before* the rsCheckEmail code blocks (around lines 4–24). Select the ASP tab on the Insert bar and click the If button. Complete the If statement as follows:

```
<% If Request.Form("Email") <> "" Then %>
```

Scroll to the end of the rsCheckEmail code blocks and insert a new line after line 24. Click the End button on the Insert bar. This ensures that the rsCheckEmail code blocks are executed only if the form is posted.

Scroll down to the "Reminder" image (reminder.gif) and insert a new line after line 86. Click the If button on the Insert bar and complete the statement as follows:

```
<% If Request.Form("Email") = "" Then 'Display the form %>
```

Scroll down to the end of the reminder form and insert a new line after the closing </form> tag (line 110). Click Else If on the Insert bar and complete the statement as follows:

```
<% ElseIf NOT rsCheckEmail.EOF Then 'Display Thank You message %>
```

Scroll down to the paragraph that reports the e-mail address wasn't found (line 116). Place your cursor before the opening paragraph (<p>) tag and click the Else button. To complete the conditional regions, scroll down to the copyright statement (line 120) and place your cursor before the opening paragraph (<p>) tag. Click the End button on the Insert bar.

Finally, select the code block that closes the rsCheckEmail recordset (lines 129–132), and drag and drop it to the end of the <% ElseIf %> region (*before* the <% Else %> tag).

Save your work and press F12 to preview the page in a browser. Enter a valid e-mail address—e.g., chip@chiphavilmyer.com—and click Submit. Your browser should look something like this:

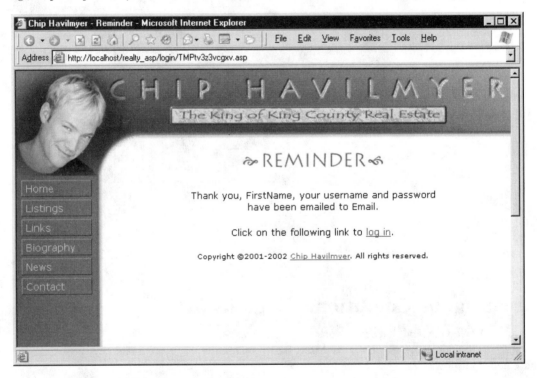

If you enter an invalid e-mail address, the last conditional region is displayed.

Creating the Conditional Regions (ColdFusion)

Before we create the conditional regions, expand CFParam in the Bindings panel and select FORM.Email. Click the minus (–) button to delete it. The reason we're deleting the <cfparam> tag is we don't want FORM.Email to have a default value.

Place your cursor inside the `reminder` form in the Document window and click the `<div>` tag on the tag selector. Select the CFML Flow tab on the Insert bar and click the isDefined button. Enter **Email** in the text box and click OK.

Dreamweaver MX switches to Split view to show you where the code was inserted. Change the closing `</cfif>` tag to `<cfelse>`.

Scroll down to line 96 and insert a closing `</cfif>` tag before the copyright statement. Switch back to Design view. The Document window should look something like this:

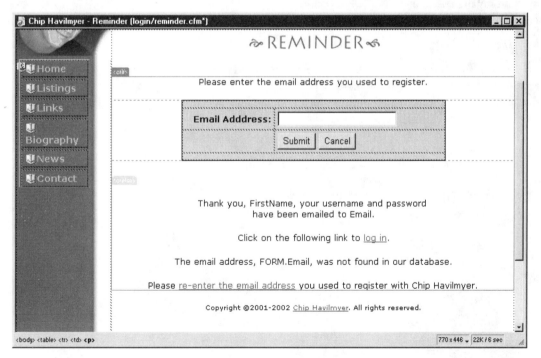

We now have two conditional regions on the page: the `reminder` form, and the messages below it. Click the `<cfif>` icon in the Document window and use the Property inspector to change the condition to `NOT isDefined("FORM.Email")`.

Switch to Code view and select the `<cfquery>` tags (lines 2–5). Click the isDefined button on the Insert bar. Enter **Email** in the text box and click OK. This ensures that the `rsCheckEmail` recordset is executed only if the form is posted.

Scroll down to the second conditional region and select everything between the `<cfelse>` tag and the closing `</cfif>` tag (lines 91–98). Click the cfif button on the Insert bar. Complete the nested `<cfif>` tag as follows:

```
<cfif rsCheckEmail.Email NEQ "">
```

Place your cursor before the opening paragraph (`<p>`) tag on line 95 and click the cfelse button on the Insert bar. If the `rsCheckEmail` recordset is *not* empty, the first region is shown. Otherwise, we inform the visitor that the e-mail address wasn't found in the database.

Save your work and press F12 to preview the page in a browser. Enter a valid e-mail address— e.g., chip@chiphavilmyer.com—and click Submit. The "Thank You" region is displayed. If you enter an invalid e-mail address, the last conditional region is displayed.

Completing the Reminder Page

To complete the Reminder page, bind `rsCheckEmail.FirstName` and `rsCheckEmail.Email` to the text placeholders in the Document window. Also replace the "Email" (or "FORM.Email") placeholder in the last conditional region with the `Email` form variable:

```
<%= Trim(Request.Form("Email")) %> (ASP)
<cfoutput>#FORM.Email#</cfoutput> (ColdFusion)
```

When you're finished, the Document window should look something like the following:

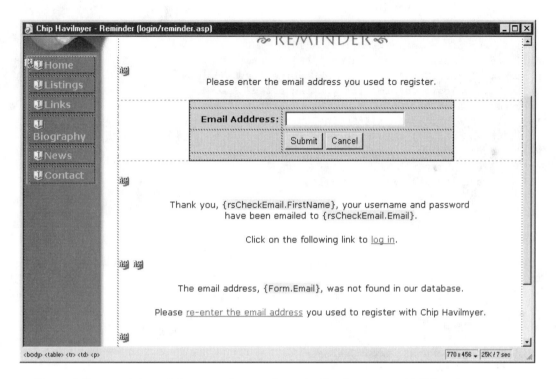

To send the visitor's login information by e-mail, use the JMail extension (ASP) or the `<cfmail>` tag (ColdFusion). Make sure to place the e-mail code inside the "Thank You" region. The completed e-mail code should look something like this (replace the sample values with your actual mail server, e-mail address, etc.):

ASP Version

```
<% '**** Send JMail if form is submitted ****
on error resume next
Set JMail = Server.CreateObject("JMail.SMTPMail")
JMail.ServerAddress = "your.mailserver.com"
JMail.Sender = "reminder@yoursite.com"
JMail.SenderName = "Chip Havilmyer"
```

```
JMail.Subject = "Chip Havilmyer Reminder"
JMail.AddRecipient rsCheckEmail("Email")
JMail.Body = "Dear " & rsCheckEmail("FirstName") & " " & ⏎
rsCheckEmail("LastName") & "," & vbNewLine & vbNewLine & _
"Below is the login information you requested: " & vbNewLine & vbNewLine & _
"Username: " & rsCheckEmail("LoginUsername") & vbNewLine & _
"Password: " & rsCheckEmail("LoginPassword") & vbNewLine & vbNewLine & _
"Love," & vbNewLine & vbNewLine & "Chip"
JMail.Execute
Set JMail = Nothing
  If Err Then 'Create error variable
  strError = Err.Description
  End If 'End check for errors %>
```

ColdFusion Version

```
<cfmail to="#rsCheckEmail.Email#" from="reminder@yoursite.com" subject="Chip ⏎
Havilmyer Reminder">
Dear #rsCheckEmail.FirstName# #rsCheckEmail.LastName#,

Below is the login information you requested:

Username: #rsCheckEmail.LoginUsername#
Password: #rsCheckEmail.LoginPassword#

Love,

Chip
</cfmail>
```

If you run into any problems, take a look at the completed version of the Reminder page in the `realty_asp` (or `realty_cf`) folder you downloaded earlier.

Summary

Can you believe it? You're one chapter away from becoming a Dreamweaver MX Master Chef!

Part of being a great chef is taking existing recipes and making them your own. In this chapter, you learned to spice up Dreamweaver's User Authentication server behaviors to create a whole new taste sensation. In addition, you learned to

- Add and remove session variables
- Enable session variables using the `<cfapplication>` tag
- Password-protect ASP and ColdFusion pages
- Restrict page access according to access levels
- Filter recordsets using session variables
- Create a Reminder page

In the next chapter, we'll tie up loose ends by completing Chip's remaining admin pages.

Chapter 20

Admin Section

INGREDIENTS

File(s)	Type	Server Model(s)	Source
realty.mdb	Access database	ASP/CF	*Sample Code*
listing-detail.asp, listings.asp, edit-details.asp, addListing.asp, addRealtor.asp, edit-listing.asp	Active Server Pages	ASP	*Sample Code*
listing-detail.cfm, listings.cfm, edit-details.cfm, addListing.cfm, addRealtor.cfm, edit-listing.cfm	ColdFusion templates	CF	*Sample Code*

 from the desk of Paul Newman

In this chapter, we're going to complete the remaining pages in Chip Havilmyer's admin section. Along the way, we're going to identify and resolve several usability issues (i.e., kill bugs dead). The first issue concerns the Add Listing page. As you may recall, in Chapter 11 we added a "linking" table, `ListingRealtors`, to accommodate listings with more than one realtor. What we haven't done yet is provide the option to add a realtor to an existing listing.

The second issue concerns the Edit Listing Details page. Right now, if Chip adds a listing to his site but doesn't add any details for that listing, the Edit Listing Details page returns an error. To remedy this, we'll apply Dreamweaver's Show Region If Recordset Is Empty server behavior.

To sum up, here's what we have to do to complete Chip's site:

◆ Revise the Listing Details page

◆ Revise the Current Listings page

◆ Revise the Edit Listing Details page

◆ Revise the Add Listing page

◆ Create the Add Realtor page

◆ Create the Edit Listing page

Looks like we've got our work cut out for us. Let's get started.

Revising the Listing Details Page

The Listing Details page is not part of Chip's admin section, but we need to revise it nonetheless. To demonstrate why, browse to the Add Listing page on your local server. Add a new listing and click the "Property Details" link on the Current Listings page.

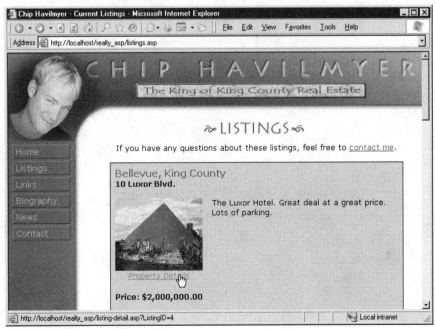

You should receive the following error:

```
Microsoft VBScript runtime (0x800A01A8)
Object required:
/realty_asp/listing-detail.asp, line 345
```

Line 345 is the code that closes the `rsListingRooms` recordset:
`rsListingRooms.Close()`. To fix this, we have to move the offending code into the
page's nested repeat region.

>
>
> This error applies only to the ASP version of the Realty site. ColdFusion users can skip ahead to the next section,
> "The Current Listings Page."

Open `listing-detail.asp` in Dreamweaver MX. In the Document window, select the
gray Repeat icon and switch to Code view. To create the outer loop, Dreamweaver MX uses the
following code:

```
While ((Repeat1__numRows <> 0) AND (NOT rsRoomCats.EOF))
```

If Chip adds a listing but doesn't add any details for that listing, the `rsRoomCats` recordset is
empty and the repeat region isn't displayed. Unfortunately, the line that closes the nested recordset,
`rsListingRooms`, is *outside* the repeat region. This raises an error because ADO is trying to close
a recordset that—as far as it's concerned—doesn't exist.

Scroll to the bottom of `listing-detail.asp` and select the following code:

```
<%
rsListingRooms.Close()
%>
```

Cut and paste it *after* the `Wend` statement on line 315.

Save your work and browse to the new listing (e.g., **http://localhost/realty_asp/listing-
detail.asp?ListingID=4**). If you arrive at the Listing Details page without incident, you solved
the problem.

Revising the Current Listings Page

To complete the admin Current Listings page, we have to edit the buttons that link to the Edit
Listing, Add Listing Details, and Edit Listing Details pages.

Expand the `adminch` folder in the Site panel and open `listings.asp` (or `listings.cfm`).
In the Document window, select the Edit Listing button—the pencil icon—and click the folder
icon on the Property inspector. This opens the Select File dialog box. Click the Parameters
button. Enter `ListingID` in the Name column, and click the lightning bolt icon in the Value

column. Expand the `rsListings` recordset and select the `ListingID` column in the Dynamic Data dialog box. Click OK.

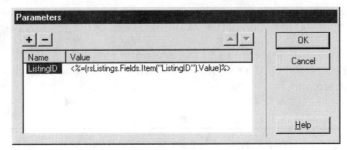

Click OK again to close the Parameters dialog box. The path in the URL text box should look like this:

```
edit-listing.asp?ListingID=↵
<%=(rsListings.Fields.Item("ListingID").Value)%> (ASP)
edit-listing.cfm?ListingID=#rsListings.ListingID# (ColdFusion)
```

Click OK to close the Select File dialog box. Save your work and press F12 to preview the page in a browser (you may be prompted to log in). Mouse over the Edit Listing button. The query string is appended to the URL (e.g., `edit-listing.asp?ListingID=3`).

Repeat the preceding steps with the Add Listing Details and Edit Listing Details buttons. In the Parameters dialog box, enter `ListingID` in the Name column, and select `rsListings.ListingID` in the Value column.

When you're finished, save your work and give the page a test-drive. Click the first Edit Listing Details button. An error occurs:

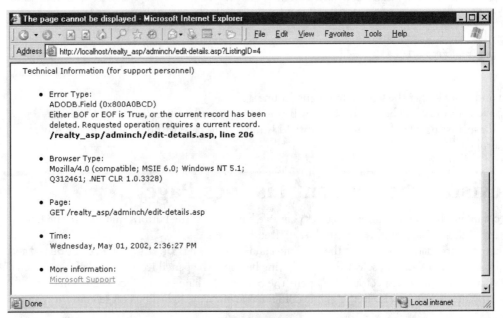

If you're using ColdFusion, the page should look something like this:

These problems occur because the `ListingRooms` table contains no records for the new listing (after all, we just added it). That's what we'll fix next.

Revising the Edit Listing Details Page

To accommodate listings that have no details—it could happen—we have to create two conditional regions on the Edit Listing Details page. One region displays the listing details (if they exist). The second region links to the Add Listing Details page. To do this, we'll use Dreamweaver's Show Region If Recordset Is Empty server behavior.

Expand the `adminch` folder in the Site panel and open `edit-details.asp` (or `edit-details.cfm`). In the Document window, insert a new paragraph after the "Edit Listing Details" image (`edit-details.gif`) and type the following message: **Click on the following link to add details to this listing**. Select "add details" in the Document window and enter the following code in the Property inspector's Link text box:

```
addDetails.asp?ListingID=<%= Request.QueryString("ListingID") %> (ASP)
addDetails.cfm?ListingID=<cfoutput>#URL.ListingID#</cfoutput> (ColdFusion)
```

In the Document window, select the paragraph (`<p>`) we just added. This is the region we want to show if no listing details exist. From the Server Behaviors panel, choose Show Region | Show Region If Recordset Is Empty. Choose `rsListingRooms` from the Recordset drop-down menu and click OK.

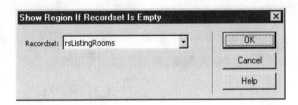

Select the conditional region we just created and switch to Code view. Locate the End If statement (or `</cfif>` tag):

```
<% End If ' end rsListingRooms.EOF And rsListingRooms.BOF %> (ASP)
</cfif> (ColdFusion)
```

and change it to the following:

```
<% Else 'show listing details %> (ASP)
<cfelse><!--- Show listing details ---> (ColdFusion)
```

Scroll down to the bottom of the page and add the following code after the "Back to Top" link (the new code is shaded):

```
<p align="center"><a href="#top">Back to Top</a></p><% End If %> (ASP)
<p align="center"><a href="#top">Back to Top</a></p></cfif> (ColdFusion)
```

Save your work and press F12 to preview the page in a browser. Add the query string `?ListingID=4` to the URL and press ENTER. Your browser should look something like the following:

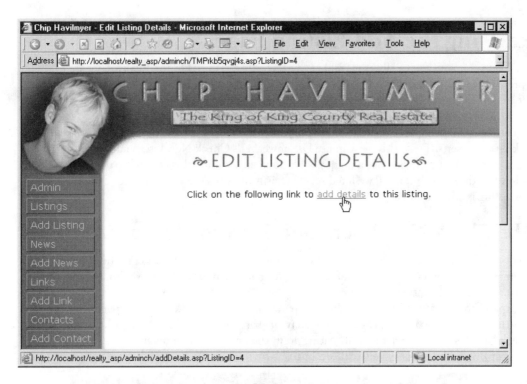

If you prefer, you can replace the alternate message with a `Response.Redirect` statement or a `<cflocation>` tag:

```
<% Response.Redirect("addDetails.asp?ListingID=" & ⤶
Request.QueryString("ListingID")) %> (ASP)
<cflocation url="addDetails.cfm?ListingID=#URL.ListingID#"> (ColdFusion)
```

This automatically redirects the visitor to the Add Listing Details page if the `rsListingRooms` recordset is empty.

Revising the Add Listing Page

In Chapter 11, we added a "linking" table (`ListingRealtors`) to the Realty database to represent a many-to-many relationship between the `Listings` and `Realtors` tables. This allows us to accommodate listings with more than one realtor. What we haven't addressed yet is how do authorized users add a realtor to an existing listing?

The solution is simple. On the Add Listing page, we check if the listing already exists *before* making any inserts. To do this, we can use Dreamweaver's Check New Username server behavior. Since each real estate listing has a unique MLS number, we'll use this column to determine if the listing already exists. If it does, we'll redirect the visitor to the Add Realtor page. Otherwise, the new listing is added as usual.

The Check New Username Server Behavior (ASP)

To query the Realty database for an existing listing, we'll use Dreamweaver's Check New Username server behavior. Instead of checking for a username, however, we'll query the `Listings.MLSNumber` column.

Expand the `adminch` folder in the Site panel and open the Add Listing page (`addListing.asp`). From the Server Behaviors panel, choose User Authentication | Check New Username. Select `MLSNumber` from the drop-down menu and click Browse to select the Add Realtor page (`addRealtor.asp`). Click OK.

Switch to Code view and locate the Check New Username code block (you can also click Check New Username in the Server Behaviors panel to select it). The Check New Username server behavior creates a new recordset, `MM_rsKey`, and filters it using the `MLSNumber` form variable:

```
MM_dupKeySQL="SELECT MLSNumber FROM Listings WHERE MLSNumber='" & ⏎
MM_dupKeyUsernameValue & "'"
```

If a match is found—`If Not MM_rsKey.EOF Or Not MM_rsKey.BOF`—the visitor is redirected to the Add Realtor page before any inserts are made.

The UploadFormRequest Collection

Now comes the tricky part. Because the `<form>` tag contains the `enctype="multipart/form-data"` attribute, we can't use the ASP Form collection to retrieve form variables. Instead, we'll use George Petrov's `UploadFormRequest` collection. In the Check New Username code block, replace `Request` and `Request.Form` with `UploadFormRequest`. The revised code should look like this (the new code is shaded):

```
<%
' *** Redirect if username exists
MM_flag="MM_insert"
If (CStr(UploadFormRequest(MM_flag)) <> "") Then
  MM_dupKeyRedirect="addRealtor.asp"
  MM_rsKeyConnection=MM_realty_STRING
  MM_dupKeyUsernameValue = CStr(UploadFormRequest("MLSNumber"))
...
```

Save your work and press F12 to preview the page in a browser. Enter an existing MLS number, such as 777777, and complete the form. When you click the Add Listing button, you should be redirected to the Add Realtor page.

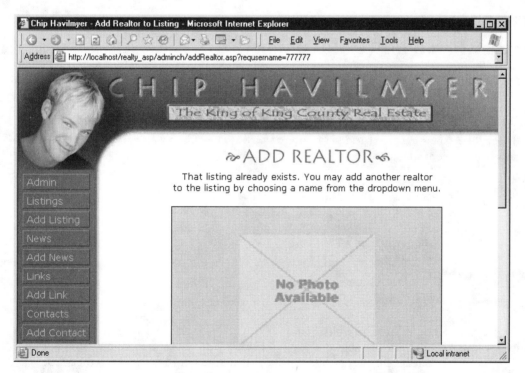

Notice that Dreamweaver MX appends the MLS number to `addRealtor.asp` as a query string. We can use the value of `requsername` to filter the recordset on the Add Realtor page.

Deleting the Uploaded Image

The only flaw with this approach is that, because the Pure ASP File Upload code block is executed before the Check New Username code block, the image is still uploaded. To address this, add the following code after the "username was found" comment:

```
' the username was found - can not add the requested username
Set FSO = CreateObject("Scripting.FileSystemObject")
strFilename = UploadFormRequest("File1")
strFilePath = Server.MapPath("../images/listings/") & "\"
If FSO.FileExists(strFilePath & strFilename) Then
FSO.DeleteFile (strFilePath & strFilename), True
End If
Set FSO = Nothing
```

Save your work and close the Add Listing page.

The Check New Username Server Behavior (ColdFusion)

Because we hand-coded so many changes to the Add Listing page, Dreamweaver MX no longer recognizes the Insert Record SB. As a result, when you attempt to apply the Check New Username SB, Dreamweaver MX prompts you to apply an Insert Record SB first.

As a workaround, we'll insert the code ourselves. Expand the `adminch` folder in the Site panel and open the Add Listing page (`addListing.cfm`). Switch to Code view and insert the following code at the very top of the page:

```
<cfif IsDefined("FORM.MLSNumber")>
<cfquery name="MM_search" datasource="realty">
SELECT MLSNumber FROM Listings WHERE MLSNumber='#FORM.MLSNumber#'
</cfquery>
<cfif MM_search.RecordCount GTE 1>
<cflocation url="addRealtor.cfm?requsername=#FORM.MLSNumber#"
addtoken="no">
</cfif>
</cfif>
```

The Check New Username code block creates a new recordset, `MM_search`, and filters it using the `MLSNumber` form variable. If a match is found—`<cfif MM_search.RecordCount GTE 1>`—the user is redirected to the Add Realtor page. Because the code appends the MLS number to `addRealtor.cfm` as a query string, we can use the value of `requsername` to filter the recordset on the Add Realtor page.

Save your work and press F12 to preview the page in a browser. Enter an existing MLS number, such as 777777, and complete the form. When you click the Add Listing button, you should be redirected to the Add Realtor page.

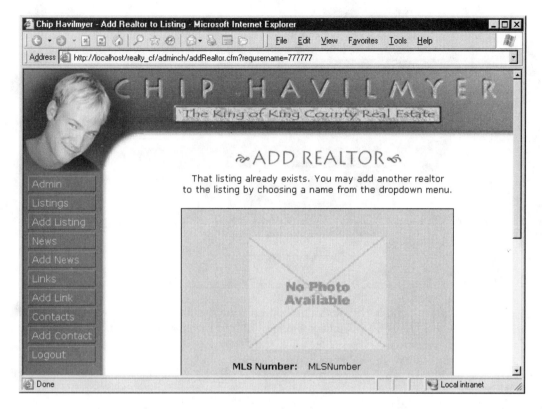

Because we placed the Check New Username code at the top of `addListing.cfm`, the file upload and insert code blocks are never executed.

The Add Realtor Page

The Add Realtor page informs the visitor that the listing already exists, and offers the option to add another realtor to the listing. To complete the Add Realtor page, we have to create two recordsets: one to display information about the current listing, and another to populate the `RealtorID` drop-down menu.

The rsThisListing Recordset

Expand the `adminch` folder in the Site panel and open the Add Realtor page (`addRealtor.asp` or `addRealtor.cfm`). From the Bindings panel, choose Recordset and name it `rsThisListing`. Choose the realty connection (or data source) and select the `qListingsAdmin` query from the Table drop-down menu. Click the Selected Columns radio button and select the following columns: `ListingID`, `MLSNumber`, `ListingAddress`, `RealtorID`, `Realtor`, `ListingPic`. Choose `MLSNumber` from the Filter drop-down menu and enter `requsername` in the URL parameter text box (this is the query string passed from the Add Listing page). Click OK to apply the recordset.

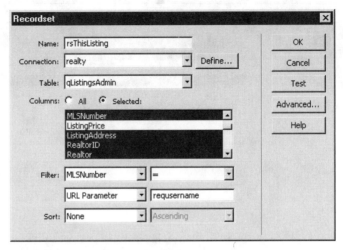

Expand `rsThisListing` in the Bindings panel and bind the database columns to their corresponding placeholders in the Document window. To bind the image, drag and drop the `ListingPic` column onto the placeholder image (`nopic.gif`) in the Document window. Use the Property inspector to complete the path:

```
../images/listings/⏎
<%=(rsThisListing.Fields.Item("ListingPic").Value)%> (ASP)
../images/listings/⏎
<cfoutput>#rsThisListing.ListingPic#</cfoutput> (ColdFusion)
```

To bind the hidden form field, drag the `ListingID` column from the Bindings panel and drop it on the hidden field marker in the Document window.

As you may recall, the third listing—54 Clover Drive—has two realtors: Chip Havilmyer and Jane Doe. To display *all* the realtors associated with the current listing, select {rsThisListing.Realtor} in the Document window and choose Repeat Region from the Server Behaviors panel. Select the All Records radio button and click OK. Select the gray "Repeat" (or "<cfoutput>") icon in the Document window and switch to Code view. Insert a break tag (`<br>`) after the `Realtor` column to prevent the realtor names from running together (the new code is shaded):

```
<%=(rsThisListing.Fields.Item("Realtor").Value)%><br> (ASP)
<cfoutput query="rsThisListing">⏎
#rsThisListing.Realtor#<br></cfoutput> (ColdFusion)
```

Save your work and browse to the Add Realtor page on your local server (e.g., **http://localhost/ realty_asp/adminch/addRealtor.asp**). Append the following query string to the URL: **?requsername= 777777**. Your browser should look something like this:

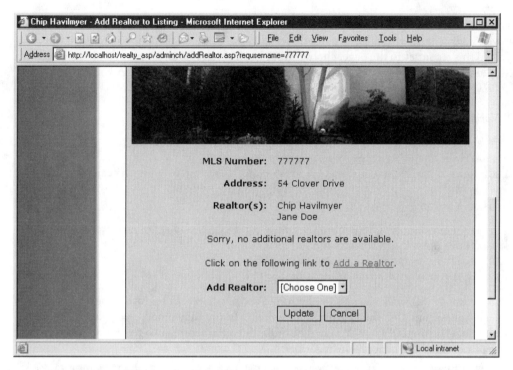

Now we have to populate the `RealtorID` drop-down menu.

The rsGetRealtors Recordset

The `rsGetRealtors` recordset populates the drop-down menu with a list of available realtors. In order to display only those realtors not already associated with the current listing, we'll write a SQL `SELECT` statement that uses a subquery. The completed SQL statement looks like this:

```
SELECT RealtorFName & ' ' & RealtorLName AS Realtor, RealtorID
FROM Realtors WHERE RealtorID NOT IN
(SELECT RealtorID FROM ListingRealtors WHERE ListingID = intListingID)
```

Confused? The easiest way to understand a query that uses a subquery is to run each query separately. The subquery queries the `ListingRealtors` table for realtors associated with the current `ListingID` number. If the value of the `intListingID` variable is 3, the subquery returns two records: 1, 2. These are the `RealtorID` numbers of Chip Havilmyer and Jane Doe. You can try this yourself by opening `realty.mdb` in Microsoft Access and running the following query:

```
SELECT RealtorID FROM ListingRealtors WHERE ListingID = 3
```

Now run the main query in Access. Enter the results from the subquery in the parentheses:

```
SELECT RealtorFName & ' ' & RealtorLName AS Realtor, RealtorID
FROM Realtors WHERE RealtorID NOT IN (1,2)
```

This example returns no results because the Realty database contains only two realtors. However, if you change the value in parentheses to 1, the query returns one record: Jane Doe.

To add this recordset to the page, choose Recordset from the Bindings panel and name it `rsGetRealtors`. Choose the realty connection (or data source) and click Advanced. Enter the following SELECT statement in the SQL area:

ASP Version

```
SELECT RealtorFName & ' ' & RealtorLName AS Realtor, RealtorID
FROM Realtors WHERE RealtorID NOT IN
(SELECT RealtorID FROM ListingRealtors WHERE ListingID = intListingID)
```

ColdFusion Version

```
SELECT RealtorFName & ' ' & RealtorLName AS Realtor, RealtorID
FROM Realtors WHERE RealtorID NOT IN
(SELECT RealtorID FROM ListingRealtors
WHERE ListingID = #rsThisListing.ListingID#)
```

If you're using ASP, click the plus (+) button to add a variable. Enter **intListingID** in the Name column, and **0** in the Default Value column. In the Run-time Value column, enter **rsThisListing("ListingID")**. Click Test. The SQL statement returns two records: Chip Havilmyer and Jane Doe. Click OK to apply the recordset.

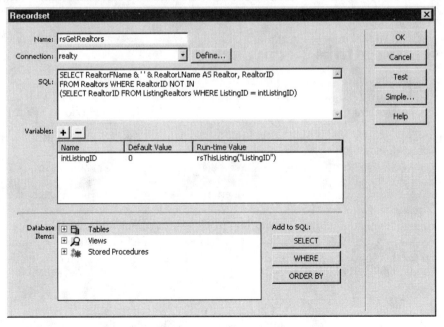

If you're using ColdFusion, you can click the plus (+) button to add a `<cfparam>` tag, but defining a default value for `#rsThisListing.ListingID#` isn't necessary.

To populate the drop-down menu, choose Dynamic Form Elements | Dynamic List Menu from the Server Behaviors panel. Select `rsGetRealtors` from the Recordset drop-down menu and `RealtorID` from the Values drop-down menu. The `Realtor` column should appear in the Labels drop-down by default. Click OK.

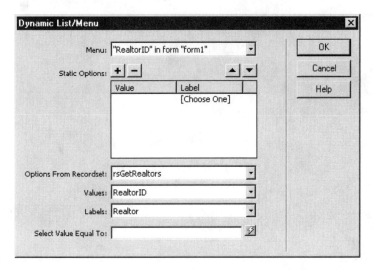

Save your work and browse to the Add Realtor page on your local server. Append the following query string to the URL: **?requsername=123456**. The drop-down menu should contain one realtor: Jane Doe. If you change the query string to 777777, the drop-down menu contains no realtors. To address this, we'll define a region that displays alternate content if the `rsGetRealtors` recordset is empty.

The Show Region Server Behaviors

To create the first conditional region, select the sixth table row (`<tr>`) in the page's form (the row that contains the "Sorry" message). From the Server Behaviors panel, choose Show Region | Show Region If Recordset Is Empty. Choose `rsGetRealtors` from the Recordset drop-down menu and click OK.

This displays the selection if `rsGetRealtors` is empty. Now select the seventh and eighth table rows in the form and choose Show Region | Show Region If Recordset Is Not Empty from the Server Behaviors panel. Select the `rsGetRealtors` recordset and click OK. The Document window should look something like this:

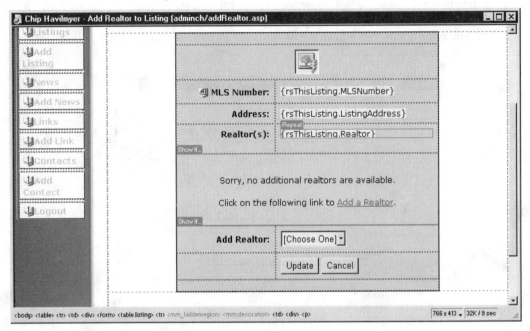

Save your work.

The last step is to apply the Insert Record SB. From the Server Behaviors panel, choose Insert Record and select the realty connection (or data source). Choose `ListingRealtors` from the Table drop-down menu and enter `listings.asp` (or `listings.cfm`) in the redirect text box. The `ListingRealtors` table consists of two columns: `RealtorID` and `ListingID`. Make sure these appear in the Form Elements (or Columns) area and click OK.

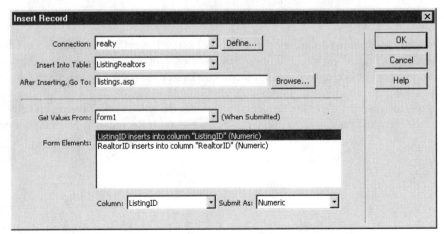

Save your work and browse to the Add Realtor page on your local server (e.g., **http://localhost/ realty_asp/adminch/addRealtor.asp**). Append the following query string to the URL: **?requsername= 123456**. Select Jane Doe from the drop-down menu and click Update. If you're prompted to log in, enter Jane Doe's username and password and click Submit.

You should be redirected to the admin Current Listings page. Notice anything different? Instead of one listing, Jane now has two!

The Edit Listing Page

To complete Chip Havilmyer's admin section, expand the `adminch` folder in the Site panel and open the Edit Listing page (`edit-listing.asp` or `edit-listing.cfm`). As you can see, the Edit Listing page is almost finished. All we have to do is bind the form elements to database columns and apply Dreamweaver's Update Record SB.

From the Bindings panel, choose Recordset and name it `rsEditListing`. Choose the realty connection (or data source) and select `qListingsAdmin` from the Table drop-down menu (make sure you're in Simple mode). Leave the All Columns radio button selected and choose `ListingID` from the Filter drop-down menu. Click OK.

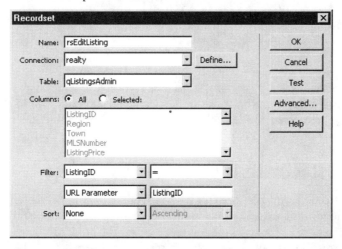

Use the Bindings panel to bind the columns from the `rsEditListing` recordset to their respective placeholders in the Document window. Skip the drop-down menus and check boxes for now.

When you're finished, create five more recordsets—`rsPropertyRegion`, `rsPropertyTown`, `rsPropertyType`, `rsBedrooms` and `rsBathrooms`—and use Dreamweaver's Dynamic List/Menu SB to populate the drop-down menus. The recordsets, values, and labels are shown in the table that follows. Use the Select Value Equal To option in the Dynamic List/Menu SB to select the appropriate `rsEditListing` column.

Recordset	Values	Labels	Select Value Equal To
rsPropertyRegion	PropertyRegionID	PropertyRegionName	rsEditListing.PropertyRegionID
rsPropertyTown	PropertyTownID	PropertyTownName	rsEditListing.PropertyTownID
rsPropertyType	PropertyTypeID	PropertyTypeName	rsEditListing.PropertyTypeID
rsBedrooms	BedroomID	BedroomCount	rsEditListing.BedroomID
rsBathrooms	BathroomID	BathroomCount	rsEditListing.BathroomID

To create the dynamic check boxes, you can use Dreamweaver's Dynamic CheckBox SB, but this server behavior rarely produces the desired results. Instead, select the `Active` check box in the Document window and switch to Code view. Add the following code to the `<input>` tag, just before the closing `>` bracket:

```
<% If (rsEditListing.Fields.Item("Active").Value <> 0) Then ↵
Response.Write("CHECKED") : Response.Write("")%> (ASP)
<cfif rsEditListing.Active NEQ 0>CHECKED</cfif> (ColdFusion)
```

Adapt this code for the other two check boxes, `Sold` and `Basement`, and save your work.

The Update Record SB (ASP)

To finish the Edit Listing page, choose Update Record from the Server Behaviors panel. Choose the realty connection and select `Listings` from the Table drop-down menu. Choose `rsEditListing` in the Select Record From drop-down menu and make sure `ListingID` is the Unique Key Column. Finally, change the Submit As value for the three check boxes—`Active`, `Sold`, `Basement`—to Checkbox –1,0. Click OK to apply the Update Record SB.

The Update Record SB (ColdFusion)

You've probably noticed by now that the ColdFusion Update Record SB has changed. Dreamweaver MX no longer creates the hidden form element (i.e., `MM_recordId`) that stores the value of the table's primary key column. To create the hidden field, place your cursor to the right of the Cancel button and select Forms on the Insert bar. Click the Hidden Field button and use the Property inspector to name the hidden field `ListingID`. Click the lightning bolt icon next to the Value text box and select `ListingID` from the `rsEditListing` recordset. Click OK to close the dialog boxes.

Choose Update Record from the Server Behaviors panel. Choose the realty data source and select `Listings` from the Update Table drop-down menu. Make sure `ListingID` is identified as the Primary Key column. Change the Submit As value for the three check boxes—`Basement`, `Active`, `Sold`—to Checkbox –1,0. Finally, select the Pass Original Query String check box. Click OK to apply the Update Record SB.

Summary

Congratulations! You are now an official Dreamweaver MX Master Chef!

Truth is, Chip's admin section isn't 100 percent complete. To earn your certification, you have to create one last page on your own: the Delete Listing Detail page (`delete-detail.asp` or `delete-detail.cfm`). This page is similar to the Delete Listing page we created in Chapter 15. The main difference is that you're deleting one record—and its associated image—from the `ListingRooms` table, rather than looping through multiple records.

To sum up, in this chapter you learned to

- ◆ Use a subquery in a SQL `SELECT` statement
- ◆ Apply the Check New Username server behavior
- ◆ Apply Dreamweaver's Show Region server behaviors
- ◆ Create dynamic check boxes
- ◆ Apply Dreamweaver's Update Record SB

Now that you're a Master Chef, it's time to start inventing recipes of your own. Stop by **www.newmanzone.com** sometime and let me know what you're cooking.

Appendix A

Sample Code

The examples in this book are presented in ASP/VBScript and ColdFusion MX formats. In addition, ASP.NET versions of the Newman Zone and Realty sites are provided to demonstrate new features of Dreamweaver MX.

If you complete the chapters in order, *The Joy of Dreamweaver MX* enables you to construct two functional web sites: Newman Zone and Realty. The Newman Zone site applies to Part II (Chapters 5–10), and the Realty site applies to Part III (Chapters 11–20). Unless you want to preview the completed sites, copy the empty versions of the sites you wish to work with to the root of your local web server (e.g., C:\Inetpub\wwwroot).

To download the supporting files for *The Joy of Dreamweaver MX*, visit **www.newmanzone.com** or **www.osborne.com/downloads/downloads.shtml**. The zip file consists of 17 folders. The first three folders contain the completed files for Chapters 1, 4, and 11 (see Table A-1). The next two folders contain the databases, and some of the extensions, used in the book.

Folder	Description
Chapter1	Completed Chapter 1 files
Chapter4	Completed Chapter 4 files
Chapter11	Completed Chapter 11 files and sample database, movies.mdb
databases	Two Access 2000 databases—newmanzone.mdb and realty.mdb—and newmanzone.sql, a SQL script to set up the Newman Zone database on SQL Server
extensions	Dreamweaver extensions

Table A-1 *The First Five Folders Contain Databases, Extensions, and Completed Files for Chapters 1, 4, and 11*

The remaining folders contain empty and completed versions of the book's two sample sites: Newman Zone and Realty (see Table A-2). The empty version (e.g., `newmanzone_asp_empty`) is what you should use to follow along with the book's recipes.

Refer to the completed versions of the sites if you run into problems and need to confirm the desired result. In some cases, a folder may also contain a readme file with information specific to setting up a particular site or chapter.

Site	Server Model
newmanzone.net	ASP.NET/VB
newmanzone.net_empty	ASP.NET/VB
newmanzone_asp	ASP/VBScript
newmanzone_asp_empty	ASP/VBScript
newmanzone_cf	ColdFusion MX
newmanzone_cf_empty	ColdFusion MX
realty.net	ASP.NET/VB
realty.net_empty	ASP.NET/VB
realty_asp	ASP/VBScript
realty_asp_empty	ASP/VBScript
realty_cf	ColdFusion MX
realty_cf_empty	ColdFusion MX

Table A-2   *The Supporting Files Include Two Sites—Newman Zone and Realty—in Three Server Models: ASP.NET/VB, ASP/VBScript, and ColdFusion MX*

Appendix B

Ingredients

A number of developers have kindly granted permission to use their extensions and reproduce their code in *The Joy of Dreamweaver MX*. You'll find a complete list of the ingredients for this book's recipes—and links to download them—at **www.newmanzone.com/downloads**. The following table lists the ingredients alphabetically.

Ingredient	Type	Chapter(s)	Author
ActivEdit	ColdFusion tag	18	CFDev.com
Alternate Row Colour	Extension	7	Owen Palmer
BUD Force Download	Extension	9	Tom Muck
CF_TwoSelectsRelated	ColdFusion tag	12	Nate Weiss
Check Form 4.66	Extension	5, 13	Jaro von Flocken
Check Image Upload 2.1	Extension	13	Massimo Foti
Conditional Region 2	Extension	5, 6	Waldo Smeets
DynaList	Extension	12	Paul Newman
Fading Text Scroller	DHTML script	10	Nicholas Poh
Horizontal Looper 2	Extension	17	Tom Muck
Insert Record With Identity	Extension	12	George Petrov
isDefined	Extension	5, 6, 13, 19	Paul Newman
JMail	Extension	5, 6, 19	Paul Newman
JustSo Picture Window	Extension	17	E. Michael Brandt
Nested Repeat	Extension	17	Tom Muck
PD Online HTML Editor	Extension	18	Public Domain
Popup Confirm Message	Extension	15	George Petrov
Preview File Before Uploading	Zip file	14	Tom Steeper
Pure ASP File Upload 2.0.8	Extension	13, 18	George Petrov

To install the extensions used in this book, download the latest version of Macromedia Extension Manager: **http://www.macromedia.com/exchange**.

Index

INTERNATIONAL CONTACT INFORMATION

AUSTRALIA
McGraw-Hill Book Company Australia Pty. Ltd.
TEL +61-2-9415-9899
FAX +61-2-9415-5687
http://www.mcgraw-hill.com.au
books-it_sydney@mcgraw-hill.com

CANADA
McGraw-Hill Ryerson Ltd.
TEL +905-430-5000
FAX +905-430-5020
http://www.mcgrawhill.ca

**GREECE, MIDDLE EAST,
NORTHERN AFRICA**
McGraw-Hill Hellas
TEL +30-1-656-0990-3-4
FAX +30-1-654-5525

MEXICO (Also serving Latin America)
McGraw-Hill Interamericana Editores S.A. de C.V.
TEL +525-117-1583
FAX +525-117-1589
http://www.mcgraw-hill.com.mx
fernando_castellanos@mcgraw-hill.com

SINGAPORE (Serving Asia)
McGraw-Hill Book Company
TEL +65-863-1580
FAX +65-862-3354
http://www.mcgraw-hill.com.sg
mghasia@mcgraw-hill.com

SOUTH AFRICA
McGraw-Hill South Africa
TEL +27-11-622-7512
FAX +27-11-622-9045
robyn_swanepoel@mcgraw-hill.com

**UNITED KINGDOM & EUROPE
(Excluding Southern Europe)**
McGraw-Hill Education Europe
TEL +44-1-628-502500
FAX +44-1-628-770224
http://www.mcgraw-hill.co.uk
computing_neurope@mcgraw-hill.com

ALL OTHER INQUIRIES Contact:
Osborne/McGraw-Hill
TEL +1-510-549-6600
FAX +1-510-883-7600
http://www.osborne.com
omg_international@mcgraw-hill.com

Complete References

Herbert Schildt
0-07-213485-2

Jeffery R. Shapiro
0-07-213381-3

Chris H. Pappas & William
H. Murray, III
0-07-212958-1

Herbert Schildt
0-07-213084-9

Ron Ben-Natan & Ori Sasson
0-07-222394-4

Arthur Griffith
0-07-222405-3

For the answers to everything related to your technology, drill as deeply as you please into our Complete Reference series. Written by topical authorities, these comprehensive resources offer a full range of knowledge, including extensive product information, theory, step-by-step tutorials, sample projects, and helpful appendixes.